(1976)

£ 3-50.

6/EC.

MONITORING BEHAVIOR AND SUPERVISORY CONTROL

NATO CONFERENCE SERIES

I   Ecology
II   Systems Science
III Human Factors
IV Marine Sciences
V   Air—Sea Interactions

III HUMAN FACTORS

MONITORING BEHAVIOR AND SUPERVISORY CONTROL

Edited by

Thomas B. Sheridan
Massachusetts Institute of Technology
Cambridge, Massachusetts

and

Gunnar Johannsen
Research Institute for Human Engineering
Meckenheim, Federal Republic of Germany

Published in coordination with NATO Scientific Affairs Division

PLENUM PRESS · NEW YORK AND LONDON

Library of Congress Cataloging in Publication Data

International Symposium on Monitoring Behavior and Supervisory Control, Berchtesgaden, Ger., 1976.
    Monitoring behavior and supervisory control.

    (NATO conference series: III, Human factors; v. 1)
    Sponsored by the NATO Special Program Panel on Human Factors.
    Includes index.
    1. Man—machine systems—Congresses. I. Sheridan, Thomas B. II. Johannsen, Gunnar. III. Nato Special Program Panel on Human Factors. IV. Title. V. Series.
    TA167.I57 1976   620.8   76-41687
    ISBN 0-306-32881-X

Proceedings of an International Symposium on Monitoring Behavior and Supervisory Control held at Berchtesgaden, Federal Republic of Germany, March 8-12, 1976, which was sponsored by the NATO Special Program Panel on Human Factors

© 1976 Plenum Press, New York
A Division of Plenum Publishing Corporation
227 West 17th Street, New York, N.Y. 10011

Preface

This book includes all papers presented at the International Symposium on Monitoring Behavior and Supervisory Control held at Berchtesgaden, Federal Republic of Germany, March 8-12, 1976. The Symposium was sponsored by the Scientific Affairs Division of the North Atlantic Treaty Organization, Brussels, and the government of the Federal Republic of Germany, Bonn.

We believe the book constitutes an important and timely status report on monitoring behavior and supervisory control by human operators of complex man-machine systems in which the computer is sharing key functions with the man. These systems include aircraft and other vehicles, nuclear and more conventional power plants, and processes for the manufacture of chemicals, petroleum, and discrete parts. By "monitoring" we mean the systematic observation by a human operator of multiple sources of information, e.g., ranging from integrated display consoles to disparate "live situations". The monitor's purpose is to determine whether operations are normal and proceeding as desired, and to diagnose difficulties in the case of abnormality or undesirable outcomes. By "supervisory control" we mean control by a human operator of a computer which, at a lower level, is controlling a dynamic system. In such systems, the computer-control normally operates continuously or at high data rates in loops closed through electromechanical sensors and motors. By contrast, the human operator normally signals or reprograms the computer intermittently or at a much slower pace. The human operator handles the higher level tasks and determines the goals of the overall system.

The conventional theory and practice of manual control and human factors has frequently proven unsatisfactory for engineering these evermore-prevalent computerized semi-manual, semi-automatic systems. Though it is generally agreed that computer and human capabilities are complementary, just how best to allocate functions between personnel and computers in most real systems remains unclear. Better models for characterizing human behavior in such systems are sorely needed, as well as better practical tools for designing of displays, of computer aids for planning and diagnosis, of computer teaching techniques, and of emergency procedures. Hopefully, this collection of papers will prove to be a significant step toward defining the problems and a start toward meeting the engineering needs.

The papers are organized into three sections. Papers in the first section describe monitoring and supervisory control of vehicles, primarily aircraft. The second section covers modeling more generally. Papers in the third section cover industrial process control. The first paper in each section is an overview or preview paper of that section. Audience questions and authors' responses appear at the end of each paper.

Following the three sections of papers are brief reports of four workshops which were held in conjunction with the Symposium. All four workshops were asked to address the same general questions : Computers and new display technology are changing the human operator's role towards that of a monitor or supervisor. What is, or what should be, the nature of this new role ? In view of this new role, what should be the priorities for research ? What implementation problems are foreseen ? What new institutional or interdisciplinary arrangements are advisable ? The workshop reports show great consensus in technical and scientific respects, but reveal differing viewpoints on the value of various problem approaches and the social relevance of applications of this technology. The editors provide further introduction and summary to these workshop reports in Section 4. We also felt it appropriate to provide at the end of the book a glossary of basic terms which are common to many of the papers, discussions, and workshops.

Finally, the editors wish to thank Dr. R. Bernotat and other members of the NATO Special Programme Panel on Human Factors and Dr. B.A. Bayraktar of the Scientific Affairs Division for helping to initiate the Symposium as well as to support it. We also thank the many authors for their fine performance in meeting tight deadlines and page limitations, the approximately 100 Symposium participants whose discussions added zest to the papers and substance to the workshops, and the many staff persons in Germany and the USA whose aid was essential.

Thomas B. Sheridan

Gunnar Johannsen

Contents

SECTION 1 MAN-VEHICLE CONTROL

SECTION 2 GENERAL MODELS

SECTION 4 WORKSHOP REPORTS

APPENDICES

Man-Vehicle Control

PREVIEW OF MAN-VEHICLE CONTROL SESSION

Gunnar Johannsen

Forschungsinstitut für Anthropotechnik (FAT)

5309 Meckenheim, F.R. Germany

1. INTRODUCTION

This lecture is the first one of three preview lectures which will be given during the symposium at the beginning of each session. The preview lecture has in view to be an introduction and a framework of the following session. The field will be structured with intent to give an insight into the main problem areas. All papers of the session will be mentioned briefly and fitted into the overall framework.

The man-machine problems in vehicle control may be differentiated according to two areas of human operation : (1) ground-based and (2) on-board monitoring and control. In the first case, monitoring and control of one or more manned or unmanned vehicles from a fixed ground-station is considered. Examples are (1) air traffic control (ATC), (2) space flight control, (3) central dispatching control of trains, other track-vehicles, buses, and ships in harbours, and (4) central control of traffic flow, e.g., on streets in cities. The human operators in these systems are called ground controllers or operators, central controllers, or - more specific - e.g., air traffic controllers. In the second case, monitoring and control within one vehicle is considered. Examples are control of all types of vehicles, i.e., aircrafts, spacecrafts, ships, and land vehicles. The human operators are, e.g., pilots, helmsmen, and drivers.

A special case in this classification is the group of remotely piloted vehicles (RPV). Although controlled from a fixed ground-station, they are more belonging to the second category, if they are piloted like an air-

3

craft. This example shows that the boundaries betwen the two mentioned classes of man-vehicle control systems are not clearly cut.

2. HIERARCHICAL MULTILEVEL STRUCTURE OF VEHICLE CONTROL

To gain a further insight into the man-vehicle control problems, see Fig. 1. Each vehicle control system can be subdivided into functional subsystems of a hierarchical multilevel structure (see, e.g., Kelley [1]). The navigation control loops form the highest level in the control hierarchy. The transport mission is the input variable of these loops and, at the same time, the input to the overall system. True position and course of the vehicle have to be determined by the navigation controller and compared with the goals of the mission. Decisions have to be derived how to change the inputs of the next lower level control loops. Accordingly, the outputs of the navigation controller constitute the input variables of the guidance control loops. These inputs are desired values of path, course, and speed-changes. The required tasks are, e.g., following a radio beam of an aircraft landing system or driving along a curved road with a car. The guidance controller produces as its outputs the input variables of the stabilization control loops, i.e., the desired values of attitude and speed.

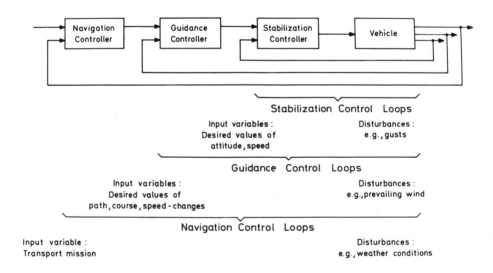

Fig. 1 : Control loops in vehicle control

In principle, all controller functions in Fig. 1 (navigation, guidance, and stabilization) might be performed only by a human controller or only by an automatic controller. However, system requirements of modern vehicles, e.g., higher speeds, higher traffic densities, and greater maneuverability, have often imposed such high demands on the controller that the human operator is not always able to do the job. On the other hand, a completely automatic controller is not the optimal solution, if the flexibility of the overall system and its safety will be restricted. Therefore, a function allocation between human and automatic control has to be chosen in many cases.

The process of automating vehicle control functions started with the inner loops (Fig. 1). This is caused by the fact that the effective signals in the inner loops show higher frequences than those of the outer loops. Therefore, automation is much more needed in the inner loops. Fortunately, the controller activity in these loops can be more easily automated than that of the outer loops. While the controller activity in the inner loops is mainly continuous tracking, i.e., sensomotor activity, the activity of the controller in the outer loops becomes more and more discrete involving decision-making and problem-solving, i.e., mental activity. In slowly responding systems however, e.g., a big ship with great time constants, the controller strategy in the inner loops is similar to that in the outer loops of quickly responding systems, e.g., an aircraft. This will be pointed out in the paper of VELDHUYZEN, STASSEN.

3. MONITORING AND DECISION-MAKING IN MANUAL VEHICLE CONTROL

Fig. 2 shows the classical manual control loop (heavily drawn lines) for a man-vehicle system. If a stability augmentation system is available as, e.g., in many aircrafts, the effective vehicle dynamics are changed and the main human controller's function is that of a guidance controller. In the other case, he has to perform the stabilization task, too. The visual information as the input of the human controller may be acquired indirectly via displays or directly from the environment. The direct inputs are cues embedded in the visual scene outside the vehicle.

Often, both types of visual information may be present at the same time. In car driving, e.g., the actual speed of the vehicle is indicated by a display, while the main guiding cues have to be extracted by the driver from the course of the street outside the window. Also, navigational input information, e.g., from the presence of other vehicles, from traffic signs, and from traffic lights, has to be gathered. The task of the driver

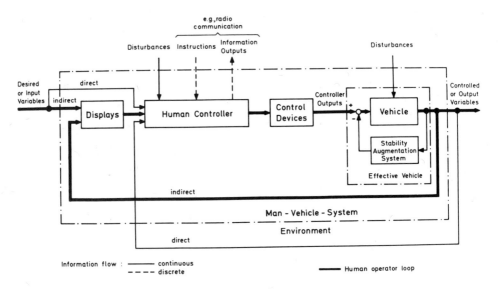

Fig. 2 : Man-vehicle control loop with indirect and direct visual information

in this situation can be characterized as a simultaneous execution of
sensomotor tracking and monitoring. Monitoring the outside world relative
to the vehicle and derived decision-making are necessary for the purpose
of safe navigation and guidance of the car. An example of this type of
human monitoring and decision-making behavior will be given in the
paper of ALLEN, SCHWARTZ, JEX. The reactions of drivers to traffic lights
and a mathematical model of the human decision-making process have been
investigated.

An additional monitoring or visual perception task of the human operator may be the identification of other vehicles, e.g., aircrafts. This
calls for a high degree of vigilance. Vigilance is defined by Frankmann,
Adams [2] as the attentiveness of the human operator and his capability
for detecting changes in stimulus events over relatively long periods of
sustained observation. The paper of MEYER-DELIUS, LIEBL evaluates
vigilance and fatigue in such tasks and shows physiological correlates.

Human monitoring in general and especially monitoring the vehicle
control process requires an internal presentation of the process dynamics.
It is assumed that the human operator is able to build in his mind an
internal model of the vehicle to be controlled. Decisions on control actions will be based on predictions of the dynamic behavior of the vehicle
achieved by the internal model. Papers which support this model idea

of the human operator are given by RAULT and by VELDHUYZEN, STASSEN.

4. AUTOMATION IN VEHICLE CONTROL : COMPUTERS AND DISPLAYS

In view of the above mentioned demanding system requirements, designers try to make use of new technologies in order to improve the overall system effectiveness of vehicles. These new technologies are computers, electronic and alphanumeric displays, and weather penetrating sensors. They supply the main foundations of automation in vehicle control. Even in such small and independently moving vehicles as cars where the costs of automation are relatively high, the first steps in this direction are done. Navigational aids for driving on highways and automatic distance controllers for driving in dense traffic have been proposed.

In Fig. 3, the automatic controller has been substituted for the human controller of Fig. 2 within the vehicle control loop. This step has been essentially facilitated by small, but powerful digital computers. Redundant systems, e.g., triplex arrangements, are used providing fail-safe capabilities. At least, e.g., safe landing of an aircraft must be possible in failure situations, although a restricted maneuverability with back-up

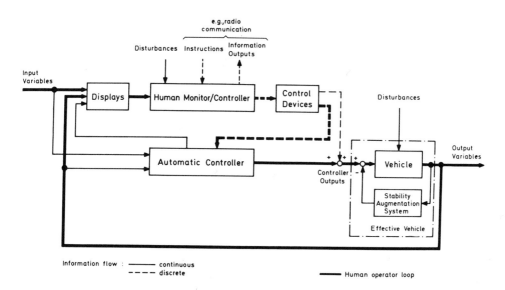

Fig. 3 : Human operator monitoring the automated vehicle control loop

systems may be tolerated. In spite of this redundancy, it seems to be
necessary in most cases to have a human operator on board as a manager
or supervisor of the overall system. He monitors the input and output variables of the automatic vehicle control loop via displays. He can change
the modes of the automatic controller via push-buttons or, as in the force
steering control concept, via continuous control devices, namely, as a
function of changing mission phases or as a consequence of failures. In
cases of severe failures, he may also take over control manually. Some
problems of automation arising in civil aircraft control are stated in the
paper of EDWARDS. More specific discussions of function allocation between human operator and computer are covered in some papers of the
General Models Session. Experiments with failures in the automatic controller are described in the paper of JOHANNSEN, PFENDLER, STEIN.

The tasks of the human operator have changed very much compared
with those in manual control. The sensomotor activities are much less
frequent whereas vigilance and decision-making behavior is more important.
The monotony of the task may increase in such a way that additional tasks
have to be invented. Correspondingly, the task of the human operator in
automated vehicle control becomes more similar to that of the human operator in process control.

Sometimes, a crew reduction results as a consequence of automation.
Also, altered man-man relationships, e.g., on ships, may occur. The
changed task requirements may lead to changed selection and training
procedures. Higher skills and education of the human operators are often
asked for.

New display and sensor devices initiate further changes in human
monitoring and supervisory control tasks. Combined with a display management computer, rather amazing possibilities are created, e.g., integrated displays with prediction capabilities and call-up displays. BAUER-
SCHMIDT, LAPORTE report on integrated display/control devices which
are arrangements of flat-panel displays and touch-panel control devices.
Less space for these devices compared with traditionally designed systems
and, accordingly, less eye movements are required.

In the paper of ROSCOE, EISELE, a design of cockpit displays based
on new technological possibilities is proposed. Weather penetrating sensor
systems, e.g., infrared sensors, yield information of the outside world
which can be converted to stylized images by means of the computer.
A superposition of this originally direct visual information with conventional
indirect visual information (see Fig. 2) can be obtained. Only a limited
number of display devices needs to be used in the cockpit.

Similar display devices with relevance to vehicle control systems are also described in some papers of the Process Control Session. An evaluation technique for integrated display formats is proposed by KIMMEL. Trans-information is used as a measure.

5. GROUND-BASED MONITORING AND CONTROL

Now, let us consider ground-based monitoring and control of vehicles. In Fig. 4, the generalized block diagram shows the central ground station and different controlled or supervised man-vehicle systems. The human operator in the central station monitors either information from these man-vehicle systems directly via radar or TV-systems or correspondingly preprocessed information from a process control computer. He can control the man-vehicle systems either by means of radio communication or indirectly via inputs to the process controller which is linked to the man-vehicle systems. Often, both communications exist in parallel as, e.g., in trains. The information flow is discrete in most cases, because connections exist mainly with the most low-frequent control loops within the vehicles, i.e., with the navigation controllers. In considerably automated systems, the main information flow involving the central operator is found within the central ground station itself, i.e., between human monitor and process controller. The tasks of the human operator are very much similar to those in process control.

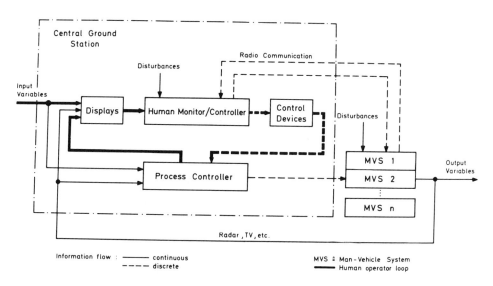

Fig. 4 : Human operator in a central ground station monitoring a number of man-vehicle systems

Two examples of this type of human supervisory behavior are given
in this session. PASMOOIJ, OPMEER, HYNDMAN report on air traffic
control. Two degrees of automation and the corresponding tasks of the
human operators are discussed. BOSSI gives an example of central supervision of urban mass transit systems. In this case, the vehicles are unmanned and automatically controlled. The radio communication links may
be used by the passengers in failure situations. The process control and
human operator functions have been extended to monitoring the passenger
flow from and to the vehicles and to scheduling sufficiently enough vehicles.

6. MEASUREMENT TECHNIQUES FOR HUMAN RESPONSE

It has been pointed out above that the demands upon the human
operator and the tasks he has to fulfill change from sensomotor to mental
activities with increasing automation. This is supported by the fact that
automation started within the inner vehicle control loops. Therefore, the
sometimes stated opinion automation unburdens the human operator is not
necessarily true. On the contrary, only a shifting from physical to mental
load may occur. In order to evaluate possible advantages of automation
to the human operator, it is necessary to measure not only system performance, but also human operator workload or, more generally speaking,
human response data in a most comprehensive way. A classification of
human response measurement techniques is given in the paper of ROLFE.
Observation, subjective assessments, loading tasks, and physiological
measures are described and compared against the criteria interpretability,
reliability, freedom of interference, and acceptability to the human operator.

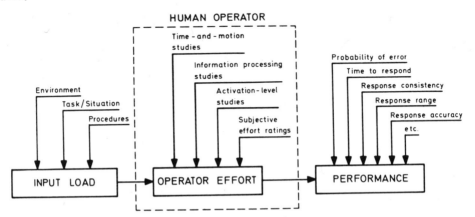

Fig. 5 : Attributes of operator workload

A most useful concept for the assessment of human response has been proposed by Johns [3] . He divides the broad area of human operator workload into three functionally relatable attributes : input load, operator effort, and performance or work result (Fig. 5). Input load is defined mainly as factors or events external to the human operator while operator effort is defined as factors or events internal to the human operator. Sometimes, the terms stress and strain instead of load and effort are used with the same or nearly the same meaning (see the paper of MEYER-DELIUS, LIEBL). Performance is defined as usual, i.e., data outputs generated through the effort exerted by the human operator which serve as inputs to other components of the man-vehicle-environment system and provide feedback on effort adequacy.

Major sources of input load may be categorized into three classes : environmental, task-induced or situational, and procedural. Environmental variables are, e.g., noise, vibration, and temperature. Task variables are, e.g., characteristics of displays and control devices, crewstation layout, and vehicle dynamics. Procedural variables are, e.g., briefing and instructions, task sequencing, and mission/task duration.

The operator effort depends on the input load and on the performance requirements of a given task. All techniques usable for the evaluation and measurement of operator effort can be classified into four groups : (1) time-and-motion studies, (2) information processing studies, (3) operator activation-level studies, and (4) subjective effort ratings. In time-and-motion studies, the execution times of all particular task elements of a certain task are assessed. A time balance is struck over the total task under consideration. Available time margins or expected time pressure characterize different degrees of effort expenditure of the human operator. This technique is used in the work of (1) BAUERSCHMIDT, LAPORTE, (2) BOSSI, and (3) PASMOOIJ, OPMEER, HYNDMAN.

In information processing studies, the human operator is regarded as an information processing element with a fixed, limited channel capacity. Secondary or loading tasks can be used to measure the spare capacity of the operator. An example is given in the paper of JOHANNSEN, PFENDLER, STEIN. Another approach applies information theory. An example is given in the paper of RAULT. He uses the same measure as KIMMEL.

Operator activation-level studies are based on the hypothesis that the level of physiological activity of the human operator depends on his effort. Examples are given in four papers : (1) MEYER-DELIUS, LIEBL, (2) PASMOOIJ, OPMEER, HYNDMAN, (3) SMIT, and (4) RAULT.

Subjective effort rating is an additional useful assessment technique. It has been investigated in three studies, i.e., by (1) JOHANNSEN, PFENDLER, STEIN, (2) PASMOOIJ, OPMEER, HYNDMAN, and (3) SMIT.

In some of the investigations described in this session, different measurement techniques are used in parallel. This is a way which might be gone more consequently in the future. It allows to find out the utility of different techniques in different situations. Moreover, it might be that the complex problem of operator workload in monitoring and supervisory control situations cannot be handled without such a procedure.

7. REFERENCES

[1]   C.R. KELLEY : Manual and automatic control. New York : Wiley, 1968.

[2]   J.P. FRANKMANN, J.A. ADAMS : Theories of vigilance. Psych. Bull., vol. 59, pp. 257-272, 1962.

[3]   D.W. JAHNS : A concept of operator workload in manual vehicle operations. Forschungsbericht Nr. 14, Forschungsinstitut für Anthropotechnik, Meckenheim, 1973.

SOME ASPECTS OF AUTOMATION IN CIVIL TRANSPORT AIRCRAFT

Elwyn Edwards

University of Technology

Loughborough, U.K.

1. INTRODUCTION

The contemporary airline pilot has witnessed in his life-time a revolution in the technology of aircraft design resulting in considerable changes in task demands.   Today it is possible for a pilot, whilst on the ground at a European airport, to depress half a dozen key switches which will activate a navigation programme to guide him to a destination in North America.   Thereafter, he may engage the autopilot at about 500' and function as a system monitor until his aircraft is on the runway four thousand miles away.

Innovations in automation have occurred simultaneously with other developmental trends.   The advent of the jet engine has doubled the typical cruising speed of aircraft over a twenty year period.   Traffic density, as measured by scheduled aircraft hours flown, has doubled in half that period, whereas aircraft weight has increased by a factor of about three over the twenty years. Each of these parameters brings in its wake both direct and indirect consequential modifications in the nature of the piloting task.   Such effects as changes in typical crew scheduling procedures or in turn-around times, although of extreme importance, will not be pursued here in view of their remoteness from the immediate problems of vehicle guidance. Neither will consideration be given to matters pertaining to general aviation or military operations;   the observations relate to civil transport aircraft.

The matter of increase in vehicle size and weight may be taken as an example of a parameter change producing deep

modifications in guidance techniques (Davies, 1967).   Three
first-level consequences may be identified, each one of which
gives rise to a set of necessary changes in technique, and
introduces possible sources of new difficulty, viz,

   A. Increase in Range of Weight and C of G.
   This produces a need for controlability over a wide range
   of values, resulting in widely differing performance figures,
   climb and descent rates, reference speeds etc.

   B. Increase in Control Loads.
   This produces a need for powered controls and hence the
   introduction of artificial feel systems, resulting in severe
   control problems in the event of malfunction.

   C. Increase in Momentum.
   This effect demands greater anticipation of the projected
   flight-path in order to achieve acceptable standards of
   guidance, and may exacerbate such conditions as wind-shear
   during take-off and landing.

   An analysis of the consequences of change, as outlined
briefly above, might form the basis of an inquiry into the ideal
form of a man-machine partnership to achieve the guidance task.
In practice, the effort expended upon the systematic examination
of such problems has been somewhat slight for several reasons
including the following:

   1. Unclear philosophies concerning the nature of the
      optimized man-machine partnership.
   2. Flux in the state-of-the-art in control components and
      techniques.
   3. Lack of dissemination of relevant human performance data.
   4. Changes in the economic climate and obscurities in long
      term predicted environment.
   5. A tendency to implement automated sub-systems where
      implementation is possible irrespective of desirability.
   6. Pressure of commercial competition.

   With respect to the introduction of automation, certain
popular misconceptions require to be dispelled.   Experience both
in aviation and elsewhere leads to the formulation of the
following two rules:-

   Rule 1: The introduction of automation does not necessarily
   ease the load upon the human operator; typically the
   operational effectiveness of the man-machine system is
   enhanced involving changes rather than reductions in the
   human contribution.

Rule 2: The requirement for ergonomics input into the design and operation of systems is in no way diminished by the introduction of automation, which changes the nature of the human factors problems without reducing their significance.

Some particular examples of the operation of these rules are discussed below.

2. SOME AUTOMATIC SYSTEMS

2.1 Flight Guidance

The pneumatic autopilots of the 1930s which assisted pilots to maintain level flight appear now as primitive ancestors of the modern flight guidance systems. These may be described under two broad categories, the former concerned with primary flight control, and the latter with flight director and autopilot functions available for the maintenance of a desired vertical and horizontal flight path.

Primary Flight Control Systems. These are available to ensure the basic stability and control of the aircraft, and are partially interfaced with the pilot. Typically the components of the system comprise pitch axis trim (either by manual or automatic input), control movement authority limiting, stall warning, spoiler mode control, direct lift control, and surface position indication. More use of active control techniques for basic stability may well be made in the future (Pinsker, 1974).

Table 1

Function	Configuration			
	Cruise	Partial Flap	Full Flap	Ground
Speed Brake	YES*	YES*a	YESb	NO
Roll Assistance	NO	YESa	YES	NO
Direct Lift Control	NO	NO	YES	NO
Ground Spoiler	NO	NO	NO	YES*c

* Under pilot control
a If speed brake fully deployed, roll assistance inoperative
b Available but not normally used
c May be engaged manually or automatically

Simplified Summary of L-1011 Spoiler Operation. (No indication is included of the differential use of the six pairs of spoiler positions, or of the limits of travel up to a maximum value of 60°).

An example of the complexity of these systems, and of the
limited available pilot intervention may be illustrated in the
case of the L-1011 spoiler system.

Flight Director and Autopilot Systems. Wholly under the
selection of the pilot, facilities are available either for the
display of pitch and roll commands, or for the inputting of these
to the autopilot.   Provision is made both to acquire a given
state or to hold the existing state, as shown in Table 2.   Mode
selection is most commonly made by push-button, and is accompanied
by a visual indication of the system state.   An additional input
to the autopilot is available in the form of Control Wheel
Steering which allows the pilot to make changes in the attitude of
the aircraft, which will be maintained automatically, by means of
the same control column used for manual control of the aircraft.

Table 2

Hold Facility		Acquire Facility	
Pitch	Roll	Pitch	Roll
IAS Mach Vertical Speed Altitude Glide Slope Climb Speed	Heading Wings level INS VOR LOC	Altitude Glide Slope Flare Attitude	Heading INS VOR LOC

Simplified Summary of DC-10 FD and Autopilot Facilities.

Roll and pitch axis control, together with automatic thrust
operation, are combined in the autoland facility.   Originally
pioneered in the U.K. for use on the DH-121 to make possible
landings in Category III weather conditions, autoland encompasses
the acquisition and tracking of the ILS localizer and glide slope,
speed control, flare at predetermined radio height, drift angle
removal, and roll-out directional guidance.   In its more recent
implementations, autoland requires the pilot only to activate a
"Land" button and to select two autopilots into their command
mode.   His next active intervention is to provide reverse thrust
for retardation on the runway.

2.2 Navigation

The traditional methods of navigation involved manual activities for both its components of data acquisition and utilization. Thus it was necessary for men to identify objects on a map, to measure drift, to make astronomical readings and, having acquired the appropriate data, to make use of a plotting chart in order to evaluate the required heading changes necessary to achieve the destination.

Both these facets have been automated. The facility of coupling the autopilot to a VOR largely solved the navigation problem for short haul operations. Area coverage systems, such as Decca, particularly after the advent of the on-board Omnitrack computer to cope with the hyperbolic signal inputs, further progressed automatic navigation.

More recently the introduction of radio-updated inertial navigation systems (INS) has brought further progress and has made possible accurate long-range navigation via economical great-circle routes by techniques requiring no additional ground facilities and independent of the magnetic compass.

Standard routes including SIDs and STARs may be stored on magnetic tape, and transferred quickly into the navigation computer. Displays describing present and future positions, tracks, distances, speeds and winds are readily available.

At present, relatively little has been done to automate the required vertical profile of the flight path.

2.3 Thrust Management

An Air Data Computer supplies Total Air Temperature values to a Thrust Computer which evaluates the limiting engine thrust (Nl or EPR). On the selection by the pilot of a thrust mode, e.g. Take Off, Climb, the Thrust Computer provides a signal to control the throttle setting. Alternatively, signals derived from a pilot-selected speed controller may, provided the demand is within the calculated thrust limits, determine thrust values.

In these ways the complexities of thrust management may be handled automatically to provide the pilot with easily selected settings which yield a speed control system, engine protection, and economical levels of performance.

2.4 Alarm Systems

Control systems operated or monitored by men require, in addition to the normal continuous displays, further devices which draw attention to existing or potential conditions which are essentially undesirable. The number of such caution and warning devices in aircraft has escalated considerably in recent years.

The circumstances giving rise to alarm signals show considerable variety and include equipment malfunction, aircraft configuration or position, change of system state, or diagnosed hazard. Similarly the appropriate response sequence varies widely from a single key depression to the re-organization of the intended mission.

Alarms may appear as visual or auditory signals to the pilot, or as kinaesthetic changes in the controls. They may occur singly, or in patterns characteristic of certain prime causes. Some signals may be cancelled by pilot response. The frequency of occurence of the alarms varies from "many times on each flight" to "never known it operate in earnest".

3. HUMAN FACTORS ASPECTS OF AUTOMATION

It is convenient to sub-divide the broad problem areas relating to flight-deck automation without, of course, implying the absence of interaction between the several aspects. Thus the analytic framework of Table 3 may be employed as a preliminary device to organize problem defintion.

Within the scope of a short paper, it is clearly impossible to attempt an exhaustive examination of the automatic systems described above in terms of the factors listed in Table 3. A few examples are discussed to indicate the nature of some of the problems arising.

3.1 The Pilot as a Monitor: the fundamental issue

Given an aircraft equipped with contemporary automatic equipment, the pilot finds himself truly in the era of the push-button vehicle in which his role is that of a system manager and monitor. His active participation in the guidance and navigation of the aircraft is minimal and even the detailed history of the flight will be automatically recorded.

Table 3

1. Allocation of function for normal operation 1.1 Automatic task performance available 1.2 Pilot(s) task performance available 1.3 Combined human-machine performance necessary
2. Pilots' interface with the automatics 2.1 Displays: machine-to-man data transfer 2.2 Controls: man-to-machine data transfer 2.3 Software: rules and procedures for system operation
3. System malfunction 3.1 Detection and diagnosis 3.2 Reversionary modes
4. Personnel factors 4.1 Pilot selection 4.2 Training and Practice 4.3 Acceptability of automatics

A framework for the definition of human factors problems in relation to flight-deck automation.

This change in the traditional role of the aircraft pilot has far-reaching consequences extending back to selection procedures which do little to seek the ability of long-term vigilant monitoring of automatic systems. Training programmes similarly have little emphasis on this central aspect of the task.

The basic design philosophy of automation owes little, of course, to considerations of the features of human performance in automatic systems, but is developed on the grounds of economic and operational advantages associated with the use of automatic control. This is a basic issue to which there is no ready solution; however, awareness of the human problems and efforts to alleviate them whenever possible are essential to the safety and effectiveness of flight operations.

In the event of malfunction or of any untoward circumstances, the pilot may be called upon to revert to manual control of the aircraft, and at the same time to diagnose and rectify the

conditions necessitating this action.   Here, problems may be
considerable.   The pilot is introduced into the control in
unfavourable circumstances and is required to perform from a
relatively "cold" start.   Skills called into use may well be ones
lacking in recent practice, so that the difficulties are
exacerbated.   In some instances, such as a late failure of the
equipment during autoland, there exists a requirement for such
skills as low-level manoeuvring in poor conditions of visibility,
about which very little experience has accrued.

The pilot, then, must act largely as a systems monitor, a
task for which he is not selected, little trained, and
constitutionally ill-suited.   Tasks demanding long-term
vigilance tend to suffer most from the effects of fatigue.   In
the event of the unexpected, the pilot must instantaneously
assume manual control employing his out-of-practice skills whilst
attempting simultaneously to diagnose and rectify the
circumstances.   There is no shortage of scope for ergonomics
expertise to contribute to the problems here.

3.2 Problems with Autothrottle

The operation of autothrottle serves as an example of a
more specific problem area.   Speed control may be achieved by
the control of either pitch attitude or thrust.   Obviously, both
these parameters cannot be employed simultaneously.   In the
event that thrust is selected, a different parameter, such as
Vertical Speed, must be employed for pitch control.   In certain
circumstances, inadvertant misoperation may result.   If, for
example, a long descent has been carried out to a preselected
altitude with autothrottle selected "Off", the aircraft will
attempt eventually to maintain the selected altitude without
power, resulting in very low speeds until such time as new modes
are selected.

A further problem arises in cases where standard operating
procedures call for regular use of autothrottle.   Manual
reversion in the case of malfunction may leave the unpracticed
pilot having more difficulty with manual thrust control than he
might have in the case of autopilot failure.

3.3 Back-up Equipment and Procedures

The system designer is faced with a difficult problem in
determining the extent of back-up required for a sophisticated
automatic system.   The INS serves as an example here.
Considerable redundancy is built into the system such that total
equipment failure is an extremely unlikely event.   Should this

happen, however, during a long oceanic sector or in the course of a polar flight, the level of facility remaining is quite primitive.

Rather more likely is the problem of an unexpected change in route demanded by ATC resulting in the temporary abandonment of the programmed inertial system.   The pilot may then have a formidable task in identifying unfamiliar way-points in a format suitable for the INS.   Alternative methods of navigation may result in reversionary operation with severely limited facilities.

3.4 Alarm Systems

Two classes of problem may be identified;   those concerned with the design features of individual alarms, and those concerned with the total integrated alarm system (Edwards, 1975). One example of each will be outlined here.

Probably the largest source of difficulty with individual alarms is the false positive, i.e. the occasion upon which a signal cries "Wolf!"   It is important to draw a distinction between reliability in purely engineering terms and the credibility of an alarm in relation to the "fail safe" concept. In hardware terms, the tendency to bias errors in favour of excessive false positives rather than less frequent missed targets is probably quite sound.   The introduction of a man into the loop introduces the notion of credibility - an item influenced by many factors, not all of which are wholly rational. Thus an alarm which gains the reputation of crying "Wolf!" will eventually assume a low value of credibility with the consequence that the fail safe philosophy is largely destroyed.

The design of an integrated alarm system should take into account the configuration resulting from causes which produce several signals to appear simultaneously or in close succession. Such a situation creates problems in diagnosis and may cause delays and difficulties in the determination of priorities in corrective action.   Various techniques are available to alleviate some of the problems in this area.

3.5 System Acceptability

The degree of acceptability of an automatic system is dependent upon several factors.   The system should have a high standard of reliability before it is installed for operational use.   It should be simple and convenient to use in terms of both hardware interfacing and procedural adaptability.   Attention should be paid to the operators' priorities in the relevance of the sub-systems selected for automation.   The modus operandi and

limitations of the automatics should be made comprehensible.
Account should be taken of the expected changes in job
satisfaction resulting from automation. Adequate programmes of
training should be available to introduce new concepts in control
technology. Such criteria are not always given adequate attention
prior to the introduction of yet more gadgetry upon the flight-
deck.

4.   REFERENCES

Davies, D.P., 1967, Handling the Big Jets. (Redhill: U.K.
       Air Registration Board).

Edwards, Elwyn, 1975, Flight-deck Alarm Systems. (Loughborough
       University of Technology, Report AERO 7).

Pinsker, W.J.G., 1974, Active Control as an Integrative Tool in
       Advanced Aircraft Designs. (Royal Aircraft Establishment,
       Technical Memorandum AERO 1596).

Material has been drawn from the published documents of
several manufacturers, notably the Lockheed-California Company
and the Douglas Aircraft Company.

DISCUSSION

RIJNSDORP :

   In order to alleviate the problem of false versus missed alarm signals,
would it make sense to introduce an intermediate display type indicating
cases where the alarm is only probable, and reserve the "real" alarms
for cases where the probability is very nearly one ?

EDWARDS :

   To some extent, this intermediate "caution" signal is already used,
and distinguished from a "warning" (the former are amber and the latter
red). The question arises - what is the purpose of an alarm signal ? It
is to alert, to inform, and to guide towards action. We must, therefore,
ask whether a signal saying "maybe" is of any help to the pilot. In some

instances (e.g. pre-take off configuration) a "maybe" should come up as a red. But in other cases the situation might be very different. In very general terms, it is difficult to see what information is being conveyed by a "maybe" and what action is being recommended. Such a system could create more problems than it solves.

WAHLSTRÖM :

You mentioned the alarm system lighting up "as a christmas tree". Are you using alarm inhibition for the alarming system in aircraft ?

EDWARDS :

Aircraft alarm systems are not yet very sophisticated. In many aircraft, a master warning (red) and a master caution (amber) are fitted directly in the pilots' line of sight. The parameter giving rise to the master signal may be identified by reference to an annunciator panel. Here, the signals are quite independent of one another ; no inhibition is used, and no attempt is made to assist the pilot to interpret patterns of signals.

Avionic systems are, perhaps, lagging behind process control technology in this respect. However, it is important to bear in mind the weight and space problems of airborne equipment, and the high standards of integrity necessary for certification.

TECHNIQUES FOR DISPLAY/CONTROL SYSTEM

INTEGRATION IN SUPERVISORY AND MONITORING SYSTEMS

D. K. Bauerschmidt and H. R. LaPorte

Rockwell International

Anaheim, California 92803

INTRODUCTION

Modern monitoring and supervisory control systems employ keyboard entry devices and cathode-ray tube (CRT) terminals as the primary control and display elements. The multi-function nature of the CRT can be used to centralize system operation but its combination with keyboard entry devices defies a high level of display/control integration. This paper was suggested by recent improvements in display and control technologies which can provide physical and functional display integration to a degree not permitted by present display and control techniques at costs allowing wide application to both commercial and military systems.

INTEGRATION DEFINED

The role of a complex monitoring system operator is to extract data from his environment, manipulate the data to provide system operating direction, and input this direction as controls upon the system. The operator performs these tasks repetitively and at a frequency appropriate for the desired level of monitoring and control. Extraction of data from his environment is accomplished by observation of data which has been sensed, processed, and displayed by the system. He may, however, augment this input by direct observation of his environment such as by the detection of smoke and the sensing of temperature changes. In most monitoring systems considerable attention is directed toward insuring the availability (i.e., sensing, and distribution) of individual data elements. Since less emphasis is often placed on the automatic processing of data for display and control integration purposes, the operator may perform a wide variety of data manipulation tasks. He may, for example,

compute or estimate individual safety margins for a particular
condition. He may collect and manipulate data, performing sample
or predictive solutions. He may convert observed data into the
dimensions and format necessary for control input. This degree of
data conversion, manipulation and translation can be used to define
display and control integration. Furthermore, this means of definition is particularly appropriate for monitoring and supervisory
control systems, where there is less direct input from the external
world in proportion to those inputs which are sensed by equipment,
and where discrete or single dimensional inputs outnumber the complex continuous control inputs of vehicular control situations.

     The level of display and control integration can be defined as
being inversely proportional to the operator activity made necessary
by the display and control system implementation. Thus, the degree
of integration increases when operator activity required by physical,
functional and temporal differences between display output to the
operator and his control input is minimized. Measurement of integration level may be accomplished in terms of time and/or error rate
attributable to operator activity. A physical separation of display
and control will result in measurable time delay from the instant
that the operator observes displayed data to the time at which a
control entry is made. Much of this delay can be attributed to the
time required for search and selection of appropriate entry devices
(Alden, et al, 1972). Functional differences, such as coding and
logical relationships, will increase the operator's activity. If
the display output is encoded differently than the control input,
additional operator time is required and a higher probability of
error exists (Welford, 1960). Operator translation from display
output to control input can be complex, requiring computation, extrapolation or other data manipulation (Crossman, 1956). The most
difficult operator transition results from situations where a control input does not result directly from a single display. This
makes a higher order of operator data manipulation necessary and
significantly increases the probability of error (Fitts and Seeger.
1953). Operator transition is made more difficult by temporal considerations of data output. If the data required by an operator to
cause a control input are not available at that time, a delay in
control input will occur. Furthermore, if multiple display outputs
are required and the operator must store data for subsequent comparison or combination with other data, a higher error probability will
result.

     Response behavior models are useful in the description of
operator activity. One model of operator response behavior, which
has been demonstrated to predict very accurately operator performance time, treats control/display operation as a series of subtasks,
each subtask involving the sum of information read in time, choice
or decision time, reach time and control manipulation time (Siegel,
Wolf and Ollman, 1962). Taking some minor liberties with the model,

read in time is typically short but may vary as a function of the difficulty involved in locating relevant information, which in turn is a function of display physical design. Choice or decision time is a function of response uncertainty and may be considered to relate to the degree of encoding used; mental computations, extrapolations and combinations of data required; and the determination of the proper control location and action required. Reach time is related to physical arrangement of controls. Manipulation time is predominantly a function of physical arrangement, but, depending on the type of control operation, may also vary with encoding and other mental requirements.

Using this model, it is clear that any configuration which improves physical arrangement or reduces decision requirements may be expected to improve operator performance time. If performance errors are considered to extend the total performance time required, this improvement would have a predominant effect on total operator performance. This model is used in a later section to illustrate the limitations of conventional control/display design and the expected improvements of emerging technologies which may achieve total integration.

CURRENT DISPLAY SYSTEMS INTEGRATION

Before the advent of the CRT and the wide use of digital data processors, display systems were almost entirely configured with display and control elements, each representing a single data output or input. Examples of these systems with relatively pure usage of dedicated displays and controls are still found throughout the range of current manned system designs. The modern submarine control station is almost entirely composed of single-function display and control elements. The engineering station of most commercial aircraft is also an arrangement of displays and controls largely dedicated to single functions. Although a relatively large body of research literature has been accumulated which suggests techniques for improved display/control integration, the performance of complex systems employing single function display and control elements will generally result in longer than necessary operator performance time.

With the CRT and associated processing capabilities, the option of relatively low-cost multi-function displays became a reality. Individual display elements may be depicted, arranged, and combined with great flexibility. Similarly, the multi-function keyboard provides for centralized data input and some flexibility in the presentation of input options. These devices are used widely in current monitoring system designs.

CRT displays have disadvantages which limit display/control integration. The low-cost CRT's in general usage are limited in brightness and do not provide display memory without additional

electronics. In many applications the CRT's high-voltage requirements, fragility, and form factor represent distinct disadvantages
that have precluded its general use. For example, in the operating
environment of many military systems, space and operator safety requirements combine to make CRT's inappropriate solutions to the
operator display problem. Similarly, the CRT's size, general viewability and cost of computer interface have impeded its introduction
into such commercial systems as banking data systems, and point-of-
sale terminals.

Keyboard options also limit integration. Common electromechanical devices limit the manner in which input data options may be
presented to the operator. Additional input options are exercised
at the expense of control duplication and panel area. Direct combination (i.e., physical association) of control input capabilities
with displayed data can be accomplished, but with restrictions on
the number and type of options presented. Entry keys may be located
adjacent to a CRT display, the display being used to identify the
nature of each entry key function. This illustrates a reconfigurable capability in which the function represented by a key may
change as indicated by the adjacent display legend. Another mechanization of reconfigurable keyboards and entry devices removes the
limitation on number of keys but in turn limits the number of display options. When each key is combined with computer-addressable
legend options, the keyboard itself may serve as the display output
device. It may be staged to provide sets of more optimally encoded
entry options in accordance with present system status. A reconfigurable keyboard of this type is employed in a sonar system
trainer instructor's console. Selection of one of the displayed
control options causes all legends to be changed to the next set of
options available to the operator. Options may be arranged in a
tree fashion with certain keys provided for access back to the top
of the tree. The number of display options per key is typically
four but can be as many as 40 with added mechanization complexity
and cost. In the sonar trainer keyboard matrix of 30 keys, over
300 separate labels are provided.

DISPLAY/CONTROL INTEGRATION REQUIREMENTS

The preceding discussion illustrated several current display
and control system designs. These existing designs have not
achieved direct physical integration and complete functional design
flexibility. A continuing need exists to provide a cost-effective
means of multi-function display and multi-function control which
can be directly combined to minimize the physical, functional, and
temporal operator transition from display input to control output.

A basic requirement of integration, as defined above, is to
minimize any physical translation between display input and control
output. Thus, display and control mechanizations must be physically

compatible, use a single viewing area, and allow operator selection of control options directly from a multi-function display surface. Since the control function will locate the device relative to the operator, viewing requirements in addition to the traditional contrast, resolution, etc., are imposed upon the display element. It must be capabile of comfortable viewing when installed in a near-horizontal position such as in a console shelf. To eliminate special requirements for the control input device to accommodate curved display surfaces, the display component should be flat or near-flat. It should also be available in various viewing areas and present no appreciable installation depth requirement. Again, this allows optimum location of the device relative to the operator for control entry purposes. The control mechanization must be physically compatible with the display and offer no obscuration of data presentation. It should be readily adaptable to any display size and should present no special mounting and/or installation requirements. It must, of course, be utilized in typical operator station ambient light environments. A further desirable characteristic is that there be no requirement for manipulation of intermediate or auxiliary control devices such as is necessary with light pen or similar mechanizations.

In addition to direct physical combination of display and control, an integrated display/control device should provide both alphanumeric and graphic output presentations and be capable of rapid reconfiguration of data presentations to best match the displayed data to the operating situation. Operator translation required, due to the manner in which display output and control input must be encoded, should be minimized.

Both the display and control mechanization must be directly compatible with digital processing and data transmission components. This allows the use of digital system components to achieve rapid input/output and reconfiguration without significant penalty in interface components. Furthermore, if both the display/control mechanizations operate autonomously, except for new data input/output (i.e., not requiring refresh), considerable savings in system cost may be realized.

APPLICATIONS OF EMERGING TECHNOLOGIES

There are several digitally-addressed x-y matrix flat-panel display technologies in various stages of development. They provide significant improvements, relative to the conventional CRT, in viewability, installation, and compatibility with data processing and transmission elements. Most importantly, their flat-panel configuration allows use with devices which sense the panel location of an operator designation. For example, a traditional keyboard may be depicted on the display. The operator action of touching the display, to indicate his choice, would be sensed by a device overlaying the display or by a device located at the periphery of the display and relayed to the system's data processing element.

Displays directly applicable to the requirements include gas-discharge (plasma) panels, light emitting diode arrays, liquid crystal panels and digital flat panel CRT's. These displays provide the capability of a random addressable x-y matrix of display elements which can be easily configured by the data processor. They all provide a flat display surface and a packaged depth of several inches.

Control input devices that are directly compatible with flat-panel displays are also in development. These devices sense the location of the operator's finger on the display surface and relay the coordinates to the data processor. One technique uses a vertical and horizontal layered matrix of conductors separated by air or liquid overlaying the display surface. When pressure is exerted on the panel, one or more pairs of conductors touch and provide the location address. Another mechanization is installed at the periphery of the display surface. It uses paired light beam sources and detectors on the vertical and horizontal axes to map the display surface. The beams are automatically scanned by the device electronics and upon the interruption of a set of horizontal and vertical beams a location address is relayed to the data processor. The present "touch panel" mechanization provides a 16 x 16 infrared light beam matrix and can be used in all normal ambient light environments.

Figure 1 presents an example of a shipboard engineering station mechanization which makes use of the flat-panel displays and touch sensitive control entry devices now in development. The four display drawings depict a sequence of formats provided at the operator's console to monitor and control an electrical failure. Figure 1a is a MASTER INDEX which provides access to lower data, as well as providing status of the subsystems under the responsibility of the console operator. By touching the subsystem legend shown in the FAILED condition (ELECTRICAL PLANT), a subindex of all electrical plant distribution and control subsystems replaces the MASTER INDEX (Figure 1b), with a failure mode showing in the PORT GENERATOR. Touching the PORT label brings up the PORT GENERATOR distribution schematic (Figure 1c) showing that the failure is in the AC power buses (AC PWR). Touching the AC PWR label displays the AC POWER bus schematic (Figure 1d), showing the voltage, amperage, and temperature on each bus. It is obvious that the AC bus 3 (AC3), which now furnishes AC power to the starboard side of the ship, is defective. The operator's task is to remove bus 3 from the circuit and shift bus 2 to the starboard distribution. The first control action will involve touching switch 3 (SW3) which will remove bus 3 from the circuit by causing a processor-controlled solenoid to open the circuit breaker (the opposite of it's current state). Feedback

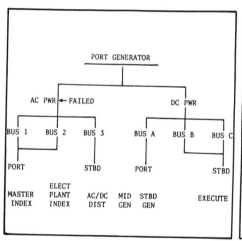

a. First-Level Indexing
    Control/Display

b. Second-Level
    Indexing Control/Display

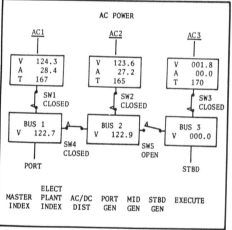

c. Port Generator
    Distribution
    Schematic

d. AC Power Distribution
    Schematic - Initial
    Condition

Figure 1. Shipboard Engineering Station Display Formats

of the circuit breaker changing state will cause the processor to change the displayed state of the switch, verifying the completion of this step for the operator.

Although this is a simplified example, it is apparent that, with proper format design, a number of advantages should accrue to the operator/system interface. In addition to centralization of controls and displays, reduction of search and movement time between information areas and control areas, and reduction of control componentry and required panel area, this concept permits a complete revision of the interface between the operator and the system through direct manipulation of the displayed information.

PERFORMANCE CONSIDERATIONS

There is little direct experimental evidence which shows the performance improvement which can be attributed to literal display/control integration of the type discussed in this paper. However, estimates can be generated by reviewing the components of reaction time and error rate performance in traditional system mechanizations. Then, those components that would be modified by the display/control mechanizations can be evaluated.

Figure 2 lists operator tasks involved in establishing a target track using a current shipboard radar console and the equivalent tasks for an integrated console using a plasma panel with a high resolution touch overlay panel. Note that only tasks expected to differ in operator response time are listed; tasks such as detection and communication would not be impacted by the type of integration illustrated.

Operator tasks times for the two sets of operations were estimated using the Siegal, Wolf, Ollman model mentioned earlier. The largest time differential occurs in this case for the two target designation tasks; using a cursor is much slower than placing a finger on the target. Other differences occur because of the reduced encoding of data, reduced visual search, and shorter reach distances. Of course, additional automation features could be added to further reduce operator response time but these reductions would not be attributable to control/display integration.

The important point to be made from the table is that the operator control/display interaction times were reduced by almost two-thirds by integration. Compariable reductions in operator error also may be expected by making use of the greater integration capabilities of the new display/control.

CONCLUSION

The purpose of this paper is to describe advanced display and control devices and to discuss the manner in which they can be employed to improve overall monitoring system performance. To this end, examples of both traditional and advanced display/control system configurations were illustrated. Furthermore, a performance

PRESENT RADAR CONSOLE		INTEGRATED RADAR CONSOLE	
Operator Task	Time (sec)	Operator Task	Time (sec)

1. DESIGNATE TARGET
   a. Activate ball tab
   b. Ball tab target
   c. Enter NEW TRACK
	9.15	1. DESIGNATE TARGET
		   a. Touch target
		   b. Touch NEW TRACK
		   c. Touch ENTER
			2.79

2. MONITOR TARGET RANGE/
   BEARING
	2.0	2. MONITOR TARGET RANGE/
		   BEARING
			1.0

3. DESIGNATE TARGET	9.15	3. DESIGNATE TARGET	2.79

4. MONITOR TARGET/RANGE
   BEARING
	2.0	4. MONITOR TARGET RANGE/
		   BEARING
			1.0

5. DESIGNATE TARGET	9.15	5. DESIGNATE TARGET	2.79

6. MONITOR TARGET RANGE/
   BEARING
	2.0	6. MONITOR TARGET RANGE/
		   BEARING
			1.0

7. DETERMINE CPA/TCPA
   a. Activate ball tab
   b. Ball tab target
   c. Enter CPA/TCPA
	9.15	7. DETERMINE CPA/TCPA
		   a. Touch target
		   b. Touch CPA/TCPA
		   c. Touch ENTER
			2.79

8. MONITOR CPA/TCPA	2.0	8. MONITOR CPA/TCPA	1.0
TOTAL TIME	44.6	TOTAL TIME	15.16

Figure 2. Comparison of Expected Response Times for Comparable
Tasks on Present Radar Console and Integrated Console

comparison of traditional and advanced configurations was included.
Improvements in performance and other factors such as cost, volume,
etc., attributable to advanced display/control applications will,
of course, depend on the specific nature of the configurations.
However, there are many potential advantages of the advanced techniques as listed below, which should be considered in future monitoring system design.

1. Improved operator reaction time
2. Decreased error rate
3. Shortened training time via dedicated training modes
4. Simplified all digital interface with processing elements
5. System modifications by changes to software
6. Centralized operator interface

7. Installation flexibility due to reduced volume, weight
    and power
8. Increased reliability of all digital components

REFERENCES

Alden, D. G., Daniels, R. W., and Kanarick, A. F. Keyboard
design and operation: A review of the major issues. Human Factors,
1972, 4, 275-293.

Fitts, P. M. and Seeger, C. M. S-R compatibility: special
characteristics of stimulus and response codes. Journal of Experimental Psychology, 1953, 199-210.

Grossman, E. R. F. W. The information capacity of the human
operator in symbolic and non-symbolic control processes. In
Ministry of Supply Publication WR/D2/56, Information theory and
the human operator, 1956.

Seibel, R. Data entry devices and procedures. In H. P. Van
Cott and R. C. Kincade (Ed) Human engineering guide to equipment
design. Washington: Government Printing Office, 1972, 311-344.

Siegel, A. I., Wolf, J. J., and Ollman, R. A discontinuous
analytic model for simulating Apollo vehicle operator actions and
information exchange. Applied Psychological Services, 1962.

Welford, A. T. The measurement of sensory-motor performance:
Survey and reappraisal of 12 year's progress. Ergonomics, 1960, 3,
189-229.

DISCUSSION

SHACKEL :

It has often been suggested, and indeed it is one of the basic assumptions of computer technology, that changes implemented via the software are much cheaper than via the hardware. I suspect, on the contrary,
that we are more rapidly into the opposite situation, with software changes
(and even software development) being more costly. Your interesting and
logical development to improve display-control compatibility for the human
depends essentially upon software design and modification to utilise this
new piece of hardware. Will it in fact prove cost-effective ?

BAUERSCHMIDT :

System software costs are indeed high and often comparable to system
hardware costs. However the basic software to support display and control
functions is generally required and available independent of the particular
display and control mechanization. The additional software cost for sup-
porting this advanced control and display mechanization will probably be
small when compared to the total system software package. Furthermore,
our concept for implementation of the flat-panel display and touch panel
is to provide a single compact design qualified for use in various environments as well as a design-oriented software package. The existance of
a "universal" qualified control and display unit would save the very
considerable non-recurring design and qualification costs associated with
"system-unique" control and display hardware. The display design software
package would provide means of translating display drawings and logic
statements into operating display software. This would allow display modes
and control logic to be easily implemented and changed by human factors
and system engineers.

ELLIS :

I was interested in the use of a touch panel for track initiation
and tracking on a radar display. But I wonder if you can achieve sufficient accuracy from such a technique. Also, have you compared a touch
system with a light-pen device ? It would seem that the light pen is
potentially more accurate but might take a little longer to operate.

BAUERSCHMIDT :

The present implementation of the touch panel provides a control input resolution of 16 x 16 over the 8.5" x 8.5" display surface. A 32 x 32 resolution can be achieved without a major change in present touch panel mechanization. This resolution should be adequate for reconfigurable keyboards or other discrete input displays structured for finger touch system purposes.

Displays of an analog nature such as radar displays may require higher input resolution for target designation and target tracking. The additional resolution can be achieved but at added mechanization expense. In addition, with this higher resolution, the finger must be replaced or augmented. A stylus may be used as the touch panel interrupt device or an auxiliary symbol can be used to precede the finger as it is moved toward the desired target. The later approach may be more desirable than using a stylus or a light-pen, in that it avoids grasping and maneuvering an auxiliary device. No direct experimental comparisons of these alternative approaches have been made.

RIJNSDORP :

a) Did you run any experiments to find the optimum geometric orientation of "touch-displays" (between that of "controls" and that of "displays") ?

b) In Fig. 1 of your paper it takes two control moves to find the cause of failure. Could this cause ("port a.c. gen. failed") not be directly indicated on the first level display ?

BAUERSCHMIDT :

a) No controlled experiments have been conducted.

b) Actually the automatic system could present the lowest level display at which operator decision and action are required. Intermediate levels with manual staging are desirable for routine evaluation of system status as well as in situations where multiple failures require operator priority assessment.

KVÅLSETH :

Has any type of predictive display been incorporated into your proposed design ? If not, why not ?

BAUERSCHMIDT :

The display systems shown during the presentation do incorporate predictive display techniques although not in an integrated fast-time analog form as studied by Kelley. The submarine example utilizes rate information to predict submarine orientation. The display mechanization, however, is not representative of the multi-function displays which are available within the state of the art. The reason for this is the emphasis on display reliability and upon the maintenance of crew proficiency to control at the lowest (i.e. unaided) control level.

The electric utility control room system can provide, depending on application, trend information to assist the operator in assessing future system status.

INTEGRATED COMPUTER-GENERATED COCKPIT DISPLAYS

Stanley N. Roscoe and Janice E. Eisele

University of Illinois at Urbana-Champaign

USA

INTRODUCTION

In the new generation of high-speed, multi-mission aircraft the role of the pilot has changed substantially. New system elements typically require the man to be an information manager or a fast decision maker as opposed to a direct controller of flight variables. Adjustment to the new demands has been greatly assisted by innovations in display and control technology and the inclusion of advanced computers on board. These innovations have increased the degrees of freedom in function allocation and display and control system design. Yet, to capitalize on these opportunities, further improvements in sensing and display are necessary for a wise use of these additional degrees of freedom.

As aircraft become more sophisticated and their missions more demanding, there is an inevitable increase in the pilot's dependence on artificial devices for sensing and display of information about aircraft performance and for control of the aircraft in flight. One approach is to determine the specific information requirements for a particular flight in a particular aircraft and to judge the adequacy of a particular display against these. However, such an approach requires eternal iteration, and there is no way of assuring that all likely missions for any given airplane will be provided for in anything like an optimum manner. A more systematic approach is needed.

To succeed in applying modern technology to long-standing unsolved flight management and control problems, what is known from research and experience in specific contexts must first be abstracted through analysis and then integrated through synthesis.

Even if all of the pilot's information requirements were exhaus-
tively known, and the required dynamics for each displayed variable
specified quantitatively, creative design would still be called
for to embody those requirements in a clearly encoded display.
The transformations between information to be displayed and its
optimum coding remain obscure because lists of information requirements do not imply anything about the relationships among
items of information. Information should be considered as an
organic, dynamic system, not as discrete items.

    Williams (1947/71) conducted a generic analysis of the pilot's
job.

        Between the knowledge of what control movements to make and
        the knowledge of the purpose of a mission lie all the areas
        of information which together result in the accomplished
        flight. Since the only course of action open to a pilot
        is through manipulation of the aircraft's controls, it
        follows that all the information he receives must even-
        tually be filtered down to this level in order for him
        to participate in the flight at all. These pieces of
        information somehow work together in an organized way and
        for purposes of analysis, must be fitted into some descrip-
        tive pattern.... Thus, the first problem is to break away
        from the notion of specific ways for presenting information;
        the second, to try to develop a scheme into which all pieces
        of information will fit in a logical way.

Williams proceeded to conceive the embryo of such a scheme, and
Carel (1965) and Roscoe (1968; 1974) have developed his concepts
as summarized in the following discussion.

                            PILOT'S TASK HIERARCHY

    Williams viewed the overall task of the pilot as the linking
of discrimination and manipulation events to bring the aircraft
to the final mission goal. A flight mission, like any other human
activity, is goal directed, as shown in Figure 1 (adapted from
Carel, 1965). The planning of a flight starts with the completion
of the mission and requires the pilot to establish the various
subgoals that must be antecedent to the accomplishment of the
overall mission goal. Thus, the pilot has to determine, moment-
to-moment throughout a flight, the altitude to fly, the heading to
fly, the speed to fly, how long to fly, and the operating condition of his aircraft and its subsystems.

    To set up all the subgoals, the pilot must take into account
the constraining facts of flight: the condition of the aircraft
itself; the traffic, which may be friendly or unfriendly; the

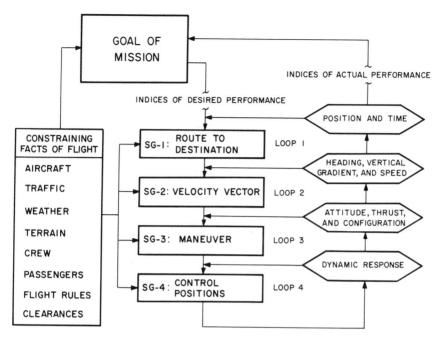

Figure 1.   The hierarchical nature of the flight task.

weather; the terrain over which he is flying, or against which he is delivering weapons; other crew members, if any, and their condition and tolerances; passengers, if any; and the rules and clearances that determine the constraints of flying in the local airspace, whether it be friendly domestic airspace or combat airspace.

The tasks that a pilot must perform if he is to complete a specific mission in a specific airplane include, first, the selection of indices of desired performance leading to all required subgoals, taking into account the constraints listed, and, second, controlling the aircraft to match its actual performance to the desired performance indices he has set up. Because the control of an aircraft is hierarchical in nature, as diagrammed in Figure 1, the pilot's job is complicated by the fact that several transformations are required between what he sees and hears and how he must move the controls at the lowest loop in the hierarchy.

If the relationships between the constraints of flight, the indices of desired performance, and the control of actual aircraft and subsystem performance were simple, there would be little for the pilot to do; but they are not simple, and the analysis of the transformations that the pilot must make in performing a given

mission defines not only the information that he must receive from
his displays or the outside world but also the things he must do
with that information to control his aircraft successfully.

Within the overall task hierarchy the major task clusters
deal with the iterative asking and answering of four questions:

1. What should be my route to my destination, and where am
    I with respect to my desired route and destination?

2. What should be my velocity vector, and what is it now?

3. What should be my attitude, thrust, and configuration,
    and what are they now?

4. What should I do with the controls to correct discrepancies
    that may exist in 1, 2, and 3?

An integrated display system should present the information necessary for the pilot to answer these questions quickly and accurately
throughout a mission.

INTEGRATED DISPLAYS

An integrated display system should be capable of generating
three basic display modes: parametric, graphic, and interactive.
Parametric displays dominate the current aircraft cockpit, presenting status indications of vital system and flight variables,
such as fuel level, engine performance, and radio frequencies,
as well as airspeed, altitude, attitude, and heading. Graphic
displays facilitate spatial and geographic orientation, thereby
providing aid in navigation, flying traffic patterns, landing the
aircraft, and performing any ground-referenced or horizon-
referenced maneuver. Interactive displays allow the pilot to
communicate with the computer for preflighting, troubleshooting,
flight planning, and managing various aircraft systems.

Display Classification

To understand the complexity of designing an integrated display
system, a knowledge of types of displays, modes of information
coding, and methods of display presentation is fundamental. Electronic sensor-generated and computer-generated displays, intended
both for orientation and for guidance and control, may be classified in many ways. Three particularly useful bases for classification are: first, the point of view presented, that is, the
spatial reference coordinates of the display; second, the mode of
information coding, ranging from the presentation of literal images

of the visual scene through full-bodied and skeletal analog representations to the abstract presentation of discrete alphanumeric
or digitally symbolic indications; and third, the manner in which
they are viewed, whether head-up or head-down and the associated
methods of presentation.

   Point of view. If the display surface represents a projection
of the aircraft's situation upon an imaginary vertical plane ahead
of the aircraft, it is called a forward-looking vertical situation
display. When the display represents a projection of the aircraft's
situation upon a horizontal plane beneath the aircraft, it is
termed a downward-looking horizontal situation display. A projection onto a vertical plane parallel to the aircraft's flight
path is known as a sideways-looking flight profile display. In
all such displays, both computed guidance commands and projections
of the flight path based on fast-time model predictions may be
presented, either in proper geometric perspective or by symbolic
coding schemes.

   In a vertical situation display, or VSD, the basic dimensions
are azimuth and elevation. Lateral displacement of translation
of display elements signifies change in aircraft heading or
horizontal flight path. Vertical translation of display elements
represents change in pitch or vertical flight path. Rotation of
display elements denotes movement of the aircraft about the roll
axis. Examples of VSDs are flight periscopes, forward-looking
infrared scopes, closed-loop TV systems, contact analog displays,
and by stretching the definition, some flight director displays.
The use of holographic optics in a reflection mode on various
areas of an airplane canopy or on the pilot's helmet visor is most
directly applicable to what we have termed forward-looking display
projections.

   A horizontal situation display, or HSD, represents the aircraft's flight path as seen from above looking down on a horizontal plane, such as the ground. The frame of reference of the
HSD may be cartesian coordinates as in road maps, azimuth and
range coordinates as in plan position (PPI) radar scopes, or a
polar grid system as necessitated at high latitudes. HSDs are
exemplified by map displays for navigation and by radar ground
maps. Sideways-looking displays have the basic dimensions of
elevation or altitude versus range or speed. Displays with this
point of view are useful for energy management, maneuvering near
the limits of the flight performance envelope, and possibly for
terrain following.

   Mode of information coding. Flight displays may be classified
along a continuum ranging from literal to abstract. Imaging displays range from direct, literal, optical projections, as in

periscopes, through electronically scanned TV, infrared, and radar
pictures, frequently scan-converted, to fully synthetic computer-
generated visual scenes analagous to animated cartoons drawn in
real time. Visual systems commonly used in modern flight simulators
project dynamic, perspective, color TV images of realistically
scaled models of airports to represent contact landing scenes as
viewed from the cockpit. Closed-loop low-light TV and infrared
sensors can present similar dynamic images on panel-mounted or
helmet-mounted displays within the cockpit.

Computer-generated imaging displays are on the threshold of
widespread use in presenting dynamic pictorial scenes analagous
to the pilot's contact view, initially in visual systems for flight
simulators and soon thereafter in airborne cockpit displays. Ad-
vocates of computer-generated imaging displays implicitly have
assumed that all information essential to the pilot for ground-
referenced maneuvers, such as takeoff and landing, terrain following,
weapon delivery, and air combat, is available from a clear view
of the outside world. A great deal of effort on these "contact
analog" displays has been directed toward generating realistic
dynamic images of airports and their surrounding terrain and
topography.

A more fundamental approach is to isolate the essential visual
cues from the contact view that the pilot uses in landing the aircraft and in other ground-referenced operations and incorporate
them into a display that may present a highly stylized contact
view in which the dynamic responses of the pictured elements are
analagous to those of their visual-world counterparts in contact
flight. A contact analog is not a camera image of the real-world
scene; it is a wholly artificial recreation of essential real-
world visual cues. A true contact analog display, however abstract or "skeletal" it may become, remains pictorial in that all
elements obey the same laws of motion perspective as their visual-
world counterparts.

Horizontal situation displays and flight profile displays
retain certain pictorial properties, but they typically differ
from VSDs in the direction of relatively greater abstraction.
Computer-generated map displays, in particular, present a skeletal
appearance, and performance envelope displays are not only
skeletal in appearance but may incorporate intentional scale
distortions. The ultimate level of abstraction is represented by
alphanumeric readouts, discrete warning indicators, and other
symbolic displays that retain no pictorial properties whatever.

Method of presentation. Displays can also be classified
according to how they are viewed. Direct-view displays, such as
those created on CRTs, storage tubes, and liquid-crystal, light-
emitting-diode, or plasma panels, present information directly to

the observed on the surface of the image-producing display medium. When the image is generated on a device out of the direct view of the observer, then projected by an optical system to a location in the observer's head-up view, the observer sees a virtual-image display. Virtual-image displays are exemplified by collimated light images reflected from a combining glass or from a holographic lens on the windshield in front of the pilot. There has been a long standing, often emotional debate over the relative merits of head-up projected displays (HUDs) and head-down direct-view displays and a more recent debate as to the relative merits of helmet-mounted CRT presentations. Each has its apparent advantages for application to specific flight operations.

Proponents of head-up presentation place great importance on the superpositioning of collimated guidance and control information on the outside visual scene, ostensibly to minimize shifts in eye fixation and accommodation during critical flight phases. However, head-up displays have been applied effectively only to landing and military weapon delivery because of the technical problems associated with their limited fields of view, restriction of pilot head movements, inflexibility of scale factors, misregistration of projected symbols with their real-world referents, and the associated penalties in size, weight, and cost.

Proponents of collimated sensor-generated and computer-generated displays projected from small helmet-mounted CRTs (1-in diameter or less) onto the pilot's helmet visor, or other integral combining elements, emphasize the advantages of free head movements, somewhat greater fields of view, variable scale factors in certain applications, accuracy of registration between computer-generated symbology and sensor-generated imagery, and the associated savings in size, weight, and cost. But helmet-mounted displays present problems in maintaining image visibility through wide ranges of ambient illumination and contrast, rivalry and misregistration between projected and real-world scenes, and despite major improvements in weight, balance, and integral packaging, some pilot discomfort and restriction of movement.

DISPLAY-CONTROL SYNTHESIS

The functions performed by any given airplane and its information-processing subsystems are highly mission dependent, and the missions airplanes are called upon to perform change both as a function of our galloping aeronautical technology and the ingenuity of flight crews. Despite extensive predesign mission and task analyses, airplane designers accept with resignation the fact that pilots will invent previously unheard of things to do with their airplanes, and other engineers will respond quickly with previously unimagined add-on devices to help the

pilots do them. The consequence is a cockpit patchwork that grows
in confusion throughout each airplane's life cycle while retaining
vestiges of confusion from earlier cockpits.

The serial consequences include increased logistic and
maintenance demands, increased pilot training requirements and
difficulty for experienced pilots both in transitioning to new
airplanes and in transferring from one old airplane to another, and
perennially renewed clamor for cockpit standardization. Engineering
test pilots frequently acknowledge that cockpit standardization is
a good idea but hasten to point out that right now is not a good
time to do it because things are changing so rapidly at the moment.
It always seems to be too early or too late to start with a clean
instrument panel and synthesize a context within which new mission
requirements may be readily accommodated.

In a sense it was too early, prior to this decade, to undertake the synthesis of a universal system that could accommodate
new requirements through software rather than hardware changes
without introducing new coordinate systems or incompatible information codes and control-display relations. Computing and display
technology now supports such an undertaking as a low-risk venture.
Within two large electronically scan-converted displays could be
synthesized essential orientation, guidance, prediction, control,
and independent flight monitoring information for any mission
function from the forward-looking and downward-looking points of
view. Two somewhat smaller displays might be dedicated to speed
and altitude information, including their derivatives and
associated commands and predictions, and a final multipurpose
display might mediate energy management, preflight and inflight
system testing and monitoring, communication management, and
assorted housekeeping.

A gross sketch of such a cockpit configuration is ventured
in Figure 2. Each of the large displays should be thought of as
an interactive electronic chalkboard on which both the computer
and the pilot can write. Both the forward-looking and downward-
looking chalkboards would accurately register dynamic real-time
sensor-generated imagery within the skeletal context of the
computer-generated forward-looking scene or the downward-looking
map, thereby accommodating specialized military requirements.
A minimum of dedicated single-parameter standby instruments would
be retained initially, for whatever comfort they may afford, and
a clock. Flight performance control would be provided through
interlocked dual sidearm controllers, thereby allowing the pilot
to fly with either hand comfortably and eliminating the visual
obstruction created by a central stick or yoke.

The computer-generated forward-looking scene, shown by itself
in Figure 3, would be quite skeletal, to accommodate the

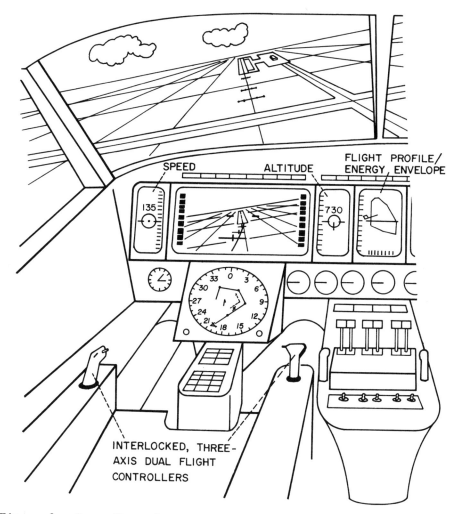

Figure 2.   Reconfigured airplane cockpit illustrating future
arrangement of integrated computer-generated displays
and computer-augmented controls.

superpositioning of dynamic forward-looking infrared or low-light
TV imagery without serious rivalry. Both command guidance and a
frequency-separated projection of the predicted flight path, as
shown by the successively smaller airplane symbols in Figure 3,
would be superposed in true perspective upon the computer-generated
scene. As shown, the airplane is low and to the left of a normal
straight in approach and banked to the right, but the pilot has made
the proper control input to pull up and roll left to bring the airplane to the desired touchdown point.

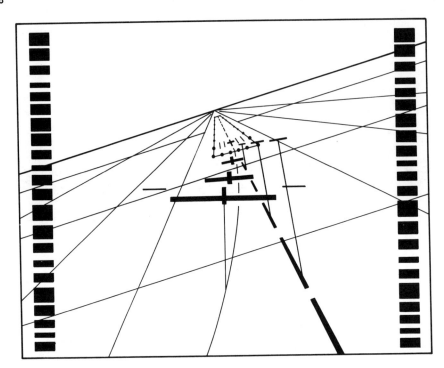

Figure 3.   Computer-generated contact analog display with fast-
time predictive flight-path projection and speed-error
and vertical-error rate fields at left and right,
respectively.

        Command guidance may be introduced selectively and presented
in ways that create a minimum of clutter to obscure the basically
pictorial presentation. The prominent vertical rate fields to the
left and right may be used to present speed and vertical flight
path guidance. By nulling the rate-field motion, the pilot nulls
the errors relative to the computed desired values of the moment.
In mission phases other than the landing approach depicted, the
rate fields might present command guidance for speed and altitude
control in 4-D navigation, inflight refueling, or other operations
requiring precise flight control.

        By bringing the outside world into the cockpit through the
superpositioning of dynamic imagery from high-resolution sensors
with limited weather penetrating capabilities, the head-up/head-
down controversy would be resolved in favor of the latter for all
flight operations other than vestigial contact maneuvers (even air
combat might be performed more effectively head-down with modern
sensing, computing, and display capabilities). Problems historically

associated with IFR and VFR transition would dissolve since, in effect, there would be none in the traditional sense. Truly all-weather (Category III) operation includes conditions in which the pilot has no contact visibility even while taxiing. In such conditions it is common for airport vehicles as well as airplanes to become lost, and the flight crew must determine not only that the airplane will land on the runway but also that the runway, or taxiway, is otherwise unoccupied.

In Category III operations, the long-standing "see to land" requirement, by definition, will be eliminated and replaced by a requirement for a weather-penetrating sensor system that will provide an alternate means of "seeing to land" or otherwise guaranteeing that it is safe to do so. Because low-visibility landing accidents are most frequently attributed to the required visual transition between instrument indications and the runway surface or its lighting configuration at a critical moment, many believe that "being able to see a little bit" creates problems that will not be present when the required visual transition is eliminated. If a true all-weather landing display were used in good weather as well as bad, Category III operations should be safer than Category II operations are today.

The quarter-century-old concept of total flight capability entirely by instrument reference, limited only by aircraft performance and human tolerance, is rapidly approaching technological feasibility. As observed by Williams in 1947, the problem is still "to break away from the notion of specific ways for presenting information ... [and] to develop a scheme into which all pieces of information will fit in a logical way." The digital transformation of sensor-derived information, including real-time literal imagery, for integral presentation with stored geographic, topographic, and aerodynamic information is now technically as well as logically feasible.

REFERENCES

Carel, W. L. Pictorial displays for flight. Washington, D.C.: Office of Naval Research, JANAIR TR 2732.01/40, 1965.

Roscoe, S. N. Airborne displays for flight and navigation. Human Factors, 1968, 10, 321-332.

Williams, A. C., Jr. Preliminary analysis of information required by pilots for instrument flight. Aviation Research Monographs, 1971, 1, 1-17 [Originally issued in 1947 as ONR Interim Report 71-16-1].

EVALUATION OF INFORMATION DISPLAYS IN CONTROL- AND MONITORING TASKS

Karl Reinhard Kimmel

Forschungsinstitut für Anthropotechnik

5309 Meckenheim, F.R. Germany

1. INTRODUCTION

The development of electronic displays opens completely new possibilities of information presentation in comparison to the use of conventional display systems. Since information presentation to the human operator or control-supervisor is of great importance it is necessary to evaluate alternative display configurations so that the one which has the lowest operator workload or permits the best performance can be selected.

Unfortunately, at the moment one is not able to evaluate display configurations for specific tasks. Therefore one must conduct time-consuming and tedious experiments in order to find out certain values from which one can indirectly judge the quality of the displays, when those were the only variables in such an experiment. So the study of displays is often carried out by including man in a continuous tracking task and characterizing the various display configurations by their respective control errors. In supervisory control tasks one would count the number of correct reactions and relate to the number of trials and could thus characterize different configurations by their respective scores.

Those methods, which are no doubt acceptable, are nevertheless very unsatisfactory since they supply non-generalizable results, perhaps valid only for the specific experimental set-up used, and tie together on the other hand uncommensurable items.

The application of the concept of information theory enables us to remove this drawback at least partially. With this concept one regards the man in the control-loop as an information-processing system, taking up visual information via the display and handing over information by way of his hand-arm system to appropriate control devices. The information theoretical methods conduct us to the calculation of the so-called "transinformation", which denotes the mean information flow per unit time, i.e. the amount of information correctly transmitted through a communication channel, in our case, the man. Therewith we have approached considerably to the informational aspects of displays and the best display configuration is then the one in which information is presented in such a manner that man is capable of transmitting the highest information rate.

The concept of information theory has already been applied among others, by Wempe and Baty [2] in 1966 in the investigation of human tracking performance with various controlled element dynamics. They also dealt in 1968 [3] with human transinformation ceilings in multiaxis tracking tasks. In this second paper they also reported on the influence of the forcing function on the information transmitting capacity of man. Etschberger [4] used transinformation in an experiment where he tested three different display set-ups which differed in degree of combination or integration of display elements in a three-axis tracking task. The first display set-up involved three monitors, the second configuration only two and the last one monitor. The elements of information presentation remained nearly the same in all cases. The differences Etschberger found in transinformation measures can be explained by the differences in eye-scan required by the different display set-ups.

2. DESCRIPTION OF THE EXPERIMENT

In the present study involving four different CRT-display configurations the influence of integration of information on the transinformation rate was investigated as well as the relationship between this measure and the root-mean-square (RMS) control error.

2.1 Experimental Task

The investigations were carried out with a three-axis control task. The subjects had to minimize the deviations of three identical controlled elements (fig. 1) with the dynamics

$$F_1 = F_2 = F_3 = \frac{1 + 1.1\,s}{(1 + s)(1 + 2s)}$$

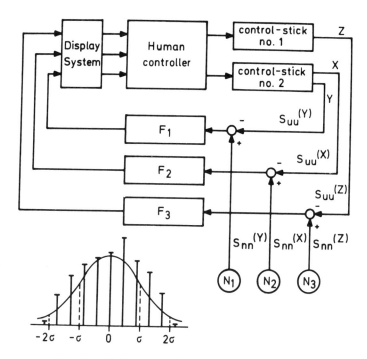

Fig. 1 : Scheme of the experimental set-up

The disturbances or forcing functions N_1, N_2, and N_3 were introduced by summing together with the operators control signals at the input of the three controlled elements (fig. 1). Three noncorrelated, nearly gaussian distributed noise sources were used as the disturbances. All three noise signals had identical statistical properties. Their amplitude distribution is depicted in the lower part of fig. 1. By using uncorrelated noise sources it is made sure, that there are no coupling effects between the three control-axes.

The next figure (2) shows the four display configurations with different degrees of integration which were used in the experiment. The orientation of the axes on the displays corresponds to the orientation of the two control sticks used. In all display configurations the z-axis was affected by the left hand by means of a one-dimensional stick and both x- and y-axes by a two-axes stick operated by the right hand. The separate x- and y-axes of configuration I are substituted by a cross in configurations II and III. The two pointers of the respective axes of configuration I are substituted in II and III by an x. In configuration III the z-deviation is represented by a stroke coming out of the x-centre vertically up- or downward according to the sign of the z-deviation. In configuration IV all errors are represented by a vector in a three-dimensional

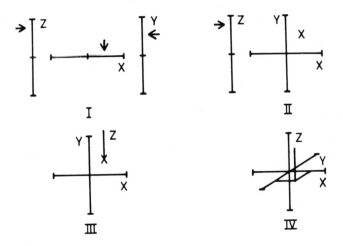

Fig. 2 : Four display configurations I-IV

coordinate system, with the special feature, that this vector is not displayed itself, but rather its three cartesian components (the three deviations).

2.2 Experimental Procedure and Evaluation

For the experiment 12 subjects were used, who had to perform the control task with each of the four displays four times. Subjects were run twice in the morning and twice in the afternoon. The sequence of presentation of the four displays was permutated. Each single trial with one display configuration lasted five minutes, so that each subject had a total trial time of 80 minutes. Subjects were trained at the beginning of the experimental series until there was practically no more improvement.

For the purpose of experimental evaluation two quantities were calculated for each trial, namely system error in the form of standard deviation of the output signal of the controlled elements and transinformation. Since the controlled element output signals were found to be gaussian distributed with zero mean, their standard deviation was used instead of root-mean-square error, because under these conditions both measures are equivalent. Systems error was divided by the maximum error in order to obtain the relative control error. The transinformation rate was calculated by using the well-known formula

$$H_T = \int_0^\infty \mathrm{ld}\ \frac{S_{uu}(f)}{S_{uu}(f) - \dfrac{|S_{nu}(f)|^2}{S_{nn}(f)}}\ df,$$

(cf. [1]or [6]), wherein S_{uu} (f) means the auto-power-density spectrum of the output signal of the final control element (the control stick), S_{nn} (f) that of the noise input and S_{nu} (f) the cross-power-density spectrum of those signals (see fig. 1).

3. EXPERIMENTAL RESULTS

The two measures relative control error R and transinformation H_T are represented in fig. 3 for the four display configurations in the form of histograms. The complete bars represent the total mean values over all subjects and for all three control axes. The marked subdivisions of the histogram amplitudes show the contribution of single axis values in relation to the total mean value error. At the first glance one will see that the values in both parts of fig. 3 have a reciprocal tendency from each other, i.e. the display with the lowest values on the left has the highest value on the right hand side of the figure. If we form the product $\pi = H_T \cdot R$ of the two values corresponding respectively, we get

Display config.	I	II	III	IV
π/(bits/sec)	1.16	1.18	1.18	1.10

i.e. a mean of 1.155 and a difference of each value above from this mean of less than five percent. So we can see that under the conditions of this experiment, the quantities relative control error and transinformation behave reciprocally to each other. We shall see below however, that this need not be true, in general.

Comparisons of results between configurations II and III indicates the equivalence of both measures in overall performance. However one can see a performance difference between these displays among the three axes. Whereas the portion for the y-axis of both configurations shows nearly the same value for error and transinformation, these values are not the same for the z-axis. The relative mean error is larger (accordingly transinformation smaller) for configuration III than for II. An equal but opposite effect in the x-axis occurs in order to equalize the overall performance. One would not expect this result, since configuration III requires fewer eye movements in comparison with display II. But obviously display II has the advantage that small deviations near the origin can be perceived easier and therefore erroneous reactions occur less frequently. Consequently, the advantage of higher integration in display III is eliminated by a reduced discriminability of small deviations as against configuration II. The subjects probably altered their strategy in permitting larger deviations in axis z and shifting their attention to the x-axis.

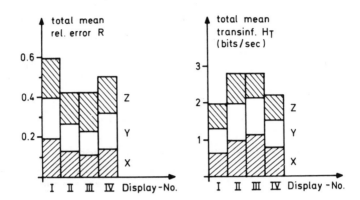

Fig. 3 : Total mean values of relative control error (left) and transinformation
(right) for the configuration I-IV

Finally, display configuration IV, which was conceptionally seen to be a
nearly ideal form of an integrated display for the three quantities, was better
than display I, which demanded the most eye movements, but was inferior to
II and III. The reason may be because of some confusion in the perspective
presentation, so that the subjects had to allow larger deviations to occur,
before they could react with certainty.

As we have seen, the total values of control-error and transinformation
behave reciprocally. To elucidate this and to assure that this result was not
due to chance, let us examine fig. 4 which relates corresponding pairs of
values H_T and R to each other for each of the three axes with displays and

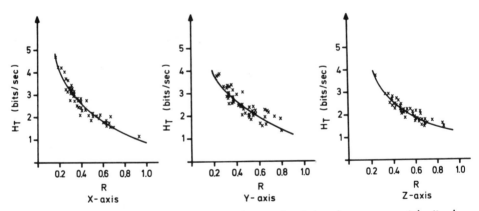

Fig. 4 : Error-transinformation curves for each of the three axes with displays
and subjects combined

subjects combined. It will be recalled that in fig. 3 the same reciprocal trend between these values was seen with respect to axes x and z. If the total values for those displays were equal by chance, then the error-transinformation curves for the three axes would show this by a large scattering of the plotted points. We can state, that this is not the case. Of course, the standard deviation of the plotted values in fig. 4 is larger compared to that of the total values. But if we realize that in single trials many factors such as motivation, fatigue, strategy and others can vary in wide ranges this would be expected. In order to judge the reliability of the values of the total means we calculated the mean-related standard deviations of the single pairs of values from fig. 4. They are given in the following table :

axis	x	y	z
mean $\overline{H_T \cdot R}$/(bits/sec)	1.12	1.18	1.19
mean-related standard deviation $\dfrac{\sigma(H_T \cdot R)}{\overline{H_T \cdot R}}$	0.1033	0.1559	0.1029

We can state that the mean-related standard deviation value for the y-axis of nearly 16 percent prevents us from assuming a rigid physical relationship between H_T and R, but the values are good enough to establish a statistical connexion between them. The larger standard deviation in the y-axis may be caused by a partial coupling of the two axes owing to the two-dimensional control stick.

Stein [5] mentioned in his 1974 report, that H_T and R can deviate severely from the reciprocal behaviour found in the present experiment, if the strategy of the subjects varies. So for example transinformation tends to infinity when a linear controller is installed into the control-loop, which, due to a small amplification constant, permits an error of nearly 100 percent, so that the product $H_T \cdot R$ also becomes infinite. On the other hand, the dynamics of the controlled element can force subjects to abandon the linear control strategy. So for instance, one would expect that a human controller would pass over to a "bang-bang" strategy in order to minimize the error, when a second-order integrating controlled system is applied. In that case, the transinformation is also minimized because the correlation between disturbance and operator control input tends to zero.

4. CONCLUSIONS

A display experiment with simple dynamics for the comparison of four display configurations presenting the deviations of three quantities each, was carried out. Two performance measures were used, namely relative control error and transinformation. As is stated elsewhere (cf. [5] or [6] the measure transinformation is not suitable for the validation of tracking performance. Difficult controlled element dynamics as applied by other authors impose additional information processing operations on the subjects which can exceed the processing load effects of visual coding, so that their negative findings concerning the reliability of transinformation are understandable.

The measure of transinformation gives a convenient description of the experimental set-up, when the characterization of displays is required. In these cases one can apply simple proportional dynamics and relatively mild disturbance functions so that there is not given rise to subjects to leave a linear control strategy. The results can then be tested and supported by the calculation of control error. In order to determine the limits of the area of application of transinformation further investigations are required.

REFERENCES

[1] FANO, R.M., Transmission of Information. Cambridge : MIT Press, 1963.

[2] WEMPE, T.E. and BATY, D.L., Usefulness of Transinformation as a Measure of Human Tracking Performance. NASA-SP-128, pp. 111-129, 1966.

[3] WEMPE, T.E. and BATY, D.L., Human Information Processing Rates During Certain Multiaxis Tracking Tasks with a Concurrent Auditory Task, IEEE Transactions on Man-Machine System, Vol. MMS-9, No. 4, 1968.

[4] ETSCHBERGER, K., Untersuchungen zur Beurteilung optischer Informationsdarstellung in Mensch-Maschine-Systemen, Kybernetik 9 (1971), pp. 112-122.

[5] STEIN, W., Vergleichende Untersuchung einachsiger manueller Regelvorgänge und Beurteilung ihrer linearen Modellierung, Bericht Nr. 21, Dezember 1974, Forschungsinstitut für Anthropotechnik, 5309 Meckenheim, Germany.

[6] SHERIDAN, T.B. and FERREL, W.R., Man-Machine Systems, Information, Control and Decision Models of Human Performance. Cambridge : MIT Press, 1974.

DISCUSSION

LAIOS :

Can you explain what are the advantages of using the measure of transinformation instead of more traditional measures of performance as RMS error, control effort, power spectrum densities of error and control effort or some combination of these measures ?

KIMMEL :

In my opinion transinformation is a convenient measure for the characterization of displays, since it is an informational measure and should therefore be most appropriate for displays which are information sources. Moreover, in cases where a mixture of analog and digital components is to be found in a display configuration, we have the possibility to sum up the partial measures, which would be difficult if other measures were used, such as RMS-error or power spectrum densities, or even different measures such as RMS-error for the analalog displays and percentage of correct responses for the digital parts of a display configuration.

SINGLETON :

The information processing rates seem rather low. What kind of subjects were used in the experiment ?

KIMMEL :

The information processing rates in fig. 3 seem low, because the total rates were divided by 3 in order to apportion the total rate to each of the 3 separate axes. This was done to permit a comparison with the values in fig. 4 where results of all runs are presented for each axis separately. The subjects used were some of my male colleagues aged 21 - 35 with a technical background and with some tracking experience.

MAN-MACHINE RELATIONSHIP IN SELTRAC*

Sandro Bossi

Standard Elektrik Lorenz AG (ITT)

Stuttgart, Germany

1. INTRODUCTION

The design of urban mass transit systems must resolve
various problems concerning man-machine relationships.
This is especially valid for fully automated rail
guided systems. SELTRAC is one possible automation
concept for these systems. SELTRAC's development is
funded by the german Ministry of Research and Technology
(BMFT). Man-machine aspects have been analysed during
the definition, development and testing of SELTRAC.

The patronage expects safety, reliability, short waiting
times, low fares, reasonable comfort, rapid transit
and simple system usage. Transport authorities require
quick response to actual demands, minimum energy consumption, minimum operating personnel and maximum availability.

Existing public transport can not entirely provide the
required services because of rigid time-tables during
the peak hours, the infrequent off-peak services, and
the rigid routeing with its associated frequent transfers and waiting times.
This paper describes the relationship between man and
SELTRAC.

2. SHORT DESCRIPTION OF SELTRAC

SELTRAC comprises one or more control centers (depend-

*SELTRAC (Standard Elektrik Lorenz Transport Control).

ing on network size) exchanging vital data with a computerized control system in each driverless vehicle. A control center contains a number of on-line computers with a central operator in supervisory and advisory control. SELTRAC has a command structure allowing operations to continue in many possible failure conditions.

SELTRAC's flexible and modular operations management provides a traffic control system with one, or a mixture of Line Haul, Line Haul Express and Personal Rapid Transit Modes.

3. THE PASSENGERS

The majority of passengers are peak hour commuters; they learn to use the system quickly by observing the person in front. For casual passengers the variance in habits and ability is extensive. This minority group includes visitors, small children, the elderly and the handicapped. Because this group uses the system outside peak travel times, the possibility of learning by observation is often lacking. Therefore station facilities should be designed to meet the necessities of this group; simplicity of the equipment and clarity of operating instructions are most important.

4. PASSENGER FLOW THROUGH A STATION

A station has a concourse with ticket automats, ticket readers and destination selectors. The concourse is separated from the platform by turnstiles.

When a passenger enters the station and is not used to the system, he looks for directions. These should be pictorial or symbolic as far as possible - a graphic strip for example. This is particularly important for visitors and foreigners. A map of the transit network and an urban map in each station should identify main orientation points and stations of the network and a 'you-are-here' indication.

When a passenger selects his destination and passes through the turnstile, his destination is indicated to the control system. This is important for PRT service.

The number of entry turnstiles, destination selectors, ticket automats and ticket readers, and their location should be based on the expected ridership for each particular station to avoid queues.

For fixed fare operation with turnstiles, fare payment

equipment, destination selectors and entry turnstiles
can be integrated. From this configuration, to enter
the system, the passenger would:

- Insert exact fare (coins or tokens).
- Select his destination.
- Check that selected destination is indicated.
- If necessary, cancel incorrect selection and re-
  select.
- Pick up the ticket (if a ticket is used).
- Pass through the entry turnstile.

If a route-dependent fare system is in operation, the
ticket automats and destination selectors are combined,
and separated from the turnstiles. One possible configuration is to group destination selectors according
to line or route, indicating, of course, the station
names. After selection, the fare is indicated; payment
accepts the indicated selection.

Items such as destination and validity are encoded on
a magnetic strip on the ticket. To reach the platform
the passenger first inserts the ticket in a reader
which transmits the destination to the Control Center.
If the ticket is valid, the turnstile is unlocked and
the passenger can pass through. This procedure, similar
to the Paris Metro, has the advantage of separating the
ticket automats from the turnstiles.

Selecting a destination, looking for coins and paying
takes longer than going through the turnstiles, so the
ratio of turnstiles to destination selectors can be
decreased considerably without causing queues. 'Off-
line' automats and destination selectors improve availability; a defective ticket automat only partially reduces passenger flow.

System personnel should be able to lock the turnstiles
to avoid dangerous platform overcrowding following
service interruption; passengers are informed of this
by an illuminated sign. For safety reasons, the entry
turnstiles rotate freely in the reverse (exit) direction.

Turnstiles should permit the inversion of the direction
of use according to rush-hour demand direction.
Destination indicators, suspended above the platform
and at right angles to the track, show the arrival
sequence of vehicles, their destination and stopping
position; indicators are updated as soon as a vehicle
departs.

Exceptions to normal service will be announced by a
central operator via loudspeakers recessed in the
station roof. Such announcements are preceded by an
audible tone to attract the attention of passengers.

5. THE PASSENGER IN THE VEHICLE

Station names should be shown on boards at the approach
to stations; a plan of the transit network is displayed
in the vehicle.

In the vehicles, clear symbolic information will explain
how to operate the doors, the emergency stop, the
'stop-next-station' button, and emergency and voice
communication equipment.

After the vehicle has stopped in a station, the doors
on the platform side can be opened. Opening is enabled
by the control system and then activated by the passenger with a push-button inside the vehicle; a push-
button on the outside of the vehicle is used by passengers wishing to board. This safety measure avoids
danger in the event of a failure, and unnecessary loss
of conditioned air in hot and cold weather.

Short headways (less than 3 minutes) do not require
vehicle operation according to a time-table. Door
opening time is a function of passenger movement;
passengers usually intend to enter a vehicle as long
as there is enough space. After a short interval the
doors will try to close; if passengers are still board-
ing or leaving, the closure of the doors will be inhib-
ited by safety edges and footboard switches. After a
programmable time, an audio-visual signal indicates
that the doors will close, gently and finally.

6. THE VOICE COMMUNCATION NETWORK

In an automated rapid transit system, communication
between passengers and system operators becomes essential; the passenger must not be given the feeling that
he is part of an impersonal computer system. A general
feeling against automated transit systems includes
the fear of abusive or criminal acts. In the event of
system failures, passengers in a selected vehicle,
or in all vehicles can be reassured by the central
system personnel. Voice communication to passengers
in stations is via a telephone network and in vehicles
is via a radio link.

The terminal equipment of both networks should be secure against vandalism. One solution is to use wall-recessed microphone-loudspeaker combinations (no hand-set). All passenger voice communication facilities are two-way; passengers may not be able to operate a press-to-talk facility, especially under stress.

Communication with the operator is established by a simple push-button. If the operator is busy, the call request is stored. When a passenger pushes the call-button in a station or in a vehicle, the identity of the calling point is indicated on the operator's control desk. The operator selects this number and the voice communication link is established. This method prevents unnecessary use, and only the operator can terminate the communication link. The operator can follow possible criminal actions and advise the police.

One of the most difficult problems is to find a good balance between the attraction of using the telephones, and the prevention of unnecessary use. One method is to cover the call button of the recessed telephones; the accessibility is psychologically reduced but not physically limited.

General information can be given to all vehicles over a radio link, and to stations via the loudspeakers re-cessed in the station roof. All announcements are pre-ceded by an audible tone to attract the attention of passengers.

An additional dedicated voice communication wire and radio network is necessary for system personnel for use in emergency, maintenance and manual operations.

7. OPERATOR ACTIVITIES

The number of operators depends on the size of the system and on the degree of implemented automation; determining parameters for a workload analysis are:

- Number of stations.
- Frequency of mode change.
- Equipment availability.
- User experience.
- Expected voice communication traffic.

Even for a small system, at least two operators are necessary per shift; each must have the skill to operate the complete system when one operator is temporarily absent. Fig. 1 shows an example of the performed workload analysis for "change of mode from PRT to line haul" in a small demonstration system.

The central operator has system responsibility and can interface with the system via 2 video display units for normal and failure data, and 2 TTYs for hard copy. In addition he can communicate with other staff members via the maintenance telephone and radio network.

A system overview is shown on a mimic located in front of the operator desk. Illuminated elements show the present vehicle locations; a flashing light indicates a vehicle failure. The precise vehicle position or the number of a vehicle occupying a track section can be retrieved via a VDU connected to the system management center.

The main task of the 2nd operator is to manage the voice communication network. The public and maintenance voice communication terminals in the control room should be duplicated; this allows both operators to handle a larger number of calls.

A mock-up of the operator interface allowing the simulation of operator activities under normal and emergency situations should be used to define the final layout of the control room. Fig. 2 shows a central operator place configuration in SEL's Stuttgart Simulation Center.

SUMMARY

This article describes some problem areas in the man-machine-interfaces with automated rail-guided transit systems. All theoretical human factor analysis examples must be verified by exhaustive testing under real environmental conditions. This required feedback is then gained by an evaluation of practical applications such as Transurban, Kompaktbahn and ICTS Toronto.

SEL's studies in this field will continue to improve constantly the human factor aspects of SELTRAC. Each implemented improvement must either facilitate the operation of the system or its usage, which in return increases the attractiveness of the system for the patronage.

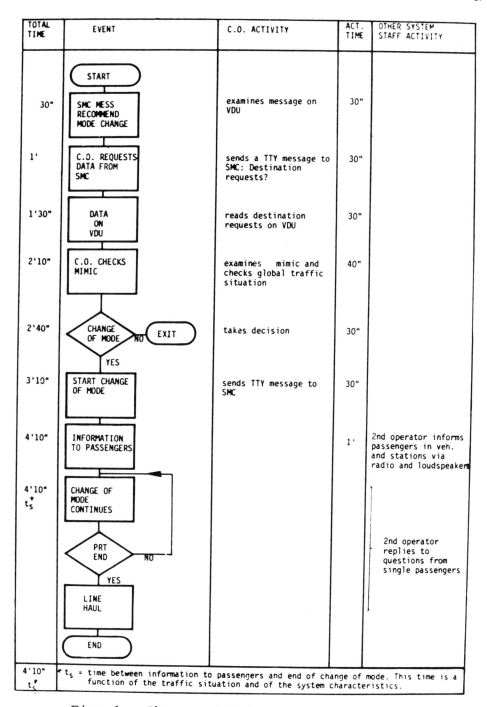

TOTAL TIME	EVENT	C.O. ACTIVITY	ACT. TIME	OTHER SYSTEM STAFF ACTIVITY
	START			
30"	SMC MESS RECOMMEND MODE CHANGE	examines message on VDU	30"	
1'	C.O. REQUESTS DATA FROM SMC	sends a TTY message to SMC: Destination requests?	30"	
1'30"	DATA ON VDU	reads destination requests on VDU	30"	
2'10"	C.O. CHECKS MIMIC	examines mimic and checks global traffic situation	40"	
2'40"	CHANGE OF MODE — NO — EXIT — YES	takes decision	30"	
3'10"	START CHANGE OF MODE	sends TTY message to SMC	30"	
4'10"	INFORMATION TO PASSENGERS		1'	2nd operator informs passengers in veh. and stations via radio and loudspeakers
4'10" t_s^r	CHANGE OF MODE CONTINUES			
	PRT END — NO — YES			2nd operator replies to questions from single passengers
	LINE HAUL			
	END			
4'10" t_s^r	t_s = time between information to passengers and end of change of mode. This time is a function of the traffic situation and of the system characteristics.			

Fig. 1:   Change of Mode: PRT to Line Haul

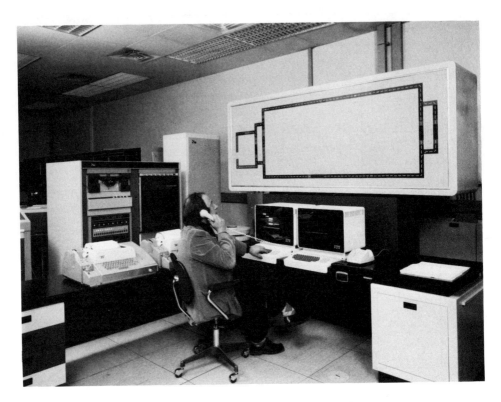

Fig. 2   The 1st Operator Place

Literature

Dr. K.U. Dobler: 'Die Betriebsablaufsteuerung SELTRAC
für Nahverkehrsysteme'.
ETR 5/1975

A. Caprasse - H. Zeopold - H. Maas - K. Stengel: 'Tarif-
gestaltung und Fahrgastbedienung in ÖPNV in Paris'.
Verkehr und Technik 1974, Heft 12

H. Kopp: 'Fahrausweisautomaten der S-Bahn, Frankfurt/M'.
Signal + Draht 66 (1974) 6/7

E. Grandjean: 'Physiologische Arbeitsgestaltung - Leit-
faden der Ergonomie'.
Otto Verlag - Thun und München, 1967

DISCUSSION

RIJNSDORP :

What type of experiments are being planned to test the actual suitability of the envisaged pictorial directions and signs for passengers ?

BOSSI :

The suitability of the pictograms for the passengers will be analysed in a later stage of SELTRAC, in direct relation to the practical implementation of public projects, like ICTS Toronto.

Proposals for generally valid symbols will be presented to competent international institutions for discussions and worldwide introduction.

DRIVER DECISION-MAKING RESEARCH IN A LABORATORY SIMULATION*

R. Wade Allen, Stephen H. Schwartz, and Henry R. Jex

Systems Technology, Inc.

Hawthorne, California, U.S.A.

ABSTRACT

This paper reviews a simulation approach to the study of driver decision-making behavior. Tasks were set up with rewards and penalties applied as performance incentives. Simulation tasks were selected that would fit into a decision context and could be efficiently implemented. Familiar driving situations were chosen to give an interesting, motivating driving scenario and cover a range of decision-making situations. The tasks were programmed to occur randomly and repeatedly in a simulated continuous drive. Expected Value Theory was used both to set up task conditions and as a means for data analysis and interpretation. Both performance and decision-making behavior were measured. Decision-making behavior was consistent with an Expected Value decision-making model interpretation.

INTRODUCTION

The simulation approach and research described here were motivated by the desire to investigate changes in driver decision making under alcohol impairment. Past studies with part task simulations have considered driver decision-making (risk-taking) behavior (Refs. 1-4) but have been inadequate in two key respects: 1) the part task simulations focused on single tasks and behavioral factors

---
*This work was supported by the Office of Driving and Pedestrian Research, National Highway Traffic Safety Administration, U. S. Department of Transportation. The views expressed in this paper are those of the authors and do not necessarily represent those of the National Highway Traffic Safety Administration.

71

unlike the multifaceted nature of typical driving situations; and
2) there was little control of the rewards and penalties which are
central to the issue of making decisions in the face of risks (e.g.,
tickets, accidents, etc.). The approach taken here was to provide
a realistic driving scenario containing a variety of tasks which
would provide a reasonable driving workload, as well as a cost functional of rewards and penalties that the driver would attempt to
maximize (i.e., make timely progress but avoid tickets and crashes).
A type of decision theory well suited to this sort of situation —
Expected Value Theory — was used to guide parameter selection and
interpret the results.

APPROACH

At the outset of this research it was necessary to select those
driving situations that would fit into a decision-making research
context and could be efficiently implemented in a laboratory simulation and (later) real vehicle field tests. During this selection
process we considered a variety of driving decision-making situations, as summarized in Table 1, with the goal of selecting a plausible cross section of situations that would be encountered in normal
driving activities. The situations in Table 1 are first categorized
according to the class of decision task they represent, which has
been grossly subdivided into situations involving: simple single-
stage decisions where the driver commits himself to a single alternative; and sequential decisions where actions on the part of the
driver lead to some change in the situation, which then provides
input for a further updated decision (a dynamic decision environment as discussed in Ref. 5).

Cases involving interaction with adjacent traffic are difficult
to simulate. With this restriction in mind we selected the three
starred situations in Table 1 and arranged them in a driving scenario that covers a range of driver decision-making situations. These
tasks were arranged to occur randomly and repeatedly in a simulated
continuous drive. The goal of this approach was to imbed individual
decision-making situations in a plausible overall driving scenario so
as to approximate the conditions under which drivers normally make
decisions. Within this scenario, we then evaluated decision-making
behavior on the individual tasks in terms of the perceptual, psychomotor, and risk acceptance factors. To date, the technique for
accomplishing this has been most highly developed for the signal
light task, which is described in detail below.

SIGNAL LIGHT DECISION TASK

The signal light decision situation is broken down into its
basic kinematic elements in Fig. 1. When the light changes from
green to amber the driver (at some arbitrary distance for the intersection) must decide whether to brake to a stop or to continue on

TABLE 1. DRIVING DECISION-MAKING SITUATIONS

DECISION CLASS	BASIC TYPE	SPECIFIC SITUATIONS
Single stage	Traffic control	Signal light[*] Course direction signs Train crossing
	Unexpected threats	Car, pedestrian, object unexpectedly enters roadway[*] Object in/on roadway
Single stage or sequential	Anticipated threats	Merging of adjacent car Approaching car at intersection Car braking ahead
Sequential	Maneuvers	Curve negotiation[*] Lane changing and merging Overtaking and passing

[*]Chosen for simulation.

through the intersection and "make the light." The original stimulus to the driver is the light change from green to amber. When the stimulus is detected and recognized, the driver must then estimate the probabilities of either "making" the light (before it turns red) or coming to a safe stop, based on current perceived speed and distance to the intersection. (The amber light time interval is normally set as a function of the posted speed limit and is known through experience by the driver.)

The signal light situation can be characterized in decision-making terms by: 1) decision alternatives, either braking or continuing on; 2) by the system performance outcomes of these alternatives, either making the signal safely or running the red light, or stopping safely or stopping in the intersection; and 3) the reward or penalty structure which provides incentives for selecting between the decision alternatives. A variety of models have been proposed for characterizing this type of single-stage decision situation (Ref. 6). A construct which seems particularly suitable for the

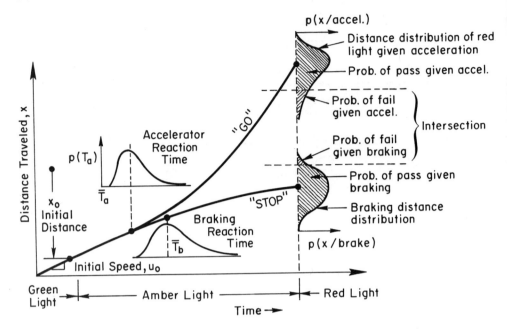

Figure 1. Driver/Vehicle Response at a Signaled Intersection

signal light task arises from Expected Value Theory (Ref. 7) where
the net value of a decision alternative is modeled as a weighted
sum of the probabilities of the various decision outcomes, each
weight being given by the value of that outcome to the decision
maker. The basic tenet of the theory is that a decision maker will
select the alternative which maximizes the expected values. The
model can be expressed mathematically in the following form:

<u>Given:</u>

    Decision alternatives, A_i

    Outcomes or consequences, X_j

    Conditional probabilities and values of X_j, given A_i:
    $P(X_j/A_i)$ and $V(X_j/A_i)$

<u>Decision Rule:</u>

    Decision Maker chooses $[EV(A_i)]_{max}$ where

$$\text{Expected Value}(A_i) = \sum_j \text{Probability } (X_j/A_i) \cdot \text{Value}(X_j/A_i) \tag{1}$$

Variations on this model arise from different interpretations of the probabilities and values. The values can be either objective (money, time, etc.) or subjective (the meaning of money or time to the driver), in which case they are referred to as utilities. Probabilities can also either be objective, as determined by physical events or subjective as perceived and interpreted by the decision maker. The distinction between objective and subjective probabilities is pertinent here because subjective probability provides a measure of risk "perceived" and, presumably, "accepted" by the driver.

Now consider the expected values for making a Go or Stop decision in the signal light case, summed across each consequence:

$$EV(Go) = \overbrace{P(Success/Go)V(S/G)}^{\text{Saving Time}} + \overbrace{P(Fail/Go)V(F/G)}^{\text{Running Red Light}} \quad (2)$$

$$EV(Stop) = \overbrace{P(Success/Stop)V(S/S)}^{\text{Safe Stop}} + \overbrace{P(Fail/Stop)V(F/S)}^{\text{Stop in Intersection}} \quad (3)$$

These equations can be simplified for our simulated situation in several ways. First of all, safely stopping at an intersection is usually not a problem because of the way signal timing is set up. Therefore, $P(Success/Stop) \doteq 1$ and $P(Fail/Stop) \doteq 0$. Also, we can assume that the value for a safe go, $V(S/G)$, is neutral or zero, while the value for a safe stop, $V(S/S)$, is negative (penalty) due to lost time.

In real life the driver is not penalized for every red light he runs, but only the portion that is detected by police or those resulting in an accident, so that the probability of a ticket or accident must be taken into account. In our simulation we have restricted the outcome to tickets, and including this factor and the conditions given above the expected value equations can be rewritten as:

$$EV(Go) = P(Fail/Go)P(Ticket)V(Ticket)$$
$$EV(Stop) = V(Stop) \quad (4)$$

These equations imply only penalties; however, in our simulation scenario a subject is given an initial stake from which the penalties are subtracted. Thus, the subject should try to minimize penalties, and the appropriate strategy for accomplishing this, based on Eq. 4, is given by the following signal light decision rule for the driver:

$$\text{GO:} \quad P(G) = 1 \quad \text{if} \quad P(F/G) < \frac{V(\text{Stop})}{P(\text{Ticket})V(\text{Ticket})}$$

$$\text{STOP:} \quad P(S) = 1 \quad \text{if} \quad P(F/G) > \frac{V(\text{Stop})}{P(\text{Ticket})V(\text{Ticket})} \tag{5}$$

The decision-making rule in Eq. 5 implies ideal behavior; however, this is not to be expected in practice due to inconsistency (noise) and bias in the driver's perceptual and estimation processes. The effect of these factors is illustrated in Fig. 2. The plot shows the probability of going versus the driver's perceived (subject) risk of failure when going. The ideal switching behavior given by Eq. 5 is shown along with the non-ideal consequences of noise in the decision process which might be modeled as shown in the block diagram of Fig. 2a. Mathematically, we can express the probability of the driver's going, P(G), as a cumulative probability distribution function with the subjective probability or risk perceived by the driver as the random variable:

$$P_{Go}[SP(F/G)] = \frac{1}{\sqrt{2\pi}\,\sigma_{SP}} \int_0^{SP_c(F/G)} \exp\left\{-\frac{[SP(F/G)-\overline{SP}(F/G)]^2}{2\sigma_{SP}^2}\right\} dSP(F/G) \tag{6}$$

where $SP_c(F/G)$ is the switching criterion between stopping and going, $P(G) = 0.5$, and $\sigma_{SP(F/G)}$ represents noise or inconsistency in the driver's perception. Here the estimation noise of Fig. 2 is assumed normally distributed. The limits of the distribution are truncated by definition, since $0 < P(G) < 1$; however, in practical cases it will be assumed that the amount of area in the tails of the distribution beyond these limits is inconsequential.

The Fig. 2b plot gives an appropriate format for interpreting signal task decision data and illustrates some possible effects between different classes of data (e.g., subject groups, normal vs. impaired, etc.). First of all, the decision maker's noise or inconsistency (σ_{SP}) may increase. Secondly, the subjective probability switching point, $SP_c(F/G)$, might shift, becoming more conservative as illustrated or more risky with a shift in the opposite direction.

SIMULATION EXPERIMENT

The decision-making concepts discussed previously have been tested in a fixed-base driving simulation including an actual car cab and CRT-line-drawn dynamic presentation of a two-lane roadway which is described in detail elsewhere (Ref. 8). The tasks selected from Table 1 were randomly presented with repeated exposure in a programmed 15-20 minute drive scenario. As part of the scenario, subjects were motivated to complete a drive by a monetary reward ($10) which would correspond to the desire in an actual situation to

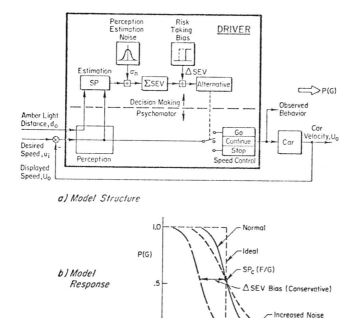

a) Model Structure

b) Model Response

Figure 2. Signal Light Decision-Making Model

return home from a tavern, party, etc. The subjects were also
rewarded for making timely progress in the drive ($2 per minute
saved) in order to provide some motivation for not stopping at signals, steering around obstacles, and negotiating curves at a reasonable speed. On the other hand, penalties were levied for speeding,
running red lights ($1-2), and crashing ($2) as defined by leaving
the edges of the defined roadway or hitting an obstacle. This
reward structure was evolved by careful preliminary testing and
evaluation.

Signal light timing was set up to give known times and distances
for arrival at the intersection given a constant speed. The amber
light duration was set at a constant 3 seconds. Signal timing, stopping distances, and available response time margins are given in
Table 2. Five different signal timings were used and randomly presented to the subjects, and a special circuit was employed to make
the timing independent of speed, as indicated in Table 2.

The data discussed here were obtained on the placebo days of an
alcohol experiment for 12 normal male subjects. The subjects were
tested four times during an 8 hour test session (roughly once every
2 hours). Each trial consisted of the regular drive scenario

TABLE 2.   SIGNAL LIGHT TIMING CONDITIONS

INTER-SECTION	TIME TO THE INTERSECTION FROM AMBER LIGHT (t_I)	STOPPING DISTANCE AT SPEED U_O (mph)						Δt MARGIN[‡]		
		MAXIMUM POSSIBLE[*] X_I			MINIMUM[†] X_s					
		35	40	45	35	40	45	35	40	45
1	0	0	0	0	0	0	0	< 0	< 0	< 0
2	2.2	113'	129'	145'	107'	133'	162'	0.12	< 0	< 0
3	2.8	144'	164'	185'	107'	133'	162'	0.72	0.52	0.35
4	3.4	175'	200'	224'	107'	133'	162'	1.32	1.14	0.94
5	5.5	282'	323'	363'	107'	133'	162'	3.41	3.24	3.05

[*]Distance at which amber light initiated in order to give desired t_I assuming a constant speed U_O: $X_I = U_O t_I$.

[†]Assuming a brake reaction time and maximum deceleration: $X_s = U_O t_{RB} + U_O^2/2a_B$

where t_{RB} = brake reaction time $\doteq$ 0.75 seconds

a_B = constant braking deceleration = 0.6 g = 19.3 ft/sec^2

[‡]Remaining time for decision making: $\Delta t = (X_I - X_s)/U_O$

employing various randomly presented tasks, and a special run of signal events used only to determine whether subjective estimates of risk were biased by a posteriori knowledge of task performance. After selected signal encounters, subjects were asked for their subjective estimate of the probability of failing (running the red light) if they decided to go, SP(F/G). During the special runs, the CRT was blanked just before the red light went on, in order to eliminate any feedback of observed task performance on the reported subjective probability.

RESULTS

Subjects were typically traveling between 40 and 45 mph on approach to the intersections. As shown in Table 2 this speed range would allow no margin for stopping for Intersections 1 and 2. With a 3 second amber light, and only 2.2 seconds required to enter intersections, the driver could easily make this signal condition and, in fact, no drivers stopped in this situation. For Intersection 3 the 2.8 second timing for entering the intersection was marginal with the

3 sec amber light, and drivers stopped roughly 25% of the time. For Intersection 4 the driver can clearly not make the signal unless he accelerates. Since the average approach speed was 40-45 mph and the speed limit 45 mph, the subjects did not have much of an acceleration option and, in fact, ended up stopping about 60-80% of the time.

The signal light results are analyzed in Fig. 3, according to the decision-making paradigm discussed previously, to determine driver decision-making behavior. In Fig. 3a the objective probabilities of going, P(G), and failing given a go, P(F/G), are compared. The probabilities are computed by dividing the total number of outcomes by the total number of opportunities (e.g., P(F/G) = number of go failures/ number of go's). As previously observed, Intersection 2 resulted in the subjects always going, P(G) = 1, and the timing was such as to preclude go failures, P(F/G) = 0. The timing was also adequate enough on Intersection 3 to allow safe go's; however, in this case the drivers did not always go (i.e., P(G) ≐ 0.75). Subjects did not go very frequently on Intersection 4 and had a high failure rate when they did, as would be expected by the timing condition shown in Table 2.

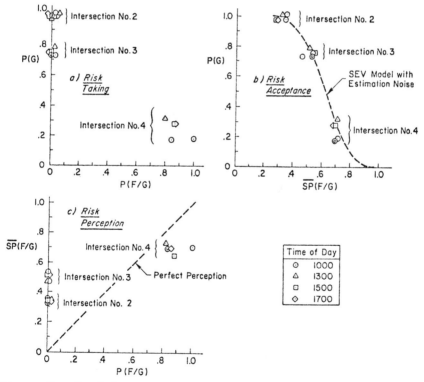

Figure 3. Decision-Making Behavior on the Signal Light Task
Averaged Over 12 Subjects, 8 Repeats
Per Intersection Per Trial

Subjects were asked for their subjective impression of the risk of going, SP(F/G), on certain signal light events during the driving scenario. Average subjective and objective measures of risk are compared in Fig. 3c to illustrate the driver's perception of risk. The reason for the lower go rate on Intersection 3 over Intersection 2 is apparent in the increased risk as perceived by the driver.

Finally, in Fig. 3b we compare the driver's probability of going, P(G), with their perception of the risk of failure, SP(F/G). Go behavior is consistent with <u>perceived</u> risk, and the relationship observed in Fig. 3b is consistent with a noisy expected value process (Eq. 6). The expected value model curve in Fig. 3b was computed for the values $SP_c(F/G) = 0.6$ and $\sigma_{SP} = 0.11$ and shows excellent agreement with the data. The σ_{SP} value was obtained from the variability between SP estimates for a given intersection, which demonstrates an important consistency within our decision-making noise model.

There is little evidence of outcome biasing of the subjective probability estimates as illustrated in Fig. 4. Data from the special runs with and without interruption are plotted versus subjective estimates from the normal drive scenario. Good correlation is evident between measures obtained with and without performance feedback, thus assuring minimal biasing of regular drive risk perception by knowledge of task performance.

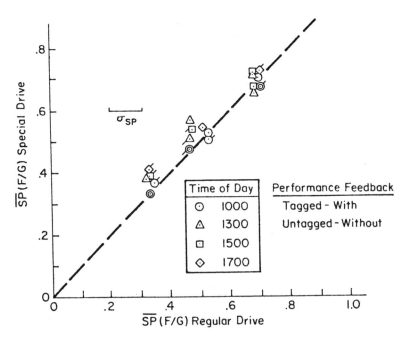

Figure 4. Comparison of Subjective Estimates With and Without Knowledge of Performance

CONCLUDING REMARKS

Expected Value Theory describes driver decision-making behavior fairly well in a simulated signaled intersection situation embedded in a larger overall driving scenario with performance incentives and penalties. This theory provides a model that is useful for data interpretation and which should be helpful in structuring and analyzing experiments involving driver stress and impairment. There are some differences between objective risk, $P(F/G)$, and perceived risk, $SP(F/G)$, which deserve further attention. Also, the effect of the reward/penalty structure on driver decision making should also be investigated.

Expected Value Theory should also be applicable to other single stage decision processes in driving such as the obstacle avoidance task employed in this simulation. Finally, further theoretical development is required to model driving situations involving dynamic decision-making situations (Table 1) which provide perhaps one of the more important classes of driving situations.

REFERENCES

1. Lewis, E. V., Jr., and K. Sarlanis, The Effects of Alcohol on Decision Making with Respect to Traffic Signals, U.S. Dept. of Health, Education, and Welfare Rept. ICRL-RR-68-4, 1969.

2. Cohen, H. S., and W. R. Ferrell, "Human Operator Decision-Making in Manual Control," IEEE Trans., MMS-10(2), 2 June 1969, 41-47.

3. Light, W. O., and C. G. Keiper, Effects of Moderate Blood Alcohol Levels on Automobile Passing Behavior, U.S. Dept. of Health, Education, and Welfare Rept. ICRL-RR-69-4, 1971.

4. Ellingstad, V. S., L. H. McFarling, and L. L. Struckman, Alcohol, Marijuana and Risk Taking, DOT HS-801 028, Apr. 1973.

5. Edwards, W., "Dynamic Decision Theory and Probabilistic Information Processing," Human Factors, 15(3), May 1972, 267-277.

6. Sheridan, T. B., and W. R. Ferrell, Man-Machine Systems: Information, Control, and Decision Models of Human Performance, Cambridge, Mass., MIT Press, 1974.

7. Edwards, W., and A. Tversky, Decision Making, Middlesex, Eng., Penguin Books, 1967.

8. Allen, R. W., J. R. Hogge, and S. H. Schwartz, "An Interactive Driving Simulation for Driver Control and Decision-Making Research," in NASA TM S-62,464, May 1975, 396-407.

DISCUSSION

LEMAIRE :

In your "signal light detection" model you expect a risk-taking bias to occur. Your experimental results, however, don't show this bias. Is there any explanation why the bias doesn't occur ?

ALLEN :

As mentioned in the introduction, the overall objective of the research was to measure the effects of alcohol impairment. Two possibilities for this impairment were given in Figure 2b : 1) noise, 2) bias. As our sober results show there was no apparent bias since the crossover point between stopping and going, P (Go) = P (Stop) = .5, occurred at a subjective probability value of ~ .6. This value is midway between the values of .4 - .8 calculated for the two penalty groups (i.e. $ 1 and $ 2).

KVÅLSETH :

It would appear to me that the events "Fail/Go" and "Ticket" are not independent. How do you justify the probability product in, e.g., equation (4) ?

ALLEN :

We should more correctly consider the event Ticket/Fail, where P(Ticket/Fail) = .3. We assume that the event Ticket/Fail is a subset of the event Fail/Go and that P(Fail/Go) P(Ticket/Fail) = P(Ticket/Go). With this modification we then rewrite equation (4) of our paper as follows :

$$EV(Go) = P(Fail/Go) \ P(Ticket/Fail) \ V(Ticket)$$
$$= P(Ticket/Go) \ V(Ticket)$$

and

$$EV(Stop) = V(Stop)$$

HUMAN PERFORMANCE AND WORKLOAD

IN SIMULATED LANDING-APPROACHES WITH AUTOPILOT-FAILURES

Gunnar Johannsen, Claudius Pfendler, and Willi Stein

Forschungsinstitut für Anthropotechnik (FAT)

5309 Meckenheim, F.R. Germany

1. INTRODUCTION

One objective of introducing autopilots into aircraft landing-approaches is always to reduce pilot's workload. Then, the changed role of the pilot is monitoring the autopilot functioning and taking over control manually, e.g., in rough turbulence and failure situations. However, the described human-automatic function allocation puts a high workload on the pilot if a severe failure occurs near touch-down. In these cases, the advantages of the autopilot under normal conditions may change into considerable disadvantages. This is a special problem with Short Takeoff and Landing (STOL) aircrafts, particularly under Instrument Flight Rule (IFR) conditions.

Instrument-Landing-System (ILS) procedures require decisions of the pilot on whether to continue the approach or to go around in failure situations. Pilots of commercial aircrafts have to discontinue the approach if certain error criteria are exceeded or a failure occurs within a component which is prescribed for the fulfillment of the ILS-procedures [1], [2]. On the contrary, this study is restricted to landing a simulated STOL-aircraft in any case, a situation which is realistic under extreme emergency conditions. The main advantage of this experimental design is that a steady-state mission phase is considered. Furthermore, manually, semiautomatically, and automatically performed landing-approaches are to be compared. Some of these are carried out with and without autopilot-failures.

One important factor determining system performance is the time needed for detecting failures [3], [4]. Another performance measure used in this study is the glide-path deviation before and after autopilot-failures. Yet, performance measures alone are generally not satisfactory for the assessment of piloted aircrafts. The pilot's effort necessary to achieve a certain performance level in a specified loading situation has at least to be estimated [5] . One class of workload measurement techniques suitable for this purpose uses secondary tasks in order to measure the operator's spare mental capacity which has not been filled up by the main task [6] , [7] . In this study, a tapping task has been chosen as the secondary task [12] . Comparisons with subjective workload rating will also be given.

2. EXPERIMENTAL SETUP AND DESIGN

A fixed-base simulator of a small STOL-aircraft (Do 28 D-Skyservant) has been used [8] . Its dynamics are linearized for the descent phase of a steep landing-approach [9] . The flight path angle is 6° and the desired airspeed is 33.4 m/s. Cross-coupling between longitudinal and lateral motion is neglected. Only vertical gusts are present. The approach-to-land geometry is shown in Fig. 1. Transitions from cruise to descent as well as flare and rollout phases are not considered. However, the sensitivity of the ILS-crosspointer display increases as usual corresponding to the approach-to-land geometry. As shown in Fig. 1, the indicated glide-path deviation changes from an angular to a linear quantity when the aircraft is 290 ft high. The angular glide-path deviation increases towards infinity near touch-down.

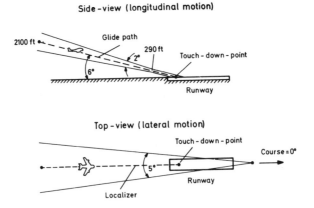

Fig. 1 : Sketch of approach-to-land geometry

Horizontal and lateral gusts are not present. Throttle and rudder are not used in this study. Hence, the pilot controls longitudinal and lateral motion only by elevator and aileron deflection through a spring-centered control stick. While the lateral motion is controlled manually or is eliminated, there exist different control modes for the longitudinal motion : manual control with and without stability augmentation and automatic control with and without autopilot-failures. The control modes for the longitudinal motion are shown in the block diagram of Fig. 2. The flight path guidance computer (FPGC) receives ILS-signals and calculates the glide-path deviation ΔGP and the height h. The vertical speed v_z results from coordinate transformations (COTR). Ordinarily, the longitudinal motion is controlled automatically in this investigation. The equation of the autopilot is :

$$\eta_{ca} = 0.833 \, \dot{\vartheta} + 0.4 \, \Delta GP + 1.0 \, \Delta v_z \tag{1}$$

where $\dot{\vartheta}$ is pitch rate ($\vartheta \triangleq$ pitch angle) and η is elevator deflection. The parameters of the autopilot are chosen so that its performance is comparable to the performance of human pilots. The task of the human pilot is now monitoring the functioning of the autopilot. Therefore, ϑ, ΔGP, v_z, and h are indicated on the electronic displays in the cockpit (artificial horizon, ILS-crosspointer, vertical speed indicator, and altimeter). In case of failure, the human pilot has to disconnect the autopilot by activating switch S which is mounted at the control stick. At the same moment, the human pilot switches himself into the control loop and, thereby, has the

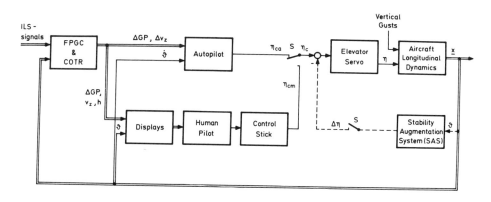

FPGC : Flight Path Guidance Computer
COTR : Coordinate Transformations

Fig. 2 : Block diagram illustrating different modes
of control of longitudinal motion

possibility of taking over control manually. In cases where a stability augmentation system (SAS) is used, this is also activated by switch S. The SAS is very simple, i.e. :

$$\Delta \eta = -0.45 \,\vartheta \tag{2}$$

The effective aircraft dynamics of the pitch axis are changed in gain, natural frequency, and damping ratio through the additional use of the SAS. The control loop of longitudinal motion is affected by vertical gusts (Fig. 2). This disturbance is a filtered pseudo-random time function which has a period of 20 s. The rms-value of the stationary disturbance is 1.24 m/s, i.e., strong gusts. The effects near the ground are simulated by a linear reduction of the rms-value starting at a height of 290 ft and ending with zero at touch-down.

The experiments are conducted in order to study autopilot-failures. Three types can be distinguished. If the autopilot output fails to zero, the detection times are considerable high and comparable with those in [3]. In cases where the autopilot output goes to an extreme magnitude bias, the failure is detected very fast. Between these two borderline cases, the autopilot works with reduced efficiency. This third type of failure is simulated in these experiments by means of a sudden enlargement of the rms-value of the vertical gusts by a factor of 3. At the same moment when the human pilot has detected the failure and disconnects the auto-pilot in order to take over control manually, the rms-value of the verti-cal gusts is reduced again to its prefailure magnitude.

One trial of the experiments starting at a height of 2100 ft above ground (see Fig. 1) takes about 180 s. The different control and moni-toring tasks and their abbreviations are :

(a) manual control of longitudinal motion (with SAS)
    and manual control of lateral motion (stationary control)   MAN/SAS

(b) monitoring the automatic control of longitudinal motion
    with autopilot-failures (with or without SAS during
    postdetection) and manual control of lateral motion
         during prefailure   SEMIAUTO
         during postdetection { with   SAS   MAN/SAS
                              { without SAS   MAN

(c) monitoring the automatic control of longitudinal motion
    (without autopilot-failures ; no lateral motion)   AUTO

The subjects of this study are 5 non-pilots. However, all of them had
a lot of training in purely manual control of the simulator in use during
preceding experiments [10] . The mean level of the subjects' performance
at the beginning of the experiments discussed in this paper is comparable
to that of a test pilot. After a first session of additional training in
manual control, the subjects had a session of training in monitoring the
automatic control of the longitudinal motion and in detecting simulated
autopilot-failures. Then, the subjects had to perform the above mentioned
control and monitoring tasks. The last trial of each subject's manual
control session is analysed in case (a). Each subject performed 6 trials in
case (b), 3 with and 3 without stability augmentation system (SAS) during
postdetection. In both of these subcases, the autopilot-failure occurs at
a different time in each trial. The three failure occurrence times are :
110 s, 130 s, and 150 s, respectively, after starting each trial. In
case (c), 3 trials were performed by each subject who had been instructed
to expect an autopilot-failure. Otherwise, it cannot be guaranteed that
the subjects are monitoring the autopilot functioning. All trials in and
between cases (b) and (c) are counterbalanced. The data of a sixth subject had to be rejected due to failures in the computer system.

Two performance measures are used : the rms-value of the glide-path
deviation ΔGP_{rms} and the detection time. The subjects had to carry out
a secondary tapping task in parallel to all experiments. The relative irregularity in the tapping task is taken as a workload measure [11] , [12].
The subjects are trained in the secondary task to a stationary basic tapping level (BTL) without performing the main task. The subjects are asked
to tap a big key in their left arm-rest as regular as possible. The mean
difference between two succeeding tapping-intervals relative to the mean
tapping-interval is chosen as a measure of the tapping irregularity :

$$BTL = \frac{\overline{|\Delta t_{i+1} - \Delta t_i|}}{\overline{\Delta t_i}} \tag{3}$$

where Δt_i is the i-th time interval between two succeeding taps. When
the same measure is taken in experiments where the subjects have to
perform the main task, i.e., the landing approach, in parallel, the
quantity of Eq. (3) is called loaded tapping level (LTL) instead of BTL.
The relative increase in tapping irregularity is the perceptual motor load
(PML) which is hypothesized to be a measure of the pilot's effort in the
main task :

$$PML = \frac{LTL - BTL}{BTL} \cdot 100 \; [\%] \tag{4}$$

After each trial, the subjects have to make a workload rating (WLR).
A pointer has to be set on a graphic scale with five steps indicating

different levels of workload. The scale is constructed according to the general recommendations described in [13].

3. RESULTS

In this study, landing approaches with autopilot failures as well as stationary approaches (without failures) are considered. From these experiments, total task results and results of selected intervals are reported. The task intervals have a length of 20 s and are located just before the occurring failure (prefailure intervals) and immediately after the detected failure (postdetection intervals). This length is a compromise between reliability on the one hand and the intention of conceiving the unstationary effects during the postdetection phase on the other hand. In most cases, the manual control adaptation process does not come to an end during the postdetection interval.

Workload ratings (WLR) and perceptual motor load values (PML) are taken as total task measures. Glide-path deviations and PML-values are taken as task-interval measures. The detection time is a performance measure of the monitoring phase. Involving 5 subjects, the mean values presented in the figures include either 1 or 3 trials per subject, i.e., 5 or 15 trials totally. Based on these measurement procedures, the following figures are containing total task measures of 15 trials or task-interval measures of 15 or 5 trials. If approaches with and without failures are compared, only corresponding task intervals are considered.

Three control modes - automatic (AUTO), semiautomatic (SEMIAUTO), and manual control (MAN/SAS) - are compared in respect to workload (Fig. 3). Simple monitoring (AUTO) causes significantly smaller PML-measures than combined monitoring/manual control (SEMIAUTO). Simple monitoring shows also significantly smaller PML-measures than manual control with SAS. Against that, there is no significant difference between semiautomatic control and manual control with SAS in respect to PML-measures. This indicates that shifting from manual control to a more perceptive task (i.e., monitoring) results in decreasing workload. It is

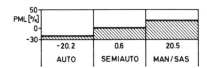

Fig. 3 : Perceptual motor load (PML) with stationary control modes
        (task-interval measures)

remarkable that the difference of PML-measures between AUTO and
SEMIAUTO is significant, whereas the difference between SEMIAUTO and
MAN/SAS is not significant. This effect may be due to the greater
difficulty of the manually controlled lateral motion compared with the
longitudinal motion. A different interpretation is based on the assumption
that two axes manual control is not significantly more loading than one
axis manual control. These hypotheses should be supported by further investigations.

From the standpoint of flight safety, detection times are of utmost
importance in cases of autopilot failures. The hypothesis has been stated
that the earlier the autopilot failure occurs in the course of the landing
approach, the longer are the detection times. This hypothesis is based on
the fact that the glide-path deviation is displayed as an angular quantity
increasing the display sensitivity by a factor of 2.6 between the first and
the last considered task interval (see Fig. 1). The mean values of detection times are shown in Fig. 4. The detection times are shorter with
later autopilot failures. Analysis of variance (after Friedman ; [14]) indicates significant differences between detection times with three different
failure occurrence times. Further tests (after Wilcoxon and Wilcox ; [14])
demonstrate significantly longer detection times with autopilot failures at
110 s compared with those at 150 s. On the other hand, there is no

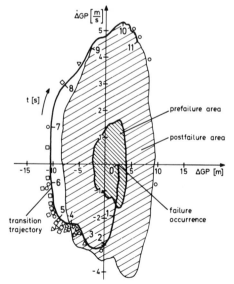

failure occurrence time [s]	points of detection time	mean detection time [s]
110	o	9.65
130	□	5.67
150	△	4.38

Fig. 4 : Phase plane of glide-path deviation
and detection times

significant difference in detection times with neighbouring failure occurrence times. Nevertheless, these results essentially support the hypothesis formulated above. The phase plane of glide-path deviation gives further information to the understanding of the detection process (Fig. 4). In most cases, autopilot failures are detected when the amplitude of the glide-path deviation exceeds the maximum prefailure amplitude about 2 to 3 times. Based on the fact that the pilot can perceive ΔGP and $\dot{\Delta} GP$, we can assume that ΔGP is more important than $\dot{\Delta} GP$ in respect to the detection process.

Another focal point of this investigation is describing and analysing the postdetection intervals. The aircraft is controlled insufficiently in the phase preceding manual taking-over. Consequently, rather high glide-path deviations have to be compensated during most of the postdetection intervals. A further question is, to what extent deteriorating performance and increasing workload can be compensated, e.g., by a stability augmentation system (SAS). Postdetection glide-path deviations and PML-measures are shown in Fig. 5. In comparison, corresponding measures of stationary, manually controlled landing approaches are presented. An expert rating and other results, which cannot presented here, point out that manual control without SAS (MAN) is ranked higher in difficulty than manual control with SAS (MAN/SAS). Furthermore, the level of difficulty with postdetection manual control is higher than with stationary manual control. These tendencies are parallelled by the PML-values of Fig. 5. The comparison of postdetection manual control results of Fig. 5 with corresponding prefailure semiautomatic control results of Fig. 3 is illustrating the increasing workload during landing approaches with failures. All PML-values of Fig. 5 differ significantly. The stability augmentation system is reducing the postdetection workload considerably. The glide-path deviations with stationary manual control are significantly smaller than with postdetection manual control. The difference is about 50 per cent. How-

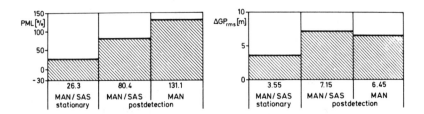

Fig. 5 : Perceptual motor load (PML) and glide-path deviation (Δ GP) with stationary and with postdetection manual control (task-interval measures)

ever, a significant influence of the stability augmentation system cannot be found out of the glide-path deviations during postdetection. The maximum glide-path deviations during these postdetection intervals amount to 3 times the presented rms-values. The mean glide-path deviation (ΔGP_{rms}) with automatic control is about 2 m.

Fig. 5 shows a remarkable effect. The performance during the more difficult task (postdetection manual control without SAS) exceeds the performance during the easier task (postdetection manual control with SAS). It may be assumed that increasing performance corresponds to increasing workload, other things being equal. Obviously, workload is increasing extraordinarily with postdetection manual control without SAS, so that not only the increased level of difficulty is compensated, but also a higher performance is achieved.

As pointed out before, the detection time is depending on the failure occurrence time, i.e., the distance to the touch-down point. From there the question arises if there is a similar influence on pilot's control performance and workload. As shown in Fig. 6, the PML-values are greater and the glide-path deviations are smaller with later failure occurrence times. Furthermore, the same tendencies in PML-measures and glide-path deviations as a function of decreasing distance to touch-down can be seen with stationary manual control. Obviously, these results are caused by the display sensitivity effect. However, only parts of the presented differences are significant. The increase in control performance and workload corre-

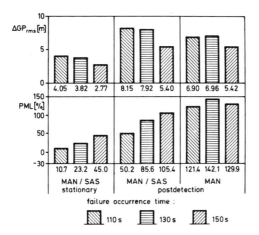

Fig. 6 : Glide-path deviation (ΔGP) and perceptual motor load (PML) with stationary and postdetection manual control as a function of failure occurrence time (task-interval measures)

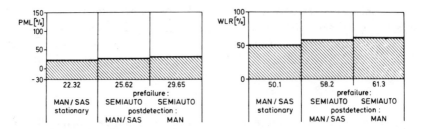

Fig. 7 : Perceptual motor load (PML) and workload rating (WLR) with
stationary manual control and with prefailure semiautomatic/post-
detection manual control (total task measures)

sponds to the increase in monitoring performance, i.e., decreasing detection times, mentioned with Fig. 4.

Fig. 7 adds corresponding total task measures to the above presented
task-interval measures. The workload ratings and the PML-values are
ranked comparably. Furthermore, the ranks of the total task PML-values
parallel the ranks of the task-interval PML-values of Fig. 5. The PML-
values of Fig. 5 differ significantly, whereas this is not true with the
results of Fig. 7. It is possible to conclude that workload ratings and
PML-results are comparable measures. The parallels between the total
task PML-measures and the task-interval measures may indicate that these
measures are reflecting dominantly the postdetection phases of the landing
approaches.

4. CONCLUSIONS

Performance and workload measures have been used in control and
monitoring tasks conducted separately and simultanously. Particularly, the
reduced performance and the increased workload immediately after failure
detection and manual taking over are brought to view. Thereby, the advantage of the more easily controllable system dynamics (i.e., aircraft with
SAS) is demonstrated. The detection times are considerably long. Other
authors have reported even longer detection times in connection with the
investigation of different types of failures. It may be assumed that there
is not always sufficient time for taking over safely and for compensating
inadmissible control errors. Obviously, man's capability in monitoring is
insufficient. Therefore, monitoring and decision making may be performed
fully automatically or aided partly by computers. Probably, detection times
will be reduced by additional presentation of past and extrapolated future

time intervals (preview, postview) of the displayed time functions. Hints at this assumption are given by the failure detection points in the phase plane of the glide-path deviation. Further work has to be done investigating performance and workload in monitoring with different levels of difficulty and in more complex decision situations.

5. REFERENCES

[1]   Richtlinien für den Allwetterflugbetrieb nach Betriebsstufe II. Nachrichten für Luftfahrer I-350/72, 1972.

[2]   Richtlinien für den Allwetterflugbetrieb nach Betriebsstufe IIIa. Entwurf, 1974.

[3]   A.R. EPHRATH : Detection of system failures in multi-axes tasks. 11th Annual Conf. Manual Control, NASA TM X-62, 464, pp.151-169,1975.

[4]   E.G. GAI, R.E. CURRY : Failure detection by pilots during automatic landing : models and experiments. 11th Annual Conf. Manual Control, NASA TM X-62, 464, pp.78-93, 1975.

[5]   D.W. JAHNS : A concept of operator workload in manual vehicle operations. Forschungsbericht Nr. 14, Forschungsinstitut für Anthropotechnik, Meckenheim, 1973.

[6]   J.M. ROLFE : The secondary task as a measure of mental load. In : W.T. Singleton et al. (Eds.) : Measurement of man at work. London : Taylor and Francis, pp. 135-148, 1971.

[7]   G. JOHANNSEN : Nebenaufgaben als Beanspruchungsmeßverfahren in Fahrzeugführungsaufgaben. Zeitschrift für Arbeitswissenschaft 30 (2NF) 1976/1, S. 45-50.

[8]   W. BERHEIDE, G. JOHANNSEN, G. NOSSING : Festsitz-Teilsimulator für anthropotechnische Untersuchungen von Landeanflügen. Bericht, Forschungsinstitut für Anthropotechnik, Meckenheim, 1976 (in preparation).

[9]   U. HARTMANN : Ein Beitrag zum Entwurf digitaler, selbstadaptiver Flugregelsysteme. Dissertation, Techn.Univ.Hannover, 1974.

[10]   G. JOHANNSEN, G. NOSSING, C. PFENDLER : Pilotenbeanspruchung und -leistung in einem simulierten STOL-Anflug. Vortrag, FA Anthropotechnik, DGLR (Köln), 1975 (FBWT-Rep. in press).

[11]   J.A. MICHON : A note on the measurement of perceptual motor load. Ergonomics, vol. 7, pp. 461-463, 1964.

[12]   J.A. MICHON : Tapping regularity as a measure of perceptual motor load. Ergonomics, vol. 9, pp. 401-412, 1966.

[13]   J.P. GUILFORD : Psychometric methods. New York : McGraw-Hill,1954.

[14]   L. SACHS : Angewandte Statistik. Berlin : Springer, 1974.

DISCUSSION

McLEOD :

There is a serious problem associated with measuring the relative difficulty of a range of tasks using tapping with the left-hand as a measure. The regularity of the taps is strongly dependent on what the subject is doing with his other hand. What you may well be showing in the PML differences found between AUTO, SEMIAUTO, and MANUAL are not differences in absolute difficulty, but differences in the number of movements made with the right hand. This artifact might explain the discrepancy between the PML measures and the glide path deviation shown in Fig. 5.

STEIN :

When measuring workload by a secondary task, there is a two-way dependency between the primary and the secondary task. On the one hand, the secondary task must be influenced by the primary task, i.e., subjects' secondary task scores reflect different degrees of difficulty in the primary task, other things being equal. On the other hand, the influence of the secondary task on the primary task should be kept as small as possible. Results of previous experiments with the same setup and the same subjects have shown that the maximum correlation between the control stick signals and the tapping signal is about 0.3 [10] .

CAVALLI :

At present, you have a measure of the pilot's effort in the main task (glide correction). When you have a deviation on the four principal parameters (glide, localizer, velocity, and heading), will you make a distinction between the decision load (cost of the strategy of choosing between the tactics) and the memorisation load (cost of the tactic which is the algorithmic sequence of elementary actions to set a parameter to zero) ?

STEIN :

The subjects were instructed and trained to use a stable strategy in both the primary and the secondary task. So there is only one detection and decision situation during one landing approach. We supposed that a secondary task is not sensitive enough to measure momentary workload effects.

ROUSE :

It would seem that BTL and/or LTL are not only measures of irregularity but also of the average rate chosen by the subject. Perhaps this factor could cause the negative value of PML found. In any case, PML can be consciously affected by the subject choosing to tap less often and thereby cancel the effects of increased irregularity.

STEIN :

The BTL - and LTL - measures as results of the tapping task become independent from the mean tapping frequency by a normalization. The normalization algorithm is comparable to that determining the heart rate irregularity. Perhaps the tapping results can be consciously affected sometimes. But in our case, the subjects did not know this algorithm.

EVALUATION OF VIGILANCE RELATED TO VISUAL PERCEPTION

J. Meyer-Delius, and L. Liebl

German Air Force Institute of Aviation Medicine

8080 Fürstenfeldbruck, G.F.R.

SUMMARY

Voluntary saccadic eye movements and the dynamics of peripheral blood flow were monitored in pilots and weapon systems operators (WSOs) performing visual perception tasks. With prolonged perceptive strain, beginning fatigue is indicated by an increase in latency and reaction times and a decrease in maximal angular velocities of saccadic eye movements. Simultaneously, after an initial rise, respiratory as well as heart rates are slightly reduced and photoplethysmography of skin blood flow reveals increasing fluctuations of the volume pulse waves.
Repetitive measurements on three subsequent days showed a shift to shorter initial values of the latency times, but still the same prolongation under visual strain. This decrease may be due to a training effect and/or to spontaneous circadian fluctuations inherent to the optokinetic system.
Vigilance and fatigue are projected into the neurovegetative control system regulating circulation. Combined perceptive and emotional stress (as experienced during the required adaptation to a new visual task) triggers an unstable "epinephrinic" type of cardiovascular response whereas perceptive stress alone results in a stable "norepinephrinic" type of reaction.

INTRODUCTION

Flight missions in today's high performance aircraft are

highly demanding with respect to visual perception. A reliable
evaluation especially of the deteriorating visual performance
as a consequence of perceptive overload and beginning fatigue
is therefore desirable to improve flight safety.
An experimental approach to this problem has to take into account several factors: On the one hand, the stress which is
acting on the physiological systems under study; in this case,
the visual task, the information is acting as stress. Under
experimental conditions, the stressor has to be standardized,
quantified, and controlled as well as the other environmental
factors. On the other hand, the strain which summarizes the
complex reactions triggered in these physiological systems;
for instance, the execution of the visual task leads to a rise
in the level of vigilance and, eventually, to fatigue. Vigilance and fatigue can, of course, not be measured directly, but
as they are modulating complex physiological control systems,
certain indicative adjustments in these systems can be detected and analyzed by observing single physiological parameters.

      One such system is the neurovegetative circulation control
system. Vigilance and fatigue are modulating the level of the
neurovegetative activity which, in turn, according to KOEPCHEN
and coworkers[1], ASCHOFF and WEVER[2], GOLENHOFEN[3], and HILDE-
BRANDT[4], controls peripheral blood flow. The blood flow of the
skin as well as heart rate and heart rate variability are easily monitored by photoplethysmography.
Another readily accessible system is the optokinetic system.
Latency time (time interval between signal and saccadic movement), maximal angular velocity, and precision of voluntary
saccadic eye movements appear to be dependent on vigilance and
fatigue.

                              METHODS

In the visual perception tasks colour light signals, the position of LANDOLDT circles, and several types of aircraft had to
be recognized and identified by pressing the appropiate push-
buttons. The signals were displayed at a distance of 3 meters
on the horizontal arc of the horopter.
In 30 min. 1,200 signals or 1,500 LANDOLDT circles had to be
recognized which, in a randomized order, appeared at 20 deg.
and 40 deg. (light signals) and 15 deg. and 30 deg. (LANDOLDT
circles), respectively, to the right and to the left of the
vertical middle axis. The silhouettes of the G-91, T-33, RF-4E,
and F-104G aircraft were mounted in aerial photos and projected with a magnitude of 36 angular min. at a distance of 20 deg.
from the middle axis. During 20 min. 300 slides were shown,
each being projected for .7 sec. The discriminating features
of all visual tasks were in the order of magnitude of 1 to 5

angular min. The experiments were performed with pilots and
WSOs.
Saccadic eye movements were recorded seperately for each eye by
bipolar electro-oculography.
The blood flow of the skin was monitored by photoplethysmography
at the ear lobe (HENSEL[5]). The volume pulse waves were displayed both directly and as relative amplitude changes via a monitor with a smoothing time constant of 5 sec. to reveal slower
oscillations of the pulse waves.
Respiratory rate was determined by a nasal temperature sensor
and heart rate was displayed as beat-to-beat frequency.
In collaboration with the German Aerospace Research and Testing
Institution recently a programme for computerized analysis of
our tape-stored data has been developed.

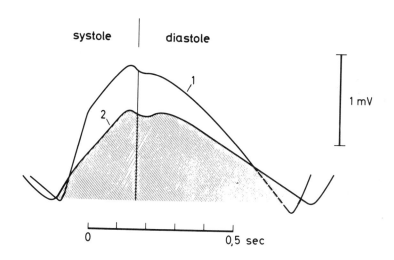

Fig. 1   Photoplethysmography of the volume pulse during rest
(1) and during visual perception (2)

Duration: systole/diastole	1) 1 : 2.5; S.D. = 0.2
	2) 1 : 2.5; S.D. = 0.5
Mean amplitude: systole/diastole	1) 1 : 0.9; S.D. = 0.1
	2) 1 : 1.2; S.D. = 0.2
Respiratory rate	1) 13 cycl./min.
	2) 21 cycl./min.
Blood pressure	1) 112/84 mm Hg
	2) 121/ 90 mm Hg

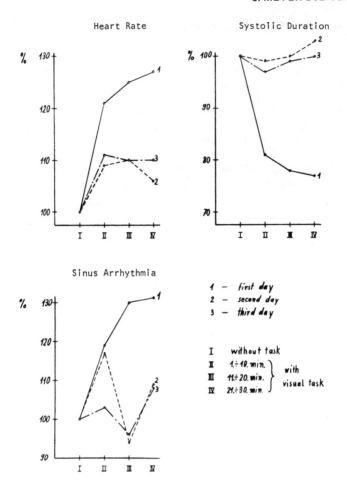

Fig. 2   Heart rate, systolic duration, and sinus arrhythmia before (I) and during visual task (II, III, and IV) on three subsequent days (1, 2, and 3)

RESULTS

Fig. 1 shows the typical change of the pulse wave under visual perception. The amplitude is decreasing as well as the slope of the ascending part and the ratio of systole to diastole remains unchanged. This is characteristic for a "norepinephrinic" peripheral vasoconstriction.

Fig. 2 shows results from our repetitive visual task experiments
on 3 subsequent days (curves 1, 2, and 3). Point I represents
the data obtained from the first 1o-min.-period without task
and is taken as 100 %. Points II,III, and IV show the averaged
data of the following 3 10-min.-periods with the visual perception task (identification of 1,500 signals) and are given as
relative values.
On the first day heart rate is rising continuously under visual
perception without reaching a steady-state. It is interesting
that this frequency increase takes place predominantly at the
expense of systolic duration, a rather unusual mechanism. Sinus
arrhythmia or heart rate variability (calculated as the sum of
the absolute differences of two subsequent pulse periods during
one min.) is also increasing. These changes show a poorly adapted cardiovascular response of the "epinephrinic" type. This
indicates an additional emotional stress posed on the subjects
by the confrontation with a new task.
On the second and third days, after an initial increase, there
is no further rise in heart rate under visual perception and
the systolic duration is kept constant, while the diastolic
duration decreases. Also a significant increase in sinus
arrhythmia is missing. This response is stable and well adapted, it is comparable to that shown in Fig. 1.

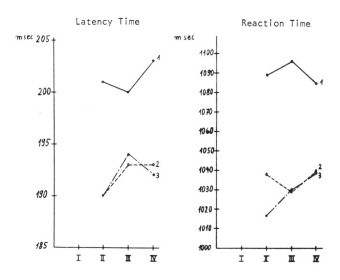

Fig. 3   Latency and reaction times of saccadic eye movements
during a 30-min.-visual-task (II: 1st - 10th min., III: 11th -
20th min., and IV: 21th - 30th min.) on 3 subsequent days
(1, 2, and 3)

Fig. 3 shows that initial values of both reaction and latency
times decrease on the second and third days. This decrease can
be accounted for by either specific training effects (ASCHOFF[6])
or spontaneous circadian oscillations caused by an inherent
rhythmicity of the optokinetic system (KRIS[7]).
In Fig. 4 the influence of visual perception on the dynamics
of peripheral blood flow can be seen. In this graph the relative changes of the mean amplitudes of the volume pulse waves
as determined every 30 sec. are plotted as a continuous line
($\bar{M}$) and the amplitude of fluctuations around this mean value
caused by pulse waves of third order is represented by the interrupted lines a and b. The right part of the graph was recorded without task, the middle and the left part during identification of optotypes of 1 and 2 min. angular magnitude, respectively. Under visual perception, a 2-min.-rhythm could be distinguished that has also been reported by GOLENHOFEN[5] who ascrib-
ed it to an increase in vascular tonus.
Fig. 5 gives frequency distributions of the relative amplitudes
of the volume pulse, on top without task, in the middle during
recognition of light signals, and underneath during recognition
of different aircraft types. The amplitudes are related percent-

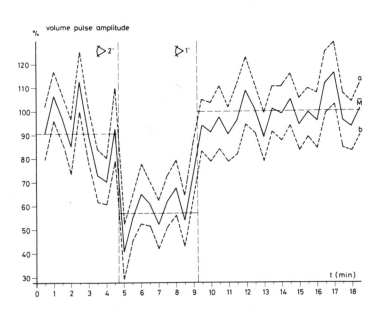

Fig. 4   Relative changes of the volume pulse amplitudes
(photoplethysmography at the ear lobe) during recognition of
PFLÜGER hooks of the magnitude of 1 and 2 angular min.

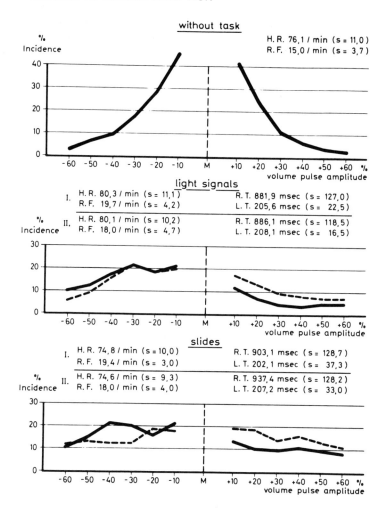

Fig. 5 Percentual distribution of the size of the volume pulse amplitude related to the mean value before task
Continuous line: 1st – 10th min.
Interrupted line: 11th – 20th min.

ually to the mean value without task. During visual perception there is a shift towards smaller amplitudes and the distributions become more flat-topped. After an initial increase, respiratory rate decreases during the task and the heart rate shows only minor and inconsistent changes. Both reaction and latency

times are being prolonged during visual perception and the angular velocities of the saccadic eye movements are decreasing
from 400 ± 26 deg./sec. to 365 ± 22 deg./sec. (for 20 deg. -
saccades) and from 500 ± 32 deg./sec. to 470 ± 26 deg./sec.
(for 40 deg.-saccades).
The flattening of the frequency distribution of the volume pulse
amplitude under prolonged visual perception can be interpreted
as beginning instability of the circulation control system and
indicates, together with both the prolongation of latency and
reaction times and the decrease in angular velocities, a lowering in the level of vigilance and the first sign of fatigue
caused by perceptive overload.

CONCLUSION

Information uptake and the concomitant arousal reaction are
projecting vigilance adjustments into the level of neurovegetative activity which, in turn, is modulating the control of the
circulatory system. To some extent, even a graded response may
be expected that is related to quantitative criteria of the
stressing input.
During visual perception, trained persons show a primarily "norepinephrinic" cardiovascular reaction with peripheral vasoconstriction and the corresponding reduction of the volume pulse
amplitudes and without significant changes in heart rate. With
beginning fatigue, as indicated by an increase in reaction and
latency times and a decrease in angular velocities of saccades,
the circulatory control system shows signs of instability ex-
hibiting a flattening of the frequency distribution of the volume pulse amplitude with larger fluctuations around the mean
value. Under these conditions, respiratory rate which is always
increasing with the onset of visual perception is reduced.
     When additional emotional factors, like performance re-
quirements related to new tasks, modify the strain due to visual
perception, a primarily "epinephrinic" response is triggered
with respect to the control of the circulatory system. Heart
rate is increasing continuously as well as sinus arrhythmia
and the systolic duration is unproportionally diminished: No
steady-state is reached. This can be interpreted as a rather
unspecific "over-all" activation of the sympathoadrenergic
system caused by combined mental-emotional overload.
Prerequisites of these studies were standardized visual perception tasks and the exclusion of uncontrolled environmental
stressing factors. The above described experimental approach
can be elaborated to give a valuable ergonomic tool for the
evaluation of vigilance and fatigue related to visual perception.

REFERENCES

1) KOEPCHEN, H.P., LANGHORST, P., SELLER, H. and J. POLSTER,
   Neuronale Aktivität im unteren Hirnstamm
   mit Beziehung zum Kreislauf,
   Pflügers Arch. ges. Physiol., 294, 40, 1967

2) ASCHOFF, J. and R. WEVER, Biologische Rhythmen und Regelung.
   In: Bad Oeynhausener Gespräche V, 1961,
   Springer Verlag, Berlin-Göttingen-Heidel-
   berg, 1962

3) GOLENHOFEN, K., Zur Rhythmik der Blutgefäße.
   In: Bad Oeynhausener Gespräche V, 1961,
   Springer Verlag, Berlin-Göttingen-Heidel-
   berg, 1962

4) HILDEBRANDT, G., Grundlagen einer angewandten medizinischen
   Rhythmusforschung,
   Die Heilkunst, 70, 117, 1958

5) HENSEL, H., Physiologie der menschlichen Hautdurchblu-
   tung.
   In: Bad Oeynhausener Gespräche VI, 1962,
   Springer Verlag, Berlin-Göttingen-Heidel-
   berg, 1963

6) ASCHOFF, J.C., Phänomene sakkadischer Augenbewegungen in
   ihrer Bedeutung für die Flugmedizin,
   Zbl. Verkehrs-Med., 17, 129, 1971

7) KRIS, E.C., Vision: Electro-oculography.
   In: Medical Physics, Year Book Publishers,
   Chicago, 1960

DISCUSSION

SHACKEL :

At the end of the paper the authors suggest that their methods can be elaborated "to give a valuable ergonomic tool for the evaluation of vigilance and fatigue related to visual perception". I cannot see how the data in the paper justify this ambitious claim.

MEYER-DELIUS :

Perhaps I should answer in this way : mental workload is correlated with neuro-vegetative sympatogenic stimulation. Here we differentiate between noradrenergic reaction, based on the degree of mental concentration, and adrenergic reaction related to the emotional stress in the workload. The increasing heart rate is a symptom of the second factor.

In assessing fatigue we don't refer to the decreasing technical performance, but to the performance in the steady state of the biological systems (heart rate, respiratory rate and peripheral blood circulation resistance), maintaining their mean value caused by the mental effort.

With increasing latency time and decreasing angular velocity of the saccades in the eye fixation movements, depending on the task duration, there was evidence of distonic regulation. This means increasing oscillation around the mean values in the waves of the skin blood flow.

To analyze in a better way the rhythmics of the above mentioned biological parameters we developed a computer program, presently applied in NOE helicopter studies.

WORKLOAD IN AIR TRAFFIC CONTROL

A field study

C.K. Pasmooij, C.H.J.M. Opmeer and B.W. Hyndman

The Netherlands Institute for Preventive Medicine
Health Organization TNO, Wassenaarseweg 56, Leiden
The Netherlands

1.   INTRODUCTION

The field of application of information processing systems in
complex man-machine systems is still expanding as a result of ever-
increasing automation. In the first stage of automation, physical
labour was replaced by machines, leaving the mental aspects of the
task to the human operator. Due to the increase of speed and capacity of information processing systems, combined with a simultaneous decrease of costprices, these systems found acceptance and
brought in the next stage of automation, in which some of the mental aspects of the task were taken over. As a result this development has led and is still leading to a modification of the task of
the human operator.

The ever-increasing number of flights to be handled during the
past decades has made it necessary to extend the capacity of the
Air Traffic Control (ATC) system. As a means to increase system
capacity the area which is to be controlled can be divided into a
number of sub-areas each under the responsibility of a separate
control position. As a consequence, renewed division of tasks between controllers becomes necessary. Moreover, by means of automation of a number of task components of the controller more time can
be given over to those task components for which automation is
either impossible or undesirable. Both methods have the underlying
basis that the human operator is a limiting factor in the ATC system, as far as the information processing capacity is concerned.

In terms of information processing the capacity of the human
operator has an experimentally proveable, but individually different
and time variant upper limit. On the other hand, this capacity is
limited on the lower side as well, due to the requirement that a

certain level of activity of the central nervous system has to be
maintained in order to avoid loss of concentration during task
execution. Nevertheless, the tendency nowadays is to create tasks
for the human operator in which merely monitoring the state of the
system is the main objective, thus lowering job satisfaction and
ultimately furthering the possibility that this lower limit will be
passed.

   A study is described, the objective of which was to assess workload of air traffic controllers resulting from the information processing associated with their task. Recordings in the real life
situation during five days in summer time have been made in order
to achieve a representative sample of the task during high density
traffic. Task parameters and observer ratings were recorded as a
quantification of the task situation, while physiological signals
were recorded as representations of the effect of task execution on
the controllers.

2.   THE HUMAN OPERATOR IN THE ATC SYSTEM

   The task of the air traffic controller is to provide a safe,
orderly and expeditious flow of traffic. For this purpose the controller has at his disposal visual and audible instrumentation aids
which provides him with information about the movements of the aircraft for which he must be concerned. The direct data link between
controller and aircraft consists of a radio-telephone (R/T) connection. The controller can be considered a system component of the
ATC system which essentially is a closed loop man-machine system
(fig. 1). Setpoint changes of the pilot/aircraft system in terms of
changes in flight level, heading or speed can be initiated by the
controller (instructions) or by the pilot (requests).
No setpoint changes can be made, however, without the final per-
mission of the controller.

Perceiving, scheduling and decision-making are the main mental processes of the controller's task and consequently condiserably contribute to his workload. Because safety rules must be obeyed under
all circumstances, fatigue and loss of concentration have to be
avoided as much as possible. Work and rest schedules are subsequently adjusted with regard to these factors, resulting in a
maximum working period of two hours without a pause and a following
resting period of 45 minutes.

   The passive role of the aircraft in the detection procedure by
the radar antenna will change due to technological advancement. The
data link between the aircraft and the information system will be
extended by creating the opportunity of digital information to be
transmitted by the aircraft. Automation of the R/T link between
controller and aircraft will complete the technological development,
but at the same time create a system under supervisory control,
leaving a monitoring task for the highly skilled controller (fig.2).
Besides the fear the controllers have that they will not be able to

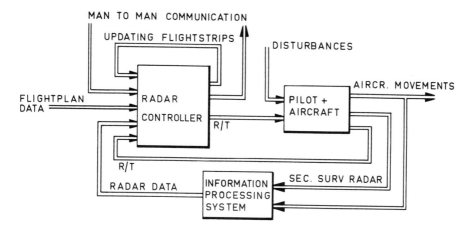

Fig.1   The Air Traffic Control System

take over control in the case of failures of the automatic system, they are also convinced that this development will ultimately make the job less challenging.

The analysis of the controllers task in the existing ATC system and the determination of workload which is imposed on the controller is necessary in order to design future ATC systems. The importance of estimating the abilities, adaptive behaviour and skill of the human operator is evident. Therefore it should be emphasized that human limitations and human possibilities with respect to the information processing capacity have to be investigated in order to arrive at a set of rules for allocating tasks to man and machine.

3.   WORKLOAD MEASUREMENT IN THE REAL LIFE SITUATION

Research on workload in ATC has concentrated for years on questions related to the capacity of a certain control position. Tools were developed with which an ATC system could be designed, one of the parameters being the amount of work to be performed at the control position (Arad 1964, GPS Ground Model 1970). These models, however, were based on an analysis of the traffic situation rather than an analysis of the characteristics of the human operator. The time spent on communications by the controller has been the subject of a number of investigations and has widely been used as a workload index for a control position (George & Johnson 1968), sometimes as a function of the amount of traffic handled in a certain period of time (Francis 1968, Spérandio 1969, Seifert 1973).

Only a few investigations have been concerned with the impact of the presumed work to be carried out at a certain control position on the human operator in terms of a load for the biological system.

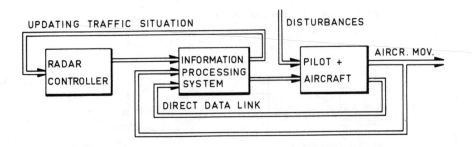

Fig. 2   ATC system under supervisory control

Increasing density of traffic does impose an increasing load on the
biological system as reflected in the increase of the mean heart
rate which has been shown in the simulation environment (Buckley
1969). The most extensive study in this field (Rohmert c.s. 1973)
has been conducted in the operational situation and is concerned
with the description of the relation between the traffic situation
as an input variable (the stressor) and the effect on the human
operator as an output variable (strain).

3.1   Subjective Rating

    Research on mental workload should ultimately lead to a set of
norms which could be applied in a preventive way. To achieve such a
set of norms instruments have to be designed in order to be able to
objectively measure workload of the human operator. Nevertheless,
subjective rating by skilled observers and the human operator himself
can be an useful tool (Philipp c.s. 1971). In our experimental situation describing, a colleague air traffic controller who was as experienced as the subject controller acted as an observer during
periods of recording. The observer evaluated the traffic without
actually controlling and gave a subjective estimation of traffic
complexity and task difficulty on a minute by minute basis. Moreover
he scored traffic density in the same way, thus providing a control
variable with respect to rating performance, since the real traffic
density could easily be measured as the number of aircraft simultaneously under control (N). Immediately after his working period
the subject controller gave an estimation of the same variables,
but in this case as a mean value of the working period.

    Correlation coefficients between the rated traffic density by
the observers and taskparameter N have values between 0.48 and 0.74.
The observers mutually differ in the mean level of their rating
which can be explained by the fact that they were not explicity
asked to count the number of aircraft under control. Some observers,
however, did not score actual fluctuations in traffic density at all,

thus making their ratings on complexity of the situation and difficulty of the task unreliable. These findings confirm the statement
that the use of one and the same observer for all recordings improves the reliability of subjective rating as a means to assess
workload (Philipp c.s. 1971), but not necessarily improves the
validity of this rating.

The observers did not, or were not able to, discriminate between
the categories complexity of the situation and difficulty of the
control task; as can be seen from the correlation 0.94 between these
categories. Moreover, high correlations between these categories
and the rated density of traffic (0.84 and 0.86 respectively) can
be interpreted to be an indication that, according to the observers,
the density of traffic can be used as a rough measure of controller
workload. The inter-individual difference, however, between the observers with respect to their rating of traffic density shows that
the objective recording of N could be used as a more accurate parameter for this purpose.

The subject controllers themselves do not appear to systematically
discriminate between the three categories either, in view of inter-
correlation coefficients up to 0.92. Unlike some of the observers
the subject controllers discriminate almost in a binary fashion between levels of density of traffic and, consequently, the same holds
for the categories traffic complexity and task difficulty. With
respect to traffic density the subject controllers generally scored
a mean value which exceeds that of the observers by about 87%. For
the two other categories this number in both cases becomes 147%,
thus showing the more subjective and personal feeling with regard
to the effect of task load.

3.2   Analysis of Communication

    Apart from the exchange of messages between controller and pilot
by means of R/T, the controller has the opportunity to coordinate
with his colleague controllers, performing their tasks at other
control positions or in adjacent centra. Generally these coordinations are very limited in number and duration and mainly concerned
with the announcement of delays in traffic, or with information
about revised flight levels. Although communications do not necessarily imply complex information processing, the time spent on
talking or listening does require conscious effort and consequently
does contribute to the workload of the controller. Expressed in
units of time the controller can be occupied by communications up
to 75% of the time for several consecutive minutes without a pause.

    As can be expected from the nature of coordinations, this
category of communications is not much influenced by different
levels of traffic density. The time spent on coordinations is relatively constant with a value of about 5% resulting in a correlation
with N of 0.25 and is not significant.

The relation between traffic density and the time spent on
R/T is fully dependant on the geographical properties of the area
which the controller is responsible for, as well as procedural aspects of the ATC system (Ratcliffe 1969).
The control position where this experiment took place was concerned
with a bidirectional airway with horizontally separated tracks.
The R/T load as a percentage of time and the number of aircraft
N for each working period (mean duration 41 minutes) have been calculated as mean values. To these data curves have been fitted, resulting in the exponential curve as a best fit, as shown in fig. 3,
explaining 70% of the variance. A possible explanation for this
nonlinear relationship is the increasing number of possible conflicts arising from greater density of traffic.

Combining the data of all working periods for this purpose is valid,
since variance analysis on the distributions of the communication
data for each value of N, and for all subject controllers separately,
has shown that no significant interindividual differences exist between the controllers, as far as the relations between N and the
communication variables is concerned. This finding allows analyses
with respect to the communication data for all controllers as a
group.

Relations between N and the communication data should be based on
the mean values of these variables over a certain period of time.
Changes in traffic density requires planning and scheduling by the
controller over a certain period which does not necessarily result
in R/T or coordination at the same moment. The calculation of a

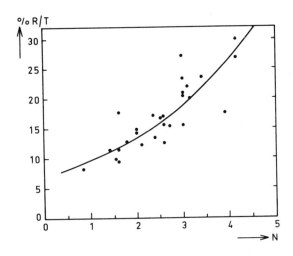

Fig. 3   R/T load versus number of aircraft

correlation coefficient between the mentioned variables on the basis of minute by minute values therefore only takes into account an interval of one minute, without taking into account the required time-shift for cross-correlation.The influence of this effect can be shown by comparing the correlation for the mean values per period as given in fig. 3 (r=0.82) with the value of the same correlation on the basis of minute values (r=0.37).

3.3   Physiological Measurements

The usefulness of physiological variables as indicators of mental workload has been shown under laboratory conditions (Kalsbeek and Ettema 1965), and in a flight simulator environment (Opmeer & Krol 1973). It has been shown that these indicators consistently discriminate between a task and a rest condition, but only in a few experiments it has been proved proved possible to discriminate between different levels of task difficulty. These findings seem to make physiological variables unsuitable as measuring instruments when a continuous signal representing the workload of the air traffic controller is desired.

In the real-life situation during working conditions the human operator processes information originating from several sources. Besides task-induced information the physical working environment can be a source as well; the social situation and self-generated information can also significantly contribute to the resulting load. With this in mind, it can be easily understood that physiological variables do not necessarily correlate with task-specific information and consequently with task-related workload.

This effect can be shown by calculating the correlation coefficient on the basis of minute by minute values between traffic density and heart rate irregularity. The latter variable is supposed to be an indicator for workoad in terms of information processing. The correlation comes to 0.16 and is not significant, in spite of the fact that increasing density of traffic, according to the subject controllers rating, leads to an increasing difficulty of the task and probably to a higher workload.

On the contrary heart rate itself has a strong relationship with density of traffic, as can be seen from an analysis on the previously mentioned set of data. A period of half an hour with low density of traffic ($\overline{N}$=1.37) and a mean communication load of 13.4% is compared with a period of the same duration and the same controller during very high density of traffic ($\overline{N}$=4.68) and a mean communication load of 40.6%. During the first "normal" working period the linear correlation between N and heart rate has the not significant value of 0.04. This value during the second "high workload" period comes up to 0.73 which is significant at the 0.001 level. The same holds for another controller during comparable periods of low and high density of traffic, the correlation coefficient being 0.18 and 0.66, respectively. These results give rise to the hypothesis that the

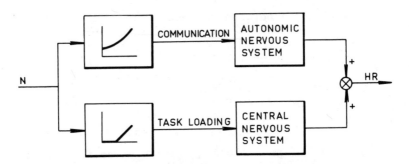

Fig. 4   Schematic representation of the relation
between traffic density and heart rate

relation between N and heart rate is non-linear.

For both controllers the mean heart rate during high density
traffic has an increase of about 6 beats/min relative to the period
of low density traffic. Opmeer has shown in a laboratory experiment
that reading aloud   (100% time occupation) compared to reading
quietly increases heart rate only by 4 b/min (Opmeer 1976) while
in both cases the mental processes involved are the same. Since
even during high density traffic the controller does not spend
100% of his time speaking, the increase in heart rate must be due
to a simultaneous increase in task loading as well. This increase
in task loading, according to the theory, should lead however to a
decrease of heart rate irregularity which, as mentioned, is not the
case. Respiratory effects due to the communications can be   an explanation for this finding. Fig. 4 gives a qualitative scheme of the
possible ways along which the density of traffic has its impact on
the heart rate of the controller.

The effect which pure emotional load can have on the heart
rate of a controller is shown in fig. 5. The registration was made
during a standard traffic situation with four aircraft simultaneously under control and a rated difficulty of the task by the observer of 10%. The arrow indicates the moment the controller reports
to a pilot that his aircraft is 12 miles off track and in military
airspace. This was a very unusual situation, because this flight
takes place each day at the same time, and therefore is a fairly
routine one for both controller and pilot. The alarm of the controller produced an excessive increase of his heart rate while
neither the controller, nor the observer outwardly showed any
emotion.

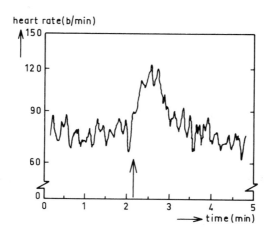

Fig. 5   The effect of emotional load on heart rate

4.   DISCUSSION

     Research on workload in the ATC environment has often been
carried out by means of simulation experiments in order to be able
to systematically vary the traffic situation with respect to traffic density (Buckley 1969, Francis 1968) or procedurial aspects
(Luczak 1971). The possibility to control the quantity and quality
of the traffic is the main advantage of the use of a simulator.
Nevertheless, research in the operational situation is necessary
in order to incorporate all those typical aspects which characterize
the real-life environment.

     The mean density of traffic during the experimental sessions,
which contained about 20 hours of recording, comes to 96% of the
mean value of the summer peak. Only during a few working periods
out of the total number of 28 however, did the controller handle
a peak load of traffic. Fig. 6 gives the frequency distribution of
the number of aircraft simultaneously under control (N) over 1150
minutes of recording, N=9 being the highest value. According to
controllers comments, N=13 is the absolute maximum which can be
handled. The conclusion can be drawn therefore that unfortunately
many more recordings in the real-life situation are necessary to
incorporate absolute peak loads in the analysis.

     With regard to the measurement of workload by means of physio-
logical variables, the recovery of the biological system from the
"working" state to the "resting" state immediately after the task
has given promising results. Hyndman (CIANS, Prague 1975) showed
that a narrow frequency band in the heart rate spectrum (0.10-0.14
Hz) which is related to blood pressure oscillations can be used
for this purpose. This variable recorded during task performance

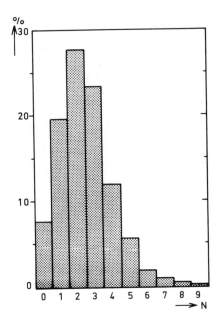

Fig. 6   Frequency distribution of the number of aircraft N

does not significantly discriminate between different levels of
workload (Hyndman & Gregory 1975), but recovery of this variable
from a period of peak workload (a 3 minute 100% binary choice task)
to the rest value was very consistent and protracted (40 minutes).
The described ATC experiment, however, was not designed with regard
to this method, and consequently recovery curves could not be determined since at least 30 minutes rest values immediately after
the working period are needed for measuring the previously mentioned
variable.

    Results of the analyses give rise to the proposition that ac-
cording to the subjective ratings of the controllers themselves,
their amount of speech workload as well as their physiological
reactions, the number of aircraft simultaneously under control gives
a rough but realistic indication of ATC workload for the described
control position. This conclusion corresponds to Rohmert's findings
with regard to ATC workload in the real-life situation (Rohmert c.s.
1973).

5.   REFERENCES

ARAD, B.A., 1964. Notes on the measurement of control load and sec-
      tor design in the enroute environment. FAA SRDS Project Report
      AD-659035, Washington DC.
BUCKLEY, E.P., W.F. O'CONNOR & T. BEEBE, 1969. A comparative analy-
      sis of individual and system performance indices for the ATC
      system. NAFEC Report RD-69-50, Atlantic City.
FRANCIS, G.H., 1968. VHF channel allocation in relation to air
      traffic density and controller workload. ATCEU Report no. 291
      RAF Farnborough-Hants.
GEORGE, P.H. & A.E. JOHNSON, 1968. Workload measurement study at
      London ATC centre West Drayton. ATCEU Report no. 289, RAF
      Farnborough-Hants.
G.P.S. SCIENCES LIMITED, 1970. The Eurocontrol ATC ground model.
      Contract no. C/57/0/68, Farnborough-Hants.
HYNDMAN, B.W. & J.L. BLOM, 1975. Comparison of central and autonomic
      nervous system correlates of information processing load.
      2nd International Congress of C.I.A.N.S., Prague.
HYNDMAN, B.W. & J.R. GREGORY, 1975. Spectral analysis of sinus ar-
      rhythmia during mental loading. Ergonomics 18, 255-270.
KALSBEEK, J.W.H. & J.H. ETTEMA, 1965. Sinus arrhythmia and the
      measurement of mental load. Communication at the London Con-
      ference of the British Psychological Society.
LUCZAK, H., 1971. The use of simulators for testing individual men-
      tal working capacity. Ergonomics 14, 651-660.
OPMEER, C.H.J.M., 1976. The influence of speech on a number of
      physiological variables. To be published.
OPMEER, C.H.J.M. & J.P. KROL, 1973. Towards an objective assessment
      of cockpit workload: I. Physiological variables during different
      flight phases. Earospace Medicine 44, 527-532.
PHILIPP, U., D. REICHE & J.H. KIRCHNER, 1971. The use of subjective
      rating. Ergonomics 14, 611-616.
RATCLIFF, S., 1969. Mathematical models for the prediction of ATC
      workload. Paper U.K. symposium E.C.A., Malvern Worcestershire.
ROHMERT, W. und Mitarb. 1973. Psycho-physische Belastung und Bean-
      spruchung von Fluglotsen. Schriftenreihe Arbeitswissenschaft
      und Praxis, Band 30, Berlin.
SEIFERT, R., 1973. Human performance analysis as basis for software
      planning in semi-automated systems. NATO seminar on Man-Machine
      relations, Utrecht.
SPERANDIO, J.C., 1969. Analyse des communications air-sol en con-
      trôle d'approche. IRIA C.O. 6909R21, Paris.

DISCUSSION

VERHAEGEN :

You showed a slide on which an important increase in heart rate was visible at the moment an air traffic controller said to the pilot of a civil plane that he was 12 miles out off his track and in military airspace. My question is : Was there any change of sinus arhythmia at that moment ?

PASMOOIJ :

As far as our visual, but not-numerical analysis of this specific period is concerned, sinus arhythmia did not change significantly. The only indication that "something was wrong" was the just-mentioned enormous increase in mean heart rate.

STOCKBRIDGE :

Have you looked at risk-bearing air misses ? These relate to number of aircraft flying. They are approximately 50 % human factor caused.

PASMOOIJ :

Thank you for your last remark about the influence of the human operator as far as air misses are concerned. During the 20 hours of recording in the real-life situation no risk-bearing air misses did take place. This possibly can be explained by the fact that no moments of real peak load, as far as the number of aircraft is concerned, did occur (see fig. 6 in the paper).

PILOT WORKLOAD ANALYSIS BASED UPON IN-FLIGHT PHYSIOLOGICAL MEASUREMENTS AND TASK ANALYSIS METHODS

J. Smit

National Aerospace Laboratory (NLR)

Anthony Fokkerweg 2, Netherlands

INTRODUCTION

During the last decades much effort has been invested to relieve pilot workload, which resulted in better handling qualities of aircraft, presentation of information in the cockpit based upon ergonomic principles, automation of functions, etc. Nevertheless there are still numerous examples of high workload conditions in aviation. For instance monitoring an automatic approach for landing in real CAT II conditions can be rather loading. In military aviation high workload situations are frequently encountered, even during training missions.

The results of pilot workload research are relevant for the design of future airborne man-machine systems. As Jahns (Ref. 1) points out: "the ultimate objective of operator workload research should be the development of techniques for reliable predictions of the effort a human operator can (or better, will) exert to meet predetermined levels of input load". It would also be of great value at the operational level if reliable methods were available to classify existing piloting tasks according to some "acceptable load"-criterium. Practical questions could be answered like: how much training is sufficient to declare a novice squadron pilot proficient for a certain type of missions. Proficient in the sense that the tasks are performed successfully and skillfully within certain specifiable "acceptable load"-limits. In other words: is it possible to make a reliable estimation of the effort the pilot has to invest to meet the demands of the specified task?

Due to the diversity and complexity of the interactions between the human operator and his taskenvironment there does not exist an adequate theoretical framework in the field of human performance. At the methodological level the discrepancy between laboratory- and fieldexperimentation, and consequently a lack of generalization of results, presents a serious impeding factor in the progress of workload research. In the workload literature the need for a more integrated, "converging methods"-approach is frequently expressed (Refs. 1, 2, 3). Also there is still a lack of reliable data, acquired during "real-life" flying conditions.

Realizing the relevance of workload research and considering the aforementioned limitations and shortcomings of currently available methods and data an experimental programme has been initiated at the National Aerospace Laboratory (NLR) to select and develop methods which offer the possibility of a more detailed and quantitative analysis of man-machine-environment interactions.

EXPERIMENTAL PROGRAM

In this paper an outline is given of an exploratory experiment which is carried out in the context of an operations research programme for the Royal Netherlands Air Force called Mission Improvement Program Air-to-Ground (MIP). This program is set up to measure the performance of pilots during standardized low level ground attack missions. A detailed analysis of the penetration- and weapondelivery phase of the mission is possible by using an instrumented F-104G "Starfighter" fighter-bomber aircraft. During approximately twenty flights by ten pilots, also physiological measures were taken and subjective ratings given to get an indication of the effort needed to accomplish these tasks. An attempt is made to account for individual differences in physiological reaction patterns (individual response specificity) by administering some paper- and pencil personality tests.

Subjective ratings of the exerted effort were asked after each flight.

The data are explored extensively by means of feature extraction methods, correlational- and multivariate analysis. This will hopefully lead to the formulation of hypotheses which can be tested in further experiments.

PHYSIOLOGICAL MEASUREMENTS

Despite a large number of unsolved problems connected with physiological measurements (Ref. 3), there are still many indications of valuable information regarding the influence of task-induced-

and environmental stress on the human operator contained in several
physiological parameters (Refs. 2, 4, 5). A general conclusion
derived from a literature survey is that due to the complexity
of the activation process it is necessary to measure more than
one physiological parameter in order to account for phenomena like
directional fractionation (Ref. 2). Three peripheral measures
of autonomically innervated response systems were selected.
  1. Heart rate signal, time between successive cardiac events
     (R-waves).
  2. Respiration signal.
  3. Skin resistance level and -responses.
The heart-rate signal is measured via three disposable electrodes
on the chest. The times between successive cardiac events are converted to voltages.
The measurement of respiration was selected for several reasons.
First of all as an indicator of autonomic reactivity.
The second reason was the strong interaction of respiration with
heart rate variability. The synchronous measurement of both signals
offers the possibility of analyzing the other components of heart
rate variability more precisely, especially blood pressure regulation effects (Ref. 6). An additional advantage of the in-flight
measurement of respiration is the gathering of data from the
pilot-oxygen mask system which are rather scarce.
The respiration signal (frequency and depth) is measured via two
flow measuring units, one for the inspiration-, the other for the
expiration phase. A measuring unit consists of two thermistors,
one is heated to $50^{\circ}C$ and measures flow, the other serves as a
temperature compensator. The device is mounted in the oxygen mask
and has shown to be very accurate and sensitive. It does not present any discomfort at all to the pilot. The output from the
measurementsystem is an analogue voltagesignal proportionate to
the in- and outflow of the oxygen mask, calibrated in liters per
minute.

The skin resistance is measured via two silver-silverchloride
electrodes at the foot of the subject. A constant current of 9
microamperes per cm^2 is applied. The resistance dependent voltage
signal is separated in a tonic and phasic component (skin resistance level, SRL, and skin resistance response, SRR.). The skin
resistance measures were selected because of the fact that they
are exclusively an indication of the activity level of the sym-
pathetic nervous system.
The four analogue signals coming from the signalconditioning unit
are digitized in a Flight Data Acquisition Unit (FDAU) and recorded on compact cassette tape, synchronously with flight data.
Special attention is paid to the safety aspects of the measuring
system. The pilot is separated from the rest of the system via a
number of medical isolation amplifiers. The powersupply is
schwitched off at an altitude of 20.000 ft.
The system is installed in the cockpit and the electronics com-

partment of a F-104G fighter-bomber aircraft in such a way that it
does not present any restrictions to the normal operation of the
aircraft or to the functioning of the pilot.

To obtain additional information about the specific physiological
reaction patterns, the pilots have to perform a critical instability tracking task with an auditory display. This offers the opportunity to get physiological reaction patterns during a task with
controlled attentional demand but without the stresses of real
flight.

A one-minute hyperventilation trial was included to elicit maximum
physiological responses (Ref. 4).

PERFORMANCE MEASUREMENTS

During the mission, which consists of the simulated attack of two
or three "targets", the following flight data are continuously
recorded in digital form:
- Pressure Altitude
- Radar Height
- True Air Speed
- Ground Speed
- Grid Heading
- Vertical Acceleration

Through computation it is possible to obtain a number of weapon
delivery performance parameters.
- Navigation Accuracy during the Run-In
- Apex Height
- Dive Angle
- Pipper Position
- Weapon Release point
- "Impact Position" of the weapon
- Recovery Manoeuvre

This offers the unique opportunity to reconstruct the mission in
terms of system behaviour synchronously with the time histories
of the physiological parameters.

The measurements are taken during the whole flight, including the
take-off, approach and landing.

DEBRIEFING AND SUBJECTIVE EFFORT-RATINGS

After each flight the pilots are debriefed. They have to estimate
their mission success and how well they adhered to preplanned
weapon delivery parameters like apex height, dive angle and true
airspeed. Special attention is paid to the reporting of events
that occurred during the mission. For instance: encountering other
aircraft or birds, system failures and other irregularities. These
events are plotted at the appropriate position at the flight's
time history.

This detailed reconstruction of the mission is necessary, in order to be able to correlate as accurately as possible the physiological data with what actually happened to the pilot (environmental stress) and what he was doing (task induced stress).

Asking the pilot to give a rating of the effort he had to invest, can render relevant data (Ref. 7). The pilot has to rate the effort he spent per mission segment on a nonadjectival rating scale (Ref. 8).

Direct questioning before and after the mission is supposed to give some insight in the attitude towards the tasks, motivation, feelings about the experimental setting etc.

Additional information about the relative difficulty of the mission is gathered by interviewing flight leaders, weapon instructors and other experienced pilots.

THE MEASUREMENT OF RELEVANT PERSONALITY TRAITS

There is ample evidence for individual response specificity (Ref. 4). Autonomic physiological responsivity is thought to be related to the "intensity" of human behaviour (Ref. 5). Therefore personality tests which indicate traits as: impulsivity, extraversion, sensation seeking and emotionality were selected.
There are some indications of a relationship between these traits and physiological reaction patterns.

A test consisting of a number of self appraisal scales is administered which is developed with the special purpose to detect this relationship (Ref. 9). Also included is an Achievement Motivation Test (the PMT of Hermans) with scales for Achievement Motivation, Facilitating Anxiety and Debilitating Anxiety (Ref. 10).

DATA ANALYSIS

The flight- and physiological data, recorded in digital form on compact cassette tapes, are converted, resulting in computer compatible tapes for processing by a Cyber 72 computer. After some preprocessing in which the raw data are converted in "engineering units" a quick-look program is carried out. As part of a large interactive graphic display programme it offers the possibility to look at the data in blocks of 256 seconds and inspect these for outliers or artefacts etc. These can be corrected on-line. In the interactive graphic display programme a number of subroutines is used for data reduction. Features can be extracted via descriptive statistics programmes, time series analysis- and frequency domain measures etc. Multi-variate analysis techniques

can be used to obtain an insight in the interactions between the
various sets of variables: physiological-, subjective- and performance measures.

REFERENCES

1 Jahns, D.W. (1973), A concept of operator Workload in Manual
   Vehicle Operations. Forschungsbericht nr. 14, Forschungsinstitut für Anthropotechnik, Meckenheim (BRD).

2 Kahneman, D. (1963), Attention and Effort. Prentice Hall, Inc.,
   Englewood Cliffs.

3 Hoffelt, W. (1973), Flugstress, eine meszbare Grösze? Wehrme-
   dizinische Monatschrift, Heft 9/1973.

4 Kok, A. (1973), Activation and Specificity, Dissertation, Vrije
   Universiteit, Amsterdam (in Dutch).

5 Duffy, E (1962), Activation and Behaviour. Wiley, New York.

6 Hyndman, B.W. and Gregory, J.R. (1975), Spectral Analysis of
   Sinus Arrythmia during Mental Loading. Ergonomics, 1975, Vol.
   18, no. 3, 255-270.

7 Rolfe, J.M., and Chappelow, J.W. (1973), The Application of
   Aircrew Opinions on cockpit tasks and equipment to Flight
   Safety research. AGARD Conference Proceedings no. 132 on
   Behavioural Aspects of Aircraft Accidents.

8 Hess, R.A. (1973), Nonadjectival rating scales in human response
   experiments. Human Factors, 1973, 15 (3).

9 Fey, J.A. (1975), Personal Communication, Psychological Department, Free University, Amsterdam.

10 Fey, J.A. (1975), An Investigation into the meaning of the
   Achievement Motivation Test: II
   Psychophysiological Correlates.
   Nederlands Tijdschrift voor de Psychologie
   30 (1975) 233 - 253.

THE MEASUREMENT OF HUMAN RESPONSE IN MAN-VEHICLE CONTROL SITUATIONS

J. M. Rolfe [*]

Royal Air Force Institute of Aviation Medicine

Farnborough   Hampshire   UK

The objective of vehicle systems design is to achieve a balance between man and machine in order to obtain and maintain the vehicle's efficiency. On one side of the balance are the requirements arising from the role for which the vehicle is designed. These will determine factors such as the vehicle's complexity, its operational profile, and its size and shape. On the other side are factors determined by the decision to employ a man or men as part of the system. There are the psychological requirements for the identification and allocation of functions between man and machine, physiological requirements for survival and efficiency and physical requirements to ensure adequate workspace under both normal and emergency conditions. In achieving an acceptable balance between these factors it is appreciated that man has the capability of enhancing the quality of the system, but he also imposes restraints on its design. For example, because man cannot fly unaided, the aeroplane is designed specifically to exceed human capabilities, but the cockpit of the aeroplane must be designed with human limitations very much in mind in order that the flow of information between the machine and the man and the return of man's responses to the machine may be effective. If the vehicle's design objectives are to be achieved it is necessary to have a means of assessing the effectiveness of the human controller with no less rigour than is applied to the mechanical, electronic and structural elements comprising the remainder of the system. A number of specific categories of response assessment can be identified, namely:-

    a.   The extent to which a total man machine system meets a given performance requirement. Different combinations of man and machine have to be compared in order to determine their relative merits. For example decisions have to be made with

---

[*] The paper was presented by B. Shackel.

regard to determination of the number of operators who will
form the team controlling the system.

b.   The relative levels of response demanded from the individual at different stages of an operation. Operations can be
broken down into a number of individual sub-phases to determine the level of operator involvement encountered during each
phase, into the nature of the responses demanded and into the
variations of responses which are demanded from the various
members of the team.

c.   The effectiveness of a particular item of equipment in
relation to some specified alternatives. Different configurations of operating equipment may be available and a choice has
to be made as to which provides the best level of response
from the operating personnel.

d.   The effect of external and internal environmental changes
on the operator's response. Extreme and unusual operating
environments may well have an effect on the operator's response
which has to be measured. Similarly, some situations may prompt
the operator to take steps to change his internal environment
in order to counteract the effects of the task situation, for
example the use of hypnotic drugs to induce sleep when work
schedules demand unusual and irregular rest periods. Again,
however, the need will arise to measure the effects of this
action on the operator's response.

e.   The evaluation of the operator in relation to either his
peers or some definable standard. Some criteria may be set up
which well define the level of response required from an operator in order to demonstrate competence. Assessments are made
against this standard in which the individual is graded with
regard to his ability to perform the task.

A second reason for taking an interest in the measurement of
operator response is that the operator himself is often an important part of the system assessment procedure. What the skilled
operator reports about the effectiveness of the vehicle is a source
of data which is used by the systems designer to assess the overall
effectiveness of the product. In aviation, for example, pilot
opinion is used to assess aircraft handling characteristics, cockpit
ergonomics and aircrew workload (Refs 1 and 2).

It is possible to identify two particular directions in which
the operator's assessments are used as measures of systems' effectiveness. The first is directed towards the assessment of the
task, the quality of the equipment provided for the performance of
the task and the variations in the nature of the task during different sub-phases of the operation. The individual is used to

undertake a task analysis, the emphasis being on the objective
aspects of the task. The second direction may be described as being
operator oriented as it requires an assessment of what the task
demands of the individual in terms of the physical and mental effort
he has to expend on particular aspects of the task.

Thus far the emphasis has been on the extent to which operator
response measures are required in the development and evaluation of
man-machine vehicle systems. Consideration must now be given to the
sorts of measures which are available and to the problems which they
present. It is logical to place direct measures of man-machine
system performance at the head of any list of measuring techniques.
However, direct performance measures are not always as informative
as may be required. Two reasons for this can be identified. The
first is the changing nature in operator's tasks in current systems.
The generation and transmission of physical energy has long since
disappeared as the major contribution that is expected of the human
operator. He is still talked about as the decision-maker, manager
and controller but, today, decisions are more often than not implemented by the operation of one switch or the press of one button
rather than by a complex combination of psychomotor actions.

The second reason relates to the assessment of task demand
factors. Knowles (Ref 3) argues "performance measures in and of
themselves seldom reflect operator load. They usually tell how
well some functional system criterion is met, for example tracking
error, missed distance, decision accuracy etc. but they seldom tell
the price paid in operator effort in meeting this criterion". So,
in addition to measures of performance which indicate how well the
task is performed, it is necessary to determine how much it costs
the operator to achieve a level of performance. The introduction
of effort expenditure measures brings into relevance the concept of
operator workload, an area of investigation which has grown in pro-
minence over the past two decades. However, this growth has been
accompanied by some confusion as it is certainly not easy to provide
a clear definition of the term workload. Jahns (Ref 4) reported
that he found himself "overwhelmed by the diversity and vagueness
in the way in which the term is defined and used". The definition
of workload is more often than not an operational one; it is related
to what the systems engineer, physiologist, ergonomist or flight
medical officer requires it to be. Two important features can be
distinguished between the various approaches. First is the technique of measurement and the assumptions underlying the measurement.
For example, the ergonomist may record overt control activity, and
argue that workload is measurable in terms of patterns of activity
exhibited by aircrew in the task situation. The psychophysiologist,
however, may record variations in heart rate arguing that physical
and mental load influence the level of activation and arousal within
the individual and this will be manifest in the magnitude and extent
of observable responses. The second discrimination feature is the

time over which the workload is studied. This can range from the
systems engineer's examination of the pilot's workload during the
last 30 seconds of a run in to a target to the flight surgeon's
interest in the cumulative workload experienced by a pilot over
weeks or perhaps years of duty.

The above points are not arguments against direct performance
measures; the reverse is more the case, for measures of performance
are essential but they may need to be supplemented by additional
measures. Very often it is the performance measures which give rise
to a hypothesis about the degree of load experienced in particular
phases of, or variations in, the task. Such hypotheses give rise
to predictions which can be verified only by resort to other
measures, which look in directions other than those of system efficiency. Four particular types of supplementary measures are encountered, namely:-

1.   Observational analysis of the subject's performance.

2.   Subjective assessments obtained from the operators
themselves.

3.   Additional performance measures using "loading tasks".

4.   Physiological measures.

Table 1 provides a brief description of the techniques, the
assumptions underlying them and examples of the application to
which they have been put.

It will be seen from Table 1 that all of the measures have
their advantages and disadvantages in relation to the direction in
which they can be applied. They also have to be assessed in terms
of other criteria, namely:-

a.   Ease of interpretability. The measure must provide information in a form which allows answers to be obtained in relation to the sort of problems which require investigation.

b.   Reliability. The measure must be consistent and not subject to distortion because it is used by different investigators. Any variability should be due to variations in the task
or operator rather than to the measure itself.

c.   Freedom from interference. The measures employed must not
increase the load upon the operator such that performance of
the task being assessed is changed by the presence of the
assessment measure.

Table 1

	Description of Techniques	Assumptions	Applications
Observation	Using check-lists, films and tape recordings, trained observers record and analyse operators' activity.	The patterns of activity exhibited by the operator give an indication of the acceptability of work-space layout and the load imposed by the task.	a. Identification of operator functions during various phases of a vehicle's operation (Ref 5). b. The analysis of ways in which work is shared between crew members (Ref 6). c. The assessment of vehicle design (Ref 7).
Subjective Assessments	Using prepared questionnaires, rating scales and check-lists the operators make quantitative assessments of the nature of the work they do and the load it imposes upon them.	The skilled operator is not only able to perform the task but is also capable of analysing and describing the nature of the task and its demands.	a. Assessment of vehicle handling characteristics (Ref 8). b. The study of the acceptability of workspace and the tasks performed by the operators (Ref 9). c. Assessment of workload (Ref 10). d. Passenger comfort under varying environmental conditions (Ref 11).

Table 1 (Continued)

Description of Techniques	Assumptions	Applications
Loading Tasks An additional standardised task (e.g. mental arithmetic), is performed simultaneously with the primary task under study. From the second task, measures are derived to indicate the extent of the load imposed upon the operator by the primary task.	The human operator is limited in relation to the amount of information he can handle at any one time. The function of the loading task is to measure the operator's spare capacity.	a. The amount of operator capacity demanded by a task (Ref 12). b. The amount of spare capacity available while controlling the vehicle (Ref 13). c. How workload affects capacity (Ref 14).
Physiological Measures The effort expended by the operator in meeting the demands of the task is assessed in terms of the physiological activity (e.g. heart rate) exhibited during the performance of the task.	Physical and mental load will influence the level of activation and arousal within the individual. This change in activation will be manifest in and measurable in terms of physiological response.	a. The relative effort demanded by different phases of a vehicle's operation (Ref 15). b. The effect of differences in crew structure (REf 15). c. The effect variations in operational load on operator effort (Ref 17).

d.   Acceptability to the operator. The technique should not
expose the operator to any discomfort or cause apprehension.

The four measures referred to above are assessed against these
criteria in Table 2.

The research which has been undertaken to date with regard to
the assessment of operator response measures indicates that no one
measure can adequately satisfy all requirements (Ref 18). Therefore
some combination of measures would appear to be the best solution to
the problem. The appropriate combination depends upon two factors.
The first is the nature of the problem being investigated. While it
is evident that the assessment of operator response should provide
information which is useful it is necessary to define what particular
elements of the human operator's response are to be studied.
Secondly, there is the question of the time at which the assessment
is undertaken. Modifications to the human and machine elements of
a system can take a long time to implement and their feasibility
becomes more limited as the system reaches the later stages of
development. Thus, there is every incentive to achieve an adequate
knowledge about the human operator elements of the task as early in
the system's development as possible. However, the sort of measures
which can be employed, when the system is at a premature design stage,
are different from those which can be employed at a point where a
prototype vehicle is available and assessments under real or simulated operational conditions can be attempted. As systems become more
and more sophisticated there is greater incentive to achieve the
correct allocation of functions between man and machine at the earli-
est possible stage. The human factors scientist may feel that he
does not possess measuring devices of sufficient sensitivity and
accuracy that can be employed to make accurate predictions from drawing board to operational use. It is perhaps that he is led to believe
that the level of accuracy demanded of his predictions is greater than
those which are expected for the remaining elements of the vehicle
system. The development of an aeroplane from drawing board to final
introduction into squadron service is one constant process of test,
modification and retest. The design engineer will only slowly modify
his opinions that 'the aeroplane will fly' to the point where he is
prepared to say 'how well it will fly'. If this is the case then
the behavioural scientist should not be ashamed of only being able
to say in the early stages of the system that the man should be able
to operate the system but defer giving precise estimates of how well
he will be able to operate it. Of course, this level of prediction
is not totally satisfactory but it is one which can also be constantly
tested, modified, and retested, during the evolution of the vehicle
system. For fuller consideration of the organisation of an "all-
through" human factors assessment system see Burrows (Ref 19).

Table 2

	Interpretability	Reliability	Freedom from Interference	Acceptability to the Operator being Studied
Observation	As the technique relies upon observable activity, its application is limited in situations where covert activity is the predominant feature of the operator's task.	Operator activity can be ambiguous and in multi-operator situations the load may be on the observer rather than on the observed. Allowing the operator under study to comment on the recorded activity can enhance the value of the technique.	The presence of an observer or additional items of equipment can be a potential source of interference.	Satisfactory as long as the operators are aware of the role of the observer and the function of any ancillary equipment.
Subjective Assessment	The use of subjective assessment allows questions to be asked about task content and load. Care must be taken to ensure that the assessment material is unambiguous.	Subjective opinion can be used to assess existing equipment or task situations. However, as a means of predicting the acceptability of proposed systems the technique has less reliability. High workload and fatigue can reduce the accuracy of assessment.	If used simultaneously with the task under performance, subjective assessment techniques may interfere if assessments have to be made while task is being performed.	Good if the right time is chosen to administer the questionnaire and if representative operators can be involved in its development.

Table 2 (Continued)

	Interpretability	Reliability	Freedom from Interference	Acceptability to the Operator being Studied
Loading Tasks	A number of indices of workload have been derived using loading tasks. The nature of the loading task, the nature of the primary task and the instructions given can all interact and influence the interpretation of the results.	Good, but care must be taken to identify where the sources of competition for information handling capacity are occurring.	The presence of the loading task may affect the performance of the primary task. This can be acceptable but it may make the use of loading tasks in vehicle control situations potentially hazardous.	Some operators find the technique's attention dividing qualities annoying and distracting.
Physiological Measures	Physiological response can best be considered as an indication of effort. For the measurement of objective task load, physiological response is difficult to interpret.	Similar changes in response can be brought about by a range of situations. Variations exist both in the magnitude of the response and the physiological system responding.	The recording of physiological response need have little or no direct interference with the task situation. However, certain techniques do impose restraints, e.g. eye movement recording where the head needs to be fixed.	Providing adequate information is given to the subject, the majority of physiological measures can be recorded without undue discomfort or apprehension.

There is no reason why a paper on the topic of the measurement
of operator response cannot end on a note of optimism. The array of
techniques which the human factors scientist possesses may not be
totally adequate. Nevertheless, if the technique is chosen with
care, valuable information can be obtained which is beneficial to
the design and operation of vehicle systems. The change in role of
the human operator in the vehicle system does present a challenge
to the human factors scientist. How this challenge can be met
depends upon the ability of the specialist not only to devise new
measures but to reappraise the potential value of well established
techniques.

References

1.   COOPER,G.E. & HARPER,R.P. (1969). The use of pilot ratings
         in the evaluation of aircraft handling characteristics.
         National Aeronautics and Space Administration.
         Report TMT-5153.

2.   MURRELL,J.F. (1968). Pilots' assessment of their cockpit
         environment. In Problems of the Cockpit Environment.
         AGARD Conference Proceedings No 55.

3   KNOWLES,W.B. (1963). Operator loading tasks. Human Factors.
         5, 151-161.

4.   JAHNS,D.W. (1973). Operator workload: What is it and how
         should it be measured? In Crew System Design, Anacapa
         Sciences Inc. Santa Barbara, California.

5.   ROLFE,J.M., CHAPPELOW,J.W., EVANS,R.L., LINDSAY,S.J.E. &
         BROWNING,A.C. (1974). Evaluating measures of workload
         using a flight simulator. In Simulation and Study of
         High Workload Operations. AGARD Conference Proceedings
         No 146.

6.   HOPKINSON,J.A. & SHACKLE,B. (1972). Summary Report of the
         Flight Deck Activity Study. Loughborough University of
         Technology. Department of Ergonomics Report LUTERG 83.

7.   SEIFERT,R., SCHMIDT,K. & DANIELS,A.F. (1971). A method of
         man-display/control system evaluation. In Guidance and
         Control Displays. AGARD Conference Proceedings No 96.

8.   MURRELL,J.F. & ROLFE,J.M. (1967). Investigation of aircraft's
         handling characteristics using subjective ratings.
         Royal Air Force Institute of Aviation Medicine Report
         No 418.

9. ROLFE,J.M. & CHAPPELOW,J.W. (1973). The application of air-
    crew opinions on cockpit tasks and equipment to flight
    safety research. In Behavioural Aspects of Aircraft
    Accidents. AGARD Conference Proceedings No 132.

10. KRZANOWSKI,W.J. & NICHOLSON,A.N. (1972). Analysis of pilot
    assessment of workload. Aerospace Medicine. 43, 993-997.

11. OBORNE, D.J. & CLARKE,M.J. (1975). Questionnaire surveys of
    passenger comfort. Applied Ergonomics. 6, 97-103.

12. ROLFE,J.M. (1971). The secondary task as a measure of mental
    load. In Measurement of Man at Work. Taylor and
    Francis, London.

13. LINDQUIST,O.H. (1971). Design implications of a better view
    of the multi-channel capacity of a pilot. In Guidance
    and Control Displays. AGARD Conference Proceedings
    No 96.

14. HUDDLESTON,H.F. & WILSON,R.V. (1971). An evaluation of the
    usefulness of four secondary tasks in assessing the
    effect of a lag in simulated aircraft dynamics.
    Ergonomics, 14, 371-380.

15. NICHOLSON,A.N., HILL,L.E., BORLAND,R.G. & FERRES,H.M. (1970).
    Activity of the nervous system during the let down,
    approach and landing: a study of short duration high
    workload. Aerospace Medicine, 41, 436-446.

16. RUFFELL-SMITH,H.P. (1967). The effects of stress in civil
    transport pilots. Proceedings of the 1967 meeting of
    the Western European Association for Aviation Psycho-
    logy, Brussels.

17. ROHMERT,W. & LAURIG,W. (1971). Work measurement; psycholo-
    gical and physiological techniques for assessing opera-
    tor and workload. International Journal of Production
    Research, 9, 151-168.

18. SINGLETON,W.T., FOX,J.G. & WHITFIELD,D. (1971). Measurement
    of man at work. Taylor and Francis, London.

19. BORROWS,A.A. (1971). The structure of an effective human
    factors effort. In Measurement of Man at Work. Taylor
    and Francis, London.

DISCUSSION

RIJNSDORP :

You have stressed the need to measure responsibility of the human monitor. Can these characteristics be obtained from current experimental methods (e.g. pay-off functions, frequency of missed signals, etc.), or do you propose to develop completely new experimental approaches ?

SHACKEL :

The simple answer is that I do not know because I have only just recognized this gap in our knowledge, as I see it, about the human when he is acting as a monitor (including intermittent action as a controller).

I suspect that many of our present measurement methods will in fact be relevant; but I consider the major need is to look at the whole problem from a very different set of viewpoints. For example, if the only real reason to have a man in the system is so that he will deal with the truly unpredicted problem, then probably our selection criteria are entirely wrong as Dr. Edwards suggested, but not our selection methods as such. What particular methods will turn out to be relevant and useful can only be discovered by a thorough reappraisal such as I have suggested.

SHERIDAN :

The control engineer might contend that having multiple performance measures with no explicit means of combining them and making explicit tradeoffs is having no useful measure at all. How would you respond to that charge ?

SHACKEL :

I consider that the aim of combining scores in some weighted manner to give a single "system goodness of fit" criterion, as is often proposed, can be very misleading. Such a procedure, even when adapted with the best of intentions to facilitate explicit trade-offs, can be counter-productive ; steering committees and procurement evaluation meetings are only human and will put too much value upon the single score, while ignoring the accompanying qualifications. Combinatorial techniques are of course available and well-known. I suspect that Dr. Rolfe was constrained from discussing this issue by the space limitation set for the length of papers.

PILOT WORKLOAD ANALYSIS

A. Rault[*]

Adersa/Gerbios

53 avenue de l'Europe, 78140 Velizy (France)

1 - Introduction

The pilot workload has been a subject of research for the past years with a double sided goal : on the one hand to prevent accidents with unknown evident causes then attributed to pilot overloading ; on the other hand to understand the pilot's behaviour in view of designing better man-machine systems.

In this paper, we shall give the results of a pluridisciplinary type of approach realized on a simulator. This analysis led us to define an approach relying basically upon pilot modelling which is presently being used to analyze the helicopter pilot task during an instrument landing procedure.

The experimental context of our research has always been a realistic one ; during the first part the analysis was carried out on the simulation of the test flight center with the help of test pilots ; the second part was realized on helicopter again with test pilots. The first part of the paper will review the results obtained by the various approaches carried in parallel.

[*] This research has been conducted under D.R.M.E. contacts n° 73/862 and presently n° 74/719 under the supervision of J.Richalet and with the cooperation of P.Leroux and J.P.Hugelé.

2 - General approach. Analysis of the results

The basic argument of our initial approach to the
problem was to consider the operator engaged in an
intelligent task as being a system much too complex to
be understood by a unique tool. Therefore, the pilot
was considered as :

- a channel transmitting and processing information.
It suggested the application of information theory tools.

- an auto-adaptive regulator which immediately
justifies the mathematical modelling of the pilot.

- a sensor through psychological questionnaire
aimed at defining the difficulty of the task.

The goal was to find a quantitative definition of
the pilot workload through these different approaches
and with a homogeneous population of pilots. One must
say that this goal has not been attained but such a
series of experiments has yielded a better insight to
the human operator behaviour. First of all the
physiological measurements and the results obtained are
going to be analyzed.

2.1 Analysis of the pilot workload through physiological characteristics

The physiological measurements were the following
ones :

- cardiac rythm
- electromyography of the neck muscles
- pulmonary ventilation by impedance measurement
- eyes movements by electro-oculographic techniques.

The electromyographic measurements proved to have a
too great variability depending upon the exact position
of the electrodes which made us reject rapidly its use.

The pulmonary ventilation although being easily
measured presented such a great personal variability
that it could not be used as a qualifiable index.

The instantaneous cardiac rythm was analysed as
follows :

- the mean value was computed every 15 seconds

on the past 30 seconds to eleminate the respiratory
variations.

- the variability was evaluated on the overall
experiment.

Experiments were carried at the simulation center
of the flight test center with test pilots. The task
was an instrument landing procedure on a transport
airplane. The difficulty was controlled by the injection
of different levels of perturbations and engine stall.
The perturbation levels were graded 1 through 5 and the
engine stall moted P.

Considering the average values over ten pilots
belonging to a homogeneous population, the mean value
of the cardiac rythm varies in the same manner as the
programmed difficulty (see Fig. 1) and is strongly
correlated with the psychological analysis (Cooper
Wanner scale, see Fig. 3, 4).

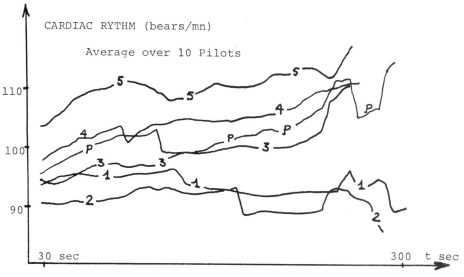

Figure 1

However, to consider the cardiac rythm as a
workload indicator is not appropriate ; indeed even with
such an homogeneous population as the test pilots,
personal dispersion appears to be large as shown in
Fig. 2. The cardiac variability appeared to present
similar characters.

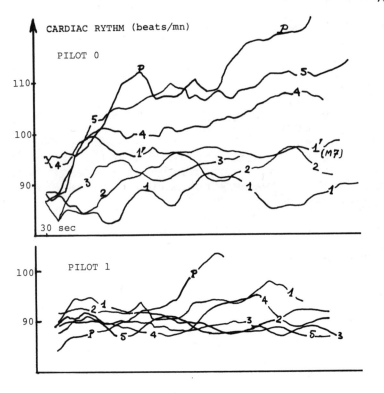

Figure 2

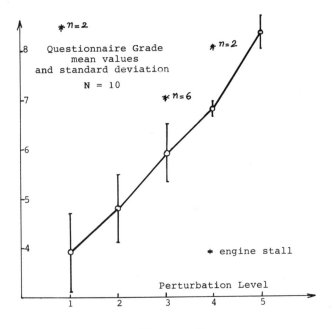

Figure 3

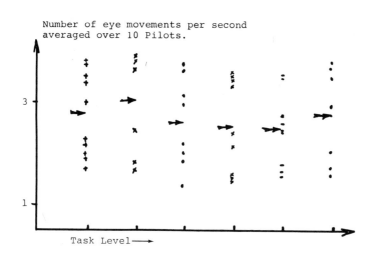

Number of eye movements per second
averaged over 10 Pilots.

Figure 4

The eyes movements have been analyzed by an electro-
oculographic technique. For this series of experiments
the system was still under a prototype version and only
the number of transitions could be counted ; it showed
that the fixation time is almost constant with respect
to the task difficulty (see Fig. 4). Lately, associated
to a better electronic treatment, a programme of
detection of the eye position has been developped.
The method is based on a learning procedure and a
Viterbi algorithm (1) finding the best finite state at
every instant. This technique proves to be useful to
comprehend the pilot's behaviour in view of modeling.

2.2 Workload analysis and information theory

The first idea of using information theory tools
to analyse the human operator was given by the psychologists. Hyman proved that after training, and considering a great number of experiments, the average reaction
time of the operator is proportionnal to the entropy
of the task. $T = 0.2 + k H$

Thus the reaction time to an event X_i could be writen as

$$t(X_i) = t_o - k \, \text{Log} \, p(X_i) \tag{1}$$

and in the case of dependent events

$$t(x_n = X_i / x_o^{n-1}) = t_o - k \, \text{Log} \, p \, (x_n = X_i / x_o^{n-1}) \tag{2}$$

If relation (1) has been experimentally verified, (2) has not. Thus one can ascertain that the use of entropy concept in the data collecting phasis of the human operator task is appropriate ; it is not clear that in a regulation task it be the same.

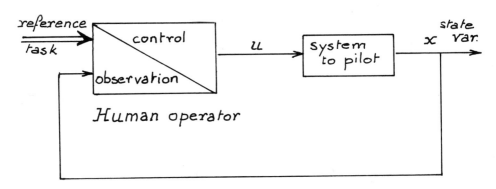

Figure 5

Considering the human operator as a transmission channel its transinformation is written as :

$$I(u,x) = H(u) - H(u/x)$$

However, the transinformation being symetric with respect to the input output relation, the notion of causality is lost and

$$I(x,u) = H(x) - H(x/u)$$

which represents the transinformation of the controlled process. Therefore in a regulation task the transinformation of the human operator $x \rightarrow u$ is equal to the transinformation of the controlled system $u \rightarrow x$. The natural concept, also used by Wempe and Baty (2), is to consider that the transinformation being the number of bits treated by the pilot, the higher his

transinformation, the more he works;thus it could be
considered as a workload index. However if one considers
the control of a purely deterministic system, then
$I(x,u) = H(x)$. At a given control criterion the strategy
yielding the highest transinformation will be that which
leaves a white residual (unpredictable and therefore
sampled at a high rate), the strategy with the lowest
transinformation will be that which leaves a sinusoïdal
residual. However, for the same control criterion the
second strategy necessitates a lower sampling rate and
thus no conclusion can be drawn. Let us also remark
that the control residuals of a human operator are often
very predictable, his policy being to maintain the state
variables within a domain of controllability ; it means
that the uncertainty on the future behaviour of the
system is somehow minimized and its transinformation
similarly.

Therefore, our initial conjecture which was to use
information theory tools as a global tool in order to
detect the workload level is far from being verified.
However it would be useful for the synthesis of a pilot
model by defining constraints on the sampling instants
and the amount of information necessary to the pilot to
perform his task.

This point of view is in agreement with the pilot
modelling as will be explained further. Thus without
talking about the actual difficulties met in the
computation of the transinformation (4) (linearity and
stationnarity) its use as a measure of workload is not
appropriate.

3 - Pilot Modelling

The experience gained through the analysis of
actual flight data has led us to the following philosophy on the pilot modelling and more generally about
the human operator's behaviour in front of the control
of a dynamic process.

3.1 General Philosophy

- First of all the objective of a pilot cannot be
formulated as the minimization of a criterion ; it is
much more fuzzy and would better be expressed as the
desire that the man machine system behave according to
a reference trajectory. This notion is well implemented

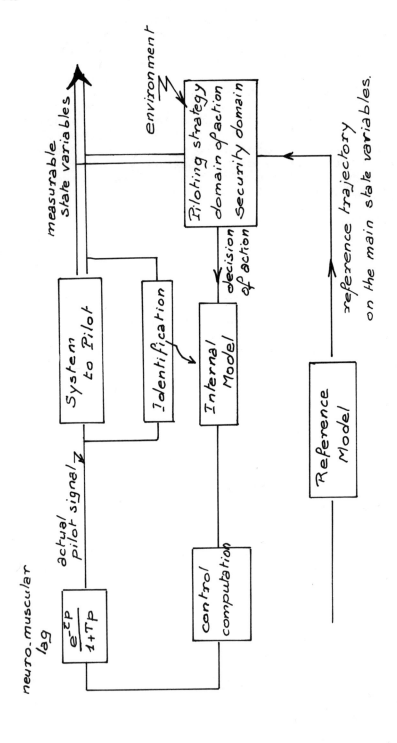

Figure 6 – Proposed Pilot Model

by a <u>reference model</u> whose structure can actually be
quite simple : gains and time constants defining a
"stability like" along the different axis.

   - The analysis of pilot behaviour reveals a strong
non linear character. As long as the representative
state variables belong to a neighborhood of its reference trajectory the pilot does not act. This can be
defined as a <u>security domain</u>, to which is closely
associated a <u>domain of action</u> corresponding to the
decision of applying a control signal.

   - Contrarily to a classical control system in
which the control signal is frequently a linear or a
nonlinear combination of the state variables, the pilots
apply impulse type of controls. Besides that, they have
a strong adaptation capability which enables them to
readjust their strategy according to circumstances or
variations of the plane dynamics. This is well rendered
by the notion of <u>internal model</u>. It is a model of the
plane (very simplified indeed) which the pilot has
acquired through his training and experience ; it is
renewed and modified by a learning procedure
(identification). This notion of internal model is
necessary to interpret the predictive aspect of a pilot
control as compared to a classical automatic pilot.

   This philosophy is summarized in the following
diagram (see Fig. 6).

3.2   <u>Application to the analysis of helicopter piloting</u>

   The task studied was an instrument landing procedure under various configurations (susceptible of
different workload levels). Each task was repeated five
times in order to obtain an average behaviour of the
pilots.

   In a first stage we shall restrict ourselves to
the lateral guiding along the localizer axis. The
problem is represented on Figure 7.

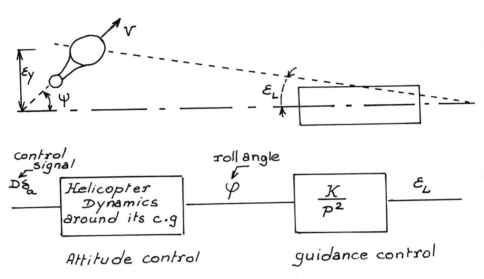

Figure 7

The helicopter dynamic are of higher frequency
than the guidance loop. Thus the pilot has two functions :
the first one is to stabilize the helicopter (attitude
control) ; the second one is to achieve a certain
trajectory. This double task generally easily achieved
when piloting a plane is very hard to perform except in
the case when the attitude control is realized by an
automatic pilot. The actual configuration we shall
analyze is given in Figure 8.

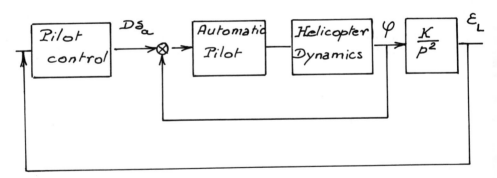

Figure 8

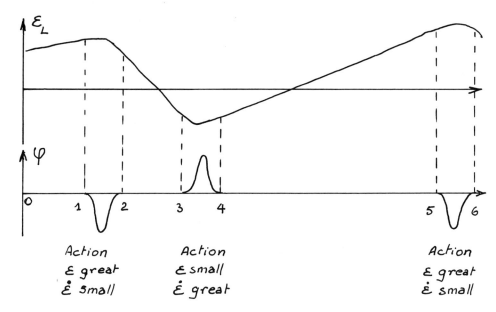

Action
ε great
ε̇ small

Action
ε small
ε̇ great

Action
ε great
ε̇ small

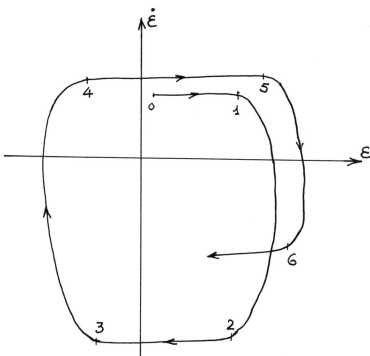

Figure 9

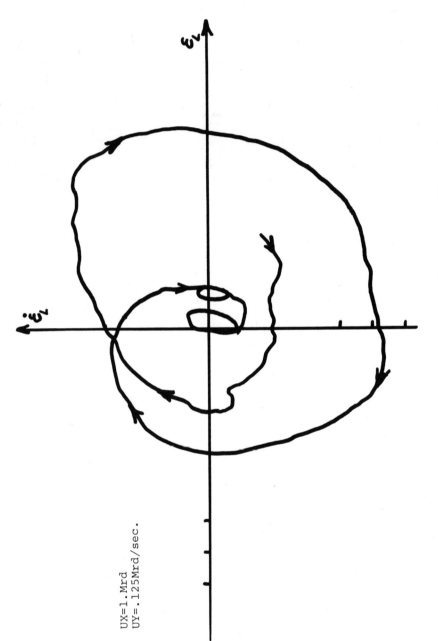

UX=1.Mrd
UY=.125Mrd/sec.

Figure 10 Actual Pilot Behaviour During a Landing Procedure

The problem is thus simplified to that of controlling a double integrator system. Actual recorded signals show a good reproductibility of control signals of the "impulse type".

Intuitively one is led to the following analysis : the pilot sends an impulsion type of signal each time his state does not belong to a certain space. This hypothesis is summarized in Figure 9 and the actual behaviour of the pilot is given in Figure 10. Note that it would be rather ridiculous to try to characterize this behaviour by a linear model.

It appears, that the important fact to explain is the law of decision to act or not. Following an action, the pilot leaves its system free, taking then care of another axis of control. The next scrutation consists in checking that the system behaves as foreseen along a reference trajectory. If it actually belong to a certain neighborhood of the reference trajectory the pilot does not act ; otherwise, he sends a control signal (see Figure 11).

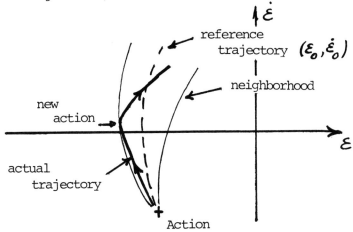

Figure 11

This strategy is implemented through the definition of a domain of action corresponding to the boundaries of the neighborhood of the reference trajectory, it is realized by a probabilistic functional of the state variables ε $\dot{\varepsilon}$ $f(\varepsilon, \dot{\varepsilon})$. When the actual trajectory touches the boundary the probability of deciding a new action tends to 1.

A function $g(\varepsilon,\dot{\varepsilon})$ defines the <u>security domain</u>
corresponding to the threshold type of behaviour of the
pilot who does not act as long as his trajectory belongs
to a neighborhood of the reference trajectory.
A schematized idea of these domains is given on Figure 12.

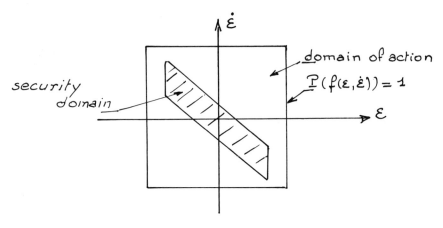

Figure 12

Thus the pilot is defined essentially by three
probabilities :

- Probability of acting at instant n given that
at (n-1) there was no action

$$P \ (1/0) = P \ (f(\varepsilon,\dot{\varepsilon}))$$

- Probability of no action at time n given that
there was one at n-1

$$P \ (0/1) = P \ (g(\varepsilon,\dot{\varepsilon}))$$

- Probability of a new action at time n given
there was one at n-1

$$P \ (1'/1) = P \ (h(\varepsilon,\dot{\varepsilon},\varepsilon_0,\dot{\varepsilon}_0))$$

This last function defines the neighborhood of the
reference trajectory $(\varepsilon_0,\dot{\varepsilon}_0)$.

These techniques are being used to analyse the
data collected on helicopter instrument landing procedure under different circumstances which have been
graded through a Cooper scale by the pilots. The final
objective is to obtain a model of the average pilot
with learning and adaptation capabilities.

This model would then be used in conjonction with
the helicopter model to test the pilotability of various
configurations and predict the actual pilot's behaviour.
The better comprehension of the pilot's strategies will
also help to understand what is the pilot's workload
and how to find a good representative index.

References

(1)   A.Rault, P.Leroux
       "Système E.O.G. - Algorithme et programmes"
       Rapport ADERSA/GERBIOS dans le cadre du marché
       ONERA n° 18377/SAT.3/AF.

(2)   Wempe T. and Baty D.
       "The usefulness of transinformation as a measure
        of human performance"
       NASA, Report SP 128, pp. 111-129, 1966.

(3)   Baty D.
       "Information-processing as influenced by the
        degree of response difficulty : a discrete
        tracking task"
       NASA, Report SP 114, pp. 157-164, 1967.

(4)   A.Rault, J.Richalet, P.Leroux, Ph.Trangosi
       "Charge de travail du pilote d'hélicoptère"
       Rapport ADERSA/GERBIOS dans le cadre de la
       convention DRME n° 73/862, Juin 1975.

DISCUSSION

EDWARDS :

In your introduction, you mention the objectives of accident prevention and man-machine system design. Could you please indicate the
ways in which your modelling studies contribute to either of these goals ?

RAULT :

In our study, goals have been evolving. The workload measurement
was the starting point. Our lack of success to attain a quantitative
measure of workload led us to a need for better comprehension of human
operator's behaviour and therefore to human operator modeling.

We believe that a good model of the average pilot will enable us :
1) to better understand man's functioning and therefore maybe get to a
workload measure, 2) have a human operator simulator on which new
systems (control laws - changes in tasks --) could be tested, thus reducing test flights and perhaps accidents.

BARGL :

Are there any experimental results concerning the question : What
influence has the mean workload before an unpredicted disturbance
(e.g., wind shear on final approach) on the level of workload to overcome the disturbance ?

RAULT :

I do not have actual experimental results to be able to answer your
question except that we noted that the pilots were more sensitive to an
engine stall when the workload level was low than when it was already
at a serious level. It seems that a threshold workload level is necessary
to stimulate the human operator attention.

KVÅLSETH :

    You mention in your paper that "... if one considers the control of
a purely deterministic system, then $I(x,u) = H(x)$". Could you please
elaborate somewhat on this ? Are you assuming that the piloted system
contains random noise ? If the answer to the last question is "yes", then
clearly the conditional entropy $H(x/u) \neq 0$.

RAULT :

    You are perfectly correct in your statement and actually I meant to
state : "... if one considers a purely deterministic control law (instead
of the human operator) then $I(x,u) = H(x)$" which assumes of course that
the system being piloted is subject to some disturbances which thus
implies $H(x/u) \neq 0$.

THE INTERNAL MODEL

What does it mean in human control?

W. Veldhuyzen and H.G. Stassen

Man-Machine Systems Group

Delft University of Technology

The Netherlands

0.   Abstract

In developing mathematical models for human performance the concept of an Internal Model has proven to be of great utility and wide spread application.
In this paper it is shown how such a concept was used to develop a model for a helmsman controlling a large ship. This example is interesting because the problem, where very long time constants are involved, tends to be more similar to supervisory control than to classical manual control. The utility of the Internal Model concept in this example suggests that the concept will also play an important role in the development of models for supervisory control.

1.   Introduction

Starting in the late forties much attention has been paid to manual control problems. The function of the human operator therein was considered to be that of a controller; an element that has to close the loop in a certain optimal way. The manual control theory thus developed has resulted into a number of useful models,

x) The research reported in this paper was partly sponsored by the Netherlands Organization for the Advancement of Pure Research (ZWO).

such as the Describing Function Model [1], the Optimal Control Model [2], the Decision Model [3], the many Non-linear Models. In going through these huge number of papers [4], one very common aspect can be recognized: In order to provide a succesful control behavior, the human operator needs some information of the statics and dynamics of the system to be controlled; this information is called an Internal Model, that is an internal representation of the knowledge the human operator has [5]. This is implicitely true for the Cross-over Model [1], where the human operator adapts his control to the dynamics of the controlled element; it is very clearly true for the Optimal Control Model [2], where for the construction of the Kalman Filter, Predictor and Optimal Controller the system dynamics should be known; and it also is true for the Decision Model [3]. Some Non-Linear Models [6,7] are based on the Internal Model concept too.

The existence of such an Internal Model can be exposed by drawing a parallel between the manual control and the design of a control loop, where in order to find an optimal solution, certain knowledge of the system to be controlled should be available. That is, the engineer or designer of the control loop should have an Internal Model of the system to be controlled. In the same way, a supervisor controlling a number of control loops of a large scale plant should be informed about the whole plant dynamics, or, he should have an Internal Model of the plant. Here it should be mentioned that the remaining task of the human operator then will change from an active manual control task to an information processing or supervisory task, where sampling of information, decision making, action pattern generation and monitoring are based upon the knowledge of the plant under supervision.

Besides the many studies executed by control and system engineers, a number of studies have been reported by psychologists. Some of these papers are related to specific situations [8;9], other papers deal with the behavior of the human operator or supervisor in a more general way [6;10]. The models are all based on the Internal Model concept, in order to plan future control actions [6;11;12]. In general these predictions are not too accurate, since:

● The structure of the Internal Model may differ from the structure of the controlled system.
● The Internal Model parameters may differ from those of the controlled system.
● The system information can be perceived only with restricted accuracy [12].
● The disturbances are often not known exactly.

The utility of the Internal Model concept is also indicated in the study of monitoring behavior; several models are reported in this area [13;14;15]. It is found that a lack of information of the controlled system, which thus means a less accurate Internal Model, does increase the sampling rate of the displayed information by the supervisor [16].

From the control and psychological papers reviewed, the
authors believe that the following statement can be made.
*All forms of human behavior involve some internal representa-
tion - the Internal Model - of the system being observed or
controlled, or can be explained in such terms.*
The study of the meaning of the Internal Model concept is therefore
of great importance in understanding human performance. Because
the monitoring, decision making, predicting or extrapolating, and
planning activities of human beings are all based on an Internal
Model, the authors believe that in supervisory control this concept can be fruitfully applied.
As mentioned before, the supervisory control of multivariable systems changes the human operator's task from a manual to a monitoring and set-point control task; it implies that the human operator experiences the system to be controlled as a slowly responding
one. A similar situation occurs in the manual control of large
scale systems, such as large ships. The slowly reponding character
of these systems will be experienced as a kind of supervisory control of a scalar system. Therefore, the study of the manual control
of slowly responding systems will be a nice introduction to the
study of supervisory control of multivariable systems.
To show the utility of the Internal Model, a model based on this
concept will be given, describing the behavior of the helmsman
controlling a large ship.

2.   Application of the Internal Model concept to the control
                        of a large ship

2.1. Experiments
      In order to describe the helmsman's behavior during the con-
trol of a very slowly responding system, a number of experiments
were executed with a maneuvering simulator. Four subjects were ordered to steer a large ship along prescribed headings during forty
minutes. During one group of tests the ordered headings were as
shown in Fig. 1; in another set of tests the deviations of the nominal heading were twice as large. The first case is indicated as
Ts A, the last one as Ts B.
2.2. Shipdynamics
      Three ships were simulated, using one model structure to des-
cribe their dynamic behavior. The model is given by Eq. 1:

$$T\ddot{\psi}(t) + a_1\dot{\psi}(t) + a_2[\dot{\psi}(t)]^3 + a_3[\dot{\psi}(t)]^{1/3} = K\delta(t), \qquad (1)$$

where $\psi(t)$ = heading angle;
      $\dot{\psi}(t)$ = $d\psi(t)/dt$ = rate of turn;
      $\ddot{\psi}(t)$ = $d^2\psi(t)/dt^2$ = angular acceleration;
      $\delta(t)$ = rudder angle,

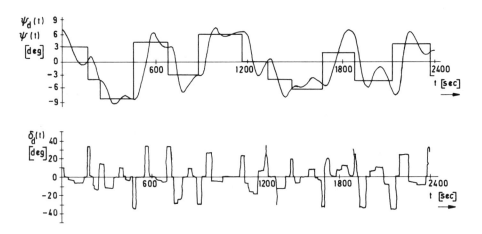

Figure 1: An example of the signals measured during a maneuvering
          test.

and where the quantities T, a_1, a_2, a_3 and K are constants. To control the position of the rudder a servo system has been applied.
The dynamics of the rudder engine are given by Eq. 2:

$$T_\delta \dot{\delta}(t) + \delta(t) = \delta_d(t) \; ;$$

$$|\dot{\delta}(t)| \leq \dot{\delta}_M \, ,$$

(2)

where: $\delta_d(t)$ = steering wheel position;
       $\delta(t)$ = rudder angle;
       $\dot{\delta}(t)$ = dδ(t)/dt = angular velocity;
       $\dot{\delta}_M$ = maximum angular velocity.

The parameters values used during the trials are shown in Table 1.

Table 1: The parameter values of the ships simulated.

Param.	Ship I	Ship II	Ship III	Dimension
T	250	250	250	sec
K	-0.05	-0.05	-0.1	sec^{-1}
a_1	1	-1	-1	-
a_2	5	5	5	$deg^{-2}sec^{+2}$
a_3	0	0	1	$deg^{2/3}sec^{-2/3}$
T_δ	1	1	1	sec
$\dot{\delta}_M$	3	3	3	$deg\ sec^{-1}$

2.3. <u>The model of the behavior of the helmsman</u>
    The helmsman's model, described in detail in [7], consists of
two main blocks (Fig. 2):
● An Internal Model.
● A Decision Making Element.

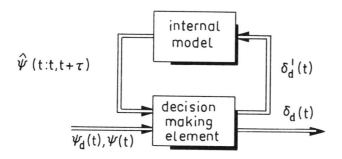

Figure 2: A block diagram of the helmsman's model.

    The Internal Model is used to make a prediction of the heading
$\hat{\psi}(t:t,t+\tau)$ on the basis of a $\delta_d'(t)$ to see whether things will go
correctly, or, to decide the proper actions if they do not. The
Internal Model is put in the folllowing mathematical form:

$$T_m \ddot{\psi}(t) + \dot{\psi}(t) = K_m \delta_d(t) ,\qquad\qquad (3)$$

where T_m and K_m are parameters in the Internal Model, and thus of
the model of the helmsman itself.

    The second block in the model is the Decision Making Element.
To understand this part, some general characteristics of the helmsman's output during a maneuvre must be mentioned. A maneuvre can
often be divided into four phases. During the first phase the
helmsman generates an output in order to start the ship rotating,
then during the second phase, the rudder is kept amidships. During
the third phase, the helmsman stops the rotating motion of the
ship and when the desired heading is achieved with only a small
rate of turn (the desired state) the fourth phase starts (rudder
angle zero). If the rate of turn is not small, there will be an
overshoot and to achieve the desired state, the cycle is repeated,
starting with the first phase again. The four phases can be easily
indicated in the phase-plane (Fig. 3).
In modelling the helmsman's control behavior, it is assumed that
this plane can be divided into four areas corresponding to the
four phases, and that the boundaries between these areas can be
approximated by straight lines, given by the Eqs.:

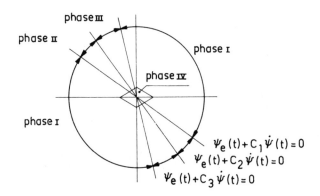

Figure 3: The four phases of control in the phase-plane.

$$\psi_e(t) + c_1\dot{\psi}(t) = 0 \; ; \tag{4a}$$

$$\psi_e(t) + c_2\dot{\psi}(t) = 0 \; ; \tag{4b}$$

$$\psi_e(t) + c_3\dot{\psi}(t) = 0 \; ; \tag{4c}$$

$$|\psi_e(t)| + c_1|\dot{\psi}(t)| = g \; . \tag{4d}$$

During the second and fourth phase the rudder angle is kept zero; during the other two phases a rudder angle must be selected in order to achieve the goals given by Eqs. 4a (Phase I) and 4d, where g=0 (Phase III). At the beginning of a particular phase, and thus when one of the boundaries is passed, a rudder angle $\delta_d(t)$ is chosen using the Internal Model, in such a way that after a time $t_p(t)$ the goal will be achieved. After the rudder angle is chosen the Internal Model is used to determine, whether the objectives will be satisfied during the following period, or whether a new rudder angle has to be chosen. A flow-chart of the Decision Making Element is given in Fig. 4.

The criteria used to judge the result of the momentary rudder angle are given by the following Eqs.:

Phase I   : $|\psi_e(t+t_p) + c_1\dot{\psi}(t+t_p)| \leqq d(t) \; ;$ \hfill (5)

Phase III: $|\psi_e(t+t_p)| + c_1|\dot{\psi}(t+t_p)| \leqq d(t) \; ,$ \hfill (6)

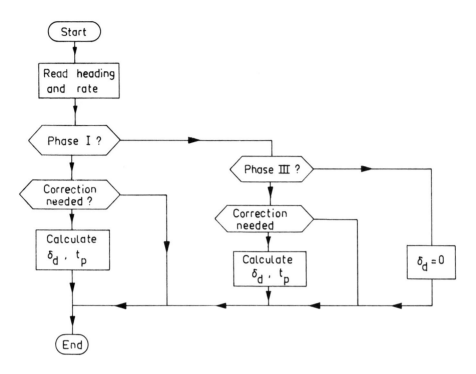

Figure 4: Flow chart of the decision making element.

where $\psi_e(t+t_p)$ and $\dot{\psi}(t+t_p)$ are predicted using the Internal Model.
The threshold value $d(t)$ depends on the heading error $\psi_e(t)$. For
great heading errors the helmsman is mainly interested to reduce
the instantaneous error, while for small errors he is in particular focussed on the difference between the predicted state of the
ship and the objectives to be reached. For the relation between
threshold $d(t)$ and error $\psi_e(t)$ the following Eq. is assumed:

$$d(t) = g(1+p|\psi_e(t)|) , \tag{7}$$

where g and p are modelparameters.
It should be mentioned that during the first phase many different
rudder angles $\delta_d(t)$ may result in the selected goal depending on

the time $t_p(t)$. Therefore it is assumed that the combination of rudder angle $\delta_d(t)$ and duration $t_p(t)$ is chosen by minimizing the following criterion:

$$J = t_p(t) + W|\delta_d(t)| ,\tag{8}$$

with W as a model parameter. Eq. (8) implies that the rudder angle $\delta_d(t)$ is weighted with the time $t_p(t)$ [7].

2.4. Parameter estimation

The parameters of the model of the helmsman's control behavior are estimated as shown in Fig. 5. The upper loop is the experimental loop with the maneuvering simulator and the helmsman; the lower loop is a simulation of ship and helmsman.

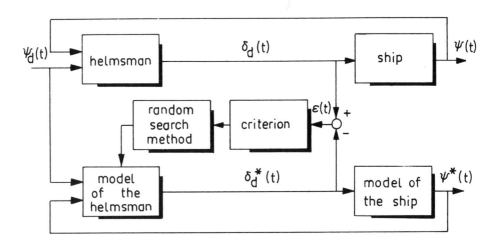

Figure 5: Estimation of the parameters of the model for the helmsman's behavior; note that one is estimating in a closed loop, sothat a biased parameter may be found.

The outputs of the helmsman and the model are used to calculate the following quantity:

$$E_\delta = \frac{\int_0^T \left[\delta_d(t) - \delta_d^*(t)\right]^2 dt}{\int_0^T \left[\delta_d(t)\right]^2 dt} \cdot 100\% \tag{9}$$

To minimize the criterion (9) with respect to the unknown parameters a random search method is used. Moreover, the time histories of the heading of the ship steered by the helmsman and the model, are compared according to Eq. (10) [7]:

$$E_\psi = \frac{\int_0^T [\psi(t)-\psi^*(t)]^2 dt}{\int_0^T [\psi(t)]^2 dt} \cdot 100\% \qquad (10)$$

2.5. Results

In Table 2 some of the results of the maneuvering tests are summarized.

Table 2: Results of the parameter optimization; the time constant of the ship in 250 seconds.

Test conditions			Par. Int. Model	Par. Dec. making element						Performance	
Ship	Ts	Subj.	T_m	g	p	W	c_1	c_2	c_3	E_δ	E_ψ
I	A	1	167	0.25	0.45	0.60	39	13	5	45	3
I	A	2	168	0.74	0.07	2.39	19	16	2	48	3
I	A	3	195	0.72	0.27	1.42	19	37	10	55	–
I	A	4	211	0.27	0.25	0.96	50	22	2	48	3
I	B	1	254	0.34	0.38	1.00	47	28	1	20	–
I	B	1	324	0.59	0.25	1.34	29	28	2	33	3
I	B	2	295	0.62	0.08	1.13	59	26	1	31	1
I	B	3	256	0.48	0.33	1.11	40	37	2	45	0
I	B	3	215	0.44	0.17	1.33	51	38	0	42	0
II	A	1	258	0.17	0.24	1.30	42	48	10	39	5
II	A	1	290	0.16	0.40	1.07	43	25	6	42	14
II	A	2	216	0.30	0.11	2.55	57	30	4	44	6
II	A	2	215	0.24	0.28	3.15	41	24	2	55	5
II	B	1	304	0.57	0.24	1.16	55	36	3	40	–
II	B	2	237	0.48	0.39	3.36	56	30	4	44	0
II	B	2	208	0.36	0.16	3.23	53	36	3	50	–
III	A	3	233	0.19	0.41	1.46	25	15	10	47	–
III	A	3	257	0.51	0.27	1.32	22	21	1	38	–
III	A	4	302	0.51	0.25	1.05	27	16	0	38	–
III	A	4	259	0.74	0.34	0.83	23	15	1	45	–
III	B	3	173	0.56	0.31	1.20	26	31	10	36	–
III	B	4	277	0.91	0.36	1.00	30	29	5	36	–

As an exemple the time histories of the heading $\psi(t)$ and the rudder angle $\delta_d(t)$, as recorded during two tests, as well as the output of the helmsman's model $\delta_d^*(t)$ and the heading $\psi^*(t)$ of the ship steered by the model are given in Fig. 6.

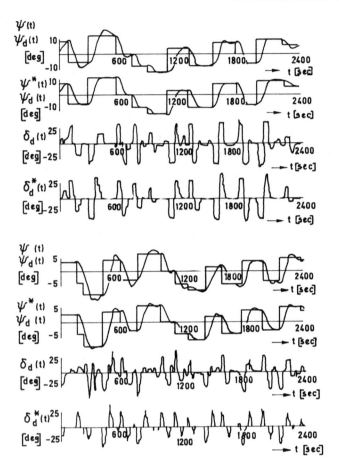

Figure 6: The actual heading and rudder angles and the model outputs for different tests.

As a result of the analyses of the tests, it was found that
the parameters of the Internal Model T_m and K_m were strongly
coupled. Fig. 7 shows the results of two tests, where the quantity
K_m was varied, and where the value of the parameter T_m was estimated according to the criterion (10) with constant other parameters:
An explanation of the cross-coupling between K_m and T_m may be the
fact that the rate of turn during a test is so small for large
ships that the damping term of the Internal Model can be neglected.
For this reason during the parameter optimization the parameter K_m
was not varied but kept equal to the real coefficient K of the
ship (as shown in Table 2).

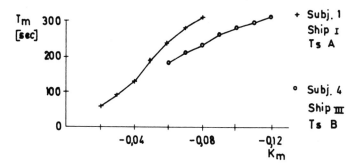

Figure 7: The optimum value of T_m with changing K_m for two tests. The other parameters are kept constant for each of the tests.

2.6. The meaning of the Internal Model in the control of large ships

The criterion values E_δ, as given in Table 2, show that the description of the helmsman's control behavior by the model leads to a reasonable match; the model accounts for about 55 to 70% of the control power.

The Internal Model used is of a much simpler structure than the model used to simulate the ship (compare Eq. 3 with Eq. 1). The coupling between the two Internal Model parameters T_m and K_m, however, indicates that even a simpler equation could be used (Fig.7). In predicting the state of systems with very long time constants, it probably may lead to the general insight that the Internal Model to describe human operator's behavior can be a rather simple one. The estimated values of the parameter T_m are of the same order as the parameter of the ship T (Table 3); the mean values η_{T_m} are in

Table 3: The mean values η_{T_m} and variances $\sigma_{T_m}^2$ of the Internal Model time constant T_m, averaged over the subjects.

Number of tests	Ship	Ts	T	η_{T_m}	η_{T_m}/T	σ_{T_m}	σ_{T_m}/T
4	I	A	250	185	0.74	22	0.09
5	I	B	250	269	1.08	42	0.17
4	II	A	250	245	0.98	33	0.13
3	II	B	250	250	1.00	49	0.20
4	III	A	250	263	1.05	24	0.10
2	III	B	250	225	0.90	74	0.30

most of the cases accurate within about 10%. In those cases where the time constants T_m were smaller than those of the ship, it has been found that the number of rudder calls increased.

The Decision Making Element parameters, in particular the threshold value g and the factor p, also influence the number of rudder calls in the model output. No relation between the parameter T_m and the Decision Making Element parameters could be found. However, here it should be noted, that the criterion (10) used, is probably not very sensitive for changes of these parameters with reference to the number of rudder calls.

3.   Application of the Internal Model concept

As indicated in the introduction the analyses of many man-machine problems can be based on the Internal Model concept. The above paragraphs indicate how the concept can contribute in building models to understand the behavior of the human operator in controlling slowly responding systems. It is amazing to see at the one side how much work has been executed in the field of manual control of relatively fast responding systems, and on the other how little attention has been paid to the manual control of a slowly responding system, although just the latter goes with increasing time constants into the direction of supervisory control. It is therefore that the authors would like to emphasize that in future more attention should be paid on the use of the Internal Model concept in the manual control of slowly responding systems. From these studies the authors believe very strongly that one can learn in solving supervisory control problems, since many important problems in human operator activities can be directly related to the Internal Model concept. As an example the following problems can be mentioned: Monitoring and decision making behavior of the human supervisor; mental load problems, task analyses and unconcious control [17] and display design.

4.   Acknowledgements

The authors gratefully acknowledge the contribution of C.C. Glansdorp of the Shipbuilding Laboratory of the Delft University of Technology. An important part of the work is done by J.F. Zegwaard, H.B.M. van Rooyen and P.C. van Holten, who completed the hybrid computer programs to optimize the model.

5.   References

1. McRuer, D.T., E.S. Krendel. Mathematical Models of Human Pilot
      Behavior. Report: NATO, 1974. 72 p. AGARD-AG-188.
2. Kleinman, D.L., S. Baron, W.H Levison. A Control Theoretic Ap-
      proach to Manned-Vehicle Systems Analysis. IEEE-Trans. on Au-
      tomatic Control Vol. AC-16 (1971) No. 6 pp. 824-832.
3. Elkind, J.I., D.C. Miller. Adaptive Characteristics of the Hu-
      man Controller of Time-Varying Systems. Springfield, NTIS,
      1968. 191 p. AD-665 455.
4. Annual Conference on Manual Control. Springfield, NTIS.
      2nd NASA-Univ. Conf., Cambridge (MIT), 1966. 417 p. NASA SP-
         126.
      3rd NASA-Univ. Conf., LA (USC), 1967. 459 p. NASA SP-144.
      4th NASA-Univ. Conf., Ann Arbor (UM), 1968. 594 p. NASA SP-192.
      5th NASA-Univ. Conf., Cambridge (MIT), 1969. 713 p. NASA SP-
         215.
      6th Conf., Dayton (WPAFB), 1970. 896 p.
      7th NASA-Univ. Conf., LA (USC), 1971. 361 p. NASA SP-281.
      8th Conf., Dayton (WPAFB), 1972. 665 p. AFFDL-TR-72-92.
      9th Conf., Cambridge (MIT), 1973. 451 p.
      10th Conf., Dayton (WPAFB), 1974. 746 p.
5. Cooke, J.E. Human Decision in the Control of a Slow Response
      System. Dis.: Oxford, 1965. 403 p.
6. Bekey, G.A., E.S. Angel. Asynchronous Finite State Models of
      Manual Control Systems. In: Proc. 2nd NASA-Univ. Conf. Manual
      Control, Cambridge, 1966. pp. 25-38. NASA SP-128.
7. Veldhuyzen, W., H.G. Stassen. Simulation of Ship Manoeuvring
      under Human Control. In: Proc. 4th Ship Control Systems Symp.,
      Den Helder, Royal Netherlands Naval College, 1975, Vol. 6.
      pp. 148-163.
8. Beishon, R.J. Problems of Task Description in Process Control.
      In: W.T. Singleton. The Human Operator in Complex Systems.
      Taylor en Francis, 1971. pp. 77-87.
9. Brainbridge, L. The Nature of the "Mental Model" in Process
      Control. In: Proc. Int. Symp. on Man-Machine Systems, Cam-
      bridge (UK), 1969. 10 p.
10. Kelley, C.R. Manual and Automatic Control, Wiley, 1968.
11. Sheridan, T.B. Three Models of Preview Control. IEEE-Trans. on
       Human Factors in Electr. Vol. HFE-7 (1966) No. 2 pp. 91-102.
12. Crossman, E.R.F.W., H. Szostak. Man-Machine Models for Car
       Steering. In: Proc. 4th Ann. Conf. on Manual Control, Ann Ar-
       bor, 1968. pp. 171-195.
13. Smallwood, R.D. Internal Models and the Human Instrument Moni-
       tor. IEEE-Trans. on Human Factors in Electr. Vol. HFE-8 (1967)
       No. 3 pp. 181-187.
14. Rouse, W.B. A Model of the Human in a Cognitive Prediction
       Task. IEEE-Trans. on Systems, Man and Cyb. Vol. SMC-3 (1973)
       No. 5 pp. 473-477.

15. Rouse, W.B. Models of a man as a suboptimal predictor. In:
    Proc. 9th Ann. Conf. on Manual Control, Cambridge, 1973.
    pp. 413-417.
16. Crossman, E.R.F.W., J.E. Cooke, R.J. Beishon. Visual Attention
    and the Sampling of Displayed information in Process Con-
    trol. In: Proc. Second Int. Congress or Ergonomics, Dort-
    mund, 1964. Supplement to Ergonomics, Taylor and Francis
    Ltd, London, p. 230.
17. Kalsbeek, J.W.H. Standards of Acceptable Load in ATC Task.
    Ergonomics Vol. 14 (1971) no. 5 pp. 641-650.

DISCUSSION

LAIOS :

What type of model have you used for your predictor display ?

STASSEN :

The predictive display was based on the internal model of the helmsman's model ; that is, the simplified first order differential equation of the ship. Experiments with an internal model like the original differential equation did not lead to better correspondence of the model with the original helmsman's output.

HAMMOND :

What are the reasons for using the helmsman within the heading control loop rather than leaving heading control to an autopilot and using the helmsman to set desired heading in a supervisory mode ?

STASSEN :

To design an autopilot in an optimal way, you need :

- Information about the system to be controlled.
- Information about possible disturbances acting on the ship.

In particular, for the ease of entering harbors or relatively narrow channels, we know that the dynamics of the ship are strongly dependent on the direct environment. For instance, a difference in water column between the bottom of the sea and the ship of several meters can change the dynamics of the ship from a stable to a totally unstable one. Therefore, an autopilot is not safe enough, in particular when one takes also into account the large to very large time constants (more than 250 seconds).

Another reason may be the economic factors. The instrumentation which really can help the helmsman is too expensive with reference to the profits to be made.

General Models

PREVIEW OF MODELS OF THE HUMAN MONITOR/SUPERVISOR

Thomas B. Sheridan

Massachusetts Institute of Technology

Cambridge, Massachusetts 02139 U.S.A.

INTRODUCTION

In past years many of us have been confronted by our non-technical friends and asked, in effect, how we have the audacity to suggest that human behavior can be reduced to mathematical equations. Typically we have retreated to the argument that we are dealing with man-machine interactions which are quite utilitarian and mechanistic to begin with. Therefore, such mechanistic mathematic models have a face validity. Anyway, when the stimulus and response are well-defined and the decision criterion straightforward, the models are useful because they are good predictors of the aspects of human behavior which are important.

Unhappily, now that the computer is gradually taking over the routine, predictable and definable tasks of vehicle and process control and performing these tasks automatically with high speed and precision, and where the human operator is now assigned the function of monitoring and supervising this robot, such generalizations about modeling seem valid no longer. To be sure, the human operator may have gained a more dignifying role. Just as assuredly, however, the mathematical modeler in his new role must beware the indignites of tripping over his own hubris.

With such caveats in place let us plunge ahead into the modeling melee. The various models presented in this section raise a whole gamut of searching questions about the nature of the human monitor/supervisor - what he <u>does</u> (the descriptive modeling problem) and what he <u>ought to do</u> (the normative modeling problem).

We will preview the modeling papers in their order of presentation, while trying to raise up those general questions and concepts which the papers themselves illustrate so well.

PREVIEW OF PAPERS IN MODELING SESSION

The first two papers of the session deal with signal detection
and the degree of participation by the human operator. On the
sensory side of the organism, Williges reviews recent development in vigilance and the "ideal observer" or "signal detection
theory" models which have now replaced classical psychophysical
theories in dealing with such problems. The commonly accepted
finding by Mackworth and others that operators simply lose
alertness after 30 minutes or so is shown by Williges to be a
more subtle secular change in the decision criterion β (stringency
or conservatism in detecting signals, i.e. avoidance of false
alarms). In fact, in terms of expected payoff he finds the subjects usually tend toward optimality (the ideal observer).

"Participation" on the motor side raises the question of
active in-the-loop control vs. out-of-the-loop monitoring – and
when is which best under what conditions. Curry and Ephrath
suggest answers to this question in the context of a failure detection experiment: in-the-loop participation is best when error
alone is insufficient or the input of motor "identification
signals" permits quick adaptation; but if control is inadvertantly
noisy or requires full attention to steering displays and leaves
little time for other displays which offer important failure cues,
the man should monitor and let the machine control.

The next paper by Curry and Gai provides us a formal normative model of detection or random process failures. It is based
upon a Kalman optimal estimator whose measurement residual determines a likelihood ratio (familiar in signal detection theory)
which in turn is compared against a decision criterion by sequential analysis to continually maximize expected value. This combination of ideas is a powerful one indeed, and provides an excellent fit to experimental data in detecting instrument failures
during simulated aircraft landing.

Moray then gives a brief respite from formal mathematics for a
comprehensive discussion of attention and sampling behavior. He
reviews earlier work regarding internal models and sampling strategies, ideas inherent in the other papers in this session, as well
as some not otherwise mentioned. He discusses, for example, the
concept of "meta-bandwidth" (ERFW Crossman's time constant for
adaptivity) and how to help the supervisor set up good cognitive
models which necessarily consist of both very normal and very rare
events. His main point, I think, is that the human monitor/

supervisor is an active creature in charge of controlling the
flow of information through his own brain, not a passive stimulus
-response (S-R) device in the classical behavioral sense.

In the next paper we are returned to mathematical rigors.
Senders and Posner, following from earlier information theoretical work of Senders et al. on visual sampling of instruments
and earlier queueing models of Posner, discuss various factors
important in modeling of instrument monitoring, including: 1)
the uncertainty of the signal due to its power, bandwidth and
time since last observation; 2) the propensity of people to
forget with increased time since observation; 3) the delay between observations and 4) the "queueing-up" of instruments
waiting for "service" (to be read). They develop a new model
based primarily on queueing theory.

Singleton again brings us away from specifics and challenges
us with a series of fundamental and unavoidable dilemmas about
behavioral models, and in particular models of the supervisor.
These are questions which we might prefer simply to evade:
complexity of mathematics vs. ambiguity of verbal models; un-
reality of controlled experiments vs. chaos of measuring reality;
having man behave like a machine vs. letting him behave like a
person and putting up with his great variability; whether to
standardize all models or "let 1000 models bloom" - with the
concomitant confusion in communication between researchers.
Singleton claims the behaviorist, instant-by instant, S-R approach
to be headed for disaster. He calls for more Gestalt modeling
of the supervisor - as a person pursuing a goal, keeping future
options open, escaping from real-time by spreading his attention
over both past and future, and finally monitoring himself at
many levels.

In a related paper, Sheridan points out that the supervisory
operator's behavior can be categorized into four rather distinct
modes: planner, teacher, monitor and intervener. He goes on to
outline a "brute force" expected-value maximizer which can be
used to model a supervisor. Fast-time internal "thought experiments" are run using an optimal selection procedure to decide
what sensory measure of the environment is used and what are the
motor responses contingent on what is sensed; the results are
input to an internalized process model and utility function.
Comparison of the process to a Kalman-Bucy control system reveals
apparent similarity in structure with a major difference being in
"off-line tuning" in the successive fast-time trials approach vs.
"on-line tuning" through use of the Kalman filter's residual
(which played a major role in the Curry-Gai model).

The next paper by Wherry describes a practical computer simulation tool for simulating human operators in a variety of tasks.
Rather than base the human operator's behavior on a unified and
highly abstract modeling scheme, in this case the operator's behavior is the total of many discrete "micro-behavior" components:
hand reaches, control device manipulations, eye shifts, absorptions of visual information, and internal decisions. A number
of empirically-based parameters (in the form of conditional
statements and subroutines) are input by the simulator user before the simulation is run for any particular task. Outputs are
distributions and sequences of task times, devices and body parts
used, etc. Validation runs in tasks of remembering, keying and
tracking are described. Wherry's approach stands in striking
contrast to most of the other models in the session, for it is a
flexible tool for aggregating "micro-models" rather than an
attempted general-purpose, unitary "macro-model". As such it
offers a number of interesting comparisons and should provoke
many questions about "how are models used?"

The last two papers in the session deal directly with that
overriding tradeoff question: how good is the man and what should
he do vis-a-vis the computer? Rouse simulates a situation where
man and computer are "parallel servers" in a multi-queue situation
i.e. where either man or computer, when free, monitors a number of
tasks and starts performing the one most in need of attention, by
a probablistic criterion. Rouse studies the effects of: number
of tasks being monitored, speed of computer relative to man, and
probabilities of computor error. He discusses in particular his
assumption that in order for such cooperative queue serving to
work, man and computer must know what the other is doing. He
notes the comparative ease of computer informing man, as compared
to man informing computer (or computer inferring what man is
doing).

The final paper, by Steeb, Weltman and Freedy takes up the
above-mentioned problem of computer knowing what (and how well)
man is doing - in this case so it can take over control. And
this, of course, ties back to the first papers in the session
which dealt with related problems of "participation". In particular Steeb et al. performed experiments with a simulated
remotely-piloted-vehicle under three conditions of decision takeover by the computer: 1) when the man asks for it, 2) when
the computer decides it can do a better job according to a
manually set threshold, 3) when the computer decides it can do a
better job according to an expected utility maximization (a
trainable linear discriminant approach previously developed by
these authors). Their results verified the advantages of the
fully-atomatic and semi-automatic control allocation by comparison
to fully manual; feedback of machine state also proved to be of

great importance.

The papers in the "models session" are by no means the only papers involving models - all of them in this symposium do, more or less. Where some of the above papers lack experimental verification, some papers in the other two sessions are particulartly interesting and provide excellent verification data.

There are no papers in the models session about modeling by verbal protocols - the verbal expression by the operator of what he is doing or thinking. Such subjective data, recorded simultaneously with overt objective task behavior (lapse-frame film or TV techniques) are often helpful in understanding task difficulties and internal models. However, experience has also shown that such expressions are often couched in abstractions at too high a level or are too general to be helpful (see, for example, papers by Rasmussen and by Drury in this volume).

PRINCIPAL QUESTIONS RAISED

If now we take stock of the principal questions to be raised by this set of modeling efforts we will find the following:

1. questions of epistemology and whether it even makes sense to model the supervisor/ monitor;

2. questions of the degree to which the supervisor/monitor is best described by input - output equations as compared to Gestalt descriptions of an active, creative matcher of tools to tasks - what Crossman calls a "polyvalent craftsman"[1];

3. questions about modeling the operator's strategy for attending to stimuli; including ideas of signal detection and queueing and the fading of immediate memory;

4. questions about the human operator's internal representation of the external process or task: what form it takes, how it is acquired, how it is tuned through experience, and how to use it when, for example, the task unexpectedly changes. (Having modeled the model of the process we might then move on to modeling the modeler's modeling of the operator's modeling, and so on!);

5. questions about the internal representation of goals, payoff function, objective function, utility function, etc. - how explicit and consistent and self-conscious it is, and the degree to which it agrees with external rewards which nominally correspond;

6. questions about the operator's strategy for truncating the taking of evidence, making a decision, taking overt motor action,

in some cases taking over control from an automatic system;

   7.   questions about the degree to which empirically-based
models of micro-elements of behavior can be combined to yield
useful aggregate models; and

   8.   questions about machine supervision of man - when the
machine should be given the power to decide what information to
display to the man or what control to allocate to him.

   To complete this preview in a somewhat lighter vein, I offer
a cartoon-model of the human monitor/supervisor which synthesizes
all of the important ingredients:

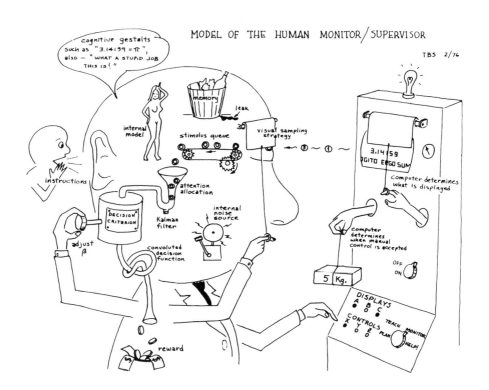

MODEL OF THE HUMAN MONITOR/SUPERVISOR

REFERENCES

1.   Crossman, ERFW, Chapter on "Automation and Skill" in E. Edwards
and F.P. Lees, Editors, The Human Operator in Process Control,
Taylor and Francis, Ltd., London, 1974.

THE VIGILANCE INCREMENT: AN IDEAL OBSERVER HYPOTHESIS

Robert C. Williges

University of Illinois at Urbana-Champaign

Champaign, Illinois 61820   USA

INTRODUCTION

In many man-machine systems the human operator performs a visual monitoring function. For instance, he may need to detect approaching aircraft during visual flight conditions to avoid a mid-air collision, or he may need to inspect a product for defects to maintain quality assurance. Often these monitoring tasks involve a single, aperiodic target that is both difficult to detect and transient. A great deal of research has been directed toward determining man's capabilities and limitations in performing such simple monitoring tasks.

One well-documented research finding is that target detection probability decreases as time on watch in the monitoring task increases thereby representing a vigilance decrement. Traditionally, most of the research in simple monitoring has concentrated only on detection performance with explanations of the classical vigilance decrement related primarily to attention processes (Buckner and McGrath, 1963; Frankman and Adams, 1962). By considering both correct detections and false-alarm errors (making a detect response to a nonsignal) one can investigate simple monitoring performance from a decision-making point of view in terms of the (Tanner and Swets, 1954) theory of signal detectability (TSD). This approach allows monitoring performance to be evaluated in terms of d', the observer's effective sensitivity to the signal, as well as β, his response criterion.

Although some researchers demonstrate a slight decrease in d' across the monitoring session (Binford and Loeb, 1966; Loeb and

181

Binford, 1968; Mackworth, 1968; Mackworth and Taylor, 1963; and
Williges, 1971), the most predominant finding is an increase in
β throughout the session (Binford and Loeb, 1966; Broadbent and
Gregory, 1965; Egan, Greenberg, and Schulman, 1961; Levine, 1966;
Loeb and Binford, 1964; Williges, 1969, 1971, 1973; and Williges
and North, 1972). An increase in β suggests that the observer is
adopting a more stringent response criterion as time on watch
continues. This increasingly more conservative response criterion
represents the usual decrease in signals detected as well as a
decrease in false alarm errors.

AN IDEAL OBSERVER HYPOTHESIS

Little research effort has been directed toward the quantitative
meaning of the typical increase in β throughout the monitoring
session. Williges (1969) posed an ideal observer hypothesis in
which he suggested that the change in the observed β approached the
normative expected value criterion (Swets, Tanner, and Birdsall,
1961),

$$\beta_i = \frac{p(N)}{p(SN)} \cdot \frac{(K_{fa} + V_r)}{(K_m + V_d)} \tag{1}$$

where the $p(N)$ equals the probability of a nonsignal event, $p(SN)$
equals the probability of a signal event, K_{fa} equals the absolute
cost of a false alarm, V_r equals the absolute value of a correct
rejection of a nonsignal event, K_m equals the absolute cost of a
missed signal, and V_d equals the absolute value of detecting a
signal. Viewed in this way, the classical vigilance decrement
expressed in terms of decreasing signal detections may actually
represent a vigilance increment when considered from a decision-
making point of view in which the human observer attempts to
optimize his decision performance across the monitoring session.

This paper briefly reviews a series of research studies which
attempted to evaluate the ideal observer hypothesis in terms of a
variety of factors that can affect the observer's response criterion.
In each study the observed β obtained from subject's detection performance was compared to an ideal β_i as expressed in Equation 1.
The results of these studies are discussed in terms of the viability
and limitations of the ideal observer hypothesis as well as the
implications of this approach in the design of monitoring tasks.

Monitoring Task

Before presenting the specific results of several studies, it
is necessary to describe the general detection task used throughout

this series of experiments. A simple monitoring task was developed
in which the observer was required to detect signals of a certain
duration brightness change during a sixty-minute monitoring session.
Periodically and at equal intervals, the brightness of a display
decreased to a lower level and remained at the low level for one
of two possible durations. The short duration was defined as a
nonsignal which the observer was instructed to ignore, whereas the
long duration was the signal which the subject was to detect. By
presenting both signal and nonsignal events it is possible to
calculate the probability of both correct detections and false
alarms. These probabilities, in turn, can be used to determine
the TSD parameters of observed d' and β as discussed by Binford
and Loeb (1966). This task was also useful in that it provided a
convenient way to manipulate the two parameters (a priori probabilities of signals and nonsignals and the costs and values
associated with various decisions) which determine the ideal
observer criterion, β_i, as defined in Equation 1.

Probability of Signals and Nonsignals

Williges (1969) first tested the ideal observer hypothesis by
maintaining a symmetric payoff of one thereby reducing the ideal
observer criterion to a simple ratio of the a priori probability of
a nonsignal to a signal. Each subject was told these a priori
values before beginning the monitoring session and given some
practice trials. It was hypothesized that observers choose an
indefinite criterion (β=1) at the beginning of the monitoring
session and approach the ideal criterion as time on task continues.
To test this hypothesis Williges (1969) used both a 1/5 and 5/1
ratio of signals to nonsignals. In the 1/5 conditions signals were
relatively rare events which is typical of the usual monitoring
task in which a vigilance decrement occurs. Consequently, an
increase in observed β was expected in this condition. In the 5/1
condition, on the other hand, signals were relatively common events,
and a decrease in β across the monitoring session was hypothesized.

Figure 1 shows the results of this study in terms of β changes
during successive 15-minute periods of the monitoring session. The
ideal β_i values of 5.0 for the 1/5 ratio condition and 0.2 for the
5/1 ratio condition are presented as dashed lines on the figure.
Clearly, these data support the ideal observer hypothesis which
indicates that the observers are approaching optimal decision
performance as time on task continues even though probability of
signal detection in the 1/5 ratio condition is decreasing during
the watch period.

Two subsequent studies were conducted to evaluate the
possibilities of manipulating the observed response criterion

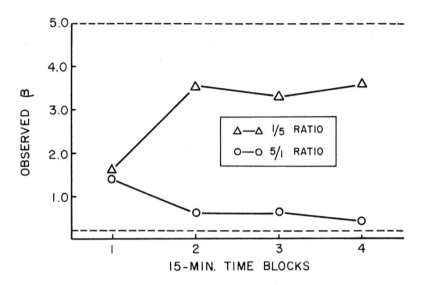

Figure 1.   Observed β values compared to ideal β_i (shown by
            dashed lines) across the monitoring session (adapted
            from Williges, 1969).

through knowledge of results (KR) and by changing the signal-to-
nonsignal ratios during the session. In both studies a symmetric
payoff schedule was used to define the ideal observer criterion in
terms of a priori signal and nonsignal probabilities. Williges and
North (1972) investigated the role of KR in hastening an observer
to adopt and maintain an optimal criterion. General KR on
frequency of detect responses and total stimulus events seen
(signals and nonsignals) as well as specific KR on correct
detections and false alarms errors were studied. Specific KR,
particularly in terms of correct detections, tended to increase the
effective sensitivity, d', during the monitoring session. General
KR, on the other hand, affected the observed response criterion as
documented in Figure 2.

    When subjects were provided KR on both the total number of
detect responses made and the total number of stimulus events seen,
they appeared to use this information to guide their frequency of
responding. Figure 2 shows that during the first two-thirds of
the monitoring session the subjects who received combined KR
adopted a response criterion which was closer to the ideal β_i than
the subjects who received no KR. But, the strategy of maintaining
a constant rate of responding resulted in more false alarms than
detections later in the session. This produced a net effect in the

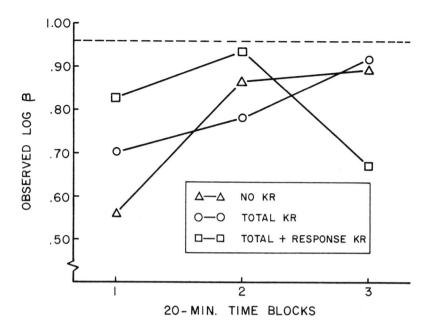

Figure 2.   Observed β values as a function of various knowledge-of-
results conditions compared to an ideal β_i (shown by
dashed line) across the monitoring session (from Williges
and North, 1972).

last third of the session of an extremely lax response criterion as
compared to β_i.   Consequently, the effect of KR on obtaining an
ideal response criterion is not straightforward.

Williges (1973) changed the ratio of signals to nonsignals
midway through the monitoring to encourage his subjects to adopt a
stable criterion throughout the session.   He demonstrated that
increasing the signal probability toward the end of the session
counteracted the usual tendency to adopt a more stringent criterion
and resulted in a stable, but lax, criterion throughout the watch
period.   These data are depicted in Figure 3 as the 1/9 signal-to-
nonsignal condition that changed to the 1/1 ratio midway through the
session.   Clearly, subjects in this condition maintained a criterion
more similar to the constant 1/1 ratio condition than to the
constant 1/9 ratio condition.   Even though target detection increased in this situation, this lax criterion also resulted in
more false alarm errors.   Consequently, it is possible to consider
the introduction of artificial signals late in the monitoring session
to maintain a constant response criterion throughout the session

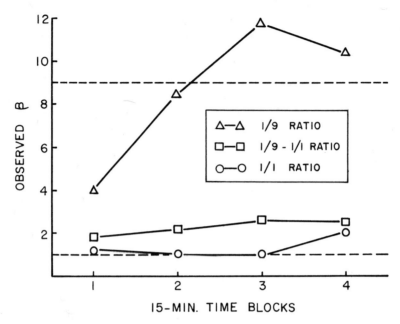

Figure 3.   Observed β values compared to ideal β_i (shown by dashed
lines) across the monitoring session (adapted from
Williges, 1973).

and thereby increase target detection at the price of more false
alarm errors.

Payoffs

In considering an ideal observer criterion both the a priori
signal and nonsignal probabilities and the various decision
payoffs must be evaluated. Williges (1972) manipulated both of
these parameters in a factorial design to ascertain their relative
importance as well as a possible interaction between them.   He
used two signal to nonsignal ratios (1/9 or 1/1) and three
different point payoff matrices (lax, neutral, or strict).   Table
1 compares the observed β values, which were averaged across the
session for each of the six conditions, to ideal β_i based on
considering either just signal-to-nonsignal ratios, just payoffs,
or the combination of ratios and payoffs.   Obviously, the obtained
β values most closely match an ideal β_i based on just the ratio of
signals to nonsignals.   From levels chosen in this study it would
seem that the a priori signal and nonsignal probabilities rather
than decision payoffs are the primary determiners of the observer's
response criterion in monitoring tasks.

Table 1. Mean Obtained β Values Compared to Three Ideal $β_i$ Values
          (Adapted from Williges, 1971)

Conditions	Observed β	Ideal $β_i$ (Ratio)	Ideal $β_i$ (Payoff)	Ideal $β_i$ (Ratio and Payoff)
1/1 - Lax	1.29	1.00	0.11	0.11
1/9 - Lax	10.33	9.00	0.11	1.00
1/1 - Neutral	1.31	1.00	1.00	1.00
1/9 - Neutral	8.07	9.00	1.00	9.00
1/1 - Strict	4.00	1.00	9.00	9.00
1/9 - Strict	10.38	9.00	9.00	81.00

Limitations

Even though these studies support a reinterpretation of the
classical vigilance decrement in terms of an increment in decision
making performance, this conclusion is limited to a specific class
of monitoring tasks consisting of low detectable signals. For
example, Williges (1973) found that it was not possible to
calculate TSD measures in a high-signal-detectability condition
because many subjects had either 100% correct detections or 0%
false alarms. But, the average probability of correct detection
still decreased over time in this condition. In other words,
factors other than decision parameters seem to be responsible for
the classical vigilance decrement in this case.

One critical assumption made in the ideal observer hypothesis
explanation is that the subject always observes each stimulus
event. Jerison, Pickett, and Stenson (1965) suggest that each
subject makes two decisions in a monitoring task. First, he must
decide whether or not to observe the display. Second, he must
decide if a signal is present given he is observing. They contend
that the change in performance over time represents primarily the
first decision, and the TSD parameters can reflect the proportions
of three types of observing -- alert, blurred, or nonobservation
of the display. Guralnick (1972), for example, presents some
data which can be interpreted as support for a blurred observing
strategy. An ideal observer explanation, however, always assumes
alert observation, and the studies reviewed in this paper tend to
support primarily an alert observing strategy due to the close
agreement of the observed β with an ideal $β_i$. Additional research
is needed to specify task parameters important in determining
specific observing strategies.

All the data presented in this paper that support the ideal observer hypothesis are limited to changes within one monitoring session. In essence, the subjects seem to realize that they are responding too frequently in a low signal-to-nonsignal ratio task and begin to respond less thereby producing an observed β which approaches ideal β_i. If this same observer continued to monitor for repeated sessions, it is hypothesized that he should begin to use a more appropriate response rate and his observed β should stabilize across subsequent sessions at a level close to ideal β_i. Although there is no direct empirical support for this hypothesis, data from Binford and Loeb (1966) indirectly support it. Their subjects completed nine, ninety-minute monitoring sessions. Average observed β for sessions 1 and 2 combined showed an increase from the first twenty minutes to the last twenty minutes of the session, whereas the average observed β for sessions 8 and 9 combined did not reliably increase within sessions. These stable values in sessions 8 and 9 also were higher than the initial value of observed β in the first twenty minutes of session 1 and 2. But, no direct comparisons were made to ideal β_i, and their subjects were not instructed as to the expected probabilities of a signal. Consequently, empirical extensions of the ideal observer hypothesis still need to be tested across repeated sessions.

IMPLICATIONS

If monitoring performance is viewed from a decision making point of view, it is reasonable to expect a decrease in detection probability as documented by the vigilance decrement because detections and false alarms are too high at the beginning of the session for an ideal observer. What may appear to be degraded detection performance at the end of the session may actually be near optimal decision performance. If the system designer views the human observer's monitoring function from a ideal observer standpoint, he can then specify the expected level of target detection as well as false alarm error rates. Additionally, he can manipulate the operator's observed β so that the operator maintains a constant response criterion. This, in turn, will affect both the overall target detection rate and error rate.

It must be remembered that these studies only refer to applications of the TSD model to a simple laboratory monitoring task. Nonetheless, applications need to be considered in terms of actual systems in which monitoring plays an important role in defining successful systems operation. Some applications of the TSD model have been suggested by Wallack and Adams (1969) for inspector performance, for instance; and, Drury and Addison (1973) demonstrated that the TSD model could be used to analyze performance of a group of on-line inspectors of glass products.

Most real systems, however, require the human operator to perform a complex monitoring function which is characterized by several dynamic displays each involving high information content and several signals. Performance in these tasks probably involves the interaction of several processes and not just a single decision process. Johnston, Howell, and Williges (1969) provided some preliminary evidence that attention, memory, and scanning processes in addition to a decision process may be present in complex monitoring. More research is needed on complex monitoring before it is possible to specify the relative weightings as well as the interactions of these processes. In any event, the limited results of both simple and complex monitoring research suggest that the system designer should consider the possible role of decision making when using the human operator in a monitoring capacity.

REFERENCES

Binford, J. R. and Loeb, M. Changes within and over repeated sessions in criterion and effective sensitivity in an auditory vigilance task. Journal of Experimental Psychology, 1966, 72, 339-345.

Broadbent, D. E. and Gregory, M. Effects of noise and signal rate upon vigilance analyzed by means of decision theory. Human Factors, 1965, 7, 155-162.

Buckner, D. N. and McGrath, J. J. Vigilance: A symposium. New York: McGraw-Hill, 1963.

Drury, C. G. and Addison, J. L. An industrial study of the effects of feedback and fault density on inspection performance. Ergonomics, 1973, 16, 159-160.

Egan, J. P., Greenberg, G. Z., and Schulman, A. I. Operating characteristics, signal detectability, and the method of free response. Journal of the Accoustical Society of America, 1961, 33, 993-1007.

Frankman, J. P. and Adams, J. A. Theories of vigilance. Psychological Review, 1962, 59, 257-272.

Guralnick, M. J. Observing responses and decision process in vigilance. Journal of Experimental Psychology, 1972, 93, 239-244.

Jerison, H. J., Pickett, R. M., and Stenson, H. H. The elicited observing rate and decision processes in vigilance. Human Factors, 1965, 7, 107-128.

Johnston, W. A., Howell, W. C., and Williges, R. C.   The components
    of complex monitoring. Organizational Behavior and Human
    Performance, 1969, 4, 112-124.

Levine, J. M.   The effects of values and costs on the detection
    and identification of signals in auditory vigilance. Human
    Factors, 1966, 8, 525-537.

Loeb, M. and Binford, J. R.   Vigilance for auditory intensity
    change as a function of preliminary feedback and confidence
    level. Human Factors, 1964, 6, 445-458.

Loeb, M. and Binford, J. R.   Variation in performance on auditory
    and visual monitoring tasks as a function of signal and
    stimulus frequencies. Perception and Psychophysics, 1968,
    4, 361-367.

Mackworth, J. F.   The effect of signal rate on performance in two
    kinds of vigilance tasks. Human Factors, 1968, 10, 11-18.

Mackworth, J. F. and Taylor, M. M.   The d' measure of signal
    detectability in vigilance-like situations. Canadian Journal
    of Psychology, 1963, 17, 302-325.

Swets, J. A., Tanner, W. P., Jr., and Birdsall, T. G.   Decision
    processes in perception. Psychological Review, 1961, 68, 301-
    340.

Tanner, W. P. and Swets, J. A.   A decision-making theory of visual
    detection. Psychological Review, 1954, 61, 401-409.

Wallack, P. M. and Adams, S. K.   The utility of signal detection
    theory in the analysis of industrial inspector accuracy.
    AIIE Transactions, 1969, 1, 33-44.

Williges, R. C.   Within-session criterion changes compared to an
    ideal observer criterion in a visual monitoring task. Journal
    of Experimental Psychology, 1969, 81, 61-66.

Williges, R. C.   The role of payoffs and signal ratios in criterion
    changes during a monitoring task. Human Factors, 1971, 13,
    261-267.

Williges, R. C.   Manipulating the response criterion in visual
    monitoring. Human Factors, 1973, 15, 179-185.

Williges, R. C. and North, R. A.   Knowledge of results and decision
    making performance in visual monitoring. Organizational
    Behavior and Human Performance, 1972, 8, 44-57.

DISCUSSION

DRURY :

What do you think of Teichner's analysis of vigilance, where he shows a vigilance effect only for signals with a high prior probability of detection and challenges signal detection theory as a model ?

WILLIGES :

Obviously, a signal detection theory model interpretation of vigilance is limited to signals of low detectability. When the signals are highly detectable, the observer either correctly detects all signals and/or fails to make any false alarm errors. When, on the other hand, the signals are difficult to detect, I feel the ideal observer hypothesis accounts for the results adequately.

RIJNSDORP :

1. How intensively were the subjects instructed about the pay-off matrix ?

2. Did they obtain any running information about the pay-off results ?

WILLIGES :

1. Each subject was given written instructions explaining the two ways in which he can make an incorrect response and the two ways in which he can make a correct response. He was also instructed as to the payoffs associated with each of these responses.

2. No.

MORAY :

1. One reason Jerison suggested non-alert observing was the discovery of very large values of beta, up to 500, which he thought were psychologically meaningless. Do you find such values ?

2. How general are your findings ? I have found huge individual differences. Did all observers show all the effects ?

3. There are some vigilance situations where d', not beta, changes ?

WILLIGES :

1. No. But, the a priori probabilities of signals and nonsignals used in the studies I reported were such that the ideal β_i was never greater than 9.00.

2. All of the values of observed β presented were averaged across subjects. Although there were individual differences, the between-subject variability was not large enough to eliminate the statistical reliability of the results.

3. Yes, there are. The usual finding, however, is that a β change accompanies a d' change. Often when only a d' change across time is reported no calculations of β are made. Although I did not discuss these data in my presentation today, I also found some small decreases in d' across time in addition to the more pronounced β changes. Details of these d' changes are presented in the specific research reports given in the reference list.

MONITORING AND CONTROL OF UNRELIABLE SYSTEMS

Renwick E. Curry[*] and Arye R. Ephrath[**]

[*]Man Vehicle Lab., Dept. of Aeronautics and Astronautics
MIT, Cambridge, MA 02139 USA

[**]NCR Post-Doctoral Fellow, NASA Ames Research Center
Moffett Field, CA 94035 USA

I. INTRODUCTION

The use of man's adaptive characteristics as a controller has a long history of providing a cost-effective method of increasing system reliabiity, from well before the Wright brothers' first flights to the present day aviation and space missions. The basic technology was a primary limitation in earlier times but is less of a constraint now, and consideration must be given to such items as operator motivation and job satisfaction as well as performance and reliability.

One of the central questions over the last few decades has been the role of the human in the control of a system: should he be an active, serial element in the control loop or should he be a supervisor monitoring the progress of the system? Arguments in favor of the active role include increased vigilance and shorter adaptation time to new environments (no "warm-up" transients); arguments for the passive role include a greater ability to assimilate more information from redundant sources and better, more accurate, system performance. There are more subtle factors at work, however, since data from aviation accident reports suggest that a pilot may become so intent on achieving the goal of landing the airplane that he may continue a bad approach beyond the point of safety.

In a comparison of controller/monitor failure detection, Wempe (1965) found that pilots, acting as monitors, were unaware of an autopilot disconnect in a simulated terrain following task. On the other hand, Vreuls (1968) compared failure detection in simulated manual and automatic approaches to landing and discovered that the

human monitor was able to detect failures more readily than the
human controller.

Most of the previous investigations of the adaptive ability of
the human operator have concentrated on sudden and usually severe
changes in controlled element dynamics. Miller (1965) and Elkind
and Miller (1966) developed models of the controller detection of
controlled-element changes in compensatory tracking based on error
and error rate criteria. Phatak and Bekey (1969) proposed decision
regions in the error-error rate plane to describe the human's
detection and adaptation strategy, as did Niemela (1974). See
Young (1969) for an exellent review of adaptive manual control to
that time.

Young (1969) notes that the Miller-Elkind criterion does not
make explicit use of hand movement information in the detection of
sudden changes in controlled element dynamics. He reported on some
preliminary experiments involving active controllers, controllers
who thought they were active but were not, and monitors of the
error signal created by the active controller. This paradigm has
been modified by Tada and Young (1976) and will be discussed in
more detail subsequently; they concluded that hand movement feedback can play an important role in failure detection.

The results discussed above are by no means exhaustive, but
they are sufficient to indicate that the question of whether the
human should be a monitor or a controller is an open one. Our
objective in this paper is to discuss some recent experimental data
which are pertinent to the problem; from these and other results,
we propose a model for failure detection which is in qualitative
agreement with the experimental data reported in the literature.
The model allows us to predict which conditions will be more favorable for failure detection by a monitor and which conditions will be
more favorable for failure detection by a controller.

II. FAILURE DETECTION DURING SIMULATED LANDINGS

The purpose of this research was the study of the pilot's
decision making behavior regarding performance evaluation and
failure monitoring. We wished to investigate the functional dependence of the pilot's ability to detect failures on the degree of
automation of the control task and the pilot's over-all workload
level, factors which were not separable in previous studies (Vreuls,
1968). Also, we wished our findings to be applicable to the population of pilots who fly low-visibility approaches in commercial
jet transport aircraft. To this end, this research was carried out
in a ground simulator and utilized fifteen professional airline
pilots as subjects. The workload index was measured by a sensitive,
non-loading subsidiary task, and the entire experiment was controlled

on-line by a digital computer. Details are reported in Ephrath
(1975).

Method

The experimental variables investigated in this study were the
pilot's participation level in the piloting task, the workload induced by the control dynamics and by external disturbances, and
the pilot's failure detection performance. The experiment involved
four levels of control participation: (a) "passive monitoring", with
autopilot coupling in all axes, including autothrottle; (b) "yaw
manual", with autopilot coupling in the pitch axis and autothrottle
coupled; (c) "pitch manual", with autpilot coupling in the yaw axis
only; and (d) "fully manual".   There were three levels of wind disturbance" (a) no wind; (b) a 45° tailwind of 5 knots, gusting to 15
knots; (c) a 45° tailwind of 10 knots, gusting to 30 knots.   Three
failure conditions were used: (a) no failure; (b) failure in the yaw
axis. In this condition, the autopilot, if coupled, or the flight
director, if manual, would steer the airplane away from the localizer course to intercept and track a course parallel to the nominal
path but translated by a distance corresponding to one dot deviation
(1.25°) at the point of failure occurrence. This resulted in a one
dot angular error about 100 seconds after the initiation of the failure. This type of failure was chosen as it was quite subtle and
therefore it provided a good measure of the limits of the pilot's
failure detection capability. (c) Failure in the pitch axis, which
resulted in a one-dot deviation (0.35° of angular error) approximately 30 seconds after the occurrence of the failure. Failures
were presented only between the altitudes of 1800 and 800 feet; each
approach was terminated either at touchdown or when a positive rate
of climb has been established following the initation of a go-around
by the subject. Workload levels and failure detection performance
were investigated in separate experiments, to avoid possible contam-
ination of failure detection data by the presence of the workload
measuring subsidiary task; the "no failure" condition was incorporated in the design so that the subjects would not anticipate a
failure on each and every approach.

One of our goals in this study was the investigation of the
pilot's failure detection performance based on his capability to
process raw flight information; we did not include any displays of
a mode progressannunciator, movable bugs or fault annunciator panel,
nor were there any warning flags. Flight director information was
provided in manually-controlled axes, but not in axes which were
controlled by the autopilot.

Results

Detection performance was analyzed in terms of detection time
and accuracy. Detection time was defined as the elapsed time between the occurrence of a failure and the verbal report by the

subject that the failure had been detected and identified. Accuracy
was measured by the fraction of failures that were missed altogether.
In all, 90 approaches were flown in which a longitudinal failure
occurred; of these, 8 went unreported; of the 90 lateral failures
presented, 9 were missed (see Table 1).

TABLE 1. Fraction of missed longitudinal (lateral) failures in %.

Participation Mode	Disturbance Level			Overall
	1	2	3	
Monitor	0. (0.)	0. (0.)	0. (0.)	0. (0.)
Control yaw	0. (37.5)	0. (14.3)	0. (37.5)	0. (30.4)
Control Pitch	12.5 (0.)	14.3 (0.)	12.5 (0.)	13.0 (0.)
Manual Control	12.5 (14.3)	14.3 (0.)	37.5 (14.3)	21.7 (9.1)
Overall	6.7 (13.3)	6.7 (3.3)	13.3 (13.3)	8.9 (10.0)

In Figures 1 and 2, the mean detection times of pitch and yaw
failures, respectively, are plotted as functions of the corresponding
mean workload levels for the four participation modes. The following
relationships are evident: (1) Detection times in a manually controlled axis are longer than detection times in an automatically
controlled axis; (2) Detection times for lateral failures are significantly longer than detection times for longitudinal failures at
comparable workload levels. We then assumed that the failure detection mechanism of the human operator acts similarly in the lateral
and longitudinal axes. Longitudinal and lateral failure detection
data were thus pooled and detection times were regressed on the type
of failure and on the control mode in the failed axis, with the workload index as a covariate, based on the following additive model:

$$T_{detection} = T_0 + \alpha(\text{control mode}) + \beta(\text{failed axis}) + \gamma(\text{workload})$$

A solution was obtained for the regression coefficients α, β and γ:

$$T_{detection} = 20.9 + 16.5 \underline{M} + 15.4 \underline{A} + 0.10 \text{ WLX}$$

where $\underline{M}$ = 1 (if failed axis is controlled manually) 0 otherwise.
       $\underline{A}$ = 1 (if the failure occurred in the lateral axis) or
           0 (if the failure occurred in the longitudinal axis)
       WLX = the normalized workload level index
and the detection time is measured in seconds.

This model does indicate the differential effects of workload and manual/automatic control. Several hypotheses can be advanced to explain the better performance of the monitor in detecting failures:
a. RMS display levels might be larger in manual control, providing a lower signal-to-noise ratio for the failure signal.
b. Different display deviations in manual versus automatic control.
c. Monitoring and control are competing for channel capacity, thus less time for monitoring when also controlling.
d. Manual control caused focussing of attention on steering symbols, not on situation displays.
Hypothesis (a) was tested and rejected, as we were   able to show through an analysis of variance that the RMS displayed error was not a significant factor in detection time, suggesting that failures were not being masked by poor system performance in one condition or the other. Also, RMS signal levels were found to be statistically the same for manual and automatic control.

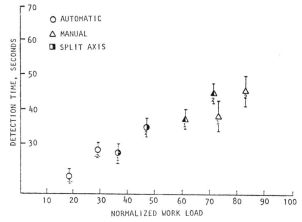

FIGURE 1.   Mean longitudinal detection times.

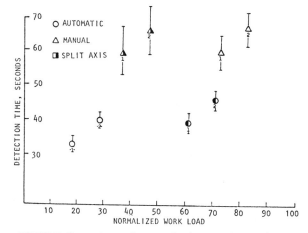

FIGURE 2.   Mean lateral detection times.

We think hypothesis (b) can be rejected for, if anything, display deviations under manual control should be larger than under automatic control. Hypothesis (c) was not tested; if true, then it follows that monitoring and controlling are separate functions requiring internal switching from one function to the other; detection time would be longer when controlling because some of the total capacity devoted to monitoring under fully automatic control must be used for the control function. Hypothesis (d) indicates that the switching between monitoring and control is done externally by the choice of displays receiving attention. In the current situation, this seems quite plausible, since it is a fact that pilots may devote a great deal of time to the flight director to the exclusion of other displays. This behavior is also predicted human controller models (Curry et al, 1975).

III. THE ROLE OF HAND MOVEMENTS IN FAILURE DETECTION

Young's (1969) preliminary experiments suggested that hand movement feedback plays an important role in failure detection. Tada and Young (1976) continued these experiments using active controllers, shadow controllers and monitors. The major difference was that each subject was an active controller, a shadow controller, and a monitor in that order. In each condition, the subject viewed his own error history generated while acting as the active controller. Although this experimental design may be susceptible to learning effects, it does provide valuable insight into the effect of hand movements on detection. The results are summarized in Table 2, showing the number of detections for which the shadow controller or monitor took longer than the active controller.

TABLE 2.   Detection performance of active controller, shadow controller and monitor.

Controlled Element Transition	Shadow/Active		Monitor/Active	
	Longer T_d	Misses*	Longer T_d	Misses*
2/s → 8/s	22/19	4/0	11/21	3/0
2/s → -2/s	16/24	3/0	24/13	11/0
2/s → -8/s	24/13	4/0	16/20	1/0
2/s → 5/s²	21/18	4/0	12/22	2/0

*Missed detections in 12 seconds.

The most notable fact regarding the the missed detections is that the active controller did not miss any, whereas the shadow controller and monitor missed up to 50%. This is not surprising since they were observing the output of an adaptive system and thus a quick adaptation by the active controller posed a difficult detection task for the shadow controller and monitor. Unlike earlier experiments of Young (1969), Tada and Young found in these experiments that the monitor may be faster at detecting failures than the active controller (even assuming learning was a negligible factor). Even if these later results supported the earlier ones in the monitor/controller comparison, the experimental protocol is biased in favor of the active controller, since the monitor is observing the output of an adaptive system. It is doubtful that any of the 2/s to -2/s transitions undetected by the monitor would have gone undetected had the transition taken place in a nonadaptive loop. Nonetheless, both experiments provide valuable insight into the use of hand-movement information in failure detection.

IV. A MODEL FOR FAILURE DETECTION

To account for the experimental results described in the first three sections, we propose the model shown in Figure 3. The serial element in the control loop is an adaptive controller; at this juncture, the details of the adaptive mechanism are not required, but may take on the characteristics of those suggested by Elkind and Miller (1966) for example. The upper branch contains a model of the closed loop system and computes an estimated error signal based on the prefailure loop dynamics. The <u>error residual</u> $\Delta e = e - \hat{e}$ is formed and is one of the two inputs to the decision mechanism. The formation of the expected error signal should be done as described in Curry and Gai (1976) and requires only the model of the prefailure system. The quantities v_e and v_u represent equivalent observation noises or uncertainties in perceived error and control respectively. The <u>control residual</u> Δu is formed by comparing the actual control, u, with the value calculated by using the prefailure control law $\hat{u}(e)$. If there is no adaptation by the serial logic, then this control residual will be small relative to the (perceived) noise in the implementation of the prefailure control law. If the human is in the role of a passive monitor then he can be represented by the upper branch alone as described in Curry and Gai (1976).

The details of the decision mechanism have been explored in detail for only one case to date viz. the detection of a change in mean by a passive monitor (Curry and Gai, 1976). It was found that a modified sequential probability ratio test (integrating the Kalman filter residuals) gave a good account of the experimental data, even when information was being derived from multiple displays with correlated information (Gai and Curry, 1976). It seems plausible that the same type of integrating effect can be used to describe the decision logic for both the error (visual) and control (hand movement) residuals simultaneously. Furthermore, an integration effect is necessary to describe the observed short detection times for large discrepancies and long detection times for small discrepancies.

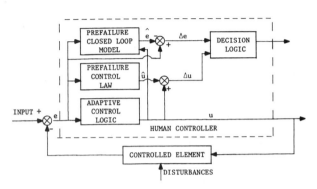

FIGURE 3:   A model of failure detection
            by the human controller

Even in its present qualitative form, the model has much to say about the conditions for which the monitor or the controller will have a shorter detection time. In general, we would expect an active controller to provide shorter detection times if the failures or disturbances are hard to detect from the visual display alone, or if adaptation is fast. Conversely, we would expect a passive monitor to provide faster detection of failures or disturbance inputs if separate steering displays do not leave enough residual attention for monitoring, adaptation is slow, or there is a low signal-to-noise ratio on the control residual. Slow adaptation seems to result from gain (but not polarity) changes, especially gain reductions (Elkind and Miller, 1966); such slow adaptation leads to small control residuals. Similarly, any facet which reduces the signal-to-noise ratio of the control residual (e.g. stiction in the manipulator, high vibration manipulators and/or environment, multiple manipulators, etc.) would be expected to lead to long detection times for the active controller.

V.   PRELIMINARY EXPERIMENTS—MONITOR/CONTROLLER FAILURE DETECTION

To test these model hypotheses, we performed some preliminary experiments with compensatory tracking (K/s dynamics) of a random input command signal. Four subjects participated in three modes each: passive monitoring (PM); active controller with a spring restrained stick having moderate force gradients (SS); and active controller with a free stick (FS). For the passive monitor condition, the control input was proportional to the error signal, as is the case for the quasilinear model of the human operator in these conditions; the control gain was adjusted for each subject to give the same RMS error as obtained when he was an active controller.

The failure in these tests consisted of a slow ramp (of either sign) added to the input signal at a random time for approximately half the trials. The three conditions were presented, balanced for order effects, and each subject had 40 trials in each condition. They responded by pressing one of two switches indicating a failure and its sign. Correctly detected failures were recorded as Hits and indicated failures when no failures were presented were recorded as False Alarms. This paradigm seems to be better suited for comparing monitor/controller failure detection by having the monitor observe a non-adaptive plant and by recording hits and false alarms to account for possible changes in the subjects' internal criterion.

The results of these preliminary experiments are shown in Table 3. The detection performance was compared by plotting the points in the P(H)-P(FA) plane as one point on an ROC curve or by plotting a reaction time ROC curve using switch activation time for Hits and False Alarms as the criterion variable; one set of RT-ROC curves for a typical subject are shown in Figure 4.

TABLE 3.   Failure detection performance for 3 experimental conditions.

SUBJECT	PASSIVE MONITOR			SPRING STICK			FREE STICK		
	P(H)	P(FA)	$\overline{T}_D$	P(H)	P(FA)	$\overline{T}_D$	P(H)	P(FA)	$\overline{T}_D$
1	.96	.11	6.9	.91	.39	5.9	.67	.46	8.7
2	1.0	.03	5.1	1.0	.27	5.5	.86	.39	6.9
3	1.0	.09	6.2	1.0	.06	6.3	.70	.27	10.7
4	.86	.83	4.6	.90	.67	5.4	.61	.68	6.1

FIGURE 4.   Reaction Time-ROC using time of detection as the criterion variable, e.g. $P(Hit|t_D \leq t) - P(FA)|t_D \leq t)$.

Termination point is overall P(H)-P(FA) performance.

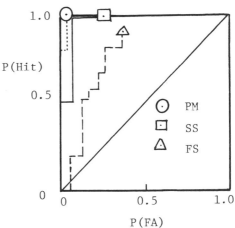

By all measures, the detection performance for the passive monitor and spring-stick conditions are nearly equal and both are much better than the free stick condition. These results emphasize the importance of the perceptual observation noise in the model, for, although the controllers are receiving more measurements, the uncertainty in applied control (especially with the free stick) increases the uncertainty of what the visual display ought to be, leading to deleterious detection performance in this task.

VI. SUMMARY

We have briefly reviewed the previous literature on adaptive manual control with the goal of determining, for failure detection, when the human should be a controller and when he should be a monitor. We suggest a model for failure detection based on an explicit comparison of both actual error and actual control with those expected for the prefailure conditions. The model is consistent with the results reported by previous investigators. The details of the decision logic must wait further experimentation to explain the shorter decision times by the monitors for transitions in which the controller is slow to adapt. Among the possible explanations are: (a) learning effects in the Tada-Young protocol; (b) near optimal processing by the controllers and monitors, but different decision thresholds; (c) reduced capacity for monitoring due to capacity expended on adaptive control; (d) suboptimal processing by the controller. However, the model in its present form can be used to predict whether the monitor or the active controller will have shorter detection times in many instances. Some preliminary experiments in detecting slow drifts in the input emphasize the masking effect of control uncertainty during manual control.

REFERENCES

Curry, R.E., Kleinman, D.L., Hoffman, W.C., NASA TMX-62464, 1975.
Curry, R.E., Gai, E.G., This Conference.
Elkind, J.I., Miller, D.C., NASA SP-128, 1966.
Ephrath, A.R., Ph.D. Thesis, MIT, 1975.
Gai, E.G., Curry, R.E. AIAA Journal of Aircraft, 1976 (in press).
Miller, D.C., M.S. Thesis, MIT, 1965.
Niemela, J., 10th Annual Conference on Manual Control, WPAFB, 1974.
Phatak, A.V., Bekey, G.A., IEEE SSC-5, 1969.
Tada, A., Young, L.R. in preparation.
Vreuls, D., Bunker Ramo Corp., Canoga Park, CA. SRDS-RD-68-9. 1968.
Wempe, T., Aerospace Medicine, 36:246, 1965.
Young, L.R., Ergonomics, 12:635, 1969.

DISCUSSION

STASSEN :

You showed a significant difference in performance when using a spring stick and a free stick. Did you look for an interpretation of this difference on the basis of what is known from neuro-physiological data about the muscular systems. Do you think that probably the proprioceptive feedback here plays an important role ?

CURRY :

The failure detection results are very recent, and we have not had time to examine them in those terms. We expected that the presence and absence of force feedback would be important but were surprised that the difference was so large.

DETECTION OF RANDOM PROCESS FAILURES BY HUMAN MONITORS

Renwick E. Curry and Eliezer G. Gai

Man-Vehicle Laboratory, Department of Aeronautics and
Astronautics, Massachusetts Institute of Technology,
Cambridge, Massachusetts, 02139, USA

I.   INTRODUCTION

This paper considers the interaction of human monitors with
systems of a stochastic nature. The problem, i.e. the dilemma, of
the human monitor is that of determining when a process is operating correctly. Monitoring is an important aspect of many human
activities and, with the likely proliferation of automatic systems
utilizing microprocessors, monitoring is likely to be even more
important for safe and reliable operation of these systems. Monitoring for failure detection and performance assessment may fruitfully be considered as a special case of decision making: "Is the
system working correctly?".

The general view of the problem is shown in Figure 1. Here
we have shown the monitored system providing both continuous-time
signals and discrete-time signals through their respective displays
to the human monitor. In addition to the system itself, there may

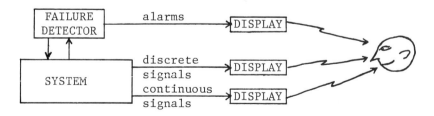

FIGURE 1.   Elements of the human monitoring problem

be failure detection systems which give off alarms when certain

criteria have been met. While it may seem reasonable that the
existence of failure detectors will ease the burden of the human
monitor, there are many instances which suggest that the presence
of a failure detector will increase the human monitor's burden
because the failure detector itself is a system which may fail.
That is, the failure detection system (which can give false alarms
as well as missed alarms) must be monitored. The monitor, then,
must continually check for a malfunction in any of the five blocks
shown in Figure 1.

Many authors (e.g. Young, 1969; deJong and Koster, 1971;
Phatak and Bekey, 1969) have pointed out that the task of the
monitor/controller in responding to changes in the process can be
decomposed into three functions of

> failure detection
> failure identification
> corrective action

There are many disciplines of ergonomics and psychology which are
related to these three tasks: psychophysics; information processing
and sampling; vigilance; learning; decision making; subjective
probabilities/utilitites; stress, fatigue and motivation. The many
studies performed in this area have a direct bearing on the failure detection of discrete processes because they have utilized simple
stimuli, usually of a discrete nature. There seems to be relatively
little understanding of what "stimuli" or features are extracted
from a continuous time process. However, if these features can be
found, then perhaps the voluminous results in these other disciplines
can be applied to predict human performance in failure detection.

The objective of this paper is to review the previous work
related to human information processing of random processes and to
examine the models that have been proposed to describe human failure
detection. Most of these models contain, either explicitly or implicitly, a set of hypotheses about the information processing
inherent in the human monitor. In Section III, we make an explicit
statement of some working hypotheses on human monitoring as a basis
for future work. In Section IV, we describe some of our work in
applying the present hypotheses to human detection of changes in the
mean value of a random process. In Section V, we suggest a paradigm
to explore other changes in characteristics of random processes and
conclude with some possible uses of models of human failure detection in Section VI.

II.   MODELS OF MONITORING AND FAILURE DETECTION

The discrete detection and decision studies that were referred
to in the previous section usually required an immediate response

after the appearance of each stimulus. There are, however, many
cases in which the stimulus is time varying and dynamic decision
making (or deferred decision making) is required. The observer's
task is therefore that of monitoring time varying signals which are
usually stochastic in nature.

Robinson (1967) described a model for the human observer in a
task of continuous estimation of time varying probability. The
probabilities governing the stimulus selection followed a pattern
of random step changes. The subjects indicated their estimate by
moving a pointer on a scale. The model for the observer's behavior
was one in which discrete changes in the pointer position resulted
when the difference between the current observation and the running
average over the previous k observations exceeded a threshold. The
results of the experiments showed that the model gave best predictions when k was between 8 and 12, and the threshold was between
12% and 15%.

Smallwood (1967) suggested a model of scanning behavior when
monitoring several instruments. His model is based on two assumptions: the human operator maintains an internal model which is
based on his perception of the environment; the human operator
behaves optimally with respect to his task and his current state of
information. As the internal model Smallwood used low pass first
or second order shaping filters driven by white Gaussian processes.
The decision function for shifting attention was the distribution
function of the current state conditioned on all previous states.
However, this previous data did not take into account the remnant
noise of the monitor, so no estimator was necessary. This decision
function was then compared to a threshold. Smallwood also compared
his model with experimental data which showed that a second order
filter gave better prediction of sampling behavior than a first
order filter.

Sheridan (1970) suggested a model to characterize the sampling
behavior of an optimal supervisor. The task of the supervisor was
to control a deterministic one dimensional process, where the value
of the return function was based upon the input process which he
monitored. The return function was defined as the expectation of
the gained value per unit time, assuming that the input is a random
process with variance increasing monotonically with time. The optimal sampling interval was defined as that value which maximized the
expected return function of the interval less the cost of sampling
per unit time. Although Sheridan solved his optimization problem
for some special cases, it seems that no experiments were conducted
to support the theory.

Levison and Tanner (1971) proposed a control theoretic model
for human decision making. This model was a natural extension of
their previous success in modelling the human controller. The

assumption was again that the observer has an internal model for
the observed variables which is the basis of their model for human
information processing. The observer's inherent limitations were
represented by a time delay and additive white Gaussian observation
noise. The data processing consisted of an optimal estimator (Kalman filter) to obtain the best estimate of the state of the internal model as well as the error covariance. The estimate of the
observation (which is linearly related to the state estimate) was
then used for the decision mechanism (based on Bayesian decision
theory) in which the instantaneous likelihood ratio is used as a
decision function. The decision function is compared to a single
threshold to determine the decision. The model was tested in an
experiment in which subjects had to detect when a horizontal bar
was outside a given border. The predictions of the model seemed
to be satisfactory for this specific task.

    In a review paper by Phatak and Kleinman (1972), the status
of models of the human operator as a controller and decision maker
were discussed. The role of the internal model and the optimal
estimator is emphasized. However, as an input to the decision
mechanism they suggested the observation error (residual, or innovations process) rather than the observation estimate. They suggest a test of the null hypothesis that the residual is a zero mean
white process with a given covariance. The authors pointed to two
possible decision functions. One based on likelihood ratio testing
with one threshold, the other based on sequential analysis. No
experiments were reported to support their theory.

            III.   HYPOTHESES FOR HUMAN FAILURE DETECTION

    The models described in the previous section contain assump-
tions about information processing by the human monitor, ranging
from Robinson's heuristic averaging to Phatak and Kleinman's normative approach. We feel that all of these approaches have as a
common basis some general principles about information processing
by the human.

    The related field of manual control summarizes the behavior
of human controllers by a set of fundamental hypotheses (Clement,
McRuer and Klein, 1971). Having a similar set of hypotheses for
the human monitor would be beneficial since it would provide a
framework for future work in this area. Because of the many simi-
larities between manual control and monitoring, we propose the
following working hypotheses based on the manual control hypotheses
to describe the human monitor:

    1. *To accomplish system monitoring functions such as monitor-
    ing the state of the system, its various subsystems (including*

displays and failure detection systems), the observer uses a variety of models about the system and its performance based on his past experience.

2.   To be satisfactory, monitoring systems, comprising both animate and inanimate components, must share certain of the qualitative dynamic features of a "good" failure detection system of the solely inanimate nature. As the adaptive means to accomplish this end, the observer must make up for any deficiency of the information displayed by appropriate adjustment of his dynamic information processing.

3.   There is a cost to this adjustment - in workload induced stress, in concentration of observer faculties, and in reduced potential for coping with the unexpected. This cost can also be traded for the cost of automatic monitoring systems. In making this trade-off, one may allocate part of the task to the human and part to the automatic failure detection system.

IV.   DETECTING A CHANGE IN MEAN

In this section, we briefly describe a model of the human's task of detecting changes in the mean or bias in a random process (Gai and Curry, 1976). This can be a very intricate problem for, as can easily be imagined, the detectability of a change in mean will depend not only on the magnitude of the change, but also on the dynamic character of the change, e.g. a sudden small jump is likely to be of the same detectability as a larger, slower change.

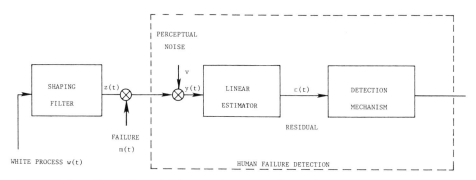

FIGURE 2:   Functional Block Diagram of Failure Detection Problem

The model includes two stages (Figure 2): an optimal estimator and a decision mechanism. The estimator is a Kalman filter which is based on the subject's internal model of the observed process (as in the optimal control model of the human operator). It is assumed that after several observations, this filter reaches steady state, and the human observer uses the observation error (residual) of the filter as an input to the second stage. Under this assumption, the first stage is a high pass filter. The residual is preferred to the estimated observation because:

It is more sensitive to the effect of the failure;

It is a white process, so successive observations are uncorrelated.

The decision mechanism is based on sequential analysis. The classical sequential analysis uses the likelihood ratio $\ell(m)$ as a decision function after m observations. Two criteria levels, A and B, are chosen, and the decision rule is

if $\ell(m) \geq A$ choose "failure"
if $\ell(m) \leq B$ choose "normal"
if $B < \ell(m) < A$ take another observation

A and B are determined by the desired probability of false alarm P(FA) and the probability of miss P(MS) as follows:

$$A = (1-P(MS))/P(FA) \qquad\qquad B = P(MS)/(1-P(FA))$$

If the involved distributions are Gaussian with equal variances and means zero and θ_1 (failure), the decision function (for $\theta > 0$) is:

$$\tilde{\lambda}(m) = \sum_{i=1}^{m} \{\varepsilon_i - \theta_1/2\}$$

where ε_i is the residual of the ith observation. The upper criterion level is $(\ln A)/\theta_1$ and the lower criterion level is $(\ln B)/\theta_1$.

The classical theory cannot be applied directly to the failure detection problem because a basic assumption in the derivation is that the same mode (either "normal" or "failure") exists during the entire observation period. A failure problem is characterized by a transition from the normal mode to the failure mode at some random time, t_f. In order to overcome this difficulty, two modifications are made (Gai and Curry, 1976).

1. Resetting the decision function to zero whenever $\tilde{\lambda}(m)$ is negative.

2. Using only an upper criterion level A_1 which is modified to keep the same mean time between two false alarms as before including the resetting.

The value of A_1 is related to A and B by the equation

$$A_1 - \ln A_1 - 1 = -(\ln A + (A - 1)\ln B/(1 - B))$$

The modified decision function is shown in Figure 3 and the block diagram of the basic decision function is shown in Figure 4. For the case $\theta_1 < 0$, the decision function is

$$\tilde{\lambda}(m) = \sum_{i=1}^{m} (\varepsilon_i + \theta_1/2)$$

and only the lower criterion level $-(\ln A_1)/\theta_1$ is used (Figure 5).

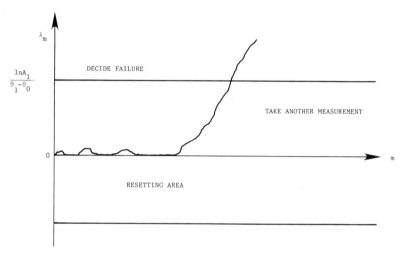

FIGURE 3. Modified decision function

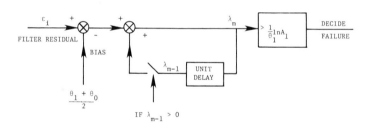

FIGURE 4. Decision Mechanism

The operation of the proposed model is actually quite simple in principle. Its basic properties are:

A high pass filter as a first stage to obtain the residuals;
Integration of the residual and comparison to a fixed threshold as a decision mechanism;
Only three parameters control the performance of the model

a.   The parameter designating the mean of a "failed"
     process, θ_1

b.   The signal to noise ratio of the observation noise in
     the Kalman filter

c.   The probabilities of the two types of error P(FA) and
     P(MS)

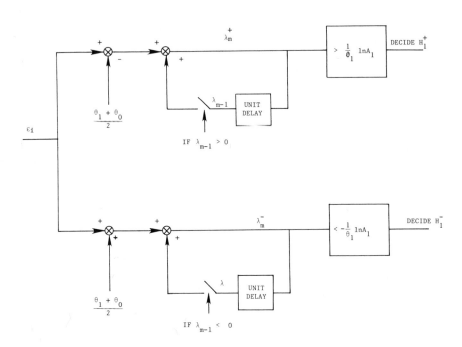

FIGURE 5:   Complete block diagram of the decision mechanism.

Experiments were run to test the validity of this model.   In
these experiments, subjects monitored the motion of a horizontal
bar displayed on a CRT.   This motion was derived by passing a zero
mean white Gaussian process through a second order shaping filter.
At some random time, the mean of the displayed process was changed
and the subject was asked to detect this change as soon as possible.
In one experimental session, the change was in the form of a step
function with four different amplitudes.   The mean and standard
deviation of the detection times as a function of the failure
amplitude for one subject are shown in Figure 6.   This figure also
shows the prediction of the model with the three free parameters
taking the values shown.   In another experimental session, the
failure had a ramp form, again with four different slopes.   The
results (for the same subject) are shown in Figure 7, as well as
the predictions of the model.

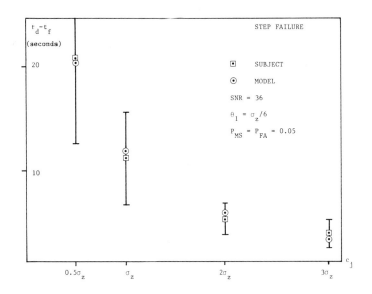

FIGURE 6.   Detection time for step failures.

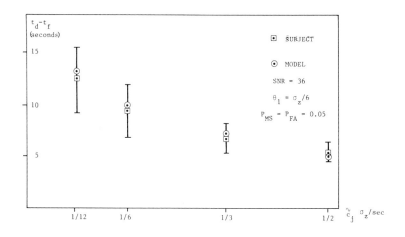

FIGURE 7.   Detection time for ramp failures.

In other cases where the decision interval was limited, it was suggested (Gai, 1975) to modify the decision mechanism by including a time varying test of probability of false alarm.

To test the model in a more realistic situation, Gai and Curry (1976a) ran experiments in which subjects were asked to detect instrument failures during automatic landing in an aircraft simulator. A linearized version of the control loop was used for the subject's internal model for this task. The time sharing between instruments was accounted for by an increase of the observation noise in the Kalman filter as is done in the optimal control model of the human operator. Again, good agreement between the model and the observed results has been obtained.

V. DETECTING CHANGES IN BANDWIDTH, POWER AND FREQUENCY

The model described in the previous section is designed to predict human performance in detecting dynamic changes in the mean of a random process. However, there are other characteristics of random processes that are subject to change (Anyakora and Lees, 1972), and many of these can be represented by a random process derived from a second order shaping filter of the form

$$G(s) = K/(s^2 + 2\zeta\omega_n s + \omega_n^2)$$

This has the advantage of specifying what we think are the three primary factors in describing a random process:

1. The standard deviation of the process (via the gain K)
2. The natural frequency of the process, ω_n
3. The frequency selectivity (damping ratio, ζ)

This transfer function is general enough to obtain spectral densities ranging from low pass to band pass.

If the Kalman filter in the animate or inanimate failure detection system has the correct parameters of the observed random process, then it is well known that the observation residual is a white noise process. Process failures or changes in process parameters can be detected by determining that the residuals are no longer zero mean and white. The Appendix contains the equations for the correlation of the residual in off-design conditions. The equations show that the characteristic modes (eigenvalues) of the residual autocorrelation function are determined by the modes of the Kalman filter which are generally higher frequency than the normal process) and the modes of the new or failed process.

Figure 8 shows the recorded detection times for 8 subjects observing changes in the bandwidth and variance of the random process. Note that an increase of frequency (decrease of period T) and an increase of variance seem to be detected more quickly than a decrease of the same size.

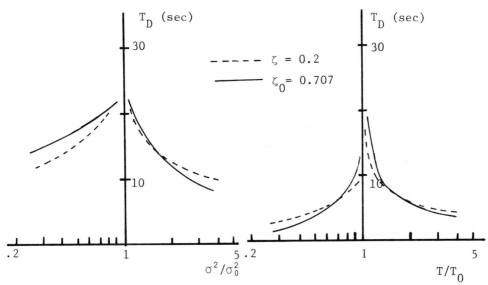

FIGURE 8:   Mean detection time for changes in variance and period
$(T = 2\pi/\omega_n)$; nominal period of $T_0 = 1$ sec.

We are currently exploring sequential hypothesis testing models
which describe these characteristics. It is interesting to note
in Figure A.1 that the residual autocorrelation function for a
comparable increase and decrease of bandwidth is much larger for
the increase in bandwidth. Thus failure detection based on residual whiteness tests would appear to be easier with an increase in
bandwidth, which is precisely the observed result in our human
failure detection experiments.

VI.   CONCLUSIONS

We look for models of human failure detection to perform some
valuable predictions of human performance. Among these would be
the determination of what errors and what failures are detectable
by the human. (If the fundamental working hypotheses stated in
Section III are confirmed by further investigation, they suggest
that those failures which the human finds hard to detect will also
be hard to detect by a hardware system.) Another utilization of
these models would be the determination of the information requirements for failure detection, i.e., what information should be displayed to the human to increase his probability of detecting certain
failures? A model would be valuable in assessing these information
requirements without the necessity for detailed experimentation.

At the present time, models for the interaction of the human
monitor with discrete random processes are fairly well understood,
that is, we are aware of the basic psychophysics and the many important results from the vigilance studies which have bearing on

this problem; however, there is relatively little knowledge in the understanding of human information processing of continuous time random processes. There have been initial steps in this direction (Levison and Tanner, 1971; Gai and Curry, 1976), but there is much more to be learned. We foresee an immediate need to determine how the human is able to interpret changes in bandwidth, power and frequency selectivity (or damping). Other problems that will need attention are the learning of the random process by the human; the effects of stress, fatigue, motivation, etc.

APPENDIX

CORRELATION OF THE RESIDUAL FOR A SUBOPTIMAL FILTER

Assume the normal process obeys the n-dimensional state equation (shaping filter)

$$\dot{x} = A_0 x + B_0 w, \qquad \text{cov } w = Q_0 \delta(t - t')$$

with m-dimensional observations

$$y = C_0 x + v, \qquad \text{cov } v = R_0 \delta(t - t')$$

The Kalman filter for the nominal system is given by

$$\dot{\hat{x}} = A_0 \hat{x} + K(y - C\hat{x})$$

and

$$K = E \, C'R^{-1}$$

$$K_\infty = E_\infty C'R^{-1}$$

where for stationary processes, the steady-state covariance of the estimate, E, obeys

$$0 = A_0 E_\infty + E_\infty A_0' - E_\infty C_0' R_0^{-1} C_0 E_\infty + B_0 Q_0 B_0'$$

Suppose the process (but not the filter) changes to

$$\dot{x} = A_1 x_1 + B_1 w \qquad \text{cov } w = Q_1$$

Let

$$e = x - \hat{x}$$

$$z = \begin{pmatrix} e \\ x \end{pmatrix} \qquad\qquad \tilde{w} = \begin{pmatrix} v \\ w \end{pmatrix}$$

Then

$$\dot{z} = \tilde{A} z + \tilde{B} \tilde{w} \qquad \text{where} \qquad \tilde{A} = \begin{pmatrix} (A_0 - K_\infty C_0) & (A_1 - A_0) \\ 0 & A_1 \end{pmatrix}$$

and $\tilde{B} = \begin{pmatrix} -K_\infty & B_1 \\ 0 & B_1 \end{pmatrix}$
$\qquad$ $\text{cov } \tilde{w} = \begin{pmatrix} R_0 & 0 \\ 0 & Q_1 \end{pmatrix} = \tilde{Q}$

The covariance of z, Z, is determined by

$$\dot{Z} = \tilde{A}Z + Z\tilde{A}' + \tilde{B}\tilde{Q}\tilde{B}'$$

The measurement residual is

$$r(t) = y(t) - C_0\hat{x}(t) \quad = C_0 e(t) + v(t) \quad = \tilde{C}z(t) + v(t)$$

where

$$\tilde{C} = [C\ 0]$$

The autocorrelation matrix for the residual is thus

$$\overline{r(t + \tau)r'(t)} \quad =$$

$$\tilde{C}\ \overline{z(t + \tau)z'(t)}\ \tilde{C}\ ' \quad + \tilde{C}\ \overline{z(t + \tau)v'(t)} \quad + \overline{v(t + \tau)z'(t)}\ \tilde{C}'$$

$$+ R\delta(\tau)$$

where

$$\overline{z(t + \tau)z'(t)} = \tilde{\Phi}(\tau)Z(t)$$

$$\overline{z(t + \tau)v'(t)} = \tilde{\Phi}(\tau)\tilde{B}(-\frac{R}{0})$$

$$\overline{v(t + \tau)z'(t)} = 0$$

$$\overline{z(t)v'(t)} = \tfrac{1}{2}\tilde{B}(-\frac{R}{0})$$

and $\tilde{\Phi}(\tau)$ is the transition matrix for the state vector z. Thus

$$\overline{r(t + \tau)r'(t)} = R\delta(\tau) + \tilde{C}\tilde{\Phi}(\tau)(Z_\infty C' - (\frac{K_\infty R}{0}))$$

It is interesting to note that if the system matrix remains unchanged ($A_1 = A_0$) then the autocorrelation matrix is determined by the modes of the new shaping filter only. Otherwise, the modes of the new shaping filter (A_1) will enter into the autocorrelation of r(t). Below we show the normalized increment to the auto-correlation function for the second order shaping filter in Section V due to changes in natural frequency and damping ratio.

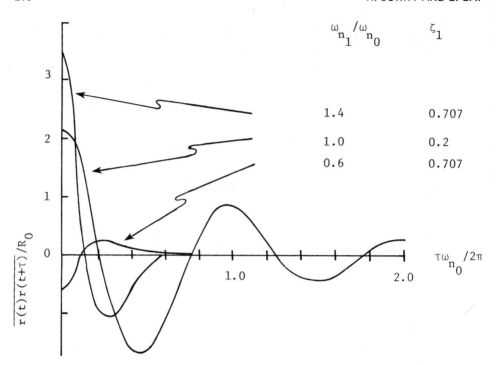

FIGURE A.1.   Normalized increment to residual autocorrelation
function for second order shaping filter ($\zeta_0 = 1/\sqrt{2}$, $R_0 = 0.01\pi\sigma_{x0}^2$).

REFERENCES

Anyakora, S.M. and Lees, F.P., "Detection of instrument malfunctions by the process operator", Chem Engin, London, 1972.

Clement, W.F., McRuer, D.T., and Klein, R. "Systematic manual
control display design", Guidance and Control Displays
Conference, AGARD Conference Proceedings #96, 1971.

Gai, E.G. and Curry, R.E. "A model of the human observer in
failure detection tasks", IEEE Transactions on Systems,
Man and Cybernetics, February 1976.

Gai, E.G., Psychophysical Models for Signal Detection with Time
Varying Uncertainty, Ph.D. Thesis, Department of Aeronautics
and Astronautics, Massachusetts Institute of Technology, 1975.

deJong, J.J. and Koster, E.P. "The human operator in the computer
controlled refinery", Proceedings of the Eighth World Petrol
Conference, Moscow, London: Institute of Petroleum, 1971.

Levison, W.H. and Tanner, R.B. "A control theory model for human decision making", NASA Contractor's Report CR-1953, 1971.

Phatak, A.V. and Bekey, G.A. "Decision processes in the adaptive behavior of the human controller", IEEE Transactions on Systems Science and Cybernetics, SSC-5, 1969.

Phatak, A.V. and Kleinman, D.L., "Current status of models for the human operator as a controller and decision maker in manned aerospace systems", Proceedings of the AGARD Conference #114, 1972.

Robinson, G.H., "Continuous estimation of time varying probability", Ergonomics, 7, 1964.

Sheridan, T.B., "On how often the supervisor should sample", IEEE Transactions on Systems Science and Cybernetics SSC-6, 1970.

Smallwood, R.D., "Internal models and the human instrument monitor", IEEE Transactions on Human Factors in Electronics, HFE-8, 1967.

Young, L.R., "On adaptive manual control", Ergonomics 12, 1969.

DISCUSSION

SINGLETON :

Could you clarify what you mean by a mental model ? Why do you need such a concept ? Is it essentially static, although parameters may vary, or does the model change ? If it does change what does this mean ?

CURRY :

Our overall goal is to predict how people will be able to perform this failure detection task under new and different conditions, and one important requirement is to summarize the observer's knowledge of his environment. This knowledge is what I call the internal model. (In our model of human failure detection we assume the observer is well practiced and uses the real-world process for the internal model.)

To use the model retrospectively (as opposed to predictively) may have some interesting implications for learning and training, for the parameters of the model may indicate various levels of learning, etc. This is a most difficult problem since the results will depend very much on the assumed structure of the internal model.

DRURY :

Does the theory predict well for the situation of a fixed observation interval rather than one which ends with detection ?

CURRY :

These data were taken with unlimited observation times. We have done some experiments with fixed observation intervals and found the trends predicted by the theory (i.e., decreasing thresholds), but we have not done a detailed study of this problem as yet. Our experiments with instrument failures during simulated landings involved fixed observation intervals, but the time limit had no appreciable effect.

RIJNSDORP :

Could the asymmetry in the speed of detection of natural frequency changes not simply be related to observation of oscillations ? If so, could the product of reaction time and natural frequency be more or less constant ?

CURRY :

I don't believe so because the display was irregular and not oscillatory, and at the present time I know of no model to describe these psychophysical data. The product of detection time and natural frequency is an important parameter for all detections since it normalizes detection time to the number of "cycles" of the process.

ATTENTION, CONTROL, AND SAMPLING BEHAVIOUR

Neville Moray

Department of Psychology, Stirling University

Stirling, Scotland

In the last twenty years there has been a remarkable renaissance in research on attention, dominated by the influence of Broadbent (1958, 1971), who has succeeded in synthesising much of the work into a coherent whole. Within the area of attention several themes have developed almost independently, in particular those of selective attention (Broadbent, 1958; Treisman, 1960, 1969; Moray, 1969) and vigilance (Broadbent, 1971; Mackworth, 1970; Jerison, 1970; Buckner and McGrath, 1963). The degree to which progress in these two fields has been largely independent is underlined by the structure of the review by Swets and Kristofferson (1970).

Even more separate has been the work on skill, which has itself been split into two almost separate traditions, that based on reaction time studies in the laboratory (e.g. Welford, 1968) and that using tasks which are much closer to the continuous complex analogue control tasks of real life (e.g. McRuer and Krendel 1974). The split is to some extent between work arising from a traditional psychological background and that done by engineers.

In the last few years a major theoretical shift has taken place, which was originally called "cognitive psychology", and more recently "information processing". Simple and even complex S-R formulations have been acknowledged as inadequate to account for the complexity of human performance, and the emphasis has changed from the human operator as a passive responder, to one in which he is seen as an active, intelligent, even rational manipulator of the information he receives. Responses are created, not

elicited.   The human operator uses both past and present information consciously and unconsciously in a tactical and strategic
interaction with the environment in the search for optimal,
adaptive, behaviour.

It now seems possible in the light of these developments
not merely to synthesise the disparate areas of attention research
but to show that certain generalisations can be made which are
applicable also to skill, monitoring behaviour, and supervisory
control.   At the same time certain methodological problems are
thrown into relief, and certain problems in training.

All problems of attention, monitoring, and supervisory
control can be thought of as concerned with a particular problem.
The observer must control the flow of information through his brain
so as to optimise his performance.   Sometimes the problem is one of
information overload, sometimes of time uncertainty, sometimes of
the exercise of control.   Two kinds of questions can be asked
about the mechanisms involved, structural and functional.   Most
questions in attention research have been structural.   Throughout
the 1960's a series of papers appeared asking whether sensory inputs were filtered, whether attention operated by selecting inputs
or responses, and what kind of analysing mechanisms were being
activated by attentional control, (Treisman, 1960, 1969; Treisman
and Geffen, 1967; Deutsch and Deutsch 1963; Broadbent 1971).
Essentially the aim was to describe the minimal hardware needed to
account for the observed phenomena.   The tasks used were almost
always laboratory tasks, and were concerned mainly with the recep-
tion of information.   Very seldom did psychologists concern themselves with tasks involving the exercise of control, (for an excep-
tion see Herman, 1965).   Functional questions on the other hand
are those aimed at answering how the mechanisms are used.   What
are the rules according to which the selective mechanisms change
their state?   How does the system decide which source to sample
next?   When should a sample be taken?   What decision rules are
to be used when the obtained information is processed?

The key to unifying the two fields lies in the concept of
an "internal model".   The observer is thought to have in his head
a model of the world, or at least that part of it which consists
of the sources of information with which he is concerned while
carrying out the task to which he is giving attention.   The model
represents more or less accurately the statistical structure in
time and space of the messages received, and the observer can run
it in fast time, so that prediction can occur.   The model also
includes the value system of the observer, embodies as weighting
functions.   When the observer processes information he uses it not
merely to make responses but also to update the model.   Since the
model can be used predictively the human operator can sometimes

abolish his reaction time lag as practice proceeds, and may indeed introduce phase lead in certain control tasks. Thus highly practised humans sometimes appear to have infinite information processing rates, at least in certain limited conditions.

The idea of such models is not in fact new, and was forseen for example, by Craik (1943). The reason for their increasing popularity may be as much technical as conceptual: only recently have many investigators had access to powerful online computers with which real time online modelling could be carried out; and without the ability to run dynamic, rather than preplanned experiments it is extremely difficult to develop a feel for the richness of the ideas involved. Probably the most extensive account of these ideas is that by Kelley (1968) which, sadly, has gone largely unnoticed by psychologists.

To develop the synthesis mentioned earlier we may begin with a well known paper by Senders (1964). Concerned with the problem of instrument panel layout, and the task of the human observer confronted by an array of sources of visual information all of which had to be sampled, Senders applied Information Theory of continuous functions (Shannon and Weaver, 1949). He postulated that the observer was a rational information seeking device whose strategy for making observations would be governed by the Sampling Theorem and the information load of each source. Since pattern vision is so poor away from the fovea the observer would have to fixate each instrument in turn in order to extract accurate information from it, and hence eye fixations could be used as a measure of the sampling rate. (Some writers have argued that overt behavioural direction of attention by movements of head and eyes should not be regarded as mechanisms of attention, but as relatively uninteresting, "preattentional" orientating devices. The logic of such an argument seems very curious. After all, while there may be arguments in selective listening over whether the listener can block off the input he receives by means of an all or none "filter", there can at least be no argument as to whether a person can shut his eyes or turn away his head! The head is opaque: the question is whether its opacity is used by the observer in a rational way, or whether it is both thick and opaque!)

Senders argued then that if the observer were rational, he would sample the sources of information in a way defined by the Sampling Theorem. The instruments were forced by bandlimited Gaussian noise of different bandwidths, and the changes in the observers' fixations recorded. Both the fixation rates and the duration of fixations were rather closely in accordance with the predictions from Information Theory. Moreover the predictions were reasonably fulfilled with pilots flying both simulators and real aircraft. Figures 1 and 2 are from his laboratory experiments.

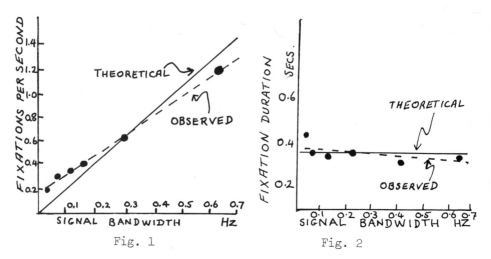

Fig. 1   Fig. 2

     Senders suggested that the failure of the data to lie ex-
actly on the predicted line was due to the inability of the observers to extract velocity information at the lowest bandwidths, but
bearing in mind that the highest bandwidths produced sampling
rates which were too low, a more plausible reason would be that
the observers were displaying the well known tendency of humans to
underestimate high probabilities and overestimate low probabilities
(Peterson & Beach, 1964).   In almost all cases where humans have
been asked to match statistical distributions they tend to com-
press the range by excluding extreme values, an observation which
may have important applications as a general principle of human
performance.

It is less important in the present case to note the details of
Senders' data than to note the model which he proposed for the
whole information flow through the organism. Those proposals are
shown in Figures 3 and 4.

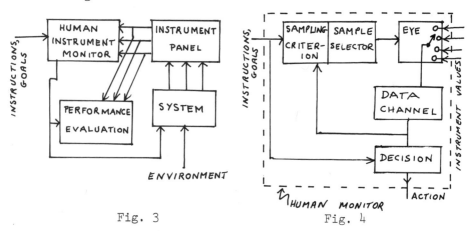

Fig. 3   Fig. 4

The boxes labled "sampling criterion" and "sample selector" receive inputs from two sources. One is the pathway labled "instructions, goals" which feeds implicit or explicit criteria to the control mechanisms based on the task demands as imposed by the situation and the experimenter's requirements. The other is the pathway carrying information about the observations made when each instrument is sampled. This pathway is a branch of that which uses the information from each observation to decide on the appropriate overt response. The control mechanism is therefore a model of the environment, in this case of the statistical structure of the messages which the observer is monitoring, weighted by the input from "instructions, goals". It should be noted that there is no room for doubt that there _is_ such a model embodied in the control mechanism. If the observer approximates closely to a sampling rate of 2W Hz when observing a source whose signal bandwidth is W Hz, then the attentional control mechanism _must_ know the value of W. And to know W is, precisely, to have a model which embodies the statistical structure of the environment.

Note also that the system produces aperiodic switches of attention. The observer does not divide his time equally among the rival sources of information, and would not do so even if there were but two of them, although most work in selective attention seems to imply that attention would be _equally_ divided between two sources. This is important, since there have been many attempts to measure attention switching time, and a large number of estimates have been made (Broadbent, 1958; Kristofferson, 1965: Moray, 1969). If attention is rationally controlled the disparity in these estimates is hardly surprising, since as we have seen the distribution of attention will be a function of task demands rather than reflecting the properties of an internal switch. No doubt there is some limitation to the rate at which attention can be redirected, but the conditions under which one would be certain that one were seeing hardware limitations rather that tactical decisions are hard to specify. In practice sampling periodicities have varied from 10 msecs to 300 millisecs or longer. Senders' work could be interpreted to mean that it could be any interval up to limits imposed by biomechanical or biophysical constraints on the structure of the switching mechanisms. (Although in the case of eyemovements there is ample evidence that not more than 4 or 5 saccades per second can ever be made.)

Some workers have been critical of the use of eyemovements as indicators of the direction of attention because of the difference between "looking" and "seeing" (e.g. Broadbent, in Buckner and McGrath, 1963). Since observers may look at a signal without seeing it, the line of regard is an unreliable estimate of sampling. While this is in general true, it is largely irrelevant in

the present context.   The regular relation between the line of
regard and the bandwidth of the source is all that is required to
make the point. (It is obvious that the model predicts that if
many of the fixations on an instrument resulted merely in "looks"
rather than observations the rate of fixations would eventually
fall, since its effective bandwidth from the observers' viewpoint
would fall.)

        Carbonell (1966) pointed out that few tasks consist merely
of monitoring without exercising control over the process monitored.   The occurrence of an error signal on an aircraft instrument
calls for action from the pilot.   The result is that the future
value of the forcing function is dependent on the action taken,
and the sequence of values is not ergodic, as was assumed by
Senders.   The future value of the function is better known following an observation and corrective action than it would be if the
forcing function were a zero mean, unit variance, Gaussian noise.
The exercise of control is predictive.   (The uses of responses as
sources of prediction is incorporated in Young's very general
model for manual control as we shall see later, (Young, 1969).

        Now once the allocation of attention as a function of time
becomes related to the exercise of control based on the value of
the sample obtained, we have moved from the "classical" account of
attention to the study of skill.   Conceptually the line between
the two is obviously very thin when viewed in this way, but historically the two have been separated.   Crossing the boundary and
following the line of thought developed by Carbonell leads to the
more recent papers by Sheridan (1970) on the concept of the Supervisor.   This work is absolutely central to an understanding of
the nature of attention and its control, but it has gone largely
unknown owing to the fact that it has appeared only in places
where few psychologists dare go (namely the terrifying pages of
Trans. IEEE!)

        As did Senders, Sheridan considers an observer monitoring
a zero mean Gaussian source and taking action on the basis of the
observations made in order to exercise control.   However the
observer is now assumed to be maximising net gain, rather than
minimising error.   Although these may often be the same, they
can in many real life situations differ, either as when a worker
may allow error to build up in order to break the monotony of a
task by struggling to regain control, or as in the case of break-
ing the speed limit while trying to get to hospital with a wife
who is having a baby. Sheridan begins by describing two extreme
strategies which the observer might use.   The observer might
continuously monitor the displayed value of the forcing function
(in the strong sense of "continuous").   In that case the accuracy
of his knowledge of the value of f(t) is limited only by the
resolution of his sense organs and of the display.   But he is com-

pletely unable to monitor any other source of information which
may be present, and may even be precluded from monitoring the
accuracy of the control movements he makes. (We assume that the
observer is a single channel processor.) Note that this strategy
is excellent for a single channel task where little control is
required, and that if a reaction time lag is acceptable, no internal model is required, or indeed advantageous. The second
extreme strategy is one which places a minimum processing load on
the system, namely to centre the control on the estimated mean
value of f(t) and to leave it there without making any observations
or control action. The mean error will be zero, but the mean
squared error will of course be the variance of the forcing function. On the other hand the observer will obviously be free for
other tasks. Note that an internal model is required even for
this strategy since the observer must estimate the mean of f(t).

Since one of these strategies takes two many samples and
the other too few, it is intuitively clear that there will be an
optimal sampling interval which will lie between the two. Sheridan
shows how the optimal sampling interval can be estimated, given
that the observer knows the statistical structure of the forcing
function, and the costs and payoffs associated with observation
and control. For a plausible set of task demands and forcing
functions the property of the Supervisor can be summarised in
Figures 5 and 6.

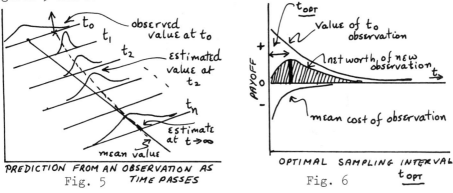

PREDICTION FROM AN OBSERVATION AS
Fig. 5   TIME PASSES

OPTIMAL SAMPLING INTERVAL
Fig. 6 t_{OPT}

The information obtained as a result of an observation at
time t_0 becomes less valuable as time passes, since it is a progressively poorer basis for predicting subsequent values of f(t)
at t_n, and when enough time has passed for the autocorrelation
function of f(t) effectively to have fallen to zero, the best
estimate of f(t) can again only be the mean, and the second
extreme case is realised. On the other hand if a cost is associated with the making of an observation, then frequent sampling
will be costly, and the longer we wait before taking a new sample
the less the average cost per sample will be. Combining the value
of information and the cost of samples we obtain a net worth for

any sampling interval, and for many plausible functions the
relation is non-monotonic, having a maximum whose position defines
the optimal sampling interval.

        We can now proceed to generalise this idea and use it to
integrate the work on skill, vigilance and attention. Let us
begin by asking what aspects of tasks may give rise to costs associated with making an observation. Two plausible candidates
immediately come to mind. The first is an essential aspect of
skilled performance at least in tasks where a graded response is
required (as against merely a go-no-go response such as pushing a
button). A human needs to observe the results of his motor response, or the internal, kinaesthetic feedback associated with its
generation in order to establish its accuracy, and to learn its
features. The clearest example of this is perhaps speech, where
delaying or abolishing auditory feedback produces devastating
effects on a speaker's output unless he can manage to learn to
observe kinaesthetic sensations rather than the sound. Other
examples can be found, and of course it is a logical necessity for
improving performance when an operator is involved in a closed
loop task.   There is considerable evidence that the more one
monitors one's own output the less effecient one is at processing
input or transforming information (Moray, 1967).   The second
source of observational cost arises as soon as there are more than
one source of information to observe. If only one source can be
monitored at a time, then making an observation on one message is
associated with a probability of missing a signal on another message. This is true regardless of the kind of target the observer
is required to detect: it may be a burst of noise, a pure tone
burst against a background of noise, an excessive value of a gauge,
or a radar echo in one part of a screen.   The cost of an observation on Message A is therefore the probability of there being a
target on Messages B . . . M during the interval of observation,
weighted by the cost of missing a target and the probability of
missing a target, if an observation were made.   A formal treatment of this model has beengiven both by Senders (1964) and Hamilton (1967).

        In laboratory experiments on selective attention it has
usually been the practice to use target schedules where the probability of the arrival of a target on any channel is uniform over
time.   Relatively little work has been done on assymetrical target probabilities.   The real world is however not like that, and
is, statistically speaking, rather predictable, at least locally.
All messages derived from the environment are of limited bandwidth, and any limited bandwidth signal is predictable at least
locally even when the signal is Gaussian noise.   In a Senders
task it is obvious that an extreme value is more likely to occur
soon after an observation near the critical level than after the
one near the mean, since the signal bandwidth is limited.   Assume

for simplicity that the probability of detecting a target given
that one is present when an observation is made stays constant
throughout a task, and that the value of a detection also stays
constant. In such a case the decision to take a sample is a
function of the conditional probability of the occurrence of a
target in each channel given the value of the observation last
made on that channel. The observer can only compute the appropriate measure if certain other information is available to him.
He must know the statistical properties of the sources, he must
have a reasonably accurate estimate of time, and he must have an
accurate memory of the values of recent observations on each
channel. If in addition he can exercise control and can estimate
the effects of his control actions then that information may allow
him to modify the next sampling interval because of the increase
in the accuracy of prediction which it allows. Thus Senders' and
Carbonell's experiments become special cases of the more general
Supervisor model. But in all cases we must postulate internal
statistical models which are used by the observer to generate his
sampling behaviour.

        Sheridan has attempted to show optimal sampling behaviour
in human observers, and found that in general they did not show it.
But it is clear that in so complex a model there are many places
at which nonoptimality may arise, and a particular failure should
not be considered a good reason for rejecting such a suggestive
and powerful normative model. The observer may not have translated the explicit payoffs into his model correctly, there may not
have been sufficient practice for him to develop good statistical
estimates of the source properties, etc. And the extent to which
practice can alter performance is known to be formidable, (Crossman, 1959).

        To make the synthesis of control tasks and selective
attention tasks complete we may consider some recent experiments
from my own laboratory where the above principles may be applied.
We have investigated strategies of attention in selective listening where the targets to be detected have included increments in
intensity, increments in frequency, letters occurring in streams
of spoken digits, and classes of nouns such as animal names occurring in streams of other nouns. Target probabilities have been
varied from 0.1 to 0.5, and various conditions of attention have
been explored, single messages, selective attention where one message is to be processed and other ignored, and divided attention
where two messages must be simultaneiously processed. In all
these paradigms certain constant phenomena were found, (Moray et
al., 1976: Ostry et al., 1976). As an example consider the following experiment.

        Listeners heard a different stream of spoken digits in
each ear, arriving at a rate of two digits per ear per second as

synchronous pairs.   Occasionally a letter would arrive instead of
a digit, and these were the targets to be detected.   The probability that a signal in a message would be a target was 0.1, but
the series were biassed so that if a target occurred in one message the probability that there was at that moment a target in the
second message was 0.5.

          The data were analysed using the Theory of Signal Detec-
tion (TSD) which yields two statistics, $\underline{d}$', a measure of target
detectability, and Beta, a measure of the observer's willingness
to be risky in deciding whether a signal is a target.   As in most
experiments in selective listening substantial changes in $\underline{d}$' were
found when the condition of attention changed, but more interesting from our point of view are the changes in Beta.   The signals
were heavily masked by white noise, and the observers practised
the task for an hour a day for ten days.   TSD can be used to
predict optimal values of Beta given an a priori knowledge of target probabilities and the payoffs associated with hits, misses,
false alarms and correct rejections.   The observers in our experiment were not explicitly told the probabilities or the payoffs,
but the instructions were such as to make it likely that the payoff matrix was unity.   If so, then Beta for a target probability
of 0.1 should be 9.0, and for a target probability of 0.5 should
be 1.0.

          Our results are shown in Figure 7.   B/CR is the value of
Beta obtained from one channel when at the moment the data were
collected the observer correctly indicated that there was no target present in the other channel.   B/H is the value of Beta based
on data collected at moments when the observer correctly indicated
that there was a target present on the other channel.

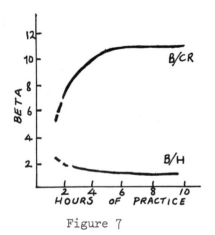

Figure 7

It is obvious that the observers
have an excellent estimate of the
general and local statistical properties of the sources and that
they are using those estimates in
a nearly optimal manner to alter
their decision criteria up to
twice a second.   The practice
curves indicated the steady growth
of the models with exposure to the
sources.   As in Senders' experiment
there is evidence of the classical
conservatism referred to earlier:
the values of Beta are slightly too
high.   This may be due partly to
the fact that not all targets were
detected and therefore the estimate
of probability will tend to be too
low.

A further point to note is that while most experiments on manual control use highly practised observers such as experienced pilots, or at least give several hours of training before data are collected, many experiments on selective attention have used only slight practice, and indeed may finish the entire experiment with less experience for the observer than ours had by the end of Day 2. Although we made no attempt to manipulate payoff in our experiment it is known that such a manipulation can be effective (Shulman and Fisher, 1972).

This emphasis on the internal statistical model is not, as was mentioned earlier, new. It is of course a version of "Expectancy Theory" as applied to vigilance tasks (Baker, 1963) and it is to such tasks that we now turn to complete the picture.

The effect of target probability on vigilance performance is too well known to need documenting here. Equally it is well known that explanations of the vigilance decrement in terms of expectancy alone have not been adequate. Indeed it seems unlikely that any theory based on a single causal variable will be successful. But there are one or two features of expectancy theory which have not yet been fully exploited and which relate to the theme of this paper.

When TSD is applied to vigilance both changes in target detectability and in the observer's response criterion can be found depending on the paradigm used (Swets and Kristofferson, 1970). As we have already seen it is reasonable to associate changes in Beta with changes in the observers' estimates of target probability. But three problems arise. The first is a practical one. If an observer is closely to approximate the predictions of TSD he must have adequate information about the distribution of target probabilities, and when targets are very rare the number of signals required to define the distribution may be too great for it to be possible to gain the necessary evidence. Secondly, with very long intervals between targets neither an observer's time estimation nor his memory are likely to be adequate to perform the necessary measurements on the incoming data. The third problem is of a different kind and is concerned with the interpretation of the TSD statistics obtained in such experiments. As Jerison (1970) observes, the values of Beta obtained are quite in order as far as the mathematical manipulations on the data are concerned, but seem to be psychologically meaningless. In most other experiments values of Beta seldom exceed 10.0, or at most 20.0. But in vigilance experiments values of the order of 200 or even 500 are not too rare. To account for these Jerison proposes that observers may be in one of three states, alert, non-attending, or an intermediate state of reduced alertness, and shows how the statistics could arise by taking into account the proportion of time that the observer spends in each state. (The

states are not directly observable). A sketch of his model is
shown in Figure 8.

The crucial feature of the model is the relatively probability of the observer being in the alert, blurred, or non-attending state. These probabilities are described by Jerison as
if they were fixed. But let us assume that they depend on the
past experience of the observer, and that they are continuously
being revised from moment to moment on the basis of the observations made during the task. (This is in contrast to, for example
Broadbent, who suggests that after a few practice runs the observer's expectancy will become constant. This seems intuitively
unlikely.) Within a run the observer computes a running estimate
or target probability based on the occurrence of the last few
targets, probably over a range of the last four or five supposed
detections (Baker, 1963). Let us now use this idea to close a
loop in Jerison's model.

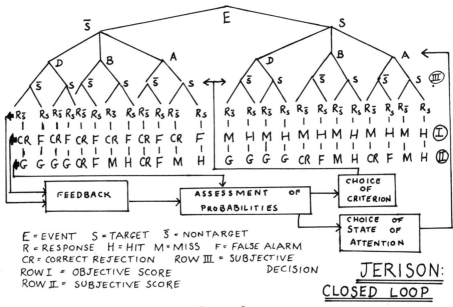

E = EVENT   S = TARGET   S̄ = NONTARGET
R = RESPONSE   H = HIT   M = MISS   F = FALSE ALARM
CR = CORRECT REJECTION   ROW III = SUBJECTIVE
ROW I = OBJECTIVE SCORE   DECISION
ROW II = SUBJECTIVE SCORE

JERISON: CLOSED LOOP

Figure 8

The observer has at any moment an estimate of the probability of a target being about to occur, and enters one of the
attentional states on the basis of that evidence, given only that
the probability of entering one of the attentional states sums to
unity over all the states. On making an observation he may decide
that there was a target or he may decide that there was not. In
either case he emits the appropriate response from the
end of the decision tree in Figure 8. But he also uses his observation (or perhaps his response) as input to a model which

embodies his expectancy, that is, a distribution of interstimulus intervals (ISIs). The model is thus updated, and the probability of entering particular attentional states at particular moments in the future is altered. (It may be more profitable to think of the attentional states as a continuous distribution rather than a set of discrete states, in which case the results would be similar to a model in which expectancy was biassed by arousal, but to pursue that suggestion would take us too far afield at present.)

This revised expectancy theory leans heavily on moment to moment changes in the observer's internal model of the statistical properties of the source, and hence if an experiment is analysed in terms of long term time averages of signal distributions it will give a misleading basis for calculating the observer's expectancy. This, it seems, may be one reason why expectancy theory has had less success than some have expected in dealing with vigilance data. The question then arises as to whether it is possible to measure moment to moment expectancy during an experiment. It might be possible in principle to use physiological measures to do this, although there are formidable difficulties in correctly identifying physiological variables. Can one devise a more straightforward behavioural method?

One way may be as follows. We recently completed a pilot experiment in which an observer performed a vigilance task in which he was required to detect occasional abnormally large readings on a voltmeter. The experiment was controlled online by a computer. The first few targets were inserted at random intervals after the start of the experiment. The computer recorded the times at which the observer claimed to have observed a target, irrespective of whether the claim was a hit or a false alarm. After sufficient responses had occurred the computer began to calculate a running average of the interresponse interval, updating this every time the observer made a response, and basing it on the most recent four or five responses. The next target was given after an interval equivalent to the current estimate of the mean IRI. Thus without knowing it, the observer was generating his own target sequence at, it was hoped, those moments when he actually expected to get one.

It was hoped that by doing this, and without the observer becoming aware of what was happening, it would both be possible to avoid any vigilance decrement and also to track the observer's expectancy in real time. Unfortunately, while there was some indication that the vigilance decrement was less for the "adaptive" than for a control group, there were huge individual differences, and the difference between experimental and control groups was not significant. There was, however, another observation which may point in the same direction. As a control for an effect due to the absolute number of targets presented, another group of obser-

vers were run. Each was run nonadaptively, but the target sequence
was a sequence which had been emitted by an observer who was running adaptively. That is, the observers were effectively "yoked"
in pairs. All observers who were run not on a random sequence,
not on one which they generated, but on one which had been generated by another observer showed very poor performance. Being
compelled to use someone else's model is a much harder task than
dealing with a random sequence, a result which may have profound
implications for training if it turns out to be general. We are
hoping to pursue this paradigm in the near future.

Let us summarise the ideas so far proposed. The observer constructs statistical models of the spatial and temporal properties of his environment. The observer uses the models both to
govern the decisions he makes about data obtained when he makes an
observation, and also to decide when and where to make observations.
The use of the models is essentially predictive, and allow the
observer to optimise the distribution of his limited processing
capacity. As Kelly, (1968), remarks, status information is mainly
useful because it allows an observer to predict the future.
While this claim is somewhat strong, since status information can
also obviously be of use in error correction, its emphasis is
probably correct. Even when the observed process is stochastic, a
good model which can be run in fact time allows an observer to
test strategies, and to generate responses even before the stimuli
colling for them occur. Thus reaction time lag can be eliminated,
and phase lead introduced in certain cases. Knowing what the
future is going to be like reduces the information processing load
on an observer drastically. Indeed in the limit the observer
need not process any information. Rather than responding to the
past or the present he generates the future - the ultimate God-
like property of adaptive behaviour!

All these ideas may be summarised in diagrammatic form by
using illustrations from a very stimulating paper by Young (1969).
The first (Figure 9) shows how a skill develops from a closed loop,
pursuit mode task in which the observer is entirely dependent upon
input and observered error for correcting his responses, to the
final state where he has models of the input, of his resonses, of
his kinaesthetic programmes, and is using an internal clock to run
these programmes in predictive mode. The second (Figure 10) sum-
marises that overall flow of information and sources of adaptation
viewed from what one might call an ecological viewpoint: the
observer in relation to the properties of the environment, task,
instructions, and his own internal adaptive processes. From what
has been said it will be clear that both of these are as much
models of attention as they are of manual control.

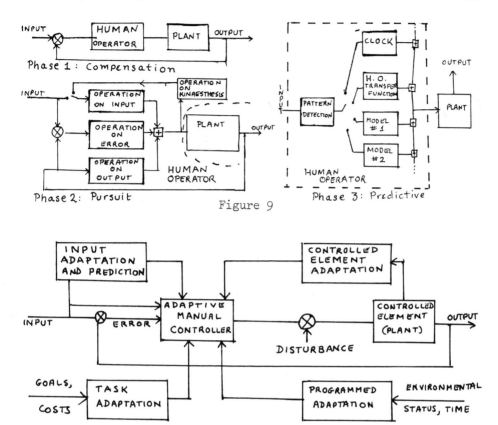

Figure 9

Figure 10

Problems of Measurement

One of the reasons for the failure of those working in
attention and those in skill to bring the two fields together may
have been problems of measurement. Characteristically quite different measures have been used in the two areas, and in the papers
where attempts have been made to integrate them a certain amount
of confusion is apparent. We have already referred to one such
problem, where Jerison claimed that mathematically appropriate
measures led to psychologically meaningless results in vigilance.
It is perhaps worth briefly reviewing some problems in the area of
measurement which must be overcome is a satisfactory synthesis is
to be made. The difficulties are not merely of interest to the
theoreticician, for they can lead to quite unrealistic assessment
of workload, level of skill, and task interference if one is not
aware of them. There does not seem to exist an overview of these
problems, although a careful reading of, for example, Sheridan
and Ferrell (1974) will reveal them, at least implicitly.

Probably the most powerful methods for analysing skills have been those related to control theory, and notable achievements have occurred in the realm of the human operator describing function (McRuer and Krendel, 1974). Continuous Information Theory has also been successful in describing certain aspects of skills, more so perhaps than the equivalent discrete theory in experimental psychology where it has largely been abandoned except in applied problems. Neither the describing function approach, nor information theory have been very successful in dealing with the problem of divided attention and secondary task interference, and of course they are hardly adapted to deal with the problem of predictive behaviour. The basic reason is that both methods are based on long term averages, quite apart from the necessity for making assumptions about linearity or ergodicity. Even adaptive control theory, while being successful in describing the change from one steady state to another, has not been used to describe momentary fluctuations in performance, and the implication of attention research is that the interference which one task causes with the performance of another is often of very short duration. It is understandable that work on transients has been slight, since most stable control systems are designed rapidly to damp the effects of transients, and long term average statistics will not show much evidence of their existence.

Crossman et al. (1964) have drawn attention to the "spectral characteristics" of vigilance and control tasks. The signal power tends to fall into two distinct bands. The tasks are characterised by long periods of very low information load, with signal bandwidths of not more than a few Hz, with occasional bursts of high frequency inputs when error signals occur. The occurence of targets may inject signals one or two decades of frequency higher than the background control task. Control tasks and control theories of the human operator, are low pass: attention and attentional theories are high pass. And never, or at least seldom, the twain shall meet.

A search through the literature can provide roughly equal numbers of papers asserting, for example, that secondary discrete tasks do or do not affect the information transmission rate of a tracking task. The reason may be connected with the nature of the tasks, the difficulty of the discrimination required, the order of control and bandwidth of the tracking task, etc. But equally it may simply be due to the nature of measurement. Consider again the experiments referred to above in which we investigated divided attention. We found marked differences between d'/CR and d'/H and between Beta/CR and Beta/H. But if one were to average data over the whole run, without making the observations conditional on contralateral events, the picture would be quite misleading. Moray and O'Brien (1967) did just that, and did not detect major systematic changes Beta. The reason is clear. The values of

$\underline{d}$'/CR and Beta/CR are no different from single channel values where there is no secondary input. It is only in connection with hits (or false alarms) that changes occur. But where, as in most experiments, the target probability is low, such events are few, and if all data are lumped together the overall change is too slight to be readily observed.

Rather little work has been done directly on the nature of distractability, but one paper (Fisher, 1972) suggests that in at least some attention tasks the effect of a distractor only lasts for about a second. Now consider the attempt to show the effect of, say, a toneburst detection task on tracking. If the targets are rare, and if each disrupts the tracking task for only a second, and if, as would be reasonable, a minute or more is spent collecting tracking data, what is the probability of detecting a change in the statistics of tracking? The net information transmission will hardly be affected by inserting two or three seconds of d.c. into one minute's tracking. The power spectrum will hardly be affected. Indeed it is difficult to think of <u>any</u> measure computed on the entire run which will be sensitive enough to detect such changes. Measures must be much more directly tied to the moments at which distractors and second task loadings occur, which itself poses difficulties for measurement, since the shorter the sampleof data the poorer the estimate of performance. But if we are to understand the laws governing sampling and control in complex multichannel tasks this is the direction in which we must go.

Again, in the light of the development of Supervisor Theory with its emphasis on the value of an observers responses rather than their accuracy, value must be introduced as a measure. Neither classical information theory nor linear control theory is particularly well suited to the task, although optimal control theory may well be, within the constraints of measurement already mentioned. As yet little seems to have been done in the direction of adaptation to changes in the cost functional rather than changes in plant or operator characteristics, but development here is clearly possible. We have already seen in the way Beta changes in attention tasks that observers can control their decision criteria, and Shulman and Fisher (1972) have also shown that they are sensitive to payoff. Indeed in experimental psychology the main reason for the rise of TSD at the expense of Information Theory was because of its ability to deal with subjective and objective payoff to the observer in addition to the statistical characteristics of the sources.

Even the implications of TSD have, however not been fully explored in relation to other measures of skills such as information theory. For example, it is intuitively obvious that if a

target is more detectable, that is, d' increases, the proportion
of available information transmitted will rise. However in some
of our experiments we found data where the opposite occurred:
rises in d' were associated with falling information transmission.
A little thought reveals that this is not unreasonable. Figure
11 shows the input output matrix for an experiment with two inputs
and two outputs. The cell entries are the number of each kind of
response that occurred to each kind of stimulus. We can obviously
analyse such an experiment in terms of information theory, in
which case we shall be dealing with terms such as

$$H_{in} = -(N_{aA}+N_{b}A)N_{tot})\log_2(N_{a}A+N_{bA})N_{tot})+....$$

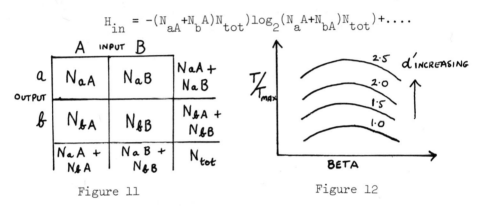

Figure 11   Figure 12

But equally we could identify a/A as a hit, a/B as a false alarm,
and so on. Then we can use TSD to provide estimates of d' and
Beta, and we have

$$p_{hit} = N_{aA}/N_{aA}+N_{bA}), \quad p_{false\ alarm} = N_{aB}/(N_{aB}+N_{bB})$$

The two sets of statistics are obviously transforms of each other,
a fact that can "readily be shown". If we then plot the proportion of available information transmitted as a function of Beta,
with d' as parameter, we obtain a family of convex upward curves,
symmetrical about Beta = 1.0 if P_A = P_B = 0.5, and skewed otherwise, (Figure 12).

      Suppose now that an observer is actually transmitting
the highest possible proportion of available information given the
discriminability of the signals. That is, he has chosen the optimal value of Beta and is at the top of the d' curve. We now
increase the strength of the signal. If he responds to the change
in the quality of the signal by becoming either more risky or more
conservative he will slide down the new isosensitivity curve, and
if he were to shift his criterion by a considerable amount he
would end below his previous level of T/T_{max}. Any changes in
subjective value of subjective expectancy may be expected to cause
such shifts.

Such considerations again emphasise the importance of Sheridan's approach. And since sampling periodicities and durations are likely to alter the value of d' indirectly if they result in degraded signals being received, we once more see the way in which information, values, and models are intimately tied together in determining the strategies of behaviours available to the observer and the uses to which he puts them.

Some thoughts on machine-aided performance

If the emphasis made here on the importance of internal statistical models is correct, then it has certain implications for the way in which training and man-machine systems may develop. It should not be overlooked that while the treatment here has been in terms of time statistics, it may also be true that spatial models are used in the same way. Some of the properties of eye-movements when static arrays are examined may be explicable in terms of spatial expectancy, spatial frequency, and the interaction of purely statistical properties of the display with subjective values. For example eye movements might be determined by factors such as spatial frequency distributions until the observer had gathered enough information to realise that he was looking at a face, and thereafter by the fact that eyes and mouths are more interesting and attractive than ears. The concepts of models should be thought of as very general. On the other hand there is no reason why the concept should not be developed rigorously.

Consider the problem of training for a skill. It is likely that most training scheduels aim to reduce error at all stages of training, and certainly the emphasis from Learning Theory of the last few years has concentrated on the idea that it is better to prevent errors than eliminate them. But such a training schedule has severe limitations where the task is stochastic and may produce rare emergency stiuations. Unless some sort of training for emergencies and indeed catastrophic situations is given, the operator may remain highly skilled for normal situations but unable to deal with situations where the exact form of response has not been practised. On the other hand, it may well be that by tolerating, or indeed encouraging errors of certain kinds (which will be task specific in many cases) a more powerful and general model will be developed which will be of much greater use to the operator in the long run.

Again, as Kelley (1968) and others have pointed out, there are many tasks which may inherently be beyond the capacities of the unaided human operator. Third order control tasks are either on the borderline or actually over it, for example. It is customary to use machine aided systems in such situations, and there is ample evidence that predictive displays, etc., can make the task of the human operator easier. But it should not be for-

gotten that part of the model which will develop will include the
subjective payoffs associated with the operator's relation to the
machine, and might include a positive worth to let error build up
to see how the system responds if it is too efficient.

A different level of modelling which would probably repay
investigation is related to adaptive control and what Crossman has
called "metabandwidth", namely the rate at which the human operator can change his parameters as the task demands change. In our
terminology this corresponds to the rate at which one model can be
substituted for another. There seems to have been relatively
little research into training for change rather than for steady
state performance.

Specifically with regard to supervisory control a major
problem would seem to be how to help an operator to set up a good
model of distributions consisting of rare or very rare events. In
many cases the length of time it will take to establish the parameters of signal distributions will be prohibitively long, and
the fallibility of human memory and the inaccuracy of time estimation may add to the difficulty. Perhaps by running an adaptive
model of the human operator in parallel with him along the lines
of the closed loop vigilance experiment described earlier it would
be possible for the model not merely to match his behaviour but to
discover the statistical properties of his periods of reduced vigilance, and to compensate for them.

The use of fast time computer models for aiding humans
is clearly of great potential. For example it should be possible
to use adaptive modelling not merely to match the properties of
the human operator, but to predict from such a model run in fast
time the moments when he was about to make errors. One can imagine a training situation where the system knows the future history
of the forcing function, but the man does not. Using its fast
time representation of the human operator the system predicts an
error and alters the nature of the display in time to force the
human operator's response into a more correct mode, for example
by increasing the gain momentarily and so making the rate of
change more obvious. Again, if human operators must be trained
on the job rather than using simulators, it should be possible to
make a similar use of a model to predict when error is likely to
occur, but to hand over the control of the plant to the model
while the trainee operator makes his response, thereafter handing
it back.

Such ideas are speculative, although we are at present
beginning to investigate some of them. In the meantime, it seems
that there are good reasons to regard the field of human skill,
vigilance, and attention as more closely related than has been
thought. In the meantime, as Keats might have said but in fact

did not,

> "Attention is skill, skill attention: this
> Is all we know and all we need to know."

Baker, C. 1963. Further towards a theory of vigilance. in Vigilance; a symposium. eds. Buckner, D & McGrath, J. 127-153.

Broadbent, D.E. 1958. Perception and Communication Pergamon.
London.

Broadbent, D.E. 1971. Decision and Stress. Academic Press.
London & N.Y.

Buckner, D. & McGrath, J. eds. 1963. Vigilance: a symposium.
McGraw Hill. N.Y.

Carbonell, J. 1966. A queuing model of many-instrument visual
sampling. IEEE Trans. Human Factors in Eelctronics. HFE-7,
No.4.

Craik, K.J.W. 1943. The Nature of Explanation. Cambridge University Press.

Crossman, E. 1959. A Theory of the acquisition of speed skill.
Ergonomics, 2, 153-166.

Crossman, E., Cooke, J., & Beishon, R. 1964. Visual attention and
the sampling of displayed information in process control.
HFT-64-11(T) Dept. of Industrial Engineering, Univ. of California, Berkeley.

Deutsch, J.A., & Deutsch, D. 1963. Attention: some theoretical
considerations. Psychological Review, 70, 80-90.

Fisher, S. 1972. A 'distraction' effect of noise bursts. Perception, 1, 223-236.

Hamilton, P. 1967. Selective attention in multisource monitoring
tasks. Ph.D. Thesis, University of Dundee.

Herman, L. 1965. Study of the single channel hypothesis and input
regulation within a continuous simultaneous task situation.
Quarterly Journal of experimental Psychology, 17, 37 - 46.

Jerison, H. 1970. Vigilance, Discrimination, and Attention. in
    Attention: Contemporary Theory and Analysis. Mostofsky, D.
    (ed.) 127 - 148. Appleton Century.

Kelley, C. 1968. Manual and automatic control. Wiley. N.Y.

Kristofferson, A. 1965. Attention in time discrimination and
    reaction times. NASA report No. CR-194.

Mackworth, J. 1970. Vigilance and Attention. Penguin. London.

McRuer, D. & Krendel, E. 1974. Mathematical models of Human
    Pilot Behaviour. Agardograph No. 188.

Moray, N. 1967. Where is capacity limited? A survey and a model
    Acta Psychologica, 27, 84-92.

Moray, N. 1969. Attention: selective processes in vision and
    hearing. Hutchinson. London.

Moray, N. & O'Brien, T. 1967. Signal detection theory applied to
    selective listening. Journal of the Acoustical Society of
    America, 42, 765-772.

Moray, N., Fitter, M., Ostry, D., Favreau, D., & Nagy, V. 1976.
    Attention to pure tones. In press. Quarterly Journal of
    experimental Psychology.

Ostry, D., Moray, N., & Marks, G. 1976. Attention, Practice, and
    Semantic Targets. In Press. Journal of Experimental Psychol-
ogy.

Peterson, C., & Beach, L. 1964. Man as an intuitive statistician.
    Psychological Bulletin, 68, 29 - 46.

Senders, J. 1964. The human operator as a monitor and controller
    of multi-degree-of-freedom systems. IEEE Human Factors i Elec-
    tronics, HFE-7, 103-106.

Shannon, C., & Weaver, W. 1949. The mathematical theory of comm-
    unication. Urbana. University of Illinois Press.

Sheridan, T. 1970. On how often the Supervisor should sample.
    IEEE Transactions on Systems Science and Cybernetics. SCC-6,
    140-145.

Sheridan, T. & Ferrell, R. 1974. Man-Machine Systems, M.I.T.
    Press.

Shulman, H. & Fisher, R. 1972. Expected value as a determinant of attention. Journal of Experimental Psychology, 93, 343-348.

Swets, J. & Kristofferson, A. 1970. Attention. Annual Review of Psychology, 21, 339-366.

Treisman, A. 1960. Contextual Cues in selective Listening. Quarterly Journal of experimental Psychology, 12, 242-248.

Treisman, A. 1969. Strategies and models of attention. Psychological Review, 76, 282-299.

Treisman, A. & Geffen, G. 1967. Selective attention: perception or response? Quarterly Journal of experimental Psychology, 19, 1-18.

Welford, A. 1968. Fundamentals of Skill. Methuen, London.

Young, L. 1969. On adaptive Manual Control. IEEE Trans. Man-machine Systems, MMS-10, 292-332.

DISCUSSION

LINN:

You have said that, the better the internal model is, the less the human operator has to respond to stimuli. But what about when the human operator has to stabilize an unstable plant, e.g., standing upright, especially on a moving platform (ship) ? In this case he must continuously respond ?

MORAY:

With an unstable system, frequent responses are indeed required. But any process – even random – is at least partly predictable over a short period, provided the disturbance or the process is of limited bandwidth, as it will be in almost all cases. My claim is that while trying to exercise control the human operator will – consciously or unconsciously – attempt to acquire a model of the process so as to perform predictively, estimate the optimal sampling interval, and allocate attention and control appropriately. Successful prediction minimizes workload.

PACK :

In a process control plant, system monitoring may cover many sub-systems. Suppose a particular subsystem can be either in condition A or in condition B. If an indicator shows neither A nor B, the supervisor probably will recognize the abnormality immediately. However, if it should read B and does read A, the supervisor may not notice the problem because the indicator complies with the model for condition A. Is it likely the supervisor carries several models for the subsystem at the same time ?

MORAY :

Yes, I believe an experienced operator will have models of all subsystems to which he has been exposed, providing their statistics are the kind and order which humans can model. Probably some subsystems are hierarchical. Hence, if a superordinate model suggests that at a lower level there is not likely to be a change, it may not be sampled. Note also that for a well-developed model, which is successful as a real time predictor, a sample may show the process to be normal and suggest that the next sample need not be taken for M seconds. If it goes ab-normal within M, the change may not be noticed. Paradoxically, a highly skilled operator may find it very difficult to detect abnormalities in a highly predictable process if his model defines long inter-sample intervals.

A QUEUEING MODEL OF MONITORING AND SUPERVISORY BEHAVIOUR

J.W. Senders and M.J.M. Posner

Industrial Engineering, University of Toronto
Toronto, Ontario, Canada M5S 1A4

I. INTRODUCTION

In many modern industrial processes the human beings involved
have been removed from direct control and placed in a supervisory
or monitoring position. Typically, a complex continuous process
is represented to the supervisor by some large number of displays
of information relating to the state of the plant. The information
may be displayed in a large number of different forms. There may
be displays of the point values at each moment in time. There may
be displays of recent past history as well as current values. In
still others there may be remote historical data which serve as a
base against which to judge the significance of current and immediately past values of the variables.

The design of work places for such supervisory activity must
be based on a number of factors. Economic and physical space
limitations obviously influence design. In addition there is a
necessary logic which relates the characteristics of the displayed
variables to the characteristics of the human supervisor. Thus
'Human Factors Engineering' usually concerns itself with the design
of individual displays and, in general, there is a sufficient understanding of the design of satisfactory information displays and of
the logical organization of large numbers of displays to make clear,
even to an only moderately skilled monitor, the displayed data and
the functions of the displays.

Two different but related problems which remain are: the calculating of the manning requirements, and the calculating of the

245

reliability of the man-machine interaction. One would prefer to
solve these before a plant is built, and surely before it is set
into operation.

I.a Manning Requirements

Any valid way of estimating manning requirements would make
possible more precise estimates of operating costs. It would
facilitate estimates of the effort likely to be involved in re-
cruiting, selecting, training, and evaluating operators, and thus
the cost of maintaining a sufficient cadre of trained operators to
keep a plant operating continuously.

I.b Man-machine Reliability

In general, the reliability of complex systems is calculable
with fairly standard analytical techniques. However, when human
beings are introduced into systems, it has usually been more difficult to estimate the probability of failure of those parts of
the system in which the human operator plays a significant role.
It is intuitively clear that reliability goes down when the load
on a human operator goes up, at least when the load is already
high. Hence, the relation between the two problems.

2. THE BEHAVIORAL MODEL

Most monitoring tasks can be described quite simply as situations in which the human monitor observes one indicator at a
time and progressively looks at, or attends to, the various instruments and indicators on which information is displayed.

In addition, of course, there are emergency indicators which
are not continuous functions of plant state, but artificially
dichotomized functions, such that when   certain continuous variables approach critical boundaries, an emergency or alerting signal might be triggered. Our concern here, however, will be only
for steady-state, normal operating conditions in which emergency
signals do not arise.

One way of conceiving the operator's task is to imagine that
each supervisory monitor consists of a 'service channel.' That is
to say, various instruments 'come,' one at a time, to be served,
much as customers approach the teller in the bank or the check-out
counter in the supermarket. Thus, it would seem appropriate to
consider the queueing characteristics of instruments. Since instruments do not in fact 'arrive' at the visual system for service in
the form of an observation but are serially fixated by the monitor,

it is necessary to construct a behavioral model for estimating both the inter-observation intervals and the durations of the observations for any instruments.

Instruments are designed predominantly for foveal viewing. In general, it is difficult, if not impossible, to get information from them if they are not directly fixated. It can rarely be the case, therefore, that an event which happens on a particular instrument elicits the response of the monitor toward that instrument. Instead, internal events in the monitor must be responsible.

2.a   Uncertainty Model

One model for such internal events is that of observer uncertainty about the nature of the data presented on the instrument. In one formulation, when the uncertainty rises above some maximum permissible uncertainty, the probability of fixation of that instrument becomes high. In a situation in which 'overload' did not exist, one would imagine that the instrument about which the operator was most uncertain would generally be fixated next. If the rates of growth of uncertainty of the instruments are widely different, a somewhat more complex algorithm can be postulated involving some weighted summation of uncertainty and rate of change of uncertainty. The latter is brought in because an observer's algorithm for choice of next point of regard may include calculation of the uncertainty of distribution one fixation hence.

The uncertainty that an observer has about a system variable depends upon two things which are related to the time since its last viewing. One of these, which is the same for all signals, is the decay of information stored in short-term memory. The second kind of uncertainty stems from variations in the system being monitored. Both the memory decay and possible plant variation generate monotonically increasing uncertainty about each variable from the moment of past observation. These two kinds of uncertainty, both increasing with time, and presumed to be linearly additive, will eventually exceed a threshold of permissible uncertainty, and elicit a fixation upon the instrument about which uncertainty is maximum or for which some weighted sum of uncertainty and uncertainty rate is maximum.

Each instrument, then, will be observed at some interval drawn from a distribution of intervals unique to that instrument, or, if there are sets of identical instruments, that class of instrument.

2.b   Probability Model

The probability model is that which was described in Senders et al (1). The task of the observer is defined as that of detect-

ing values of any of the signals which exceed arbitrary limits.
The limits are assumed to be characteristic of the individual
variables being monitored. The model calculates the interval between observations as a function of two alternative strategies on
the part of the monitor. In one strategy, the observer samples
when the probability that the signal exceeds the limit is a maximum; in the other, he samples when the probability itself exceeds
some threshold probability. These different goals yield different
values of interval between samples. In addition, the interval is
itself a variable since it depends on the value of the signal last
observed as well as upon the bandwidth and memory of the monitor.

2.c General Comment

The earlier work did not include the effect of forgetting in its
solution but that omission is easily overcome. The critical point
is that the two models briefly described here: uncertainty-based
sampling, and probability-based sampling yield widely differing
values of the interobservation interval. Consider the case where
the observed value of a signal is very near the limiting value. The
probability model predicts a next observation almost immediately
after the preceding one since the probability that the signal will
exceed the limit is very great. The uncertainty about the value
of the signal is still, however, at a very low value, and the uncertainty model would predict a sample at a much later time quite
independently of the value previously observed.

3. THE SAMPLING MODELS

In all cases the calculations of the intervals between samples
is a function of the bandwidth of the signals. If forgetting were
assumed absent, the mean intervals would be in strict proportion
to the bandwidths, although the actual values would vary with the
model. The uncertainty model, if the maximum permissible uncertainty is the same for all signals as assumed, yields fixed intervals. The probability model yields distributions of intervals.
Since the queueing model which follows requires only the mean intervals between observations, we will not here consider the distribution
functions.

3.a The Uncertainty Model

The externally generated uncertainty (on the observer's part)
about the value of a signal is the information generated by that
signal during the period of non-observation. For bandlimited
Gaussian signals, the information rate, and therefore the un-

certainty growth rate is:

$$\dot{U}_s = 2W \log_2 \sigma \sqrt{2\pi e} \text{ bits per second,} \tag{1}$$

where W is the bandwidth in Hz and σ is the average power of the signal. This rises to a maximum of:

$$U_{max} = \log_2 \sigma \sqrt{2\pi e} \text{ bits,} \tag{2}$$

which is the information of a Gaussian distribution after $\frac{1}{2}$ W seconds, the Nyquist interval.

Added to this is uncertainty generated by the forgetting process. If one assumes that the original perception is correct, i.e., within some acceptable limits of error, and that the memory trace becomes contaminated with Gaussian error with the passage of time, then the uncertainty will be:

$$U_f(t) = \log_2 \sigma \sqrt{2\pi e} \; (1-e^{-.1t}) \text{ bits} \tag{3}$$

assuming a time constant of forgetting of .1 second. The total uncertainty $U_t(t)$ will therefore be:

$$U_t(t) = U_s(t) + U_f(t) = 2Wt \log_2 \sigma \sqrt{2\pi e} + \log_2 \sigma \sqrt{2\pi e} \; (1-e^{-.1t}) \tag{4}$$

The maximum value of the sum will still be the value of equation U_{max}. The observer will sample when the sum reaches some threshold amount U_p. If there were no forgetting of the previously read value of the signal, then the durations for the various signals would be in strict proportion to their bandwidth. What actually happens is that very slowly varying signals will be sampled more often than on the basis of bandwidth alone. See figures 1 and 2.

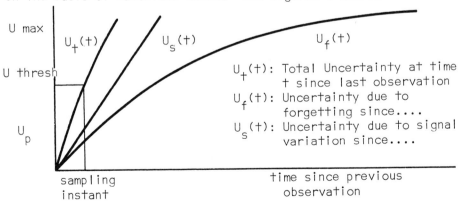

U max

$U_t(t)$ $U_s(t)$ $U_f(t)$

U thresh

$U_t(t)$: Total Uncertainty at time
            t since last observation
$U_f(t)$: Uncertainty due to
            forgetting since....
$U_s(t)$: Uncertainty due to signal
            variation since....

U_p

sampling
instant

time since previous
observation

Figure 1

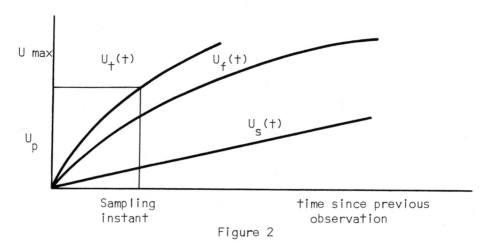

Figure 2

3.b The Probability Model

The analysis shown in reference I yields the following results.

Since the sample interval is a function of bandwidth, the solutions have been expressed in terms of the value of the autocorrelation function. For any bandwidth, these can be converted back into time.

For the case where the observer samples when the probability of exceeding the limit is maximum, the mean value is:

$$\frac{1}{r_m} = \frac{\sigma}{L\sqrt{2\pi}} \left(1 - e^{-\frac{L^2}{2\sigma^2}} \right) + \frac{1}{2}\left[1 - \phi\left(\frac{L}{\sigma}\right) \right] \tag{5}$$

where ϕ is the normal probability integral, L is the arbitrary limit and σ^2 is the variance of the amplitude density distribution of the signal.

For the case where the observer samples when the probability of exceeding the limit itself exceeds some probability threshold, the mean value is:

$$\frac{1}{r_+} = \int_0^L r_T\ r(Y)\ dY + \frac{1}{2}\left[1 - \phi\left(\frac{L}{\sigma}\right) \right] \tag{6}$$

To the results of both of these for any specified function of a given bandwidth limit value, and variance, must be added the same forgetting term used earlier. However, the value of the forgetting' variance would be added to the variance resulting from the diminishing value of the autocorrelation function with increasing time since previous observation.

4. THE QUEUEING MODEL

Posner and Bernholtz (2) have considered a broad class of closed queueing networks in which customers possessing different characteristics circulate among a number of service stations. A particular subclass of those models studied appears applicable in the present context. Specifically, assume that the system being considered consists of m different instruments which arrive for service (for observation by a single human monitor) on a first-come-first-served basis (see Figure 3). That is, when an instrument requires observation, (because its value may be at the threshold) it may be viewed as moving into a queue to await attention by the observer. The service or attention time requirement for instrument type j (j = 1,2,...,m) is assumed to be an exponentially distributed random variable G_j with mean $1/\mu_j$. After completion of service, instrument j (indicated by I_j) undergoes a random delay having mean U_j before it is again ready to be observed, and enters the queue. Note that in practice only the mean delay to readiness is required for this model, the results being independent of the shape of the delay distribution.

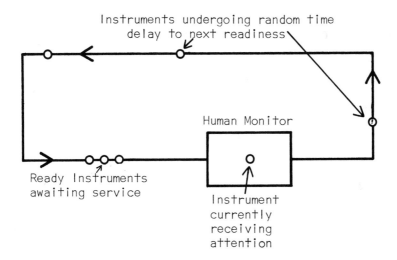

Figure 3

It is assumed throughout that the process has been ongoing for a considerable time so that steady state conditons prevail, and all limiting distributions to be defined exist.

Let $P(i_1, i_2, \ldots, i_m)$ be the joint stationary probability that i_j instruments of type j ($j=1,2,\ldots,m$) are under observation or awaiting attention by the human monitor. Since instruments are presumed to possess distinct characteristics, $i_j = 0$ or 1 for $j=1,2,\ldots m$. Thus, a suitable particularized form of model solution taken from Posner and Bernholtz yields

$$P(i_1, \ldots, i_m) = K(i_1 + i_2 + \ldots + i_m)! \; \rho_1^{i_1} \rho_2^{i_2} \ldots \rho_m^{i_m} \quad (7)$$

where the normalizing constant K is obtained by summing $P(i_1, \ldots, i_m)$ over all possible combinations of $i_1, \ldots, i_m$ satisfying $0 \leq i_1 + i_2 + \ldots + i_m \leq m$, and where

$$\rho_j = (\mu_j U_j)^{-1}, \quad j = 1,2,\ldots,m$$

is the ratio of mean attention time to mean interdemand time for i_j.

For $i_1 + i_2 + \ldots + i_m = n \leq m$, let P_n denote the stationary probability that n instruments are under observation or awaiting attention. Hence P_n is obtained as the summation of the $P(i_1, \ldots, i_m)$ over all possible values of $i_1, \ldots, i_m$ such that $i_1 + i_2 + \ldots + i_m = n$. Carrying out this summation operation on (7) yields

$$P_n = K n! \; S_{m,n} \quad (8)$$

where $S_{m,n}$ is generated using the following recursive procedure. If

$$S_{r,j} = \Sigma \ldots \ldots \ldots \ldots \ldots \Sigma \; \rho_1^{i_1} \rho_2^{i_2} \ldots \rho_r^{i_r}, \quad 1 \leq j \leq r \leq m$$
$$i_1 + i_2 + \ldots + i_r = j$$

then in general

$$S_{r,j} = S_{r-1,j} + \rho_r S_{r-1, j-1} \quad (9)$$

with

$$S_{r,o} = 1 \qquad , r = 1,2,\ldots,m$$

$$S_{r,1} = \sum_{n=1}^{r} \rho_n, \quad r = 1,2,\ldots,m$$

Furthermore, since $P_o + P_1 + \ldots + P_m = 1$, the normalizing constant K is determined from (8) as

$$K^{-1} = \sum_{j=o}^{m} j! \, S_{m,j}$$

so that a closed form solution for P_n is

$$P_n = \frac{n! \, S_{m,n}}{\displaystyle\sum_{j=o}^{m} j! \, S_{m,j}} \quad , n = o,1,\ldots,m \tag{10}$$

Thus, $P_o = K$ is the proportion of time the observer is idle, and

$$P_o + P_1 = K(1+\rho_1+\ldots+\rho_m)$$

is the proportion of time that no instruments are queueing to await the observer's attention.

4.a Waiting Time to Observation for I_m

Suppose we are concerned with how long a particular instrument m (say) must wait in the queue before the human monitor is prepared to make his observation on that instrument. As noted, this (random) time is important since the plant under control of the human monitor might go out of limits during this waiting period of non-observation.

Let the random variable W_m denote the (stationary) waiting time in the queue for I_m. Furthermore, let $\vec{N}_m^{(r)} = (i_1,\ldots,i_{m-1}) \equiv \vec{i}$ denote a particular subset of exactly r other instruments already in queue or in service at the moment of arrival of I_m. Thus, for example, if $i_j=o$ in this vector, then I_j is not present in the queue or in service when I_m arrives, while $i_j=I$ indicates that I_j is present when I_m arrives.

Now W_m has a mixed probability distribution with the probability of no wait given by

$$Pr\{W_m = o\} = P_o / \sum_{r=o}^{m-I} \sum_{i_1+i_2+\ldots+i_{m-I}=r} \ldots\ldots\ldots\ldots\ldots\Sigma\, P(i_1,i_2,\ldots,i_{m-I},o) \tag{11}$$

and the density function associated with positive wait denoted by $f_{W_m}(\cdot)$ and distribution function given by $F_{W_m}(\cdot)$. Therefore

$$Pr\{W_m>\tau\} = I-F_{W_m}(\tau) = \sum_{r=I}^{m-I} \sum_{\vec{i}=(i_1\ldots\ldots i_{m-I})} \ldots\ldots\ldots\ldots\Sigma\, Pr\{W_m>\tau\,|\vec{N}_m^{(r)}=\vec{i}\}.$$

$$\cdot Pr\{\vec{N}_m^{(r)}=\vec{i}\} \tag{12}$$

where the multiple summation is carried out over all elements of $\vec{i}$ satisfying $i_1 + i_2 +\ldots+i_{m-I}=r$.

Now, since $Pr\{\vec{N}_m^{(r)}=\vec{i}\}$ is the conditional probability of a specific subset $\vec{i}$ of size r in the system at the moment of arrival of I_m we can therefore write

$$Pr\{\vec{N}_m^{(r)}= \vec{i}\} = P(i_1,i_2,\ldots,i_{m-I},o)/$$

$$\sum_{k=o}^{m-I} \sum_{j_1+\ldots+j_{m-I}=k} \ldots\ldots\ldots\ldots\Sigma\, P(j_1,\ldots j_{m-I},o) \tag{13}$$

where $j_\gamma = o$ or I for $\gamma = I,2,\ldots,m-I$. From equation (7) and (8) we then have

$$Pr\{\vec{N}_m^{(r)}= \vec{i}\} = r!\,\rho_1^{i_1}\ldots\rho_{m-I}^{i_{m-I}} / \sum_{n=o}^{m-I} n!\, S_{m-I,n} \tag{14}$$

Denote the service time of I_k $(k=1,2,\ldots,m-1)$ by

$$G^k_{i_k} = \begin{cases} G_k & ,i_k=1 \\ 0 & ,i_k=0 \end{cases}$$

Then

$$Pr\{W_m > \tau \mid \vec{N}^{(r)}_m = \vec{1}\} = Pr\{G^1_{i_1} + G^2_{i_2} +\ldots G^{m-1}_{i_{m-1}} > \tau\}$$

Since, for $i_k=1$, G_k is exponentially distributed with parameter μ_k and since all service times represent mutually independent random variables, it can easily be shown that

$$Pr\{W_m > \tau \mid \vec{N}^{(r)}_m = \vec{1}\} = \sum_{\gamma=1}^{m-1} \delta_{i_\gamma,1} \prod_{\substack{k=1 \\ k\neq\gamma}}^{m-1} \left(\frac{\mu_k}{\mu_k-\mu_\gamma}\right)^{i_k} e^{-\mu_\gamma \tau} \quad (15)$$

where $\delta_{i_\gamma,1}=1$ if $i_\gamma=1$ and is o otherwise. Combining (14) and (15) into (12) yields

$$Pr\{W_m>\tau\} = \sum_{r=1}^{m-1} r! \sum_{i_1+\ldots+i_{m-1}=r} \cdots \sum \sum_{\gamma=1}^{m-1} \delta_{i_\gamma,1}\, \rho_\gamma \cdot$$

$$\cdot \prod_{\substack{k=1 \\ k\neq\gamma}}^{m-1} \left(\frac{\mu_k \rho_k}{\mu_k -\mu_k}\right)^{i_k} e^{-\mu_\gamma \tau} / \sum_{n=0}^{m-1} n!\, S_{m-1,n}$$

$$= \sum_{r=1}^{m-1} \sum_{r=1}^{m-1} \vec{T}^\gamma_{r,m-1}\, e^{-\mu_\gamma \tau} \quad\quad (16)$$

where

$$\vec{T}^\gamma_{r,m-1} = r!\, \rho_\gamma\, \vec{T}^\gamma_{r-1,m-1} / \sum_{r=0}^{m-1} n!\, S_{m-1,n}$$

$$\vec{T}^\gamma_{r-1,m-1} = \sum_{i_1+i_2+\ldots+i_{m-1}=r} \cdots \sum \delta_{i_\gamma,1} \prod_{\substack{k=1 \\ k\neq\gamma}}^{m-1} \phi_{k,\gamma}^{i_k}$$

$$= \sum_{i_1+\ldots+i_{\gamma-1}+i_{\gamma+1}+\ldots+i_{m-1}=r-1} \cdots \sum \prod_{\substack{k=1 \\ k\neq\gamma}}^{m-1} \phi_{k,\gamma}^{i_k} \quad (17)$$

$$\phi_{k,\gamma} = [(\mu_k-\mu_\gamma)\, U_k]^{-1}$$

Thus, the form of (16) reveals that the waiting time for I_m has a mixed exponential form involving the service parameters μ_γ ($\gamma = 1, 2, \ldots, m-1$) of all other instruments. The mean and variance of its waiting time to observation are therefore given by

$$E\,(W_m) = \sum_{r=1}^{m-1} \sum_{\gamma=1}^{m-1} \bar{T}^\gamma_{r,m-1} \,/\, \mu_\gamma$$

$$V\,(W_m) = \sum_{r=1}^{m-1} \sum_{\gamma=1}^{m-1} \bar{T}^\gamma_{r,m-1} \,/\, \mu_\gamma^2$$

In order to obtain analogous expressions for any other particular instruments, the method of this section is merely repeated using another instrument in the assumed m^{th} position. The mathematical formulations are symmetric in form so that implementation of these calculations is easily realized. In particular, to assist in creating similar constructs the formula for $\bar{T}^\gamma_{r-1,m-1}$ in (17) may be obtained in a simplified recursive manner. By successive partitioning of the multiple summation and product form, it can be shown in general that

$$\bar{T}^\gamma_{j,n} = \bar{T}^\gamma_{j,n-1} + \phi_{n,\gamma}\,\bar{T}^\gamma_{j-1,n-1}, \quad 1 \leq j \leq n \leq m-1, \; \gamma = 1, 2, \ldots, m-1$$

with

(1) $\quad \bar{T}^\gamma_{j,\gamma} = \bar{T}^\gamma_{j,\gamma-1}$

(2) $\quad \bar{T}^\gamma_{j,j} = \prod_{k=1}^{j} \phi_{k,\gamma}, \quad j = 1, 2, \ldots, \gamma-1$

(3) $\quad \bar{T}^\gamma_{j,j+1} = \prod_{\substack{k=1 \\ k \neq \gamma}}^{j+1} \phi_{k,\gamma}, \quad j = \gamma, \gamma+1, \ldots, m-2$

(4) $\quad \bar{T}^\gamma_{o,n} = 1$

4.b Probability of Plant Failure

Suppose that historical plant statistics indicate that the time τ_m required for instrument m to go out of limits measured from the time it is ready to be observed, is a random variable having some distribution function $F_{\tau_m}(\tau)$. Then the probability P^m_f that

I_m will go out of limits during a wait for observation is given by

$$P_f^m = \int_{\tau=0}^{\infty} Pr\{W_m > \tau\}\, dF_{\tau_m}(\tau)$$

$$= \sum_{r=1}^{m-1} \sum_{\gamma=1}^{m-1} \overline{T}_{r,m-1}^{\gamma} \int_{\tau=0}^{\infty} e^{-\mu_\gamma \tau}\, dF_{\tau_m}(\tau)$$

$$= \sum_{r=1}^{m-1} \sum_{\gamma=1}^{m-1} \overline{T}_{r,m-1}^{\gamma} \, L_m(\mu_\gamma)$$

where

$$L_m\{s\} = \int_{0}^{\infty} e^{-s\tau}\, dF_{\tau_m}(\tau)\ ,\ Re\{s\} > 0$$

is the Laplace-Stieltjes transform of the time to plant failure due to instrument m. Thus, for example if τ_m is known to be approximately normally distributed with mean α_m and variance σ_m^2, then

$$P_f^m = \sum_{r=1}^{m-1} \sum_{\gamma=1}^{m-1} \overline{T}_{r,m-1}^{\gamma} \, \exp[-\mu_\gamma \alpha_m + \tau_m^2 \mu_\gamma^2/2] \qquad (18)$$

As previously noted, analogous failure probability terms can be determined for other instruments underconsideration. Denote these by $P_f^1,\dots,P_f^{m-1}$. Since these failure probabilities are assumed to be quite small, failures due to each instrument going out of limits may be treated (approximately) independently so that a good estimate of plant failure is given by

$$P_f = \sum_{r=1}^{m} P_f^r \qquad (19)$$

4.c Number of Plant Failures in Time V

Consider a reasonably long period V. How many plant failures are anticipated during this period on the basis of assumed observer behaviour? We have determined that I_m will go out of limits during a wait for the observer with probability P_f^m. Thus, on each cycle through the observer system instrument m will go out of limits with

that probability. The mean cycle time for I_m is given by
$U_m + E(W_m) + 1/\mu_m$ so that the expected number of failures during
period V due to instrument m is

$$\frac{\mu_m \ V \ P_f^m}{1 + \mu_m U_m + \mu_m E(W_m)} \qquad (20)$$

By treating instrument failures independently, the expected total
number of plant failures is given by

$$\sum_{r=1}^{m} \frac{\mu_r \ P_f^r}{1 + \mu_r U_r + \mu_r E(W_r)} \ V \qquad (21)$$

4.d General Comment

At this point the question of how to improve the reliability
of the system in terms of reducing the expected plant failure rate
to an acceptable level can be addressed. It is clear that it would
be possible to apportion the care of instruments among several
human monitors so that each would be responsible for a specific
subset of the instrument array. From the analysis presented,
subsystem reliablity corresponding to a subset of instruments under
the care of a single operator can be evaluated, leading to a
reliability measure for the entire system with several operators
working simultaneously. An iterative procedure can then easily
be developed for allocating instruments to operators in order to
further improve the total system reliability. This allocation
procedure could continue until an acceptable performance level
is obtained, or possibly until an optimal allocation results. The
analysis serves, therefore, to provide solutions both to the problems
of reliability and to the problem of manning requirements. Further
applications of the results to questions of training, simulation,
and operator evaluation are readily seen.

5. REFERENCES

1. J.W. Senders, J.E. Elkind, M.C. Grignetti, and R.P. Smallwood,
        "An Investigation of the Visual Sampling Behavior of
        Human Observers," NASA Cr 434, (1965).

2. M. Posner and B. Bernholtz, "Closed Finite Queueing Networks with Time Lags and with Several Classes of Units," Operations Research, 5, 977-985, (1968).

THE MODEL SUPERVISOR DILEMMA

W. T. Singleton

Applied Psychology Department, University of Aston

Birmingham B4 7ET, United Kingdom

INTRODUCTION

When a computer is available to assist a human operator in controlling a complex set of hardware the computer normally takes over the more routine tasks involving data sensing, control and manipulation and simple logical choices among a range of alternative strategies while the human operator retains a longer-term planning function, an overall monitoring function, and a consultant function when unusual situations arise. In these circumstances his role is better described as a supervisor rather than an operator. (Sheridan, 1972). Models of man the supervisor are obviously going to be more complex and diffuse than those which were appropriate for the more traditional manual control operator. In psychological terminology it looks as though we will need to move from a stimulus/response model to a gestalt, field or cognitive model. Models of man the controller based on servo-theory and communication theory are stimulus-response type in that a unitary response is related to a unitary error signal, but there is one field theory characteristic in that the development of stimulus and response in time are recognised as significant. Greater complexity is now required in that at least two other parameters are needed to adequately model supervisor behaviour; one is the pattern of events in space and the other is the purpose of the activity specified perhaps at several levels. This suggests models utilising sampling and queueing theory (Carbonnel, 1966; Sheridan, 1970) and Kalman filtering (Baron et al, 1969; Kleinman et al, 1971) but before reaching for these tools it is worth pausing to consider the inevitable methodological issues which can be posed in dilemmatic form.

1.   Theoretically we feel more secure when we are able to use
a rigorous mathematical approach but, at present, the available
mathematics are tiresomely complex and yet inept as descriptors
and predictors of supervisor performance. On the other hand, to
use the flexibility of verbal methods is to invite ambiguity and
difficulties of communication.

2.   Scientifically we seem to make progress most readily by
taking measurements from simulated situations in the laboratory.
The simulation of purpose is not satisfactory. We have a choice
of studying controlled but unreal laboratory tasks or real but
uncontrolled practical situations.

3.   Operationally the behaviour of the kind of technically
advanced system under discussion must be predictable within very
rigid limits but the supreme advantage of the human operator is his
intelligence which implies variability between situations and between
individuals. Predictability can be enhanced by information
presentation and by training but each step in this direction
decreases the potentiality of the human performance. We can steer
him into behaving like a machine but he won't like it and anyway
that is not why he is there.

4.   Research studies in such a problem area must inevitably
and desirably incorporate a wide range of models and techniques
but greater variety makes for greater difficulty of communication.

The purpose of stating the extremes in this way is to highlight
the difficulties of work in this area. The solution in each case
is, of course, to avoid the extreme and use some kind of intermediate
and compromise approach but this makes great demands on the skill
and experience of the investigators.

METHODOLOGY

We are contemplating a system which has three main components:

1.   A hardware component, that is machines invariably with their
own power supplies and probably also with effectors and sensors
which interact with the physical environment.

2.   A computer component, that is one or a set of combinations
of hardware and software which collectively can accept, store,
manipulate, and sequence data and perform logical operations on it.

3.   A human component, that is a team of people who accept and
comprehend the goals of the system and who understand the functions
of the machines and the computers so that they can set them up

within a particular context, monitor and control them and their
environmental interactions and detect and remedy malfunctions.

One can analyse or design such a system from four starting
points:

1.   An engineering approach which starts from the characteristics and limitations of the machinery and then considers ways of
compensating for these by the use of computers and of people.

2.   A systems ergonomics approach which poses the problem
as one of optimal allocation of function between the three
components: man, machine and computer.

3.   A systems analysis approach which in effect (although
many of the practioners like to deny this) starts with the
characteristics of the computer.

4.   A psychological approach which starts from the
characteristics and limitations of the people and then considers
ways of compensating for these by the use of machines and computers.

In practice of course the analyst or designer always uses a
combination of these approaches, the balance being dictated by
the nature of the problem and by his own personality and training.
The weight of tradition and expertise is in favour of the
engineering approach. The raison d'etre of the engineer is
designing and making things. It is unfortunate that this has in
the past been seen as requiring professional expertise in
mathematics and the natural sciences but not in the biological
or human sciences. The 'allocation of function' method is always
used but usually intuitively rather than formally. Everybody knows
roughly what the machines, the computers and the people are best at
and this determines the primary allocation but the exact location
of the interfaces between the three is settled as a matter of detail
specific to the particular system, generalities are not of much help.
At least this seems to be the lesson of the history of the simpler
problem of man/machine allocation of function and it will be
interesting to see if it remains true with the increased complexity
of the three-way allocation problem. The systems analysis approach
has been used most extensively in systems with minimal hardware but
extensive information processing such as management.

The psychological approach would seem at least as important as
the others but there are inherent dangers because of the dilemmas
already mentioned. These all stem from the conflict between
precision and validity of analysis and description. The pursuit
of precision can lead to the serious underestimation of the
complexity of the human function.

Even within psychology the fashion over the past thirty years has been for stimulus-response descriptions of human behaviour. This invites design decisions and man-machine and man-computer interfaces which favour presenting the man with a stimulus and expecting an appropriate unique response. It can safely be predicted that any supervisor system designed on this basis will be a disaster. The whole point of man as a supervisor as opposed to an operator is that he needs to be able to make intelligent responses which in turn implies that he reacts in terms of concepts and not in terms of stimulus-response units. He needs an unrolling map on the basis of which he can check progress towards a goal rather than a stimulus. This suggests that we must start with a gestalt-type psychology. One of the many possibilities is to use the concept of human skills. This is based on the varied and changing nature of human activity and it incorporates the concept of purpose or goal. Perhaps most important of all it recognises and utilises the extent of individual differences which are treated as a source of evidence rather than of error.

This approach is still not well understood although it was developed from gestalt psychology by Lewin (1936) who thought in terms of topological and vector psychology and Tolman (1932) who, although a behaviourist, thought at the molar rather than the molecular level and acknowledged the dominance of purpose in behaviour. These German and American contributions respectively were taken up in Britain and developed as the theory of human skill by Bartlett and his associates during the 1940's (Bartlett, 1943; Davis, 1948; Welford, 1951). The approach has progressed slowly on the psychological side (Miller et al 1960; Fitts, 1964; Bruner, 1970) and has strongly influenced some approaches to technologically advanced systems (Crossman, 1960; Kelley, 1968). Nevertheless it must be accepted that most of the effort of psychologists over the past thirty years has gone into human performance studies which are fundamentally stimulus-response type rather than gestalt type. For a more detailed description of the differences see Singleton (1976).

It must be accepted also that another reason for the slow development of skill psychology is the extreme difficulty of applying these concepts. Recognising for example that skills are both hierarchical and heterarchical, that although timing is always critical time is often unimportant, that movement sequences in time and patterns in space are by no means consistent and yet there are underlying constances and so on makes intuitive sense but it really does complicate skills analysis.

SKILLS ANALYSIS

There are not, at present, and perhaps there never can be any standard procedures for carrying out the analysis of skills. There has to be a strong element of what proponents of this approach would call creativity and sensitivity but which opponents would call inconsistency and arbitrariness. As Miller (1967) puts it "no numbers or very few of them, uncertain validity measurements aside from practical usage, no objective, invariant definitions. The requirement of interpretive judgement".

Nevertheless the general role of the human operator from this gestalt and skill viewpoint can be described so that we know what to look for in a specific analysis. He is pursuing a goal which ought already to have been defined by the designers within the systems objectives. At a given time he may be concentrating on a particular case or a sub-goal which needs careful identification because it need not obviously be in direct line with the main goal. He may be avoiding an anticipated obstacle or pursuing a strategy which keeps a variety of future options open. He will be economical of his own efforts and will do nothing unnecessary except for cases where he is 'keeping his hand in' to maintain the skill or to keep up his arousal level. In the extreme case he pushes the system off-course just for the pleasure of pulling it back on again, and this must be accepted as a legitimate indeed an essential activity. He has many sources of information to do with the current state of the system and even more to do with the context in which he is operating. He can make discriminations which are not obvious between minor perturbations which will right themselves, those which need positive corrections and those which indicate possible malfunctions. His relationship with the system in the time domain is complex and indirect. His effector interaction can, if necessary, be beautifully phased with the system but his receptor and effector activities go along in parallel rather than in direct alternation and similarly his information gathering need not be directly linked to external events. In short he escapes from real time and the more skilled he is the more his attention spreads into the past and the future.

In order to avoid missing the subtleties and complexities of human behaviour we must not attempt to be too exact in describing it but reasonable precision is desirable and another aid to this end is available from consideration of the purpose of the analysis. A skills analysis is not merely an intellectual exercise, it is carried out as a step towards improving human performance as a system component and the number of avenues through which we can do this is very limited. We can change the man/machine and man/computer interfaces, we can change the selection and training methods and we can change the procedures or drills but that is all. Thus a useful anchor for the analysis is whether further analysis

or exploration of a particular facet of the skill could, in
principle, effect one or other of these three design activities
and which one.

In summary, this approach to skills analysis has two
foundations; the potentialities for improvement and the general
model of the role of the human operator in such systems. How it
works in practice is best illustrated by examples. It has already
been pointed out that in such complex systems the human component
is bound to be a team of individuals such as hardware adjusters,
programmers, monitors, operators, maintainers and so on. These
analyses concentrate on the supervisor who controls by monitoring
and intermittent adjusting and also has responsibilities for
checking system integrity.

CASE STUDIES

The Operator of Numerically Controlled Machine Tools

Contrary to some original expectations this man has turned out
to be not a deskilled machine minder but an important craftsman
with additional skills added to those developed during his
apprenticeship (Taylor, 1976). His objective is to turn out a batch
of elaborately machined parts and to be able to switch to making
another batch rapidly and economically. Unlike many systems there
is little danger to persons and also little perturbation due to
environmental changes or inconsistencies in materials. The system
is reliable once it is set up for a particular component but the
problem is to set it up. This involves a difficult skill or thinking
within a three dimensional space where there are continuous changes
with time, sometimes rather misleadingly called a four dimensional
problem. The specific problem solution is in the form of a
programme and although this may be written in the first instance
almost as geometry it has to be checked operationally. This is
done by the skilled operator who will go through the whole cycle with
cutting metal to check for example that the tools never foul the
work piece, or that physically impossible sequences of movement
have not been demanded. He will also make various checks against
the original drawings by using digital readouts from the machine or
by taking direct measures from the first piece off. At this setting-
up stage he is using the real machine as a simulator which aids his
thinking about the situation.

There is an interface problem in providing him with facilities
to modify the programme. Once the system is functioning on-line he
still may use override facilities for speeds and feeds to avoid
distortions and periods of vibration. Training is mostly by trial

and error assuming one starts with a manually skilled machine tool
operator, the trial and error crystalises into procedures of do's
and don'ts for given conditions and problems which are not easily
formalised. They involve, for instance, the critical specification
of sub-goals, obstacles, direction changes and so on. There are
new problems of allocation of function between product designers,
programmers and operators.

Distribution Station Controller

This is normally thought of for national or regional grids in
electricity and gas but similar problems arise for large oil and
water systems (with the difference that storage is easier) and they
are emerging also in frozen food distribution particularly white
fish and vegetables. Generally there is a cyclically fluctuating
demand which is roughly predictable but which must be met exactly
and economically. The system uses current data to do 'fine tuning'
within the regular major variations and copes also with malfunctions
such as the failure of particular sources or supply lines. The
computer is arranged to cope with the general plan and with sub
routines such as standard malfunctions. It may do this on-line or
it may merely advise the human operator who remains in manual control.
The supervisor writes new routines off-line and making choices
on-line. Timing can be critical but unless he is in manual control
phasing is time only rather than displacement/time matching. His
receptor activity is the characteristic supervisory roaming to
maintain an overall model of the success of the computer control.
He may have additional data about future trends which the computer
does not have, e.g. for a power distribution system the state and
forecast of the weather and the planned occurrence of a particular
national event such as a TV programme. In this mode he modifies
predictions made by the computer. By contrast he may act first and
allow the computer to complete the process after he has selected
solution space. He plays sometimes by doing manual line switching
to try alternative routes, like the machine tool operator he is
using the real system as a simulator which aids his problem solving.
There are the standard problems of adequate interfacing, training
is by experience which again crystallises into procedures on-line
and off-line which are mutually understood between supervisors but
which are difficult to formalise and sometimes even to justify.
There are problems of allocation of functions and responsibilities
between levels of operator and of handing over from one shift to
another.

Air Traffic Controller

One of his main problems is to generate orderly queues of

aircraft in and out of airports (Whitfield and Stammers, 1976).
Again there is a fluctuating demand roughly predictable but which
must be met exactly and economically. There are dramatic safety
problems. Continuity must be maintained, there are some storage
facilities for aircraft in flight and on the way to take-off
although these are severely limited in capacity and time. Economy
is a matter of minimising time delays. As in the case of the
machine tool operator there is a rapidly changing three dimensional
space situation. Handing over and taking over between shifts are
again key aspects of the skill. Effector activity is confined to
implementing choices but timing is critical and so is style of
verbal implementation which must be authoritative but polite and
reassuring. Receptor activity is roaming again to keep the dynamic
picture, continuous loading and shedding of items is required.

    We are currently in a phase where there are many proposals for
much greater participation by computers in the decision making
process. The objectives are to generate more economical continuous
solutions and also to attempt problems which have previously been
regarded as too complicated, e.g. heavy traffic landing and take-off
from two runways in parallel rather than confining take-offs to
one and landings to the other. At present computer assistance is
confined to data storage and presentation. It should not be too
difficult to move to the next phase where the computer provides
more sophisticated decision support e.g. by simulation of possible
solutions or future developments in fast time which the human
controller can use to check feasibility. A radical change in
required skills will occur if the computer eventually takes over
the on-line decision making. Extensive theorising has appeared
in the literature (Whitfield, 1975) but this is mainly of the systems
analysis kind and lacks the discipline of practical experience.
There has been little progress in what should be the parallel line
of theoretical activity above what happens to the skills of the
controllers with automation of this kind.

    Whatever the computer does the human controller will still
need to know what the situation is and what should happen.
Thus his 'picture' of the situation will need to be continuously
updated and to do this he must function at many different levels
concurrently. At the lowest level he is an information processing
device using eyes to scan instruments and hands to select data
streams but he does this in the context of rules, procedures,
flight plans, aircraft performance characteristics and so on -
his general situational knowledge. He is also monitoring his
own performance in relation to long term and short term objectives,
changing his and the computers strategy, adjusting his arousal
level and even switching objectives. The computer will presumably
aid him at different levels and participate in monitoring computer
performance and human performance as well as hardware performance.

We need new symbolic systems or languages to describe and comprehend what is required. (Miller, 1975)

CONCLUSION

These descriptions of cases are necessarily brief and superficial but nevertheless they illustrate the earlier theses. In particular gestalt models of supervisor behaviour are a better fit than stimulus-response models. There are problems of staying within limits which themselves vary with the context, there are changes of direction in a functional sense, timing is always critical. Dynamic three dimensional space modelling or picture building seems to be a key control skill, but there are also situations with many more than three-quarter dimensions which are impossible to 'picture' spatially as a whole although even here the supervisor may select two or three key parameters from which to generate a picture which he can use to make a decision. He seems to be able to operate in a figure/ground or foreground/background mode where interactions within 1-3 dimensions are considered in detail but also in the context of other dimensions. Perhaps the most difficult aspect of skill to describe is the multi-level self-monitoring. There are also some problems new to man-machine systems but classical in management, in particular interactions between individuals which involve allocation and sharing of functions and responsibilities and handing them over at points in time.

REFERENCES

BARON S. & KLEINMAN D.L. (1969) The human operator as an optimum controller and information processor. IEEE Trans. MMS-10 9-17.

BARTLETT F.C. (1943) Fatigue following highly skilled work. Proc. Roy. Soc., B 131, 248-257.

BRUNER J.S. (1970) Beyond the Information Given. Edited by J. M. Anglin. (London: George, Allen and Unwin).

CARBONNEL J.R. (1966) A queueing model of many-instrument visual sampling. IEEE Trans. HFE-7 157-164.

CROSSMAN E.R.F.W. (1960) Automation and Skill. Reproduced in Edwards E. & Lees F. B. (1974) The Human Operator in Process Control. (London: Taylor and Francis).

DAVIS D.R. (1948) Pilot Error. Air Ministry Publication AP3139A. (London: HMSO).

FITTS P.M. (1964) Perceptual-Motor Skill learning. In Melton A.W.
    (ed) Categories of Human Learning.

KELLEY C.R. (1968) Manual and Automatic Control. (New York: Wiley)

KLEINMAN D.L., BARON S. & LEVISON W.H. (1971) A control theoretic
    approach to manned-vehicle system analysis. IEEE Trans.
    AC-16 824-832.

LEWIN K. (1936) Principles of topological psychology. (New York:
    McGraw Hill)

MILLER G.A., GALANTER E. & PRIBRAM K.H. (1960) Plans and the
    Structure of Behaviour. (New York: Holt, Rinehart and Winston).

MILLER R.B. (1967) Task taxonomy: Science or Technology. In
    Singleton W.T., Fox J.G. & Whitfield D. (eds) The Human
    Operator in Complex Systems. (London: Taylor and Francis).

MILLER R.B. (1975) A break with the bondage of absolute design
    notations. IBM TR No. 2691.

SHERIDAN T.B. (1970) On how often the supervisor should sample.
    IEEE Trans. SSC-6 140-145.

SHERIDAN T.B. (1972) Supervisory control of teleoperators. In
    Bernotat R.K. & Gartner K.P. (eds) Displays and Controls.
    (Amsterdam: Swets and Zeitlinger).

SINGLETON W.T. (ed) (1976) The Study of Real Skills. (London:
    Academic Press).

TAYLOR R.G. (1976) The metal working machine tool operator. In
    Singleton W.T. (ed) The Study of Real Skills. (London:
    Academic Press).

TOLMAN E.C. (1932) Purposive behaviour in animals and men.
    (New York: Appleton-Century).

WELFORD A.T. (1951) Skill and Age. (Oxford: University Press).

WHITFIELD D. (1975) Man-computer symbiosis: a 1975 review.
    AP Report 57, Applied Psychology Department, University of
    Aston in Birmingham.

WHITFIELD D. & STAMMERS R.B. (1976) The Air-Traffic Controller. In
    Singleton W.T. (ed) The Study of Real Skills. (London:
    Academic Press).

TOWARD A GENERAL MODEL OF SUPERVISORY CONTROL

Thomas B. Sheridan

Massachusetts Institute of Technology

Cambridge, Massachusetts 02139 U.S.A.

INTRODUCTION: SUPERVISORY CONTROL

The supervisory control paradigm applies to situations where a person allocates his attention among various graphical or alphanumeric displays and intermittently communicates new programs to a computer which itself is in continuous direct control of a physical process. It applies, for example, to piloting or ground control of modern aircraft, to supervision of nuclear power plants and large chemical plants, to monitoring and reprogramming of industrial robots (see preview paper on models in this volume). Figure 1 illustrates the supervisory paradigm. The functions of each of the five elements are listed in the figure below the corresponding box.

The supervisory controller (and consequently the whole system) can be said to operate in four modes:

1. Planning

This is self-paced and "off-line" (loop A of Figure 1). It can also be done without assistance from the computer. It is done in anticipation of response to future events rather than in response to immediate control requirements. It involves consideration of:

  a) what sensors to employ and how to process and display the results
  b) what alternative response sequences will produce what changes in the process, and
  c) what the relative worth of these changes will be given the current state of the process

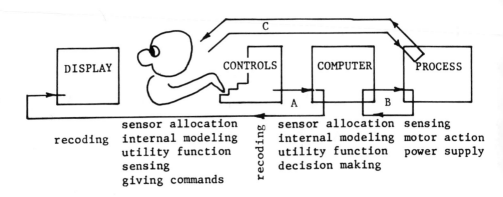

Figure 1.   Supervisory control paradigm

Table 1.   Examples of computer roles in man-supervised system

	PLAN	TEACH	MONITOR	INTERVENE
SENSING AND PRESENTING RELEVANT INFORMATION ABOUT PRESENT PROCESS STATE				
-display data to human operator in given format	✓	✓	✓	✓
-find and display data which meets given criterion	✓	✓	✓	✓
-apply given measure (extrapolation, correlation,etc)	✓		✓	
-find best sensory process to meet criterion	✓		✓	
-make diagnosis of measured symptoms			✓	✓
EVALUATING ALTERNATIVE ACTIONS				
-indicate to operator command doesn't meet criterion	✓	✓		
-determine model response to given test input	✓			✓
-determine which control is best by given criterion	✓			✓
-test whether actual response matches model response			✓	
-suggest an action to human operator	✓	✓	✓	✓
-request data from operator, process recommendation	✓	✓	✓	✓
IMPLEMENTING ACTIONS				
-request data from human, process it for action			✓	✓
-take certain action when operator gives signal			✓	✓
-take control action unless operator gives signal			✓	✓
-take control action independently of human operator			✓	✓

2. Teaching

This constitutes a commitment of the necessary and sufficient
specification of commands to the computer to make it run automatically for an interval of time, and make it stop or change to a
different program under specified conditions of its sensors. It
is also executed in loop A of Figure 1.

3. Monitoring

This consists of the supervisor allocating attention among the
displays to make sure everything is working in loop B properly, and
if not, to diagnose what might be wrong. The workload pace is forced
by the process events. The pace at times can be dull and cause in-
attention, at other times can be stressful and cause information
overload, or can change from one level to the other rapidly. It
can involve loop A only to call up displays of information which
loop B makes available to loop A through the computer.

4. Intervening

This involves interruption by the human operator of the programs which are running in loop B, and requires more or less direct
interaction between him and the process (loop C). This is done
under emergency conditions or for routine maintenance or repair.

POTENTIAL ROLES FOR COMPUTER

In each of the above supervisory modes the computer has a potential role. Obviously these can be multiple and richly varied.
Table 1 gives some examples, categorized into sensing actual process state, evaluating alternative actions, and implementing action.

Check marks indicate the most probable uses of the computer in
the four supervisory control modes. Note that both the sensing and
evaluating are represented in each of the modes. In the case of
intervening, this means the use of the computer as an off-line diagnosis tool. Actions on the process itself are not implemented in
the planning mode. In the intervention mode the actions by-pass the
computer. In the teaching mode, actions are to start programs.
In the monitoring mode actions are to stop them.

FRAMEWORK OF A MODEL: A GENERALIZED EXPECTED VALUE APPROACH

Many aspects of the human operator have been characterized
by well-defined experimental paradigms or tasks. Some of these,
such as the signal detection task, the absolute judgement task, or
the compensatory tracking task have relatively sophisticated and
well validated decision, information or control models to accompany
them.[1]

The "supervisory control task" is hardly a single task, however.

It is doubtful that any single experimental paradigm or mathematical model can encompass the whole of it. For the present it is
more likely that a variety of models will be useful to describe
and predict different aspects of supervisory control.

If any model - or "modeling framework" for trying out component
models to provoke thinking about theory and experiment - were viable, it would have to meet several tests. First it would have to
accommodate the different functions being done by either person or
machine or both, and help keep account of the trading relation.
In this sense it would have to be a model of a complete man-machine
system, not just the human operator.

Secondly, it would be convenient to have the model organized
in terms of functions which are classically separated in the literature:

   a) sensory mechanisms for acquiring information about the
       world
   b) internal cognitive mechanisms for evaluating alternative
       actions which might be taken in response to what is sensed,
       and
   c) mechanisms for implementing action.

Each of the supervisor modes (plan, teach, monitor, intervene)
embodies these functions, but in different ways.

The model, or modeling framework, proposed is a synthesis of
five assumptions which heretofore have appeared separately in various modeling efforts:

1) The human operator's (and/or computer's) purpose is to
maximize an implicit or explicit utility function.

2) The human operator (and/or computer) repetitively evaluates
"sensory measures" (ways of using his senses) in combination with
alternative "motor actions" and in light of prior expectation of
alternative state variables (of the environment or process).

3) The human operator (and/or computer) in order to estimate
the worth of having taken various actions when various changes in
the state of the process obtain, utilizes an "internal model" of
the process. This internal model predicts the new process state
resulting from any given action and initial process state. A
utility function then specifies the worth of this change in state
at the cost of that action.

4) Concurrently with such thought experiments, the human operator (and/or computer) effects control of an actual process based
upon the above steps, i.e. he employs the "best" sensory measure
based on his expectation, and implements the "best" motor action
based on what that sensory measure tells him.

5) The human operator (and/or computer) repetitively updates
his expectations concerning the process or environmental states he

is likely to encounter.

The model is represented in Figure 2, with what is human function and what is computer function left unspecified. It should be
emphasized that while the diagram as drawn may resemble a continuous control system there is nothing in the description below which
restricts it in terms of continuity, linearity or dimensionality.
It assumes only a sequence of separable time periods, t. During
each time period, u,x,y and t are constant vectors, presumably of
high enough order to represent everything that happens of interest.

Selection of a Sensory Measure

The second step above is best explained in terms of a decision tree, Figure 3. Beginning at the left, there is a decision
concerning which of a set of sensory measures to make, including
the option "none". The result of this measure is an estimation
y, of the true process state, x_i. Based upon the state of knowledge
$p_n(x_i|y_j)$ following the measurement, an appropriate action u_k must
then be taken. From this action, and depending upon the true state
of the process x_i (which cannot be known until this point) a net
value V_{ik} results, which includes both the benefit and the cost of
the action u_k itself. The purpose is to select that sensory measure which, in view of the best information available over the distribution of process states likely to occur, $p(x_i)$, and based upon
the presumably known precision of the various sensory measures
$p_n(y_i|x_i)$ as well as the cost K_n of implementation for any measure,
yields the greatest net expected value.

Referring to Figure 3, if on the first branch of the decision
tree there is no measure, the greatest expected value is

$$EV_{NM} = \max_k \left[\sum_i p(x_i) V_{ik} \right] \qquad (1)$$

If a measure yields perfect information (see second branch) the
choice of action u_k is then simply based upon the greatest V_{ij}.

$$EV_{PM} = \sum_i p(x_i) \left[\max_k V_{ik} \right] - K_n \qquad (2)$$

The difference between (1) and (2) above is the net value of the
perfect measure itself, sometimes called the value of "clairvoyance".

In the case of imperfect information $p_n(x_i|y_j)$ will be other
than zero when $i \neq j$. In this case we must take the expected value
over all $p_n(x_i|y_j)$, in place of $p(x_i)$ in Equation 1, and take the
expected value of the final result over all $p(y_j)$.

$$EV_{IM} = \sum_j p(y_j) \left\{ \max_k \left[\sum_i p_n(x_i|y_j) V_{ik} \right] \right\} - K_n \qquad (3)$$

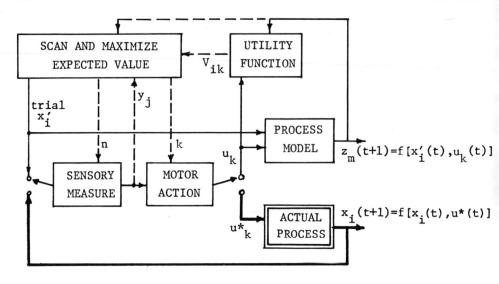

Figure 2.   Generalized expected value seeker

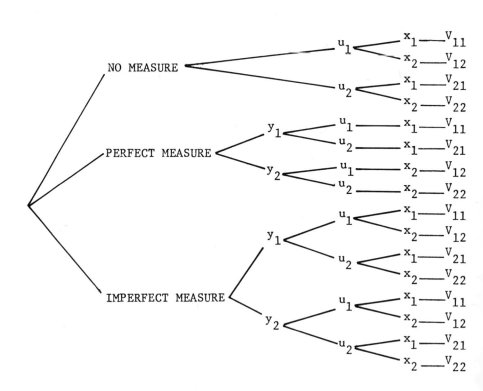

Figure 3.   Decision tree of fast-time trial computation

Using Bayes theorem

$$p(x_i|y_j) = \frac{p(y_j|x_i)\,p(x_i)}{p(y_j)} \tag{4}$$

and substituting, we have

$$EV_{IM} = \sum_j \left\{ \max_k \left[\sum_i p_{\mathbf{n}}(y_j|x_i)\,p(x_i)\,V_{ik} \right] \right\} - K_n \tag{5}$$

Finally, choosing the best measure from among the various n,

$$EV* = \max_n \left[\sum_j \left\{ \max_k \left[\sum_i p_{\mathbf{n}}(y_j|x_i)\,p(x_i)\,V_{ik} \right] \right\} - K_n \right] \tag{6}$$

The $p_{\mathbf{n}}(y_j|x_i)$ ingredient is the error (or precision) characteristic of the sensory measure. $p(x_i)$ is the a priori expectation of what might happen.

In Figure 2 the above calculation is carried out by the "scan and maximize" box on the basis of scanning through suitably wide ranges of x_i, n and u_k. The distribution $p(x_i)$ is determined from preknowledge of task requirements or from an extrapolation on y in the previous cycle (see below). Thus for each value of x_i' fed in on a trial basis a corresponding value of y_j is determined by the sensory measurement box and made available for the calculation of (6). V_{ik} is determined by other parts of the system as described in the next section.

Evaluation of Alternative Actions to Find their Utility

Equation 6 poses a need to determine V_{ik} associated with each combination of action u_k and the process state x_i'. This can be done by feeding x_i' into a simulation of the process which, run in "fast time", i.e. with time constants many times faster than the actual "real-time" process. The process vectors z at beginning and end of the interval and the control vector u for that interval then determine V_{ik}, based on a utility function which must be given.

It is important at this point to note that the determination of V_{ik} does not depend upon y_j. Further, Equation (6) does not demand knowledge of z. V_{ik} need only be referred to the prior process state x_i'.

In Figure 2, scans of k are nested in the do-loops with trial values of x_i' and n, while V_{ik} is determined and fed back to the "scan and maximize" calculation of (6). The "motor action" box in (2) must keep track of which u_k was best for each y_j, since it will use this information later as described in the next section.

Intermittent Real-Time Control of Actual Process

All of the fast-time computations described thus far utilize
the thin signal flow lines of the upper part of the diagram. Between each fast-time computation cycle the two switches are changed
to put the sensory measure box (with n fixed for now) and the motor
action box (now having a basis for outputting a different u_k for
each different y_j estimated) in a control loop with the actual process.

Updating

Prior to the next fast-time computation cycle, the recently
encountered and/or projected trend of y_j in the real-time loop is
noted and becomes the basis for the set of x_i' for the next fast-
time computation cycle. There is also the potential opportunity
to compare $\partial z/\partial u$ in the fast-time mode to $\partial y/\partial u*$ in the real time
mode for the same y_j and use the difference to refine the process
model. This is not shown in the Figure.

Comparison to Kalman-Bucy Control System

Figure 4 shows a conventional Kalman-Bucy estimator control
system.[2] It is interesting to note that this system achieves optimal
control by continuously "trimming" the process reconstruction model to
yield an accurate estimate of process state, and accordingly (continuously) adjusting control parameters to their best values. The sensor
measure C is left constant.

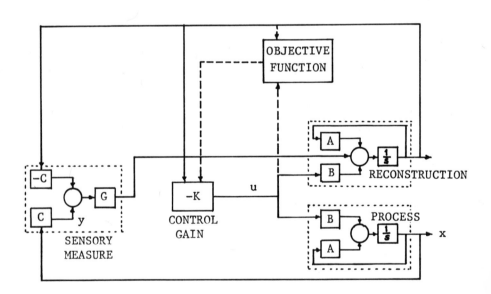

Figure 4. Kalman-Bucy control system

The comparable optimization is accomplished in Figure 2 by "trimming" the sensory measure and the control parameters on each successive iteration, leaving the process model constant. Feedback from the actual process manifests itself in Fig. 2 by determining the "trial x_i'" values for the next off-line iteration.

Preview of Queued Stimuli

x_i' and u_k are vectors characterizing any stimulus and any response. Thus, as is so characteristic of multi-task situations, it may be necessary that each x_i' be a queue or list of stimuli which need not be responded to in the same temporal order in which its components first appeared. A single u_k can be a schedule of responses to the list of stimuli, and be best executed in some other temporal order. Thus, the fast-time model would be used to evaluate various u_k sequences to compound x_i' situations. Since the computation time may get large in such cases, dynamic programming and other "short cut" algorithms have been employed to make such evaluations.

This in effect amounts to a second level of nested subroutines to exercise the process model. In relatively slow response situations the extra level of computation can be quite easy. Such a computational technique was demonstrated by the author and his colleagues in a two-level fast-time-modeling experiment in robot manipulation.[3]

USE OF THE MODEL

With part of a system embodied in hardware/software, the remainder can serve to model the remaining (human operator) portion of the system. Alternatively, the human operator can duplicate functions embodied in the computer. This model is merely a representation of functions which must be done somewhere.

If any model such as this can be made to perform significantly better than the human operator on experimental tasks then it is fair to use the model as a yardstick to measure the operator's performance. (If some other model does better than this one it should be substituted as the yardstick).

If the human operator does significantly better than the model, the model is of questionable value as a yardstick. This leads to the standard dilemma with the human operator: the very thing we seek most to understand, namely how he is more clever than the automatic machine, we probably cannot explain by reference to mechanistic models.

USE AND ABUSE OF SUPERVISORY CONTROL

As supervisory control becomes more commonplace certain undignifying human tasks will be replaced by computer operation, and supervisory operators may delight in their new power. On the other hand, the operators may suffer from isolation and remoteness from the actual work. They may find their skills degraded when called upon to take over in emergencies. While they marvel at - or become alienated by - their powerful computer-slaves, they may abandon to the computer responsibilities which they as people should retain. And they may become even more confused between mechanical productivity and human fulfillment.

The trend toward supervisory control promises to engage us in a variety of challenges.

REFERENCES

1. Sheridan, T.B. and Ferrell, W.R., Man-Machine Systems, M.I.T. Press, Cambridge, Mass., 1974.

2. Kalman, R.E., "A New Approach to Linear Filtering and Prediction Problems", JOURNAL OF BASIC ENGINEERING, Trans. ASME, Vol. 82D, 1960, pp. 33-45.

3. Hardin, P.A., Whitney, D.E. and Sheridan, T.B., "And Tree" Computer Data Structures for Supervisory Control of Manipulation : Proc. 1972 IEEE Intl. Conf. on Systems, Man and Cybernetic October 9-12, 1972, Washington, D.C., 72-CHO-6478-SMC.

DISCUSSION

RIJNSDORP :

The fourth mode of supervision you've called "intervention", i.e. switching to a lower level of automation.

However, in partially automated systems the supervisor has also the task of a master controller, which could be labelled "adjustment" or "trimming". Can the fourth mode of supervision be generalized to encompass these actions ?

SHERIDAN :

I use "intervention" to mean any act by the supervisor to change in any significant way the automatic control of the process. At the extreme this can mean stopping the process for emergency or routine repair. It can mean a complete change from automatic to manual control. It can mean a change to a "lower level" of automatic or partially manual control mode. Or, finally, it can mean adjustment or trimming of the automatic control system parameters.

THE HUMAN OPERATOR SIMULATOR - HOS

Robert J. Wherry, Jr.

U.S. Naval Air Development Center

Warminster, Pennsylvania 18974 U.S.A.

The Human Operator Simulator (HOS) digital computer program developed over the past seven years, is capable of simulating the performance of a goal-oriented, adaptive, trained human operator in a complex weapon system down to the level of hand reaches, control device manipulations, eye shifts, absorptions of visual information, and internal information processing and decision making.

The combined effects of an operator's role, the displays and controls he would be given and their layout, and the various situations with which he would be confronted are obviously complex. Existing human performance prediction techniques do not handle such complex, interactive situations in which there are hundreds of variables that could effect his performance. It is axiomatic that such complex situations must be created and exercised to find out what will really happen to the operator.

While poor design elements might be suspected intuitively by the human engineer he could not prove that such was the case without dynamic simulation; and dynamic simulation results are usually too late to greatly impact system design. The inability of prior human engineering techniques such as task analysis and timeline analysis to document in a truly objective and convincing manner, the deleterious impact of the hundreds of variables on human performance and consequently on system performance led directly to heavy reliance on "expert" opinion rather than data with a resultant feeling by others that human engineering is only "common sense" and that all one really needs to do to come up with a good operator station is to "think about the problem." Unfortunately, we have too many self-appointed experts and too few real ones.

The need to create the situation and to collect human performance data from the created situation led to the conclusion that simulated man-in-the-loop, dynamic simulation would be an acceptable substitute if human operator behavior in a complex crew station could be simulated with sufficient accuracy and detail. With the advent of high speed, digital computers, a sufficiently sophisticated model of how a human operator behaves became feasible. HOS is an attempt at such a model.

Recognizing that real human operators adapt their performance to the varying demands of a changing situation, HOS had to be designed as a goal-oriented, trained human operator rather than an "unthinking" robot. The idea of a "goal-oriented, trained human operator" implies concepts which require further definition. In the first place a trained operator knows what needs to be done. In HOS this capability is, in part, represented by the simulated human operator's long-term memory of various procedures which must be defined in detail and read into the HOS program. The use of HOPROC, an English-based Human Operator Procedures language, which was created specifically for this purpose, permits human engineers to easily describe to HOS the tasks and subtasks the operator will be performing.

Secondly, a real human operator must deliberately choose to work on one of several simultaneously on-going tasks. In HOS this capability is simulated by various "strategy algorithms" which constitute the modeling of operator "volition." They include algorithms which take into account the criticality and type of various "active" procedures, how long it has been since he worked on that procedure, whether the procedure is awaiting the completion of another procedure, etc. The determination of the changing criticality of various monitored displays is also handled by the strategy algorithms. Such algorithms also include decisions on whether the operator should continue attempting recall of an item of information or spend the necessary time to access and gather desired information from a display.

Not only is a real trained operator familiar with the various steps in a procedure but he also knows how to accomplish each step. In HOS this function is taken care of in a variety of ways. First, there is an instruction handler for each type of instruction permitted by HOPROC. Secondly, these handlers make use of more "micro" subroutines which simulate the behavior necessary to obtain estimates of items of information, to integrate two or more pieces of information together, and to enable and adjust control devices as desired. The subroutines use even more micro routines which simulate such behaviors as short-term memory recall, information absorption, decision making, and anatomy movement to bring the operator's eyes, hands, and feet into visual or physical contact with desired displays and controls.

RATIONALE FOR 'MICRO' MODELS OF HUMAN BEHAVIOR

The use of "micro" models as a basic HOS approach yields several desirable features. First, they allow the usage of single, often complex, equations to apply whenever a particular type of behavior is being simulated. This ensures that all assumptions about how that type of behavior works are logically consistent throughout the simulated run as well as from one run to the next. Secondly, the particular path through the micro models is determined while the simulated run is being conducted. Thus, for one instruction which requires an estimation of some item of information, the simulated operator may rely on recall if the short-term memory model indicates a high probability that he should be able to recall and extrapolate a good estimate. For that same instruction, at a different time in the mission, the micro models may indicate the necessity for the simulated operator to turn his head and eyes to the appropriate display and absorb the needed information. Since at different times in the mission his eyes may be fixated on different displays or controls just prior to the execution of that instruction, the time charges to accomplish needed movements of the anatomy may differ.

While some may question the necessity for such micro models it seems clear that data from models can address levels of detail only down to the level of detail within the model itself. If one believes that the layout and choice of types of displays and controls in a crew station are important then one requires detailed data on eye and hand usage and the amount of time being consumed in accessing and absorbing displayed information and for reading, grasping and manipulating various controls. The question of whether such micro models should be used cannot be settled by whether an investigator likes a micro-model approach or not; it can only be settled by whether the type of data desired demands the use of micro models or not. On the other hand, if one does not have a good (i.e., sufficiently valid) model of human behavior, then one should never claim to be simulating human behavior. Human engineering techniques, currently in vogue, which summate across time some human engineer's estimates of task times and accuracies and which utilize his "best-guess" estimates of frequency of task performance are not simulations of human performance! In the first place, there is no guarantee of a consistent model of the various important aspects of human behavior present within the technique. Such techniques may represent a more sophisticated way of using "expert" opinion, but they don't ensure the "expert" is a good estimator of human performance. Further, accretion of estimated task times assumes a similarity of how the operator will perform the task each time he performs it and/or random (i.e., unpredictable) variation around the estimated time. Neither of those assumptions are true in most complex situations and usage of them merely ensures an inadequate simulation of human performance.

Various equations appear in HOS which were derived in part
by studying actual human performance data which were reported
in the literature over the years. The functional relationships
between a variety of situational variables and the time consumed
by human operators to accomplish various human behaviors has been,
this author believes, established well enough to commence simulating human behavior with sufficient validity that HOS can be expected to produce highly useful results. Among those behaviors
which are considered to be well modeled and predicted by HOS are
arm and hand reach times, grasp and manipulation times for a
variety of control device types, head and eye movement times, information absorption times for a variety of display types, short-
term recall time and accuracy and decision making time. Among
those human behaviors which are not, as yet, modeled and predicted,
and must still be estimated are internal information integration
and extrapolation (internal mediated functions).

Since a very large majority of an operator's time is spent
in behaviors which are well modeled, HOS can be used advantageously
in human engineering crew procedures and crew station design, test
and evaluation endeavors even in its present state.

The arm reach equation is one example of a "human behavior"
equation which is used in HOS. Prior to deciding what it should
be many studies were obtained from the literature. Experimenters
whose data were studied included Fitts, Briggs, Sharp and
Topmiller. Of particular interest is that no two studies seemed
to cover the same distances reached or to be studying the
same direction of movement. Fitts' data, for example, studied
only left-to-right movements in the horizontal plane; S.J. Briggs
also studied horizontal movements, but in all directions and over
longer distances than Fitts; Sharp and Topmiller studied movements in both the horizontal and vertical planes simultaneously
and were only interested in movements which were essentially
away from the operator.

In spite of the differences in experimental procedures and
interests of the investigators, it appears that time to reach is
a fairly linear function of distance with a relatively faster
movement for distances greater than five inches. This indicates
that movements involving shoulder and elbow movements take less
time than movements involving only wrist movement, however, all
movements make at least some use of wrist movement. Further,
it appears that movement time is slowed by a constant percentage
for a given weight object being moved.

A similar approach has been used to derive other human
behavior micro model equations. While no pretense is made that
HOS contains the "ultimate" equations, it has at least made a
beginning in an appropriate direction.

HAL, HOS and HODAC

HOS is actually three computer programs as shown in Fig. 1.
The first of the three programs, the HOPROC Assembler and Loader
(HAL) accepts information written in the HOPROC language. The
type of information entered into HAL includes (1) the words which
will be used to refer to the various settings, displays, symbols,
controls, procedures, etc. (each name can be a maximum of 20 characters), (2) the operator internal processing equations (written
in FORTRAN type format but allowing the use of the above names),
(3) the various operator procedures which pertain to the operator
of interest, (4) hardware internal processing equations (used to
describe functional relationships within the hardware system
being simulated) and (5) hardware procedures (used to describe
logical relationships within the simulated hardware system).

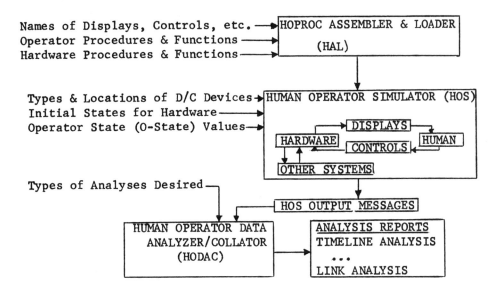

FIGURE 1. - FLOW OF INFORMATION AMONG HAL, HOS AND HODAC

The second program is the Human Operator Simulator (HOS)
which contains the various strategy algorithms and micro models
of human behavior. HOS is actually a generalized simulated human
operator and becomes a specific trained operator in a specific
system only after having been given additional inputs. These inputs include knowledge of operator procedures and internal functions (input from HAL) and the types and locations of displays and
controls (input separately to HOS) constitute the operator's
knowledge about how his system works and represent the operator's

long-term memory. HAL also inputs to HOS the compiled HOPROC
statements which permit the simulation of the operator's own hardware system as well as other systems. A final input to HOS are
the initial states of all displays, controls, equipment, etc. and
what are referred to as "O-states" which represent levels of capability of the individual operator being simulated during the next
HOS run. O-states represent individual differences and include
such things as "short-term memory capability," "willingness to
rely on memory," "reaction time," etc. The O-states permit the
testing of the importance of differences in various human attributes to system performance. For example, an individual with poor
short-term memory may spend more time absorbing information from
displays. If this does not degrade overall system performance,
then the system is relatively "insensitive" to that type of individual difference. Since the types and locations of displays and
controls are input separately to HOS, it is feasible to make separate runs using different crew station designs to determine if
system performance is sensitive to either changes in types of interface or rearrangement of these interfaces.

The outputs from HOS are in the form of coded messages which
record all events occurring. Each "message" contains the time,
the type of behavior occurring, and the display, control, function, procedure, etc. to which the behavior was directed.

The third program is the Human Operator Data Analyzer/Colla-
tor (HODAC) which decodes the output HOS messages and performs
various types of desired analyses and outputs reports. Available
analyses to date include: (1) TIME LINE ANALYSIS which provides
a listing of actions performed by the operator, by body part
(left hand, right hand, eyes, etc.) throughout the simulation;
(2) DEVICE-BY-BODY-PART which accumulates statistics on time
spent by each body part in moving to, absorbing, grasping, manipulating each symbol, display or control; DEVICE-BY-USAGE which
accumulates statistics on time spent performing a variety of
actions associated with each device; (4) DEVICE-BY-PROCEDURE which
accumulates statistics on device usage, broken down by which procedures used them; (5) PROCEDURE ANALYSIS which provides relevant
data, by procedure, on number of times and amount of time spent
performing a variety of actions; (6) LABEL ANALYSIS which describes
the number of times and amount of time spent performing various
steps within a procedure; and (7) LINK ANALYSIS which analyzes the
time spent on "interactions"between groups of devices.

These reports provide relevant data to the human engineer to
help him decide if and what changes either in procedures or
crew station design might be advantageous. Testing of suggested
changes is accomplished by subsequent runs of HOS which incorporate those changes. Thus, the crew station and operator procedures
may be improved through iterative runs of HOS.

THE HOPROC LANGUAGE

The HOPROC (Human Operator Procedures) language is an important aspect of HOS and while a complete presentation of HOPROC is beyond the scope of this paper a brief introduction to the language is appropriate for a basic understanding of how it works. The HOPROC language is used to instruct the simulator on (1) the names or titles used in statements to refer to various settings, displays, controls, mediated functions, procedures, etc., (2) the statements which form each defined operator procedure, and (3) the statements which form the hardware simulation.

It has long been recognized that even the most complex job of an operator may be broken down into tasks and subtasks which become progressively more detailed. The HOS program is also task oriented, but each task is referred to as a procedure. A basic premise within HOS is that while an operator can only work on one procedure at a time, he may be in various stages of completion of several procedures at any one time. The procedures for which he is currently responsible are all those which appear on the "active" list. The procedure which is entitled "Mission" is the highest level procedure and is assumed at the start of a HOS run to be on the active list.

A procedure is merely a series of allowable HOPROC statements which have been given a unique title through the use of a "DEFINE procedure-name" statement which introduces the procedure to the HAL program. In general, the choice of a procedure name is left to the user, however, there are three types of procedures - ENABLE, ADJUST, and SHUTDOWN - to which HAL itself assigns a title. An "ENABLE device-name" procedure is defined whenever a device must be activated before it can be used. A single ENABLE procedure may contain actions to be taken which result in the joint enabling of many different devices. One may think of the MISSION procedures requiring the accomplishment of several lower level procedures which might be entitled "PREFLIGHT-BRIEFING," "PREFLIGHT-CHECK," "START-UP," "TAXI," "TAKEOFF," etc. One may imagine the procedure named "START-UP" as requiring accomplishment of quite a few of the procedures to ENABLE various devices. Of course some device may not be enabled until a later stage in the mission but when it is finally required it will be accomplished by a procedure to "ENABLE device-named" which will place the device(s) in an active state when completed.

An "ADJUST device-named" procedure describes the process required to change a named-device to a desired value. For example, if a simulated pilot reads a display and finds that it is outside of desired limits, he invokes an ADJUST procedure which itself may require the obtaining of various information, control manipulations, etc. A device cannot be adjusted unless the device is already "active." If a given procedure, for one reason or another, should require the adjustment of some device, HOS will automatically check to ensure that the device is active. If it is not active, HOS will automatically place its ENABLE procedure on the active procedure list. This feature of HOS permits the writing of all operator procedures as if the referred-to devices are already active, and constitutes a great simplification in the writing of procedures in complex weapon systems.

A "SHUTDOWN device-named" procedure contains those actions necessary to change the status of that device to "inactive." A device which has been SHUTDOWN will have to be enabled before it can be used again.

In addition to the HOPROC statement (DEFINE) which introduces the title for a given procedure, other statements in the HOPROC language are used to indicate the sequence of actions which constitute the procedure. It is a premise of the model that all operator actions are actually composed of relatively few basic activities. One basic activity type deals with starting and stopping other procedures.

Procedural statements relating to the starting and ending of other procedures are handled in HOPROC by the following types of statements:

> ACTIVATE "P" - the procedure named "P" is added to the "active" procedure list and thus becomes one of the procedures on which the simulated operator can work

> END 'P'   - the procedure named "P" is to be removed from the "active" procedure list

> ACCOMPLISH "P"-same as "ACTIVATE 'P'", but, additionally, no further progress can be made in the current procedure as long as "P" is on the "active" list

> COMPLETE "P" - if "P" is currently on the active list, cease work on current procedure until "P" is not on the "active" list

Procedural statements relating to the monitoring of specific information are handled in HOPROC by the following types of statements:

> MONITOR "X" - the procedure for monitoring and adjusting 'X' is placed on the "active" list

> END MONITORING "X" - the procedure for monitoring and adjusting X is removed from the "active" list

Procedural statements are normally executed sequentially, and each statement can be thought of as one step in the procedure. Any statement, other than a DEFINE statement, can be given a "step-name." A "GO TO step-name" statement permits transfer of program control to another statement elsewhere in the procedure. Transfers can be either immediate (GO TO step-name NOW) or possibly delayed (GO TO step-name) if a more critical procedure is found on the active procedure list.

The "ALTER named-parameter of 'X' TO value." statement can be used for changing a variety of parameters of "X" which may be a display, control, symbol, function or procedure. Parameters of 'X' include its DESIRED VALUE, UPPER LIMIT, LOWER LIMIT, and CRITICALITY. If an ALTER statement does not contain a named parameter the HOPROC compiler assumes the statement refers to the DESIRED VALUE OF 'X'. When the "ALTER X TO value" statement is executed, the desired value of "X" is immediately changed. The simulated operator will then obtain an estimate of the current setting or value of X (through the use of the ESTIMATOR subroutines). If a discrepancy does not exist then the operator will continue with the next statement in line. If a discrepancy is believed to exist and if X is a control device and if there is no procedure to ADJUST X then the simulated operator will commence movement of its appropriate anatomy to reach, grasp, and manipulate the control device to the appropriate desired setting. If the device is not a control or if an ADJUST X procedure exists then the procedure to ADJUST X will be placed on the "active" procedure list.

Decisions are handled in HOS through the use of an "IF test condition THEN allowable-statement." The test-condition can be a phrase such as "ALTITUDE IS LESS THAN 2000 FEET" while the "allowable-statement" might be "GO TO STEP CLIMB" or "ACCOMPLISH PROCEDURE TO SHUTDOWN RADAR." The test-condition can become quite complex by the chaining of test-conditions with a logical "and" or "or" as in "IF ALTITUDE IS LESS THAN 2000 FEET AND AIRSPEED IS GREATER THAN 100 KNOTS THEN ..."

While several other basic statement types exist in the HOPROC language, the vast majority of procedural statements are handled by one of the above mentioned ones. Using only 15 basic statement types, a task-processing situation can be specified to HOS and accurately simulated.

The HOPROC language permits a relatively free use of synonyms in writing various statements. For example, END, CEASE, STOP, HALT, and TERMINATE all have the same meaning to HAL. Other words such as TO, THE, A, etc. are permitted but are ignored by HAL. This flexibility in the syntax permits relatively easy sentence construction.

RESULTS OF HOS VALIDATION RUNS

Space permits only the briefest overview of the results of various HOS validation runs conducted to date. It should be remembered that studies which have been replicated using HOS were originally conducted by different experimenters using a variety of population samples. Often the actual "procedures" which subjects used in these studies were unknown as were their requisite skills and training level. With these problems in mind, what was believed to be appropriate procedures were written and runs were conducted using simulated people of average capabilities.

Five different <u>Reach</u> studies have been validated and, in general, show that HOS reach times are within a tenth of a second of reported average reach times obtained from real subjects. This is believed to be well within expected sampling differences. Several classic "<u>Display Reading</u>" studies have been replicated using HOS and a variety of types of visual displays. They have shown that HOS results correlate very highly with reported results. This indicates that HOS can be used to test and evaluate the relative "goodness" of two or more proposed display types. Actual time spent in reading a given type dial is again quite close to reported results. <u>Simultaneous Dial Monitoring</u> has been simulated using HOS and results show that as the dials' readings become more variable and approach or exceed allowable limits the simulated operator spends more time monitoring those dials which are most likely to exceed allowable limits. This indicates that the strategy algorithms for choosing what to work on next are forcing the simulated operator to behave as a real operator behaves.

Several <u>Short-Term Memory</u> studies have been replicated with what are believed to be fairly remarkable results considering the inaccessibility of determining what is really happening internally in the operator. This indicates that the micro model for short-term memory is probably sufficiently accurate. Several <u>Keyset-Entry</u> studies, which utilize a variety of the micro behavior models, have been replicated and show that decision making and sequential entry of data through keysets, by the simulated operator produces data highly similar to human data. <u>Tracking</u> problems, both compensatory and pursuit, have also been studied on HOS. Results indicate that HOS performance is similar to human performance. Comparison of the relative effectiveness of HOS tracking versus other simulated human tracking is planned.

At the time of this writing, the most ambitious of the validations is currently underway. This validation attempts to simulate an airborne tactical officer performing an ASW mission. The displays, symbols and controls number in the hundreds and the number of different operator procedures exceeds fifty.

REFERENCES

1. Briggs, S.J.: A Study in the design of work areas, un-
    published doctoral dissertation, Purdue University,
    Lafayette, Indiana, August 1955

2. Fitts, Paul M.: The information capacity of the human
    motor system in controlling the amplitude of movement.
    Journal of Experimental Psychology, 46, No. 6, pp 381-391,
    1954.

3. Topmiller, Donald A. and Sharp, Earl D.: Effects of
    visual fixation and uncertainty on control panel layout.
    Wright-Patterson Air Force Base Technical Report AMRL-
    TR-65-149, Aerospace Medical Research Laboratory, Air Force
    Systems Command, Ohio, October 1965.

ADAPTIVE ALLOCATION OF DECISION MAKING RESPONSIBILITY

BETWEEN SUPERVISOR AND COMPUTER

William B. Rouse

University of Illinois

Urbana, Illinois 61801

ABSTRACT

Multi-task situations where supervisor and computer have intersecting decision making responsibilities are discussed. Adaptive allocation of task responsibility is espoused and formulated as a multi-queue, multi-server situation with a pre-emptive but non-competitive service discipline. Average delay in task performance and percent of decisions performed by the computer are predicted via simulation as a function of number of tasks, human-computer speed mismatch, and probabilities of various types of computer error. Prerequisites to the real-world realization of adaptive human-computer multi-task systems are considered and two laboratory investigations in this area are discussed.

INTRODUCTION

One of the crucial issues in the design of human-computer systems focuses on determining how responsibility should be divided between human and computer [1]. Several researchers have developed taxonomies of roles appropriate for the human and computer. Some of these ideas are reviewed in reference 1.

This paper approaches the issue somewhat differently. Succintly, it is assumed that while some tasks are best performed by the human and others are best performed by the computer, there are many tasks that could be successfully performed by either human or computer. Whichever partner has the time to devote to the task in question, should be allocated the responsibility for that task.

Further, the division of responsibilities for the overall set of
tasks should be dynamic (i.e., situation dependent) and not fixed
by some a priori analysis of task requirements.

There are two motivations for this approach. First, a static
allocation of responsibility implies that each partner keeps track
of his own set of tasks and has "faith" that the remaining tasks
will be successfully performed by his partner. While the computer
might blindly adopt such faith, the human would not have such infinite confidence in the computer and might spend considerable time
monitoring the computer. With a dynamic allocation of responsibility, the human would have supervisory responsibility for all
tasks which he might possibly perform. He would scan the displays
looking for assurance that all tasks were being completed. Whenever he felt it to be appropriate, he could perform particular
tasks himself. Hopefully, the computer would successfully perform
most tasks whose requirements fall within its abilities and thus,
the human would spend most of his time as a supervisor.

The second motivation for the dynamic approach comes from
simple queueing theory ideas. Briefly, a multiple queue system
where servers are strictly assigned to particular queues results
in much more customer waiting time than occurs if servers can move
among queues and serve customers at any of the queues. Thus, dynamic allocation of task responsibility would improve performance
in the sense that tasks would be more quickly processed (i.e.,
they would not queue-up).

In this paper, we want to pursue a general understanding of
adaptive allocation of decision making responsibility between
human and computer. To this end, we will first develop a general
mathematical formulation of the human-computer multi-task situation. With this general formulation, we will discuss some specific
situations and consider the impact of the numerous variables involved. Finally, we will consider specific applications currently
being pursued in the laboratory and how such applications might
impact real-world technology.

A GENERAL FORMULATION

Assume that there are N tasks in the multi-task situation of
interest. Each task can be characterized by a state vector $\underline{x}_i$,
i = 1,2,...,N while the entire state space is characterized by
$\underline{X} = (\underline{x}_1, \underline{x}_2, \ldots, \underline{x}_N).*$

---

*In an effort to simplify notation, time dependencies have not
been explicitly noted although they are, of course, implied.

Upon scanning his displays, the server (human or computer) observes $\underline{Z} = (\underline{z}_1, \underline{z}_2, \ldots, \underline{z}_N)$ where $\underline{z}_i$ is his best estimate of $\underline{x}_i$ and may include partial and/or noisy observations. Further, since the server may not scan all of his displays during every scan, $\underline{z}_i$ may be a prediction or extrapolation of the observation obtained when he last scanned the ith display.

Given an observation $\underline{Z}$, the server must decide whether his attention is needed for task i (i.e., Should he perform task i?) or whether he should continue scanning his displays. More formally, the server's motivation for diverting his attention to task i is based on his perception of the possibility of some event of set $\underline{e}_i$ having occurred that requires an action of set $\underline{a}_i$.

The server's observation $\underline{Z}$ leads to probability estimates of the form $p(\cdot|\underline{Z}) = p(\underline{e}_1, \underline{e}_2, \ldots, \underline{e}_N|\underline{Z})$ and he must trade off the cost of ignoring this information against the cost of ignoring N-1 tasks while he implements some action of set $\underline{a}_i$.

The costs of not monitoring N-1 tasks depends on what events might occur in those tasks over the time interval of interest. Let $f_i(\underline{t}_e|\underline{Z})$ be the joint probability distribution of time between events for task i conditioned on observation $\underline{Z}$ and $f(\cdot|\underline{Z}) = f(\underline{t}_{e_1}, \underline{t}_{e_2}, \ldots, \underline{t}_{e_N})$ be the joint distribution of time between events for all tasks. The server's perception of $f(\cdot|\underline{Z})$ characterizes his feelings for what might occur in the N-1 tasks if he were to ignore them over some interval.

The time interval of interest is related to the time required to implement the desired action. Let $g_i(\underline{t}_a|\underline{Z})$ be the joint distribution of action times for task i and $g(\cdot|\underline{Z}) = g(\underline{t}_{a_1}, \underline{t}_{a_2}, \ldots, \underline{t}_{a_N}|\underline{Z})$ be the joint distribution of action times for all tasks. The server's perception of $g(\cdot|\underline{Z})$ and more specifically $g_i(\underline{t}_a|\underline{Z})$ characterizes his feelings for how long it may take to perform task i.

We would like to "solve" the problem formulated above in the sense of determining optimal allocation of server attention and the resulting system performance. Since we will resort to simulation to obtain a solution, we need not restrict our choices of $p(\cdot|\underline{Z})$, $f(\cdot|\underline{Z})$, and $g(\cdot|\underline{Z})$. A specific measure of performance or cost and a planning horizon must also be chosen. Some alternative choices and their impact are discussed in reference 2.

Since solution requires some choice of probability distributions and there is no inherent reason to pick any particular set, we will look at a situation that is relatively easy to simulate and interpret and, for which there is ample literature available.

A SPECIAL CASE - INDEPENDENT TASKS

Assume that the time between events is random and independent among tasks. Then, $f(\cdot|\underline{Z}) = f_1(t_e)f_2(t_e)..f_N(t_e)$ where $f_i(t_e)$ is exponential with mean $1/\lambda_i$. Similarly, assume that the time to implement an action or perform a task is random and independent among tasks. Thus, $g(\cdot|\underline{Z}) = g_1(t_a)g_2(t_a)...g_N(t_a)$ where $g_i(t_a)$ exponential with mean $1/\mu_i$.

We have at this point what appears to be a classical queueing situation which resembles Carbonell's instrument sampling model [3]. However, we are dealing with multiple servers which adds another dimension to the problem especially since we assume that any server can perform any task (i.e., serve any queue).

The crucial issue here is the queue discipline. We have a priority queueing situation that roughly fits the formulation of Cox and Smith [4]. The main differences are that we will assume batch service (i.e., servers empty the queue whenever they attend to a particular task) and, that finite time is required to observe the state of each queue. Nevertheless, we will adopt the pre-emptive strategy of Cox and Smith and assume that a server performs the task with largest $c_i\mu_i$ where c_i is the cost of delay in performance of task i. The only restriction on this strategy is that a server cannot attempt to perform a task that another server is already performing. While this appears to be a rather weak restriction, we shall see in later discussion that it has rather important implications.

Now let us briefly restate the queue discipline. Server j scans the task displays, in order of decreasing $c_i\mu_i$, at a fixed rate of t_j per display. He services the first task for which he perceives some action-evoking event, subject to the constraint that no other server is performing that task. He performs all actions necessary to complete the task (i.e., empty the queue) and then returns to scanning, starting again at the highest $c_i\mu_i$ task.

EXAMPLES

In this section, we will consider some specific examples of a human and a single computer in the above situation. The purpose of these examples is to illustrate the effect of various computer parameters on overall performance.

In general, the human is a reasonably good decision maker but fairly slow while the computer, as yet, is a somewhat poor decision

maker but very fast.* To characterize the speed mismatch, we will
assume that a human can scan a display in 1.0 second while a computer requires 0.001 second. Further, we will let the computer
perform tasks at a rate S faster than the human (i.e., $\mu_C = S\mu_H$).

To characterize the ability mismatch, we will assume that the
human never makes mistakes but that the computer can have false
alarms, missed events, and incorrect actions. To be specific, a
false alarm requires the computer to devote one, randomly generated,
service time to realize its mistake. A missed event simply means
that the computer scans the display for a task that needs performing without perceiving it on that scanning iteration. An incorrect
action results in the computer's service being unsuccessful in the
sense that the task is still waiting in the queue even though the
computer left that task thinking it was completed.

As measures of performance, we will adopt average delay in
completing a task (time waiting for service plus actual time in
service) and percent of decisions performed by the computer. These
measures will be referred to as average delay and percent decisions.

Given N, arrival rates (λ_1, λ_2,..., λ_N), service rates (μ_1,
μ_2,..., μ_N), S, and probabilities of false alarm, missed event, and
incorrect action, we would like to predict our performance measures.
This problem statement significantly exceeds capabilities of analytical methods available in queueing theory [5]. Thus, we have
resorted to simulation. All the results that follow were obtained
using a FORTRAN simulation of our problem. Data points are averages
of three runs where each run constituted the service of 1000 events.

The first example we will consider used $1/\lambda_i$ = 100 seconds and
$1/\mu_i$ = 10 seconds (for the human) for all N tasks. The speed mismatch parameter S as well as N were experimental variables. Results
are shown in Figure 1. As one would expect, average delay increases
with N and decreases with S while percent decisions decreases with
N and increases with S. The interesting result here is that while
great improvements in performance are achieved as S increases from
1 to 2, further increases yield quickly diminishing returns. This
effect is more dramatic for higher values of N but still evident at
lower values of N which shows that the effect is not merely a rami-
fication of the queue utilizations (λ_i/μ_i) chosen. These results
lead one to conjecture that the computer need not be much faster
than the human as long as the probability of computer error is low.
(All three probabilities of error were zero in this example.)

---

*The artificial intelligence programs that might be characterized
as adequate decision makers usually have not retained a speed
advantage over the human.

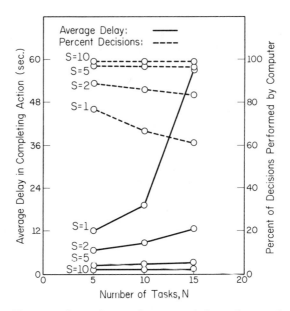

Figure 1: Effects of Number of Tasks (N) and Speed Mismatch (S)

In the next example we consider the impact of computer error. In this case, N and S were both fixed as 10 while the three probabilities were varied, one at a time. Results are shown in Figure 2. The obvious conclusion here is that false alarms are crucial while missed events and incorrect actions have less impact on performance. Missed events present little difficulty since the computer can scan so quickly. In other words, barring other arrivals, the computer will scan the same display N milliseconds later. Incorrect actions have marginal impact because they can only occur during an actual service while false alarms can occur during any scan. Of course, we have only considered the time lost and incorrect actions could have disastrous effects which we have not included here.

As a third example, we will consider a situation where $1/\lambda_1$=10 seconds while $1/\lambda_2$ through $1/\lambda_N$=100 seconds. Also, $1/\mu_1$=2 seconds while $1/\mu_2$ through $1/\mu_N$=10 seconds (for the human). Finally, we will fix N and S both as 10 and let the probability of computer false alarm vary. Thus, we have a situation where more events occur in one task than in all the others combined. Results are shown in Figure 3. The service rate for task 1 is five times greater than in previous examples while the arrival rate is ten times greater than before. Thus, one might expect the overall performance to suffer. However, while more events must be serviced, each servicing action requires less time and the computer can scan the other tasks between event occurrences in task 1 and thus assume more of the decision making responsibility than in our previous

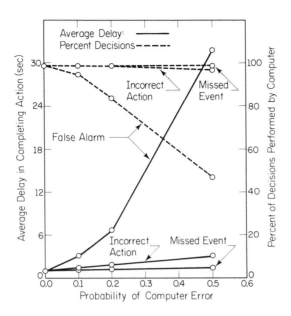

Figure 2: Effects of Computer Error (N = 10, S = 10)

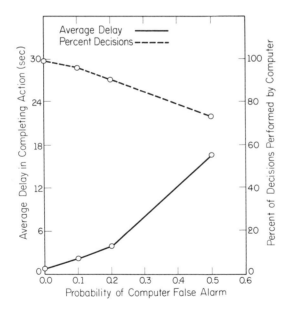

Figure 3: Effects of Non-Uniform Distribution of
Events and Computer Error (N = 10, S = 10)

example. Thus, performance improves by making task 1 a situation with higher utilization. This may not agree with the reader's intuition.

The above examples have one specific feature in common that we want to stress. It is assumed that each server knows what the other server is doing. We will now pursue in detail that aspect of the human-computer interaction.

PREREQUISITES

In an earlier paper [2], we considered the impact of a lack of cooperation between the human and computer in the sense that they did not plan their respective actions in light of what the other was doing. This situation was termed competitive intelligence (in a laissez faire benign sense) and simulation studies showed, as one might expect, that competition had severe effects on performance.

Instead of studying competitive situations (perhaps via game theory instead of queueing theory), it seems appropriate to assume cooperation or cooperative intelligence between human and computer. Thus, our previous discussion in this paper has started with that premise. Now we want to briefly consider how cooperation might be achieved.

The basic difficulty is in devising some method of letting human and computer know what each other is doing. It also would be of value if they know what each other is planning to do [2], but we will not pursue that issue.

It is not very difficult for the computer to tell the human what it is doing. Some type of status indicator on each display could inform the human of the computer's actions. An indicator of computer confidence in its own performance would also be possible. This feedback combined with the human's supervisory perogative of taking responsibility for any task he chooses, should result in quite satisfactory computer-to-human communication.*

Human-to-computer communication presents more difficulties. While natural language input by the human appears desirable and feasible within a limited range [6], this assumes that the human

---

*
This assumes that the human is not overloaded by all the status displays he would have to scan which seems reasonable since the status displays would have lower information generation rates than the physical variable displays associated with the tasks in question.

can express his knowledge and that the computer can interpret the language in a semantic and contextual sense. The use of physiological measurements such as EEG [7] avoids the difficulties of natural language processing but does not solve the interpretation problem or the human's inability to formalize "tacit" knowledge [8].

The computer must have some way of inferring the human's state of knowledge. In other words, in engineering terms, the computer must construct a model of the human with which it is dealing much in the same way that humans construct models of other humans when pursuing joint endeavors. Several researchers are currently pursuing this idea [9,10,11], and it is far from an easy problem. However, it will be very difficult to design cooperative human-computer systems with any degree of generality if this aspect of human-to-computer communication is ignored.

APPLICATIONS

Now, we will consider two laboratory investigations that fit the general human-computer multi-task situation discussed throughout this paper. Enstrom [10] has considered simultaneous tracking and monitoring with emphasis on telling the computer how the human has allocated his attention between pursuit tracking and randomly occurring sidetasks (arithmetic problems). Using fading-memory system identification methods [12,13] and discriminant analysis [14], he can consistently detect changes in the human's control characteristics as attention is allocated to the sidetasks. The real-time realization of this method was motivated by a situation where a pilot interacts with an on-board computer that detects and corrects aircraft failures. Enstrom's method has potential for telling the computer what the human is doing in this situation. It might also be applied in automobile situations to sense vigilance problems or otherwise unfit drivers.

Greenstein [11] is pursuing a multi-task monitoring situation somewhat analogous to failure detection and correction in industrial operations. Initially, the emphasis has been on the computer "watching" the human so as to learn how to detect failures via discriminant analysis [14]. The next phase of the work will emphasize dynamic allocation of responsibility and the comparison of the theoretical formulation presented here with empirical findings.

It takes very little imagination to think of possible real-world applications of ideas presented in this paper. Pilot-aircraft situations, driver-automobile situations, air traffic control, and industrial monitoring are a few potential avenues of application. However, a great deal of laboratory research is needed before applications will be realized.

ACKNOWLEDGEMENTS

This work was supported in part by the Joint Services
Electronics Program (U.S. Army, U.S. Navy, and U.S. Air Force)
under Contract DAAB-07-72-C-0259 and in part by the U.S. Air Force
Systems Command under Contract F33615-73-C-1238.

REFERENCES

1. W. B. Rouse, "Design of Man-Computer Interfaces for On-Line
    Interactive Systems," Proceedings of the IEEE, Special Issue
    on Interactive Computer Systems, Vol. 63, No. 6, pp. 847-857,
    June 1975.
2. W. B. Rouse, "Human Interaction With An Intelligent Computer
    in Multi-Task Situations," Proceedings of the Eleventh Annual
    Conference on Manual Control, NASA Ames Research Center,
    pp. 130-143, May 1975.
3. J. R. Carbonell, "A Queueing Model of Many-Instrument Visual
    Sampling," IEEE Transactions on Human Factors in Electronics,
    Vol. HFE-7, No. 4, pp. 157-164, December 1966.
4. D. R. Cox and W. L. Smith, Queues, London: Meuthen, 1961.
5. L. Kleinrock, Queueing Systems, Vol. 1, New York: Wiley, 1975.
6. J. Martin, Design of Man-Computer Dialogues, Englewood Cliffs,
    NJ: Prentice-Hall, 1973.
7. L. R. Pinneo, "Persistent EEG Patterns Associated with Overt
    and Covert Speech," Bulletin of the Human Factors Society,
    Vol. 18, No. 2, pp. 1-2, February 1975.
8. M. Polyani, Knowing and Being, Chicago: University of Chicago
    Press, 1969.
9. R. L. Weisbrod, K. B. Davis, and A. Freedy, "Adaptive Utility
    Assessment in Dynamic Decision Processes: An Experimental
    Evaluation of Decision Aiding," Proceedings of the 1975 IEEE
    Systems, Man and Cybernetics Conference, San Francisco,
    pp. 302-308, September 1975.
10. K. D. Enstrom, Real Time Adaptive Modeling of the Human
    Controller with Application to Man-Computer Interaction,
    MSIE Thesis, University of Illinois at Urbana-Champaign, 1975.
11. J. S. Greenstein, Ph.D. Thesis in progress, University of
    Illinois at Urbana-Champaign.
12. N. Morrison, Introduction to Sequential Smoothing and
    Prediction, New York: McGraw-Hill, 1969.
13. J. M. Mendel, Discrete Techniques of Parameter Estimation,
    New York: Marcel Dekker, 1973.
14. M. M. Tatsuoka, Multivariate Analysis, New York: Wiley, 1971.

DISCUSSION

ANDOW :

Could you comment on the problems that can arise with "Multi-Server" systems when either the computer or the man fails in some way during processing of tasks ?

ROUSE :

Until recently, we have assumed that failure of either human or computer only resulted in the task (being performed at the time of failure) not being computed. Since it was assumed that either server could perform any of the tasks, failure of one server only resulted in a higher load on the remaining server.

While this is unrealistic, we decided that a specific context was necessary to be able to consider the impact of server failure (as opposed to error). We are currently considering the application of the proposed human-computer concept to aircraft operations and industrial monitoring. These contexts should allow study of server failure. One immediate question concerns the transfer of the mass of information necessary when a server fails in the middle of a task. In other words, how does the remaining server know the state of the task in which the failure occurred ?

SHACKEL :

I would expect it to be more important for the man and computer to tell each other what they are going to handle next, rather than what they are doing now ; have you looked at this ? Further, the time taken for either, but especially the man, to scan the information display in order to find out what the other is doing, or will do, may be a significant component of task load and hence may degrade performance ; have you studied this aspect ?

ROUSE :

A knowledge of each other's planned actions as well as current actions can improve performance in the human-computer system envisioned. This is noted briefly in the paper and discussed in more detail in reference 2.

Considering information loading due to the feedback between human and computer, status displays generated by the computer should impose less loading than the displays for the original unaided tasks. Information on what the human is doing can hopefully be gained covertly, and thus not impose an additional load on the human.

We need not be too concerned about overloading the computer since we can always employ more than a single computer.

MAN/MACHINE INTERACTION IN ADAPTIVE COMPUTER-AIDED CONTROL

Randall Steeb, Gershon Weltman, and Amos Freedy

Perceptronics, Inc.
6271 Variel Avenue
Woodland Hills, California 91364

ABSTRACT

Shared decision making between man and intelligent machine is becoming an important part of advanced systems. The research described in this paper is directed toward developing human factors criteria for the man/machine interaction. The research effort includes evaluations of task allocation techniques, information feedback, operator training, and decision analysis methods.

The paper presents the results of a series of experimental investigations of adaptive computer-aided control. The results of the investigation suggest that control allocation and machine state feedback are perhaps the major factors in these interactions, and that automatic allocation should be a primary function of the machine component.

INTRODUCTION

Computer aiding systems have recently evolved from inflexible routines to adaptive programs capable of high-level interaction and initiative. Adaptive (or intelligent) components are taking over many of what were once considered uniquely human functions, such as learning, pattern recognition, problem solving, and inferential decision making. Employing such functions, an intelligent aiding system can analyze alternative actions, recommend responses, and even perform various tasks autonomously.

It is just this potential for flexible, autonomous action, however, that leads to a variety of new human factors questions. Man/machine factors which need definition include the dynamics of parallel human and machine learning, the forms of information feedback necessary for operator cognizance of system operation, the assignment of functional responsibility as capabilities change, and the types of operator training necessary for acceptance and effective use of the aid.

This paper describes a series of exploratory studies of these aspects of shared control between man and intelligent machine. The overall goals of this work have included the development of techniques for modeling the man/machine interaction, examination of the major factors influencing the dynamics of man/computer interaction in simulated tasks, and establishment of guidelines for application of adaptive computer-aided control to operational man/machine systems.

Computer Aiding. Computer aiding systems are devices that simplify or otherwise facilitate the performance of some specific task. Present and planned applications cover such diverse situations as continuous dynamic control of remotely piloted vehicles, sonar signal processing, and information flow in command and control operations. The emphasis in these advanced systems is on the aiding of decision making processes, including such contributions as data organization and display, establishment of procedures to select courses of action, mathematical optimization (linear programming, optimal control and their ilk), and decision analysis (Weisbrod, Davis, and Freedy, 1975; Nickerson and Feehrer, 1975).

For the most part, experimental studies of computer-based decision aids have shown that operators are able to function effectively with machine support. Hanes and Gebhard (1966), in a realistic simulation of anti-aircraft warfare, found that naval commanders freely accepted computer advice in a tactical command action. Similarly, Miller and his associates (1967) demonstrated the efficiency of combining human value judgment and machine policy selection to perform aircraft dispatching in a tactical air command system. The interaction was found to be superior in performance to unaided human dispatching. But, probably the most powerful demonstration of computer aiding is found in the U. S. Army's Simulated Tactical Operations System (SIMTOS). SIMTOS is an interactive information system for command and control operations designed to complement the man's information processing and decision making capabilities. The system has been used to test the effects of a number of procedural and information control factors on system performance (Baker, 1974).

Models and Function Allocation. The modeling techniques proposed to deal with man/computer interaction have been diverse, including such disciplines as information theory, operations research methods, optimal control theory, and decision analysis (Carbonell, 1969; Nickerson and Feehrer, 1975). Among the most promising of these techniques have been the information processing constructs

of Carbonell (1969), decision methods based on expected utility
(Miller, Kaplan, and Edwards, 1967; Weisbrod, Davis, and Freedy,
1975) and seat-of-the-pants intuition. An expected utility analysis
approach has been relied on in the present work because this technique is reasonably descriptive of the operator's cognitive processes (Krantz, Luce, Suppes, and Tversky, 1971), provides a guide
for normative (optimal) behavior, and is of a linear, additive
form suited to pattern recognition algorithms.

Training and Acceptance. It is generally agreed that human
decision makers must understand the capabilities and limitations
of their decision aids. For example, the findings of Ferguson and
Jones (1969) indicate that rigorous training procedures are necessary to overcome the complexity that the introduction of an aid
temporarily adds to the decision situation. Other factors contrib-
uting to the operator's attitude toward computer advice are his
opinion of its performance and his compatibility with its style of
presentation. Halpin, Thorneberry, and Streufert (1973) found that
exposure to an initially inaccurage computer decreased later utilization of an accurage aid. The second factor, presentation style,
has to do with the content and structure of information provided
by an aid. Using such dimensions as "abstract/concrete" and "ac-
tive/passive", Levit, Alden, Erickson, and Heaton (1974) found that
if there is a mismatch between the particular recipient's decision
style and his mode of information presentation, large decrements
in cognitive task performance can be expected. For the most part,
these factors were examined in the content of preprogrammed, rather
than adaptive, aiding. The present study provides a chance to
examine many of these considerations in the context of decision
making shared with an intelligent machine.

SYSTEM CONFIGURATION

An experimental system incorporating an adaptive computer aiding system was used to explore a series of hypotheses about man/
machine interaction. The experimental system consisted of a learning control system, an adaptive decision model of operator behavior,
a variety of means of allocation of control between man and machine,
and software for assessment of performance and behavior. Figure 1
illustrates the essential structure of the system.

Autonomous Control System. Aiding in the form of control
automation comes from a trainable "machine learning" computer program, the autonomous control system (ACS). The ACS (Freedy, Weisbrod, and Weltman, 1973) is an adaptive system which observes task
conditions, operator behavior and resulting outcomes, and adjusts
its behavior toward optimal performance.

Decision Analysis. Decisions regarding delegation of control
in man/machine systems require a continuing analysis of task cir-

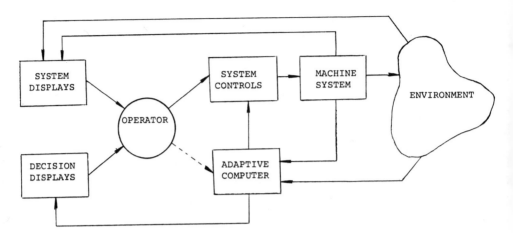

FIGURE 1.   ADAPTIVE AIDING SYSTEM

cumstances and requirements. In most man/machine systems, objective performance criteria for the immediate task are not well defined, or are only indirectly related to specified system goals. As a result, objective performance maximization is difficult and such systems may rely heavily on the operator's subjective evaluation of the situation at hand. In such systems, allocation decisions should be based accordingly on subjective preferences (utilities) inferred from the operator.

One way to perform the necessary in-task, dynamic utility assessment is to use pattern recognition techniques to fit decision model parameters to observed operator behavior. A method of this type was developed by Freedy, Weisbrod, and Weltman (1973) using a trainable linear discriminant function based on an expected utility model. The expected utility model is a very general model of decision making under risk where the operator is presumed to choose that alternative whose expected (probability weighted) utility of outcome is highest (Krantz, Luce, Suppes, and Tversky, 1971). A detailed explanation of the underlying assumptions, adjustment techniques and performance of the utility estimator is given in Freedy, Weisbrod, and Steeb (1973).

Once the operator's utilities have been accurately assessed, they can be used in an analysis and feedback of decision quality. Also, the utilities can be incorporated in a model capable of unburdening the operator of a portion of the control allocation task.

Automatic Control Allocation. Allocation of control responsibility between the operator and an adaptive aiding system should be organized in such a way as to utilize each controller's unique capabilities and to ensure operator acceptance of the partnership. Such decision by decision allocation can be performed entirely by the operator (manual allocation), by a threshold device set by the operator (semi-automatic allocation), or by a fully automatic system based on decision rules.

Manual Allocation is present when the operator physically allocates control to himself or to the machine on each decision. While simple, manual control is time consuming, as the operator must not only continuously evaluate his own capabilities along with the machine's, but must physically take the action of overriding.

In Semi-Automatic Allocation, control is transferred to the machine when a threshold level of expected machine performance is exceeded. Thus semi-automatic allocation relieves the operator of the decision-by-decision override function and replaces it with an occasional threshold adjustment. If conditions are relatively constant and if operator performance and capabilities vary little, few adjustments are necessary.

Fully Automatic Adjustment removes the primary allocation decision from the operator and delegates it to a formal decision rule. The decision rule may be based on objective performance using expected utility maximization, or on subjective performance using expected utility maximization. The objective approaches are less involved than the subjective ones, since constant, objective costs rather than estimated utilities are used in the decisions. The subjective, utility-based approach uses as inputs the apparent preferences for human and computer control outcomes. As described earlier, these utilities are estimated continuously from behavior.

EXPERIMENTAL STUDIES

Task Simulations. Two task simulations were used to study shared control between man and an adaptive aiding system. The earlier configuration was a generalized control task resembling aircraft control through a winding flight corridor. The operator moved a cursor dot over the face of a large oscilloscope display using a two-dimensional, variable rate joystick. The task was to traverse a "safe" but invisible corridor as rapidly as possible while hitting the boundaries as little as possible. The Autonomous Control System (ACS), in turn, acquired the path trajectories by monitoring the operator's successive attempts to run them, and gradually was capable of taking over more and more responsibility for control. In some studies, a secondary task of detecting repeated digits on a single digit display was added.

The second, later type of task simulation was more realistic and specific and required greater amounts of inferential decision making. The operator's task resembled the control of an intelligent remotely piloted vehicle (RPV) through a "hostile" terrain. The operator used a one-dimensional, single-speed velocity stick to control the vehicle, with control actions and obstacle terrain displayed on a moving map display. The obstacles, which are presented singly or in pairs, have associated with them probabilistic distributions of "success" and "hit". These obstacles appear at the top of the display screen and move toward the bottom at a constant velocity. The object was to fly the vehicle through the obstacle terrain, either by manual or computer control, minimizing the probability of hitting the obstacles. Figure 2 gives a view of the CRT Simulation.

<u>Variables</u>. The types of variables that have been examined in these studies include the following:

1) Task Difficulty--The number of turns and rapidity of change in the path negotiation task, and the number of possible combinations of obstacles in the RPV simulation.

2) Payoffs--The payoff matrix listing costs and payoffs for hits and misses under each type of control, human or machine.

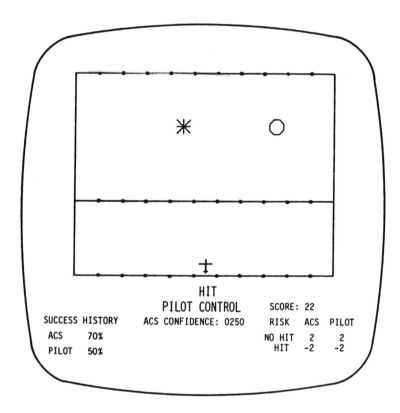

FIGURE 2.   SIMULATED REMOTE PILOTED VEHICLE DISPLAY

3) Allocation Technique--Manual and semi-automatic modes were compared in the path negotiation task. Manual and automatic modes were examined with the RPV simulation. The automatic modes were performance (EV) based and utility (EU) based.

4) Information Feedback--Conditions with and without display of a control takeover light and machine confidence indicator were examined using the path-following task; using the RPV-task, the level of machine confidence, predicted ACS action, immediate expected utilities and expected values of each controller, and estimated operator preference for control, were compared.

5) Operator Training--Indoctrination in principles of machine learning, general decision making, and specific task requirements was investigated using both types of simulation.

In something of an evolutionary approach to studying man/machine interaction, the more basic variables were introduced, observed, and refined in a course of sequential experiments. As the studies progressed, it became apparent that the allocation of control, the switch that determines functional responsibility, was of major importance. Thus, more emphasis was placed in the later experiments on aspects of allocation.

Performance Measures. In the path negotiation task, the overall system performance was described by the number and cost of errors and by the speed of completion of the task. Overall performance in the later RPV task simulation was reduced to a single figure of merit, the score resulting from the number and cost of errors. Speed was eliminated as a variable by presenting the task at a set pace.

Individual contributions to the task were characterized by the frequency of success of the particular controller. Each controller's probabilities for success and failure were weighted by the respective payoffs for success and failure, providing an indication of the average expected scores for the decisions undertaken by each partner.

Allocation behavior and effectiveness was specified by the proportion of decisions made by each controller, man or computer, and by the efficiency of allocation. Measures of efficiency were the difference in expected values between the optimal and the observed allocation, the amount of inconsistency and the number of control allocation overrides. Generally, the smaller the number of overrides, the more accurately the allocation reflects the operator's control allocation criterion.

Subjects. Throughout the series of experiments, subjects were selected to be as much as possible like the probable users of Navy computer aided systems. For the most part, the participants were recruited from nearby military units and had several years of college experience. During the program, fifty-three subjects completed a total of 302 one to one-and-a-half hour experimental sessions.

Findings. A brief summary of the findings of the series of studies follows. The reader is directed to Weltman, et al (1972), Freedy, et al (1973), and Crooks, et al (1974) for more complete descriptions of the experimental circumstances and results.

Task Conditions. Operator responses to the task conditions of difficulty and payoff structure were widely varied and typically were specific to each individual. Increases in task difficulty in the path negotiation task resulted in the operators allocating significantly greater amounts of control to themselves. When payoff structure was changed, control allocation and estimated utilities for control both moved significantly in the direction of the favored controller, although not as much as that proscribed by objective measures.

Utilities. The estimation of utilities for control outcomes, human and ACS success and failure, was obtained both in the present work and in related studies in an intelligence gathering context (Weisbrod, Davis, and Freedy, 1975). In the RPV task simulation, it was found that the estimated utilities were responsive to changes in task conditions and were successful at predicting a major portion (85-95%) of the operators behavior under different conditions. Also, a high correlation (.82, p < .01) was found between estimated and operator expressed preferences using a similar program in an intelligence gathering task in a simulated dynamic environment (Weisbrod, Davis, Freedy, 1974).

Control Allocation. With the path negotiation task, semi-automatic allocation (where the operator sets a threshold of minimum acceptable machine confidence) was found to be significantly more effective than manual allocation. A fourteen per cent improvement in total score came from a fifteen per cent higher ACS score, and a fifteen per cent increase in secondary task scores. These were apparently the result of a more consistent allocation strategy, and of operator unburdening. Studies with the RPV simulation, in turn, showed that automatic control allocation based on expected utility produced behavior essentially identical to that found with the semi-automatic mode. The performance score, allocation percentages, and utility measures all showed less than a ten per cent disparity between the two allocations, and no measures differed at a significant level. Expected value allocation, based on objective costs rather than utilities, resulted in an observed allocation closer to the optimal amount, and scores tended to be higher, although the scoring differences did not reach significance. EU allocation, on the other hand, resulted in significantly more consistent behavior and higher operator probability of success than was seen with EV allocation.

Indoctrination. Effects of indoctrination in the principles of machine learning, decision making, and task specifics were inconclusive. Indocrinated subjects in the path negotiation task had significantly higher performance scores than did a non-indoctrinated group. But these results were not seen in the RPV task.

Feedback. Studies with the RPV simulation showed that feedback of the machine level of confidence, and of the predicted ACS action, increased the operator's use of aiding, but in a somewhat counterproductive manner. With feedback, the operator allocated a lesser amount of control to the ACS, lowering overall score compared to the no-feedback conditions. The decisions the operator gave the ACS, however, were those for which it was most effective. Essentially, he improved machine performance at his own expense. The most beneficial types of feedback were the immediate expected values associated with each controller and the estimated net preference. EV information had an effect similar to that of EV based allocation. It resulted in a shift in allocation towards the objectively correct amount. Information regarding the net preference (an index of relative utility for manual over machine control) was effective in reducing the operator's inconsistencies and overrides, and in increasing the operator's probability of success.

CONCLUSIONS

The studies briefly summarized here represent an attempt to examine some of the factors influencing shared control between men and adaptive machines. The results of a decision analytical approach to modeling the interaction, and the findings of several experimental studies, led to the conclusions that the factors of greatest importance in shared control were control allocation and feedback of machine state.

Assessment of the operator's utilities for control decisions was accomplished using a pattern recognition technique to fit parameters of a decision model to observed behavior. This method makes it possible to obtain on-line estimates of the operator's utilities as he performs the task. Experimentally, the utilities estimated by the adaptive program were responsive to conditions, compatible with preferences expressed directly by the subjects, and effective in predicting behavior. Automatic allocation of control based on the estimated utilities or on objectively defined values appeared to be of major advantage in shared control. Automatic allocation relieves the operator of a continuous monitoring and control transfer task and reduces often costly communications. The utility based allocation corresponded closely to allocation manually set by the operator, indicating minimal interference with operator needs.

Feedback of machine state was also important when it provided information about available aiding and criteria of allocation. Display of the expected value of each controller, human or machine, was

similar in effect to performance-based allocation in drawing behavior toward objectively correct distribution of control.

In future applications, automatic allocation techniques and
their associated feedback appear appropriate to analysis and transfer
of costly information as well as control. The degree of aiding provided by such automatic allocation is expected to increase as the
number of computer controlled systems increases. Potentially, such
an aiding system can direct the limited supervisory capabilities of
a human operator to the critical parts of a multi-machine assembly,
provide the necessary decision-making information, and sharpen its
capabilities for future actions by observing the operator's response
to the immediate situation.

ACKNOWLEDGMENT

This research was supported by the Office of Naval Research Engineering Psychology Programs and Information Systems Programs Contract
N00014-72-C-0093.

REFERENCES

1. Baker, J.D., SIMTOS: A Man-in-the-Loop Interactive Simulation
of a Tactical Operations System. Paper presented at the NATO Special
Program Panel on Sysems Science. Munich, Germany, August, 1974.

2. Carbonell, J.R., On Man-Computer Interaction: A Model and Some
Related Issues, IEEE Transactions on Systems Science and Cybernetics,
SSC-5, 16-26, 1969.

3. Crooks, W.H., Artof, M., Freedy, A., and Weltman, G. Man/Machine
Interaction in Adaptive Computer Aided Control: Analysis of Auto-
mated Control Allocation. Perceptronics, Inc., Woodland Hills, Calif
Technical Report No. PATR-1008-74-12/30, December, 1974.

4. Freedy, A., Steeb, R., and Weltman, G., Man/Machine Interaction
in Adaptive Computer Aided Control: Initial Study, Technical Report
#72-10, Perceptronics, Inc., Woodland Hills, Calif., November, 1972.

5. Freedy, A., Weisbrod, R., May, D., Schwartz, S., and Weltman, G.,
Adaptive Computer Decision Aiding in Dynamic Decision Processes.
Technical Report PTR-73-101, Perceptronics, Inc., Woodland Hills,
Calif., NTIS-AD 769 113, 1973.

6. Freedy, A., Weisbrod, R., Steeb, R., A Pattern Recognition Approach to Subjective Value Estimation for Task Control Allocation,
Journal of Cybernetics, in press, 1976.

7. Freedy, A., Weisbrod, R., and Weltman, G., Self-Optimization of
Task Allocation in Shared Man/Computer Control, Proceedings of the
IEEE Conference on Decision and Control, Paper #FP5-3, San Diego,
Calif., December 5-7, 1973.

8. Ferguson, R., and Jones, C. A Computer Aided Decision System, Management Science, 1969, 15 (10), B-550-B-561.

9. Halpin, S.M., Thornberry, J.A., and Streufert, S., The Credibility of Computer Estimates in a Simple Decision Making Task, Purdue University, Technical Report No. 5 (ONR Contract N00014-67-A-0226-0030), January, 1973.

10. Hanes, R.M., and Gebhard, J.W., The Computer's Role in Command Decision, U.S. Naval Institute Proceedings, September, 1966.

11. Krantz, D.M., Lane, R.D., Suppes, P., and Tversky, A. Foundations of Measurement: Additive and Polynomial Representations, I. New York: Academic Press, 1971.

12. Levit, R.A., Alden, D.G., Erickson, J.M., and Heaton, B.J., Development and Application of a Decision Aid for Tactical Control of Battlefield Operations. Vol. 1; Honeywell, Inc., Contract DAHC19-73-C00069, 1974.

13. Miller, L.W., Kaplan, R.J., and Edwards, W. JUDGE: A Value-Judgment-Based Tactical Command System. Organizational Behavior and Human Performance, 1967, 2:329-374.

14. Nickerson, R.S. and Feehrer, C.E. Decision Making and Training. Bolt, Beranek, and Newman (Cambridge, Mass.) Technical Report NAVTRAEQUIPCEN 73-C-0128-1, July, 1975.

15. Weisbrod, R.L., Davis, K.B., and Freedy, A. Adaptive Utility Assessment in Dynamic Decision Processes. Proc. Conf. on Systems, Man, and Cybernetics, San Francisco, Calif., September, 1975.

16. Weltman, G., Steeb, R., Freedy, A., Smith, M. and Weisbrod, R., Experimental Study of Man/Machine Interaction in Adaptive Computer Aided Control, Technical Report No. 73-10, Perceptronics, Inc., Woodland Hills, Calif., November, 1973.

Process Control

PREVIEW OF PROCESS CONTROL SESSION

Elwyn Edwards

University of Technology

Loughborough, U.K.

1. INTRODUCTION

The most distinctive occupational consequence of technological progress in control is, of course, the increased use of the human controller as a monitor and supervisor rather than as a continuously active element within the system. The controller's primary task, therefore, comprises the receiving of information about the process, making the broad decisions concerning its required control parameters, and communicating these requirements to the hardware which provides the moment-to-moment control. Additionally, the operator is concerned to detect, diagnose and correct any malfunction within the system; faults may originate in the plant itself or in the automatic control system. Subsidiary duties may be concerned with the recording or transmission of data, with minor maintenance, or with tasks not directly connected with the control of the process.

The relevant model of the process controller would seem to be one depicting a multi-channel decision-maker embedded within a fairly slow-response dynamic system, the variables of which are to be stabilized or optimized over a period of time. The construction of such a model is not without difficulties of several types. The amount of observable behaviour may be small and not easily interpretable; different operators may employ varying strategies to attain their immediate goal; the effect of operators' decisions may be highly complex and remote in time from the initiating action; skilled performers are frequently unable to analyse and describe the nature of their own skill.

For purposes of this Preview, two types of taxonomy are outlined, and the twelve contributions are located within these
structures.   Firstly, control systems are described in terms of a
four-element model (SHEL) which includes the human operator who
must be correctly interfaced with other system components.
Secondly, a six-fold classification of research and development
techniques is described, within which studies of control systems
may be organized.

2. THE SHEL MODEL

Control Systems may be conveniently analysed into four basic
types of component, viz,

SOFTWARE: The rules, procedures and programmes describing how
             the system should work.
HARDWARE: The fabricated components of which the system is
             built.
ENVIRONMENT: The prevailing physical, economic and social back-
             ground in which the system functions.
LIVEWARE: The human beings which contribute to the operation
             of the system.

The knowledge necessary to design a system, to understand and
control its workings, to modify it, or to investigate its malfunctions, comprises information concerning each of the four types
of component.   But more than this;   system knowledge is largely
concerned with the problems of interfacing the elements.   The
concept of a system described in terms of these four component
types and emphasising their interactions has been called the SHEL
Model.

Some of the interfacing problems are better known and have
received more attention than others, e.g.,

H-E interface: The effects of temperature, vibration, impact,
                 and moisture on components.
H-H interface: Standardization of power supplies, plugs and
                 sockets, rack and case sizes for components.

An anthropocentric version of the SHEL model is illustrated
in Figure 1.   Here, the four interface involving the L component
are shown.   Each of these requires proper attention in design.

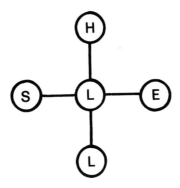

Figure 1. The SHEL Model. In this representation, the four
components and their interfaces are configured in a way which
illustrates the relationship between LIVEWARE and other system
components.

L-H interface: The "man-machine" interface; the most
                widely researched aspect of ergonomics.
L-S interface: The somewhat neglected area of study concerning
                the fitting together of men with operating
                procedures, rules, conventions, codes,
                languages, laws and traditions.
L-E interface: Environmental and organisational aspects.
L-L interface: The interaction within crews, teams and
                small groups.

A comprehensive investigation into the optimization of each of
these four interfaces would involve an ambitious programme of
research and development to precede any human factors applications
work. Indeed, it is unlikely that any such programme has yet been
attempted in the process industries. To date, ergonomics effort
has been confined to relatively restricted areas within the total
system in order that development work may be carried out at a cost,

and within a time-scale, which make viable the implementation of resulting recommendations. Thus progress has been achieved within such particular areas as display design, control room layout, and operator training.

A further problem which has hindered the widespread application of research findings in process studies is the high degree of specificity appertaining to controllers' tasks. Only little may be said concerning the nature of the job of the process controller when this job is divorced from the individual characteristics of any particular SHEL system. The nature of the interfaces vary substantially in different situations dependent upon the type of feedstocks involved, the type of reactions employed, the economic value of the products, the extent to which the process may be defined quantitatively, the sophistication of the technology, and many other such factors. This rich interaction between the component parts of the system leads inevitably to a lack of simple and general solutions to the problems of the human operator in process control.

3. CONTROL TASKS AND THEIR ALLOCATION

Different levels of analysis may be used to arrive at a definable "task" element. Using a fairly coarse analysis, a typical process may involve the operator in some or all of the following functions:

*Measurement	*Optimisation
*Data Inputting	*Communication
*Data Processing	*Data Logging
*Continuous Tracking	*Scheduling
*Sequential Controlling	*Fault Diagnosis
*Monitoring	*Fault Rectification

To a large extent, the job of an operator depends upon the relative significance of these functions within a given process, and the extent to which the functions are carried out automatically. The variety of possible allocations of function - and consequently the nature of the man's role - is wide.

Within a single control loop, the various functions may be carried out by the operator, by automatic equipment, or by some combination of the two. The allocation decision may be made on the basis of a systematic consideration of the relative merits of men and machines, or may owe its origin to tradition, oversight, or some other less desirable reason. Some examples of allocations for the seven elements within a control loop are shown in Table 1. To a large extent, the role of human factors expertise in process control is concerned with the optimization of

Table 1: Examples of possible allocation decisions for different component parts of a control loop.

FUNCTION	EXAMPLE	ALLOCATION
1 Detect	Measure X-ray radiation	Machine
	Liquid viscosity	Man or machine
2 Transmit data	Convey temperature value to controller	Machine
	Inform plant manager of daily output	Man or machine
3 Process data	Identify unusual flow rates	Man and machine
	Calculate mean hourly temperatures	Machine
4 Record	Record conditions at shut-down	Man
	Log hourly plant values	Machine
5 Compare	Compare sample colour with standard	Man
	Compare flow-rate with set-point	Machine
6 Decide	Adjust valve position by 10%	Machine
	Diagnose cause of instability	Man and machine
7 Act	Operate control to initiate start-up	Man
	Increase coolant flow-rate	Machine

of such allocations, and of the consequent system interfaces.

4. METHODS OF INVESTIGATION

Numerous approaches to the study of system design and operation are possible. One classification of techniques is set out below. Some of these techniques are discussed in Drury's paper and are illustrated in the papers within this session.

*System Analysis, i.e. a priori analysis of the requirements
    necessary for the system to meet its specification.
*System Performance Assessment, i.e. objective and subjective
    measures of the level at which the system performs in relation
    to a criterion.
*Activity and Strategy Analysis, i.e. studies of what people do;
    why and how they do them.   The basic data may originate with
    either an observer or the performer.
*Workload Assessment, i.e. the evaluation of the physical or
    mental "cost" to the operator of his performance.
*Experimental Studies, i.e. the collection of data from situations
    controlled and contrived by the experimenter.
*System Failure Analysis, i.e. the examination of errors, mal-
    functions, problems and accidents.

4.1 Experimental Studies

Each of these methods has its own particular advantage and the relative merits of the methods may be considered only in relation to the objective of the study.   Traditionally, a good deal of attention has been given to Experimental Studies, and the results of these have been extrapolated in the form of recommendations relevant to system design.   In the present session, Kvalseth et al. describe subjects' trade-off decisions in a situation where both data sampling and performance errors involve a notional penalty.   McLeod compares the tracking ability of naive and experienced subjects in a control task which simulates the positioning of neutron-absorbing rods in a nuclear reactor.

In his paper devoted to a review of the methodology of process ergonomics, Drury explicitly indicates his support for the more comprehensive and grandiose assault as advocated by Lees (1974):

"Serious progress would now seem to depend on sustained and systematic long-term research involving the study of the totality of the operator's job in all its complexity and probably using sophisticated and expensive equipment". (pp. 410-411).

4.2 Activity and Strategy Analysis

The "black box" approach provides an incomplete analysis of complex task performance. The investigator requires to construct a description of the way in which an operator "sees" the plant, in order that the operator's behaviour may be interpreted in terms of a strategy. "Measures of strategy go one level deeper than performance measurement - they provide some of the reasons for observed changes in performance". (Drury)

The technique of modelling the operator's model is discussed by Rasmussen. The procedure utilises several sorts of data collection and interpretation. "...... the analysis of verbal protocols collected from process operators can serve only as a guide or intermittent indication of his activity at several levels". Part of the problem, of course, stems from the fact that experts in the performance of skilled activities are by no means experts in understanding the nature of their own expertise. The investigator plays the role of a detective, utilising a variety of methods and system engineering concepts in an attempt to reveal the nature of the operator's skills.

Sampling strategies of subjects, described by Kvalseth et al. was shown to be affected both by sampling cost and error cost. Analagously, the experienced subjects in McLeod's sample exhibited a conservative control strategy derived, presumably, from their knowledge of the penalty associated with overshoots on the real reactor. Smith describes analyses of different search strategies adopted by his subjects in the solution of problems.

4.3 System Failure Analysis

Lees and Sayers discuss the function of the operator in dealing with emergency conditions. This is essentially a three-part procedure involving Detection, Diagnosis and Action. Errors may occur at any one of these stages. One basic difficulty in studying this type of behaviour is the paucity of data resulting from the inevitable rarity of the events either on real plant or on a realistic simulator.

5. L-H INTERFACING

The problems of man-machine interfacing in control may be sub-divided into three broad areas, viz,

H-to-L information flow: Display Design
L-to-H information flow: Control Design

H and L dynamic matching: Optimising the hardware
                             characteristics in relation to
                             human control capability.

Of these areas, that of display design has received the
largest amount of ergonomics attention to date.   With the advent
of the computer together with the CRT and other electronic
components, displays have reached a high level of sophistication
and efficiency.   Conversely, and in spite of a wide range of
computer input devices including joy-sticks, light-pens, keyboards,
track-balls, pressure tablets, and rho-theta pens, it is still
comparatively difficult in many situations for men to communicate
conveniently with the hardware.

Zimmerman describes some techniques for the production of
video displays having versatility in content and format.   Shackel
describes two types of visual display; one a low-cost simple-
technology "stateboard", the other an experimental computer-driven
predictor display.

The problem of serial versus parallel information display in
the caseof typical d.d.c. operator panels was discussed by Edwards
and Lees, (1972).   The following features of the serial display
were noted (p 150):

* The value of only one variable is displayed to the Operator at
     a time.
* The presentation is digital rather than analogue.
* There is no spatial coding in the information display and
     the layout of controls.
* No recent history of values is displayed.
* Specific behaviour is required in order to generate a display.
* Foremen, managers and maintenance fitters have no access to
     plant information without disturbing the operator.

Geiser and Schumacher examine the parallel versus serial
controller problem in the context of manual control, and conclude
that the former are superior.   They go on to examine the use of
multi-variable polar displays with compatible controls.

Such polar displays are also used in studies described by
Smith.

Both displays and controls are included within the
experimental "input-output-colour-screen-system" (IOC) described
by Grimm.   This comprehensive system includes a colour display
comprising both graphic and alphanumeric elements, and attempts to
ease the human output task by using a virtual keyboard.

Pack's paper describes an ergonomics review of existing control

rooms in nuclear power plants, and goes on to outline a projected
research programme using a sophisticated plant simulator.

Human outputting and its imitation by hardware is discussed
by Thompson, who describes the problems of using robots to perform
assembly tasks and related manipulative skills.

6. SUMMARY

The papers presented within this session display a wide
range of orientation.   In SHEL terms, there is a preponderance
of emphasis on man-machine (L-H) interfacing.   In terms of
methodology, the emphasis is upon experimental investigations and
strategy analysis.   The technical difficulties associated with the
assessment of performance or with operator workload assessment
remain daunting.   The extent to which formalized models of the
human operator are used appears to be fairly slight.

7. REFERENCES

Edwards, Elwyn and Lees, Frank P., 1972 Man and Computer in Process
      Control.   (London: The Institution of Chemical Engineers).

Lees, Frank P., 1974, Research on the Process Operator in Edwards,
      E. and Lees, F.P. (Eds.) The Human Operator in Process
      Control (London: Taylor and Francis).

THE BEHAVIOUR OF PROCESS OPERATORS UNDER EMERGENCY CONDITIONS

F.P. Lees[1] and B. Sayers[2]

1) Department of Chemical Engineering
   Loughborough University of Technology
   Loughborough LE11 3TU, U.K.

2) U.K. Atomic Energy Authority, Systems Reliability
   Service, Wigshaw Lane, Culcheth, Warrington WA3
   4NE, U.K.

INTRODUCTION

On many types of large-scale plant the penalties of a serious failure are now very great. This has been underlined by recent events such as the disaster at Flixborough. When a fault does occur on such a plant it is dealt with by the control system, which includes both the instrumentation and the human operator. As other control functions become more automated, attention focuses increasingly on fault administration.

In process plants generally there are differing philosophies on the allocation of function in fault administration between man and machine. In some the operator deals with fault conditions with few automatic aids and is thus required to assure both safe and economic operation. In others automatic protective systems are provided to shut the plant down if it is moving close to an unsafe condition and the operator has the economic role of preventing the development of conditions which will cause shutdown.

In a plant without protective systems the process operator is effectively given the duty of keeping the plant running if he can, but shutting it down if he must. This tends to create a conflict of priorities in his mind. Usually he will try to keep the plant running if he possibly can and may tend to take necessary shutdown action too late. There are numerous case histories which show the dangers inherent in this situation (Lees, in press(b)).

The nuclear industry in the U.K., and elsewhere, has a well established practice of automatic protection. The approach is that if an unsafe condition can credibly occur a protective system is provided to guard against it (Green and Bourne, 1966). This philosophy assigns to the operator the essentially economic role of keeping the plant running. The chemical industry is beginning to adopt a similar approach and the number of protective systems is growing rapidly, though it should be emphasised that many existing plants have only partial automatic protection. In practice, and particularly in the process industries, this clearcut allocation of function is not easily realised and the process operator tends to retain a residual safety role.

In the first place, although high integrity protective systems with 2/3 voting are used on particularly hazardous processes (Stewart, 1971), many trip systems do not have this degree of integrity.

Protective systems have other limitations. One is that it is very difficult to foresee and design for all possible faults, particularly those arising from combinations of events. It is true, of course, that even if a process condition arises from an unexpected cause a protective system will usually handle it safely. But there remains a residual of events, usually of low probability, against which there is no protection either because they were unforeseen or because their probability was estimated as below the designer's cutoff level.

Another problem is that a protective system is only partially effective against certain types of fault such as a failure of containment. In such an event the instrumentation can initiate blowdown, shutoff and shutdown sequences, but while this may reduce the hazardous escape of materials, it does not eliminate it.

Yet another difficulty is that many hazards occur not during steady running but during normal startup and shutdown or during the period after a trip and startup from that condition. A well-designed protective system is designed, of course, for these transitional regimes as well as for continuous operation. Nevertheless this remains something of a problem area.

Even with automatic protective systems, therefore, the process operator tends to retain a residual safety function. Since high probability hazards will be dealt with by the automatic equipment, the events which the operator has to handle will have low probability. The reliability of the operator in carrying out such tasks tends to be low. Thus the designer can only rely on the operator to reduce the probability of low probability hazards by a small factor. These last remarks apply specifically to safety. The situation with respect to economics is quite different. Here the operator has the task of preventing the development of conditions which will trigger the shutdown system. Although he is aided to various degrees by the automatic controls he retains a primary role in this area.

An emergency situation occurs when the fault, or the situation resulting from it, is unexpected, may have serious safety and/or economic consequences and requires rapid remedial action. In these conditions the operator is under various kinds of stress, particularly anxiety, information overload and time stresses.

It is not assumed here, therefore, that the prime feature of a process emergency is necessarily safety considerations. On the contrary the presumption is that it will normally be economics. It is recognised, however, that there will be some cases where safety predominates.

The first part of the paper describes experimental work on the behaviour of process operators under emergency conditions. In this work the fault condition, the allowable response time and the corrective action required were relatively well defined. The data obtained may be regarded, therefore, as a contribution to the estimation of an upper limit of operator reliability in emergencies.

An emergency normally implies the need for a quick response. In the work described the allowable response time never exceeded 90 seconds. Under these conditions the probability of success correlates strongly with the allowable response time.

Data on operator reliability in emergencies are increasingly required for reliability studies. The application of reliability engineering is now proceeding very rapidly in the process industries. The control system was one of the first aspects to receive attention and there is inevitably a demand for reliability data on operators. Workers in human factors have now done a considerable amount of work on human error in industrial tasks, notably Swain and coworkers (Swain, 1964, 1969 and 1972a). Human error data banks have been built up (Altman 1964; Rigby 1967) and are being used (Swain, 1964 and 1974;Ablitt 1969). The specific problem of process operator reliability has been discussed by both the authors (Edwards and Lees, 1973; Lees, 1973 and in press(a); Sayers, 1971). Studies of process hazards, often using fault trees, now frequently include estimates of operator error (Lawley, 1974). The well-known study of accident risks in nuclear power reactors by N.Rasmussen and coworkers (U.S. Atomic Energy Commission, 1974) also uses this approach. However, there is very little quantitative information available on operator reliability in emergencies.

There is also relatively little information on the proportion of emergencies for which operator error is responsible. This is discussed by Rasmussen (1969) and Lees (in press(b); the latter quotes a study by Moore (1966) in which 10% of major faults on some nuclear research reactors were attributed to human mal-operation.

The second part of the paper reviews the present situation in respect of fault administration by the process operator. In general, work in this area places rather less emphasis on the allowable response time and tends to be concerned with more complex decision situations. In this context it is convenient, where the situation is generally similar but the allowable response time is larger than that defining an emergency, to refer instead to a serious fault. A serious fault can turn into an emergency if time runs out. Work on fault administration has not yet reached the point of being able to quantify operator reliability in serious fault conditions

with complex decision-making, but nevertheless considerable
progress has been made.

EXPERIMENTAL WORK ON EMERGENCY BEHAVIOUR

The U.K. Atomic Energy Authority has carried out over a
period of years a programme of work on process operators. Three
stages of this work are described here.

Laboratory Experiments on a Simple Panel

An initial series of experiments was conducted to gain a feel
for the basic response characteristics and reliability of subjects
performing a simple but industrially relevant task and to investigate some of the factors which might influence performance.

The basic experiment was the surveillance of a simple
instrument panel consisting of a dial, a pushbutton and a lamp.
The instrument indicated a steady reading under normal conditions
but could be made to approach or pass a higher reading, the danger
condition, at various rates. After the danger point had been passed
the warning lamp would light. The subjects were instructed to
press the pushbutton immediately it became apparent that the danger
condition was inevitable. After a predetermined time the signal
reverted to normal.

Experiments conducted on this apparatus gave data on the
distribution of response times and on the probability of failing to
respond at all within the specified period. A value of about 10^{-3}
was obtained for the latter.

Tests were also carried out to investigate the effect of
various factors which might influence performance: physical environment, equipment design, job instructions, stress factors, boredom,
individual background. It is possible here only to state qualit-
atively some of the stronger conclusions as they relate to industrial operators: 1) no effect of physical environment was
observed, within normal control room limits; 2) no effect of
length of watch (vigilance effect) was observed, within normal
8-hour shifts; 3) boredom can lead to a marked deterioration in
performance.

Industrial Experiments Using HORATIO

These experiments were set up to explore in greater depth,
over a longer time period and in actual industrial environments,
much the same factors as in the initial experiments.

The equipment used was HORATIO (Human Operator Response
Analyser and Timer for Infrequent Occurrences). This device automatically produces signals which are reasonably representative in
form and time distribution of certain types of fault indication
and measures the time interval between the onset of the signal and
the operator's response to it. The actual control room instruments may be used as the displays if desired. The signals may be
programmed to be systematic or random. The signal duration is
limited to a predetermined time after which the signal reverts to

its normal value. Signal rates can be made to vary in the range 10 to 10^{-4} per hour. The unit provides the facility for presenting visual or audible alarms and has a pushbutton to allow cancellation of the signal.

A series of experiments was done with process operators in nuclear reactor control rooms using this equipment. The subjects were asked to respond to a simultaneous visual indication and audible alarm by pressing the pushbutton. In Test 1 the reactor was a small research reactor with day working only, while in Test 2 it was a power reactor with 3-shift working. The signal rates were 1.5 and 0.35 per hour respectively. The response times are shown in Fig.1 and have a log normal distribution. In these experiments the probability of failure to respond at all within the allowable period was again about 10^{-3}.

A further series of experiments, Test 3, was conducted in which the number of decisions involved in the task was increased. In these there was a visual indication only, the pointer moved in both directions and there were two buttons to push. The instructions were to press a green or a red button depending on whether the signal had violated or was about to violate, the lower or the upper limit respectively. The signal rate was 10 signals in 10 minutes. The response times which again give a log normal distribution are shown in Fig.1. But in these experiments, where failure could occur either by not responding at all within the allowable time or by pressing the wrong button, the probability of failure was about 6×10^{-3}.

A further description of work using HORATIO is given by Green (1969).

Simulator Experiments of Reactor Faults

The object of these experiments was to study operator behaviour in response to more realistic fault conditions. The work was done on training simulators in the U.K. Atomic Energy Authority and the Central Electricity Generating Board. The simulators closely resemble the equipment on the plant and give a realistic 'feel' for its operational characteristics. The simulator rooms resemble plant control rooms.

The experiments consisted of simulating a number of plant failures and assessing the operator's response and reliability. Before the fault appears the operator is occupied with normal control of the plant. His reactions when the fault occurs are therefore somewhat complex. Initially he is expected to attempt to control the situation, but when it appears that a genuine and uncontrollable fault has occurred he should shut down the plant.

The faults simulated were those shown in Tables 1 and 2. The task of the operator was in all cases to trip the plant, using a single pushbutton, before the trip level was reached. The demand rate was 10 per hour.

The results given in Tables 1 and 2 suggest that for this type of task operator reliability is low for an allowable response

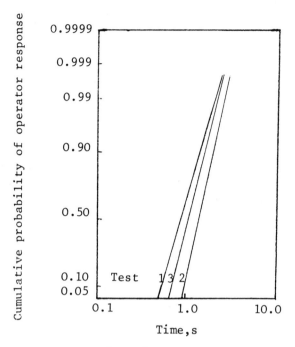

Fig.1. Operator response times in nuclear reactor control rooms

Table 1. Operator behaviour in simulated fault conditions (1)

		Fault condition			
		Control rod runout	Blower failure	Gas temp. rise	All
No. of tests	a	9	15	10	34
Time to reach trip level from onset of fault(s)	b	64	3	28	–
Actual response time(s)					
Minimum		20	1.5	7	–
Maximum		64	65	39	–
Mean	c	33.6	7.9	19.6	–
Actual response time/ allowable response time	c/b	0.53	2.6	0.7	–
No. of failures to trip	d	0	7	2	9
Probability of failure					
Mean	d/a	0	0.47	0.2	0.26
9 9% confidence limit		0.41	0.77	0.61	0.49

time of less than 30 seconds, high for a time greater than 60
seconds and intermediate in the range 30–60 seconds. Several
features of this task made success more probable than in industrial
emergency responses. The required response was to push a single
button. The demand rate was very high compared with that for an

Table 2. Operator behaviour in simulated fault conditions (2)

| | Fault condition | | | | | | | |
	Control rod runout		Coolant flow fault				Gas temp. rise		All
No. of tests	9	9	14	7	4	5	10	10	68
Time to reach trip level from onset of fault(s)	43.5	64.0	3.0	7.9	10.8	16.2	21.0	28.0	-
Actual response time(s)									
Minimum	2.0	20.0	1.5	5.4	7.8	5.4	10.2	7.0	-
Maximum	30.6	64.0	13.0	10.8	9.6	9.6	21.6	39.0	-
Mean	14.4	33.6	3.8	7.6	8.7	7.8	14.9	19.6	-
Actual response time/ allowable response time	0.33	0.53	1.27	0.96	0.81	0.48	0.71	0.70	-
No. of failures to trip	0	0	6	3	0	0	0	0	9
Probability of failure									
Mean	0	0	0.43	0.43	0	0	0	0	0.13
99% confidence limit	0.41	0.41	0.75	0.83	0.65	0.59	0.39	0.39	0.27

industrial manual trip which might be 10^{-4} per hour. The data may
therefore be regarded as setting an upper limit to the reliability
of operators in an emergency. For a more complex and less frequent
task the reliability will be lower.

It is interesting to compare the mean probability of failure
in this task, which for Tables 1 and 2 combined is 0.18, with that
for aircraft emergencies. There is a study of these by Ronan (1953),
while Swain (1972b) quotes probabilities of ineffective behaviour
per emergency of 0.31 and 0.32 for real and simulated emergencies.
The latter figure breaks down into 0.14 failure to detect a signal
within a specified time and 0.18 other ineffective behaviour. More
recently Swain (1974) has given a figure of 0.16 ineffective behaviour per emergency; it is not clear if this excludes detection of
the signal.

In conclusion two points may be emphasised. The tasks simulated were related to the safety rather than the economic function
of the operator, but the data are equally applicable to the latter.
The study described was fairly limited and there is need for much
more work.

DEVELOPMENTS IN FAULT ADMINISTRATION

There is also now a considerable body of work on fault administration which is relevant to process operator behaviour in emergencies in so far as it provides a basis for more informed decision-
making in areas of system design such as allocation of function,
personnel selection, task analysis and training, job aids and
computer-based aids, information display and so on.

It is often convenient to consider fault administration as
consisting of three stages: fault detection, diagnosis and
correction.

As already stated the operator's most important function is to
try to prevent the development of serious fault conditions. This

aspect cannot really be isolated from manual control in general, on which much has been published, but mention may be made in particular of the work on information sampling by Crossman, Cooke and Beishon (1964), on information sampling and mental models by Bainbridge and coworkers (Bainbridge, Beishon, Hemming and Splaine, 1968; Bainbridge 1974) and on information sampling and fault administration by de Jong and Köster (1971).

West and Clark (1974) have studied the behaviour of operators in fault administration on a computer-controlled pilot plant. They found that operators may have difficulty in distinguishing the gradual development of a disturbance from the slow drifting which can sometimes occur. The same problem occurred in the simulation experiments described above.

Considering first fault detection, there is much scope for improvement of ordinary process alarm systems, conventional or computer-based. This has been discussed by Andow and Lees (1974).

Another related area is the detection of faults, particularly incipient faults, which are not signalled by the instruments or which occur in the instruments themselves. Operator detection of instrument malfunction has been studied by Anyakora and Lees (1971). There are also more general discussions of malfunction detection by operators and computers (Anyakora and Lees, 1972; Edwards and Lees 1973).

Some work has been done on computer graphic displays for process state assessment and fault administration. Survey displays which allow the operator to make an 'at-a-glance' assessment of process state are probably most important. But several special fault displays have also been developed such as the status array (Stainthorp and West, 1974) and alarm displays using grouped equip-ment symbols (Rasmussen, 1974). West and Clark found that chart recorders were of particular value in fault situations.

Duncan and coworkers (Duncan 1974; Duncan and Shepherd 1975 and in press) have done much work on the development of task analy-sis for training design and have studied fault administration on an acid purification plant and a chlorine cellroom. The task analysis involves interviewing personnel and developing an explicit statement of the hierarchy of tasks. A task is then redescribed into a set of subordinate 'operations' whose execution is governed by a 'plan'. This task analysis furnishes the training officer with an appropriate methodology and provides a rational basis for task training, including fault administration.

In this work panel fault diagnosis procedures are given in the form of fault-symptom matrices (equivalent to truth tables) and decision trees (equivalent to fault trees but including one-one fault correction instructions). In one series of tests on fault diagnosis on a simulator panel with two groups of trainees of which one practised diagnosis but had no decision tree and the other had a decision tree, the performance of the latter was much better. In another series of tests using slide projection of a panel showing static fault displays, subjects achieved high performance by

cumulative part task training in which they gradually acquired the
ability to recognise the pattern associated with a particular fault.

An alternative to the use of a logic tree in diagnostics is
the use of probability information. Man's tendency to try first
the high-probability path is well known and has been studied in the
context of process control by Rasmussen and Jensen (1974). Anyakora
and Lees (1971) have discussed the operator's use of probability
in detecting instrument malfunction. Duncan and Shepherd (1975)
recommend the use of probability information strategies for some
unstructured search tasks and process state assessments.

There are a number of developments in the use of the computer
to assist the operator in fault administration. Alarm analysis at
nuclear power stations is described by Patterson (1968) and Welbourne (1968). Here the computer scans the process measurements
for alarm conditions and then analyses these alarms to diagnose
the fault. This facility requires great technical effort and the
only example in the chemical industry appears to be the experimental one described by Barth and Maarleveld (1967). Work has been
reported recently on more fundamental and economical methods of
producing the analysis logic using information flow concepts
(Powers and Tompkins, 1974; Andow and Lees, 1975). However, computer alarm analysis also involves considerable human factors
problems. These have been discussed by Rasmussen (1968).

Corrective action by operator or computer is typically fault
reporting, equipment changeover, change of operating point, re-
scheduling/balancing or partial/complete shutdown. In general,
this is a neglected field. One of the few pieces of work in this
area is that of Duncan described above which includes reporting
and restoration procedures following from the diagnostic task and
also deals with difficulties involved in particular operations such
as identifying hand valves. However, there has recently been some
interesting work by Rivas, Rudd, and Kelly (1974) on computer-based
interlocks which may presage further developments.

There appears to be scope for work on the ranking of process
emergencies on the lines of the aircraft emergency ranking scale
developed by Rigby and Edelman (1968), though the diversity of
process situations is a difficulty here.

Finally the large amount of work on stress is very relevant.
In process emergency situations this is likely to arise from anxiety
about physical danger or management reprimand, from information
overload or time stress. Only two points will be mentioned here.
One is that one of the objectives of training as developed by Duncan
is to reinforce the operator's confidence by success in task execution during training. The other is that there exists the phen-
omenon of operator indecision. Bainbridge (1974) describes how
some subjects in an electric arc furnace simulation study can choose
what action to take, but cannot bring themselves to take it. A
similar effect was found in the simulation work described earlier,
where in one case the operator's mind went completely blank. The
provision of confirmatory information, in display design or in

diagnostic procedures or facilities (Rasmussen 1968), may be helpful
in this context, but is not the whole answer.

REFERENCES

Ablitt, J.F., 1969, U.K. Atomic Energy Authority, Rep. AHSB (S) R160.

Altman, J.W., 1964, A central store of human performance data,
Symp. on Quantification of Human Performance, Albuquerque, N.Mex.

Andow, P.K. and Lees F.P., 1974, Loss Prevention and Safety
Promotion in the Process Industries (Ed.C.H.Buschmann) (Amsterdam:
Elsevier), p.299.

Andow, P.K. and Lees, F.P., 1975, Trans.Instn.Chem.Engrs., 53, 195.

Anyakora, S.N. and Lees, F.P., 1971, Chem.Engr., Lond., 264, 304.

Anyakora, S.N. and Lees, F.P., 1972, Decision, Design and the
Computer (London: Instn.Chem.Engrs.) 6: 7.

Bainbridge, L., Beishon,J.,Hemming, J.H. and Splaine,M., 1968,
Opl.Res.Quart., 19, Special Conf. Issue, p.91.

Bainbridge, L., 1974, in Edwards, E. and Lees, F.P., op.cit,p.146.

Barth, J. and Maarleveld, A., 1967, The Application of Automation
in the Process Industries (Ed.J.M.Pirie) (London:Instn.Chem.Engrs.),
p.23.

Crossman, E.R.F.W., Cooke, J. and Beishon, R.J., 1964, Univ.of California, Berkeley, Calif.,Hum.Factors in Technol.Res.Gp.Rep.HFT64-11-7.
See also Edwards, E. and Lees, F.P., op.cit., p.25.

Duncan, K.D., 1974, in Edwards,E. and Lees, F.P., op.cit., p.283.

Duncan, K.D. and Shepherd, A., 1975, Analysis and training of fault
location tasks in the chemical industry, Chem.and Allied Prod.Ind.
Training Board, Staines, Middlesex, Rep.

Duncan, K.D. and Shepherd, A., A simulator and training technique
for diagnosing plant failures for control panels, Ergonomics, in
press.

Edwards,E. and Lees,F.P., 1973, Man and Computer in Process Control
(London: Inst.Chem.Engrs.).

Edwards,E. and Lees,F.P., (eds), 1974, The Human Operator in Process
Control (London: Taylor and Francis).

Green, A.E. and Bourne, A.J., 1966, U.K. Atomic Energy Authority,Rep.
AHSB(S) R117.

Green, A.E., 1969, U.K. Atomic Energy Authority Rep. AHSB(S) R172.
See also Instrum.Pract., 1970, 24, 109.

de Jong, J.J. and Köster, E.P., 1971, The human operator in the
computer controlled refinery, Proc.Eighth World Petrol,Cong.,Moscow
(London : Inst.Petrol.). See also Edwards,E.and Lees,F.P., op.cit.,
p.196.

Lawley, H.G., 1974, Loss Prevention Vol.8, Chem.Engng.Prog.Tech-
nical Manual (New York: Am.Inst.Chem.Engrs.), p.105.

Lees, F.P., 1973, I.E.E.E. Trans.Reliab., R-22, 124.

Lees, F.P., Design for man-machine system reliability in process
control, Generic Techniques in Systems Reliability Assessment (NATO
Advanced Study Institute, Liverpool) (Amsterdam:Nordhoff),in press(a).

Lees, F.P., The reliability of instrumentation, Chemy.Ind.,
in press (b).

Moore, J.C., 1966, Nucl.Engng., 11(118) March,195, and 11(119) April, 306.
Patterson, D., 1968, Proc.I.E.E., 115, 1858.
Powers, G.J. and Tompkins, F.C., 1974, A.I.Ch.E.J., 20, 376.
Rasmussen, J., 1968, Atomic Energy Commission, Res.Est., Risö, Denmark, Rep.Risö-M-686. See also Edwards,E.and Lees, F.P., op.cit., p.222.
Rasmussen, J., 1969, Man-machine communication in the light of accident records, Man-Machine Systems, I.E.E.E.Conf.Rec.69C58-MMS.
Rasmussen, J., 1974, private communication.
Rasmussen, J. and Jensen,A., 1974, Ergonomics, 17, 293.
Rigby,L.V., 1967, Sandia Laboratories, Albuquerque, N.Mex.,Rep. SC-R-67-1150.
Rigby, L.V. and Edelman, D.A., 1968, Hum.Factors,10,475.
Rivas,J.R., Rudd, D.F. and Kelly, L.R., 1974, A.I.Ch.E.J.,20,311.
Ronan, W.W., 1953, Am.Inst.Res.,Pittsburgh,Pa.,Rep.AIR-153-53-FR-44.
Sayers, B., 1971, U.K. Atomic Energy Authority, Systems Reliability Service, Rep. SRS/GR/9.
Stainthorp, F.P. and West, B., 1974, Chem.Engr., 289,526.
Stewart, R.M., 1971, Major Loss Prevention in the Process Industries (London: Instn.Chem.Engrs.), p.99.
Swain, A.D., 1964, Sandia Laboratories, Albuquerque, N.Mex., Rep. SC-R-64-1338.
Swain, A.D., 1969, Sandia Laboratories, Albuquerque, N.Mex., Rep. SC-R-69-1236.
Swain, A.D., 1972a, Design Techniques for Improving Human Perform-ance in Production (London: Industrial and Commercial Techniques Ltd.)
Swain, A.D., 1972b, private communication. See Edwards,E.and Lees, F.P., (1973), op.cit., p.92.
Swain, A.D., 1974, Sandia Laboratories, Albuquerque, N.Mex.and Livermore, Calif., Rep. SAND 74-0051.
U.S. Atomic Energy Commission, 1974, Rep. WASH 1400 (Washington, D.C.).
Welbourne, D., 1968, Proc. I.E.E., 115, 1726.
West, B. and Clark, J.A., 1974, in Edwards, E and Lees, F.P., op.cit., p.206.

EVALUATION OF MAN-MACHINE RELATIONSHIPS IN U.S. NUCLEAR POWER PLANTS

Randall W. Pack

Electric Power Research Institute

Palo Alto, California, USA

The Electric Power Research Institute (EPRI) began operations in 1973 for the purpose of expanding electric energy research and development under the voluntary sponsorship of the United States utility industry, public, private, and cooperative. Its goal is to develop a broad, coordinated, advanced technology program for improving electric power production, transmission, distribution, and utilization in an environmentally acceptable manner. More than 500 member organizations, accounting for approximately 80% of the U.S. electric power generating capacity, support the EPRI program. For 1976 the members have agreed to contribute 0.140 mills per kilowatt hour of sales, giving EPRI a 1976 research and development planning guideline budget of $150 million.

The EPRI research programs described in this paper concern nuclear power plant operator performance and control system design. Problems and developments in the area of control room design were discussed at a recent International Atomic Energy Agency specialists meeting in San Francisco [1]. Changing conditions mentioned at that meeting included the following:

- Increased system complexity due to both larger plants and additional automation of protective circuitry.

- Introduction of digital computers as integral parts of the indication and control loops.

- Planned increase in use of such variable format display devices as cathode ray tubes (CRTs).

● New regulations, standards, and technical specifications.

The absence of design standards and the large number of organizations involved in control room and control system design have generated a plethora of approaches. The initial EPRI projects are directed largely towards evaluating the effectiveness of the various approaches taken.

HUMAN FACTORS REVIEW OF CONTROL ROOM DESIGN

The Reactor Safety Study WASH-1400 [2], performed for the U.S. Atomic Energy Commission (AEC), criticized the design of controls and displays and their arrangements on operator panels in nuclear plants as deviating from human engineering standards generally accepted in other industries and specified for the design of man-machine systems. In response to this and similar criticisms from within the utility industry, EPRI retained an experienced team from Lockheed Missiles & Space Company, Inc., to review the human factors aspect of the control rooms of nuclear power plants which recently have become operational. The review covers five plants and evaluates current nuclear practices in the light of knowledge developed in other industries and estimates the significance of the differences in terms of their potential effects on reactor safety and reliability. The review is focusing primarily on the training simulators corresponding to the selected power plants due both to the high accessibility of simulators relative to operational plants and to the availability of opportunities to study operator actions during simulation of major plant transient operations. The following five designs are being included in the study:

Nuclear Power Plant	Plant Location	Simulator Location
Dresden 2	Morris, Ill.	Morris, Ill.
Rancho Seco	Clay Station, Ca.	Lynchburg, Va.
Zion 1	Zion, Ill.	Zion, Ill.
Calvert Cliffs	Lusby, Md.	Windsor, Conn.
Indian Point 2	Buchanan, N.Y.	Buchanan, N.Y.

The project, EPRI RP 501, began in June 1975 and completion is scheduled for April 1976. NUS Corporation is providing the Lockheed team with training, consulting, and liaison services. To date, visits associated with the Indian Point and Zion designs have been completed.

Pilot Study

Indian Point was used for the project pilot study, a two week visit, in which the effectiveness of candidate human factors measurement methods were studied. Some of the methods used were guided interview forms, human factors engineering checklists based on aerospace industry standards, direct observations of operator performance during simulator and plant operation, evaluations of procedures, analyses of operator tasks, and investigations of operator errors described in events reported during the past several years. After the pilot study the guided interview forms were reworded to eliminate ambiguity discovered in the phrasing of some questions and several unproductive questions were deleted. In general, however, the forms were evaluated as very useful methods of obtaining human factors information based upon the experience of the plant operators and simulator instructors. The checklists and direct performance observations were valuable supplements to the interview forms.

A task analysis was performed on two simulations of steam generator tube ruptures. The specific sequence of events was different in each case because of the interdependencies of system parameters and variations caused by control manipulations, and because of differences in operator actions allowed within the generalized procedures. The study team recommended that any future task analyses on training simulators be made with the assistance of the simulator computers for event documentation.

Project End Products

The ultimate program objective is to improve the effectiveness of reactor operator performance with accompanying benefits in reactor safety and reliability. The following end products are expected for project RP 501:

- An authoritative and well-documented qualitative and quantitative assessment of the present generation nuclear power plant control rooms in terms of human factors considerations.

- An assessment of the degree of commonality between control room simulators and corresponding operational sites.

- Guidelines required for human factors engineering standards that may be applied to the development of control room designs.

- Suggested follow-on simulation studies, research, and analyses in the human factors field.

- Human factors implications associated with the designs of future generations of control rooms, e.g., increasing levels of automation.

- Recommendations regarding operator training programs, especially training equipment.

- Suggested improvements for the content and format of operator procedures and manuals.

- Observations concerning the selection of operator personnel based on performance monitoring during participation in the training program.

- Computer modeling concepts for nuclear power plant control room design and evaluation.

Regarding the study of guidelines for design standards, the Institute of Electrical and Electronic Engineers (IEEE) is preparing a guide for control room display and control facilities design [3]. The guide is general in nature and concerns design methods more than it addresses design product standards. Preliminary results from the EPRI study indicate many areas in which specific design standards are needed.

PERFORMANCE MEASUREMENT SYSTEM FOR TRAINING SIMULATORS

The EPRI staff is planning a one-year project to install and test run on the Tennessee Valley Authority's Brown's Ferry nuclear power plant training simulator a system capable of automatic recording of statistical information about operator actions. The project would be part of an EPRI program to investigate the use of training simulators for the following purposes:

- To provide an empirical data base which could permit the statistical analysis of operator reliability.

- To provide an empirical data base for allocating the responsibility for the operation of safety and control systems between operators and automated controls.

- To improve current methods of operator selection and training, procedure preparation, and control room and system design.

The first phase of the program was a feasibility study [4] conducted by the Simulation Products Division of the Singer Company. In the project being planned, the contractors will develop several operating and casualty drills for performance recording by both the

simulator computer and the instructors. Hardware and software
modifications will be made as necessary, and the monitoring system
will be used in as many training situations as are available.

Use in Safety and Reliability Analyses

The draft version of the previously referenced Reactor Safety
Study [2] contains the following statement:

> "An actuarial data base for human error rates in
> nuclear power plants does not exist. Although the
> AEC does collect information on human errors
> associated with abnormal power plant incidents,
> the data are not generally in a form usable for
> human reliability analysis." (Appendix III, p. 121)

Training simulators are powerful, but essentially yet unused, tools
for collecting performance data for safety and reliability analyses.
The validity of the simulator data taken will be checked against
data from operating plants wherever statistically practical.

The project will include both a survey of applicable methods
of modeling operator performance and a study of how the monitoring
system can be used to verify and calibrate candidate modeling
methods. F.P. Lees states, "Models which fit data on human
reliability are important not only as a means of correlating
experimental data but as a guide in collecting it." [5]

Use in Function Allocation

The American Nuclear Society (ANS) is drafting for American
National Standards Institute (ANSI) approval criteria [6] for
determining which safety functions must be automated completely and
which can rely upon operator action. The criteria involve time
tests which vary according to the event severity. All protective
functions which must occur sooner than specified by any time test
must be automated.

Qualitative information useful for drafting such criteria is
scanty. The development and validation of modeling techniques and
the comparison of predicted operator performance with predicted
automatic safety system performance should provide a better foundation for the address of function allocation questions than is
available presently. The modeling techniques should be capable of
describing the operator's ability to analyze and control failures
in power plant systems during dynamic and stressful conditions.

The complexity of function allocation study is compounded by the problem of common mode failures. Although the frequency and severity of such failures require their inclusion in any complete analysis, their unpredictability creates doubts about the accuracy which can be achieved by analytical methods. The planned EPRI program will approach the problem using both analytical and empirical techniques.

Use in Selection, Training, and Design

In 1968 the American Institutes for Research (AIR) reported the completion of the first phase of a project for the AEC [7]. The objective of Phase I was to develop ways of measuring the performance of operators, while Phase II was to have developed predictor methods for the selection of job applicants most likely to become effective operators. The report describes the formulation of a Reactor Operator Performance Checklist, which was used by supervisors in evaluating observed operator performances as "above standard requirements" or "below standard requirements." Items checked were weighted and scored to form measures of an operator's overall performance. Based on inconsistency of reports from different supervisors and from the same supervisor in different reporting periods, the reliability of the scores was evaluated by the researchers as less than fully satisfactory. Phase II of the project was not undertaken.

Improvements in operator selection and training methods require extensive and reliable measures of operator job performance. The training simulators provide observational opportunities for aspects of job performance which are difficult or impossible to obtain otherwise. The EPRI project is intended to exploit these opportunities with a measurement system which will place minimal reliance on observer subjectivity.

·The simulator performance measurement system also will be useful in evaluating the effectiveness of procedures and design. For example, statistically significant rates of maloperation of particular control devices may point the need for redesign. The differences in maloperation by novices and by experienced operators will be examined from such aspects as cultural stereotyping, i.e., where operators "naturally tend" to make errors before such errors are trained away. The potential for reversion to stereotype under stress can then be evaluated.

FUTURE WORK

The widespread use on training simulators of automated performance measuring systems depends on two factors: their effectiveness in accomplishing the program objectives described in the preceding section, and the opinions of training staff members about their use in training programs. Simulator time is expensive; performance measurements must be an integral part of training programs to keep research program costs reasonable.

If some simulator time is dedicated to research purposes, it could be used to isolate components of performance. For example, perceptual components might be isolated by interrogating the operator about parameter values with indicators available. Cognitive components might be identified by freezing the problem and quizzing the operator about state changes and parameter values with indicators unavailable. Correlations of simulator performance, both with written tests on theory, systems, and procedures and with supervisors' evaluations of on-job performance, would be desirable to establish.

The high cost of simulator time may also require that some analysis be performed on partial simulations. Research on the most effective display schemes for CRT use might be performed with less than full simulation, for example.

In summary, EPRI research in man-machine relationships presently is directed towards development of evaluation methods for use in nuclear power plant control rooms. Expansion of the research both into fossil fired plants and beyond control rooms may be undertaken in the future. EPRI hopes the research program results will provide the utility industry with helpful guidance through an expanding maze.

REFERENCES

1.   Proceedings of the IAEA Specialists Meeting on Control Room Design, San Francisco, California, July 22-24, 1975, IEEE publication 75CH1065-2.

2.   "Human Reliability Analysis", Section 6.1 in Appendix III - Failure Data, of WASH-1400 (Draft): Reactor Safety Study - An Assessment of Accident Risks in U.S. Commercial Nuclear Power Plants, U.S. Atomic Energy Commission, Washington, D.C.

3.   IEEE Proposed Standard, "Guide for the Design of Display
     and Control Facilities for Central Control Rooms of Nuclear
     Generating Stations," P566, Draft 2, July, 1975.

4.   K.D. Feintuch, "Operator Performance Measurement Using Simu-
     lation Techniques," Singer report No. 8358-7526, October, 1975.

5.   F.P. Lees, "Quantification of Man-Machine System Reliability
     in Process Control," IEEE Transactions on Reliability Vol. R-22,
     No. 3 (Special Issue on Human Performance Reliability), August,
     1973, pp. 124-131.

6.   ANSI Proposed Standard, "Criteria for Safety-Related Operator
     Actions, "N660, Draft 11, September, 1975.

7.   R. Fitzpatrick, D.W. Dysinger, and V.L. Hanson, "The
     Performance of Nuclear Reactor Operators," American Institutes
     for Research report AIR-491-9/68-FR, also issued under NYO-
     3288-10, Reactor Technology (TID-4500), September, 1968.

DISCUSSION

THOMPSON :

Recommending that nuclear system designers use human factors
principles or specifications may not be sufficient as the military services
found. H.F. specifications, that your IEEE group will develop, or
similar ones, should be required to be used, and checked on.

CONTROL STRATEGIES OF NOVICE AND EXPERIENCED CONTROLLERS WITH A SLOW RESPONSE SYSTEM (A ZERO-ENERGY NUCLEAR REACTOR)

Peter McLeod

M.R.C. Applied Psychology Unit, 15 Chaucer Road

Cambridge, England

A zero energy nuclear reactor may be defined as one in which the thermal effects of fission have a negligible effect on the reactor's behaviour. Such reactors are used as research and instructional tools. They are also relevant to control problems with power producing reactors because these behave in the zero-energy mode when starting up and their dynamic operation is fundamentally affected by their zero-energy component.

Reactor power is controlled by neutron absorbing rods, typically driven by constant speed motors. In the reactor which was simulated in these experiments the controller manipulated the rods via a three position switch. The central position left the rods stationary; moving it to the left (Lower) drove the rods at a constant velocity into the reactor, reducing the reactivity; moving it to the right (Raise) drew the rods out, raising the reactivity.

The relationship between reactivity, power and control position can be seen in figure 1. The lower half of the figure shows reactivity as a function of time: the upper part shows the corresponding power level. When the reactivity slope is positive the control rods are being raised; when the slope is zero the rods are static and when the slope is negative the rods are being lowered. To maintain a constant power level the reactivity must be zero. (Thus in figure 1, when the steady new value of power level is reached, the reactivity has returned to zero.) In principle it is possible to change power level in two movements. (This would leave a triangle on the plot of reactivity against time.) In practise the lag in the system makes it too difficult to estimate the correct time to change the sign of the reactivity. The problem can be seen in figure 1. About 8 sec elapse after the

INCREASING POWER

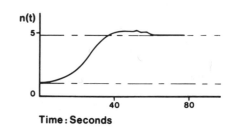

FIGURE 1. The relationship between control position, reactivity and power (n) when power level is being raised.

DECREASING POWER

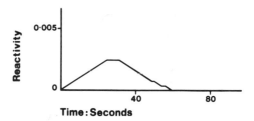

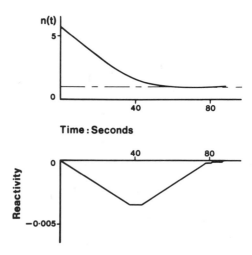

FIGURE 2. The relationship between reactivity, power level and control position when power is being reduced.

control is moved to Raise before any change in power level is perceptible; then the power level accelerates as long as the reactivity slope is positive. It is known (e.g. Fuchs, 1966) that the human operator is not efficient at extracting information from accelerating error functions. [The controllers task is not simply trying to switch his control half-way between start and desired finish level because the reactor's response to changes in reactivity is not constant, but dependent on absolute power level. So, for example, a different timing of control responses is required to reduce rather than raise power over the same range. See figure 2.]

In general control system terms this may be regarded as a system with a response lag of about a minute. The object of the research reported here is to elucidate the strategies followed by naive and experienced operators when faced with this system.

Apparatus and Design

The defining equations of a standard model for simulating zero-energy dynamic behaviour were programmed on an analogue computer. (See Lamarsh, 1965, p. 423). The equations were solved in terms of n, the neutron population. This quantity was displayed on a dial, radius 5 cm, placed 30 cm in front of the subject. The permissible range of neutron populations, 0–100, occupied an arc of 50°, with graduations every $2\frac{1}{2}^o$ (equivalent to n = 5.)

The naive subjects were 12 Naval Ratings. On each of 8 days each subject performed one of the sets of three runs shown in Table 1. On day 1 all subjects performed the first set of three runs (i.e. starting at n = 10, 30 and 50, and finishing at n = 60), and on day 2 they all performed the second set. On the following six days each subject performed each of the six sets once, the order of testing being selected from a digram balanced Latin square. On any one day each set was performed by two subjects.

Table 1

Starting Power Level					
10,30,50;	30,50,70;	50,70,90;	10,30,50;	30,50,70;	50,70,90;
60	90	30	70	80	20
Finishing Power Level					

The experienced subjects were three operators with an average
of 6 years experience controlling a real zero-energy reactor. They
performed on one day only. After several practise runs they each
performed six of the runs detailed in Table 1. Between then they
performed all the runs in Table 1 once.

Subjects were told to change power level as quickly as
possible, but to avoid overshoots. An overshoot of 10 caused the
run to be terminated by the experimenter. These were fairly rare.
For example, on the last day only one run was terminated. The
criterion for completing the run was to be on the finishing power
level with an acceptably low drift rate. (The maximum acceptable
drift rate was defined in terms of the reactivity of the 'reactor',
a quantity which was available to the experimenter but not the
subject. (i.e. in figures 1 or 2, the reactivity had to be within
a criterion distance of zero.) The corresponding rate of change of
n varied with power level.)

The integrated modulus error for the duration of the run, and
the time to complete the run were recorded. Movements of the
control switch were also recorded.

Results

Figure 3 shows the time to criterion and the error to criterion
for the last six days. Each point is the mean for all runs on that
day, i.e. 1 run by two subjects on each of the 18 runs in Table 1.
The open points give data from the naive subjects; the filled
points from the experienced operators. Two points are clear.
1. There is little change in the measures between Day 3 and Day 8.
2. The naive subjects are better than the experienced operators.

The second somewhat paradoxical observation may result
partially from the difference between real experience and the
experimental conditions. The naive subjects treated the task as a
game: the 'winner' was the one who reached criterion fastest. The
experienced operators, on the other hand, treated the task as an
extension of their normal job where there was no prize for a fast
run, and a considerable penalty associated with an overshoot. They
were naturally more conservative.

Control Strategy

Of greater interest are the control movement data in figures
4 and 5. Figure 4 shows the average number of Raise and Lower
movements per run made on the runs where the final power level was
greater than the initial. The lone points after Day 8 show the
number of movements for the experienced operators. Figure 5 shows

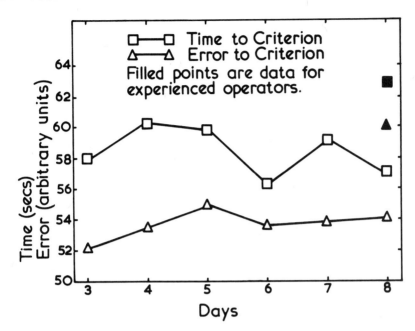

Figure 3. Error and time scores for naive subjects (open points) and experienced controllers (filled points).

the equivalent data for runs where the final power level was lower than the initial.

For raising power all subjects on all days make fewer movements in the initial Raise direction than they do in the correcting Lower direction. By Day 8 80% of the raise power runs are completed with the theoretical minimum of 1 Raise movement. This is accompanied by 3 or 4 Lower movements. The strategy which gives rise to this difference seems clear. One Raise movement is made which puts reactivity into the system. As the power approaches the desired level the controller removes the reactivity with a Lower movement whose duration underestimates the reactivity of the system. Under the action of the prompt neutrons the power level needle is slowed down or brought to a halt. The control switch is returned to the central position, when, under the action of the delayed neutrons (it is these that constitute the lag in the system) the power level begins to rise again. (If the system reactivity is positive, the power level will rise with the control lever in the central position. See figure 1.) The operation of putting the switch to Lower and centring again is repeated several times until the power level is that required and the reactivity nearly zero. (An example of this strategy being followed can be seen in figure 1.) That the subject is following the strategy of removing the reactivity in steps

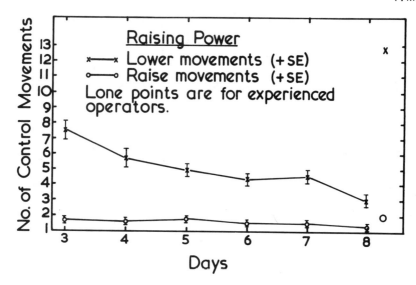

Figure 4. The number of Raise and Lower movements made when raising power.

deliberately and is not simply slowing the power needle down too early is shown by the infrequency with which he makes further Raise movements. These would be required if the reactivity was reduced to zero before the final power level was reached.

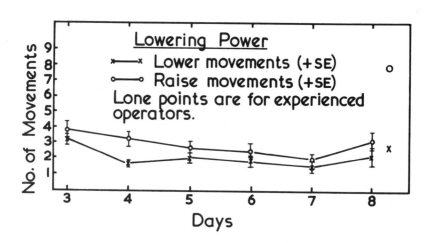

Figure 5. The number of Raise and Lower movements made when lowering power.

For lowering power the same pattern, fewer movements in the initial direction than the correcting direction, is apparent, although clearly less marked. The reason for this change is that runs which reduce power tend to end at lower points on the power range than runs where power is raised because of the restricted range used. The displayed power level is less sensitive to changes in reactivity at lower power levels than at higher ones. Thus a given movement produces less apparent effect at low power levels. An effect of this is that the first correcting movement when lowering power tends to be longer than the equivalent movement when power is raised. Hence there are fewer correcting movements, and the probability of an extra movement in the initial direction tends to be increased.

An intriguing point is the comparison between the control movement patterns produced by the naive operators and those produced by the experienced men. The lone points on figures 4 and 5 show that the two groups produce an identical pattern of movements. (i) More movements in the correcting than the initial direction (ii) a smaller difference between the two directions for lowering than for raising power (iii) Raise movements approaching the theoretical minimum of 1. It thus appears that in their first weeks training, and with no instruction, naive subjects adopt the same strategy as that used by controllers with many years experience.

Discussion

A point which is frequently at issue in the modelling of human response in control systems is the relative weight which should be attached to open and closed loop modes of control. That is, to what extent the controllers actions are determined by attempts to follow some function of the error and its derivatives, and to what extent by preprogrammed responses unconnected with the error. It seems clear that the strategy followed with the system studied here is not linearly related to any displayed error function, although the moment at which the next step in the control pattern is executed may well be determined by some error function.

The immediate, uninstructed adoption of an open-loop control strategy seen here may explain why Brigham and Laios (1975) with another slow response system found that allowing subjects to watch an automatic controller, which was driven by a weighted sum of the error and its first two derivatives, was of little use as a training aid. With a slow response system subjects are trying to develop a control strategy which overcomes their perceptual and memory limitations, not one which is primarily controlled by the error. Showing then a device which is error controlled is likely to be an active hindrance to the development of such a strategy.

Describing work with slow response systems Attwood (1970) stated, 'An understanding of the system is the first requirement for controlling it.' There is little evidence to support this apparently self-evident assertion. Crossman and Cooke (1962), Landeweerd (1971) and, under some conditions, Brigham and Laios (1975), found that specific instructions about plant dynamics had little effect on performance. In the present study the naive subjects showed that the experienced operators, who knew how the system worked, were too conservative: understanding of the system dynamics actually hindered performance. Rather than trying to explain the system, perhaps attempts to train people in the use of slow response systems should concentrate on ways of helping the operator to understand what his own preprogrammed strategy really is, and getting him to work deliberately on that. Once he understands what he is doing, perhaps he will do it more effectively.

One final aspect of the data might repay further research. Previous studies of naive controllers with slow response systems (Crossman and Cooke, Attwood) typically show oscillatory behaviour about the desired mean, caused by corrections which are both too frequent and too large. This form of behaviour was absent from the reactor control. If the essential difference between the control loops in this and the previous studies could be established, this might lead to the design of a control mechanism for slow response systems which would be effective in reducing hunting by bad or by inexperienced operators.

References

Attwood, D. 1970. The interaction between human and automatic control. Reprinted in: Edwards and Lees (Eds.) The Human Operator in Process Control. Taylor and Francis: London, 1974.

Brigham, F.R. and Laios, L. 1975. Operator performance in the control of a laboratory process plant. Ergonomics, 18, 53-66.

Crossman, E.R.F.W. and Cooke, J.E. 1962. Manual control of slow response systems. Reprinted in: Edwards and Lees (Eds.) The Human Operator in Process Control Taylor and Francis: London, 1974.

Fuchs, A.H. 1962. The progression-regression hypothesis in perceptual motor skill learning. Journal of Experimental Psychology, 63, 177-182.

Lamarsh, J.R. 1965. Introduction to Nuclear Reactor Theory. Addison-Wesley: Reading, Massachesetts.

Landeweerd, J.A. 1971. The influence of instruction on performance when controlling a slow response system. Eindhoven University of Technology (Unpublished report.)

HUMAN PERFORMANCE IN MANUAL PROCESS CONTROL

Colin G. Drury

State University of New York at Buffalo

Amherst, New York   14260

INTRODUCTION

Manual Process Control tasks in industry are legion. The
operator must control such a complex process in real
time with strict limitations on any deviations from optimum
performance if the process is to be economically viable. Chemical
processes (Kragt & Landeweerd, 1974)[*], steel making processes
(Bainbridge et al, 1968)[*], paper mills (Attwood, 1970)[*], and glass
manufacturers (Drury & Hill, 1973) have been studied with a view
to improving operator performance.

Such processes, Figure 1, can be characterized (Drury & Baum,
in press) as having:

1. many controls which interact with each other in their
   effects and may have long time lags between action and
   effect.

2. more than one output variable which must be controlled.

3. variable inputs in the form of material quality from
   previous process stages, uncontrolled environmental
   disturbances and changes in product specifications.

4. no precisely known model or equation to predict the
   process outputs given the process inputs.

These give rise to symptoms such as low process reliability,
a yield dependent upon operator skill, long training times, long
start-up times, distinct operator "styles" in control behaviour
and the presence of blindly-followed "rules of thumb" among operators,

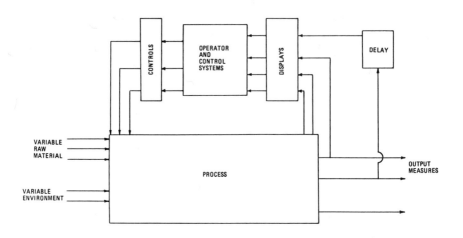

FIGURE 1: Schematic of Process/Operator/Environment System.

foremen and managers.

Such processes have received increasing study over recent years
(see reviews by Edwards & Lees, 1973, 1974). In general there is
agreement on both the complexity of the problem confronting industrial practitioners and researchers and the potential payoff in
improving the functioning of an operator with such a central effect
on process economics. Rather than attempt a thorough review of the
literature or even a simple listing of what is known about operator
performance and the factors causing it to vary, this paper will concentrate on the methodological issues of the subject. With the
advent of relatively cheap and powerful mini-computers for process
control has come the need to define the process more exactly so that
parts of the control function can be pre-programmed. This has led
to a number of interesting paradoxes and related issues.

If an engineer wishes to describe a process in sufficient detail
for it to be automated, how can such a description (model) of the
process be obtained? Most of the processes involve a complex combination of continuous and discrete controls so that the normal
methods of physics are usually inapplicable. Statistical experimental designs to cover all possible interactions are prohibitively
costly. The usual approach has been to use the skilled operator's
knowledge of the process to provide a structural model of its
operation and then to use quantitative techniques to parameterize
this model.

But to do this (and the following steps of function allocation between operator and computer) with anything like certainity the investigator must know how the operator's "mental model" is likely to differ from the "true" model of the process. The paradox is that most studies in the literature attempt to model the operator in a situation where there is no "true" model of the process! There are arguments about whether or not a study in an off-line situation, even if it has enough complexity <u>and</u> a "true" process model, can have any applicability in the real world. Such studies (e.g. Bainbridge et al, 1968)* are few, costly and produce complex results, as is to be expected when studying a complex behaviour.

These difficulties are compounded when an attempt is made to construct a unified description of what is known about the process operator. The "models" assumed by investigators, however unconsciously, have influenced both the independent variables chosen for study and the dependent variables measured. This point will be discussed after a brief review of factors which have been found to affect human process control behaviour or performance. These findings are taken from laboratory and field studies reviewed earlier by the author (Drury & Baum, in press). References have been omitted and can be obtained from the earlier paper.

FACTORS AFFECTING CONTROL

Task Factors

1. <u>Access to Output Information</u>: if the rate at which the operator can obtain feedback from the process output is reduced, performance suffers.

2. <u>Accuracy of Output Information</u>: the addition of random noise to the output before it is displayed to the operator degrades performance.

3. <u>Access to Intermediate Information</u>: if displays of important intervening variables are available, control is improved.

4. <u>Access to Controls</u>: operators often make more control actions than necessary and control can be improved by restricting the number and range of control changes.

5. <u>Access to Historical Information</u>: a time-history of the process improves performance when the task is above a fairly low level of complexity.

6. <u>Process Complexity</u>: the addition of time lags to a process and the degree of interaction between controls both degrade performance. Number of controls may have a positive or negative effect depending upon their type and interaction.

7. <u>Input Complexity</u>: the greater the bandwidth of the input to

the process the faster the operator must sample to maintain control.

Operator Factors

8. <u>Student vs. Industrial Operators</u>: industrial operators and naive (students) subjects perform very differently. On a task simulating the operators' task closely, industrial operators do better, whereas on a more abstract laboratory task students have higher performance.

9. <u>Practice on Task</u>: as expected practice on the task, even with no formal training scheme improves performance.

10. <u>Type of Training</u>: practical instruction and simple heuristics appear to be more effective than teaching the basic physics and chemistry of the process.

MEASURES OF BEHAVIOUR AND PERFORMANCE

There is an intimate connection, as noted earlier, between the independent variables listed above, models of behaviour and the measurements used by the investigators. It is worthwhile re-examining the measurement alternatives open to the investigator, whether it be of an industrial or a laboratory situation. It is convenient to consider a heirarchy of levels of measurement with respect to involvement with the operator.

System Specification Measures

The first level of measurement involves a description of the process and the operator's intended role in its control. It can be done before the process is operational, but is more commonly met with as a first step in analysis of actual operation. Beishon (1967) describes Signal Flow Graph analysis, a technique used by control engineers to analyze complex networks. The process (and its operator) are graphed by connecting circles representing variables (input, intervening or output) by effect lines, annotated with as much knowledge as is available on the transfer function for each line. He shows the application of this method of analysis to control of paper mills. A similar method is reported by Savoyant (1971).

Duncan (1974)[*] uses Task Analysis to describe the operation of an acid purification plant. This technique, combining the largely North American Function and Task Analysis ideas with the largely European Skills Analysis methods analyses the heirarchical control processes required of the operator. Some of the higher level tasks (called <u>plans</u>) may require many of the lower level tasks (<u>operations</u>) for their successful execution.

Both of these techniques can be used to analyze complex processes required of the operator but they say nothing of the actual strategies employed by the operator nor of the level of performance achieved by the operator.

System Performance Measures

The ultimate criterion of interest to managers and systems designers is systems performance. This is usually measured by cost per unit of product, or in many cases, times and errors which are assumed to be related to cost. Thus Ketteringham & O'Brien (1974)[*] used throughput as a measure of performance in their study of soaking-pit scheduling in the steel industry. Bainbridge et al (1968)[*] used a number of measures of error and also total power consumption to quantify performance on a steel furnace control simulation.

When the process output is a single-valued function such as process yield or cost it is possible to quantify the variation of yield with time (the yield-time curve) in a number of ways. A clear distinction should be made here between performance in the start-up condition (search for an optimum) and that of continuous control to keep the process within limits when an optimum has been reached (tracking).

In the former case some quantification of the rate of increase of yield is required. Crossman, Cooke & Beishon (1964)[*] used a time-on-target measure in their laboratory task. Obviously as the optimum conditions are approached, time on target increases. In the same way Kragt & Landeweerd (1974)[*] and Brigham & Laios (1975) measured the mean absolute deviation from the target output. Rigby (1972) and Coe, Baum & Drury (unpublished) used a number of measures based on the rate of increase including time to optimum, number of moves to optimum and mean rate of progress to end of trial if an optimum was not reached. A rather different approach was taken by Buck & Hancock (1975). They allowed a number of moves in each of their tasks proportional to the number of possible control setting combinations. They then measured maximum performance (yield) during each task. This really measures deviations from the results predicted by a random search strategy and thus some of their conclusions could be biased as random search was found to be an inappropriate model for subject's strategy.

One of the main problems with the measures of "hill climbing" performance is that they are very sensitive to luck in initial choice of settings by the subject or operator. The more random the strategy becomes, the greater the variance within experimental conditions and hence the lower the ability of the experiment to reach significant conclusions. Another, more serious criticism is that such measures can only contribute to understanding of the process operator if the results are compared to predictions from some theoretical model. But when precautions are taken to standardize measurements with respect to the known predictions of a model (e.g. Buck & Hancock, 1975) the experimental results become very difficult to interpret with respect to other models.

For continuous tracking performance Crossman & Cooke (1962)[*] and West & Clark (1974)[*] used an integrated error score, either total or root mean square, by analogy with human performance measurement in other continuous control tasks. These measures are less subject to chance than those of hill climbing performance but they still make small contribution to understanding operator performance.

Observed Strategy

To overcome some of the objections to performance measures, many investigators have attempted to observe the strategy of operators and investigate independent variables which have an effect on strategy. The simplest way has been analysis of the frequency of various activities such as:

1. output sampling frequency - Crossman & Cooke (1962)[*], Crossman, Cooke & Beishon (1964)[*]

2. communications between operators - Chadwick-Jones et al (1970)

3. control setting frequency - Kragt & Landeweerd (1974)[*], Bainbridge et al (1968)[*], Beishon (1967), Spencer (1962)[*]

4. number of computer predictions requested and accepted - Ketteringham & O'Brien (1974)[*]

5. classified strategies (number and size of control changes) - West & Clark (1974)[*], Bainbridge et al (1968)[*]

6. number of controls changed at one time - Coe, Baum & Drury (unpublished).

More complex observations of strategy involve comparison of observed strategies with some model of strategy. Indeed, in these studies the strategy results are only reported in terms of deviations from model strategies:

7. number of regions of each control setting used as compared to the number of regions expected on a random search model - Buck & Hancock (1975)

8. number of controls varied at one time as compared to the number expected on various control strategies - Buck & Hancock (1975)

9. the ratio of the subjects' rate of increase of yield
    at each trial to the maximum possible rate of increase
    at that trial (Tangent Ratio) - Coe, Baum & Drury
    (unpublished)

10. ratio of the "distance" moved on one trial to the
    distance from the start of the trial to the optimum -
    Coe, Baum & Drury (1975).

These latter two measures imply that a "rate of steepest
ascent" strategy is optimum and judge subjects' behaviour against
this standard. Figure 2 shows an example of the difference in
Tangent Ratio between instructions emphasizing that the problem was
either abstract or applied. Over the middle part of the trial the
tangent ratio remains at about 0.5 for the abstract instructions
whereas with the application instructions it takes half the trial
to reach this value. Obviously the last step in each trial has a
tangent ratio of 1.0 when the optimum is reached.

Measures of strategy go one level deeper than performance
measurement - they provide some of the reasons for observed changes
in performance. However, in the context of analyzing complex
control behaviour such simple, omnibus measures can only detect
major differences in strategy.

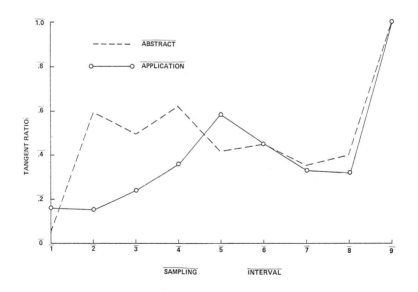

FIGURE 2: Effect of Instructions on Changes in Tangent Ratio.

Reported Strategy

In order to probe more deeply into the behaviour of individuals
in a process control task the methods of post-performance interview and analysis of verbal protocols have both shown some utility.
In a laboratory task Brigham and Laios gave a questionnaire to their
subjects after their performance on the task. Analysis of these
responses combined with observed strategy records enabled them to
explain the differences in performance between their different
experimental conditions in terms of the type of predictive model
developed by the subject.

In an industrial context Spencer (1962)[*] used interviews with
experienced operators to split operators into two groups: "technical"
and "empirical" but his number of subjects was too small for him to
draw conclusions with any certainty. Drury & Hill (1973) showed
how a simple interview with different levels of operator could be
used to produce an input/output matrix of perceived relationships
between controls and displays. This could then be used to improve
control strategy training and to change display design.

The most thorough use of reported strategies has been the continuing work of Bainbridge (1974)[*] on the analysis of verbal
protocols from subjects controlling a complex simulator of steel
furnace scheduling. Her subjects are required to "think aloud" as
they perform the task and a tape recording of this, together with
observed strategy measures, is used to analyze the "thought
processes" which lie behind the strategies. Given a large enough
sample of performance certain routines and subroutines can be seen
to repeat themselves, each concerned with calculating or estimating
some particular parameter. The overall control of which routines
are called in which order is modelled as a loose goal-directed
program with the possibility of various levels of interrupt.

These reported strategies suffer from not being quantified in
the usual sense and from being very different between subjects.
However the behaviour in controlling a complex process must be
complex and there is ample evidence of large subject differences in
performance and observed strategy for it to be less than surprising
to find reported strategies to be idiosyncratic.

DISCUSSION

The research and application literature has reached a stage
where reviews such as those mentioned in the introduction are
possible and fruitful. However the practitioner waiting to use this
body of knowledge in industry finds very little that is substantial.
There have been many studies of very simple analogies of process
control tasks, whose results have not been incorporated into higher

level models of behaviour. We can only predict performance and behaviour in a set of largely unrelated and very simple subtasks. The author agrees with Lees (1974)[*] that the time has come for large scale integrated studies which treat one class of process control tasks at each of the levels described above.

There is another way of elucidating roles and skills in complex tasks which does not seem to have been used in the process control field. This is the correlational study as exemplified by Fleishman & Hempel (1954). Here individual differences in task performance are correlated with appropriate measures of ability on a preliminary test battery. This method has been useful in a range of occupational skills: there is no a priori reason why it should not be used successfully to study manual process control performance.

ACKNOWLEDGEMENTS

The author would like to thank the Department of Industrial Engineering at State University of New York at Buffalo (Chairman, W. H. Thomas) for providing the facilities necessary to carry out the research reported here, and to A. S. Baum and D. D. Coe for helpful discussions of manual process control measurement techniques.

REFERENCES

References marked in the text with ([*]) can be found in Edwards & Lees (1974). They are not listed separately for reasons of space.

Beishon, R.J. (1967), Problems of task description in process control. Ergonomics, 10, 177.

Brigham, F.R. and Laios, L., Operator performance in the control of a laboratory process plant. Ergonomics, 18, 53-66, 1975.

Buck, J.R. and Hancock, W.M. Manual optimization of ill structured problems. Proceedings of Human Factors Society 19th Annual Meeting, 321-328, Dallas, Texas, 1975.

Chadwick-Jones, J.K., Sheppard, C., and Carceller, A., Search strategies used by process operatives in continuous flow technology: Performance and learning, Perc. Mot. Sk., 31, 775-785, 1970.

Coe, D.D., Baum, A.S. and Drury, C.G. (unpublished) Laboratory simulations of process control tasks, submitted to Human Factors, 1975.

Drury, C.G. and Baum, A.S. (in press) Manual Process Control - A case study and a challenge, submitted to Applied Ergonomics, 1975.

Drury, C.G. and Hill, J.W. Studies of manual process control in
    the glass industry. Paper to 5th IEA Congress, Amsterdam,
    1973.

Edwards, E. and Lees, F.P. Man and Computer in Process Control,
    Institute of Chemical Engineers, London, 1973.

Edwards, E. and Lees, F.P. The Human Operator in Process Control,
    Taylor & Francis, London, 1974.

Fleishman, E.A. and Hempel, W.E. Changes in factor structure of a
    complex psychomotor task as a function of practice.
    Psychometrika, 19, 239-252.

Rigby, R.H. Studies of a manual process control task using a
    laboratory analogue. Unpublished B.S. thesis, University of
    Liverpool, 1972.

Savoyant, A. Diagnostic dans une etude de poste de l'industrie
    chimique, Travail Humain, 34, 177-182.

DISCUSSION

STASSEN :

The different strategies of human operators you mentioned can all
be formulated as the problem "What cost criterion is the human operator
minimizing ?" Do you believe that you will be able to distinguish from
your actual measurements which cost criterion is used ? Measurement on
arm motion shows that the results were very poor, the choice of the cost
criterion was very insensitive on the final result. I expect in your case
similar problems.

DRURY :

The problem is to collect enough data on the operator when he/she
is using a single internal model. Given this there is no reason why
standard parameter estimation techniques cannot be used to derive estimates
of the weights in the criterion function. If the model is insensitive to
these weights so much the better from the practical point of view – but
such a result would not be very satisfying theoretically.

PASMOOIJ :

You stated that system performance measures are the main contribution to the measurement of workload. Is not this statement merely based on system efficiency and economic factors, rather than factors such as health and well being of the human operator ? It seems to me that human factors agreements are neglected in this viewpoint.

DRURY :

My point was that over the next few years legal regulation may cause clients to include workload limits in the design specifications (e.g., OSHA in the USA). These workload measures then become performance measures in the systems sense.

LAIOS :

I agree with you that real-life process control tasks are very different from the tasks studied in the laboratory. Have you any evidence that the general conclusions drawn from these laboratory studies are not valid (or irrelevant to real-life control tasks) ? Could you report some examples ?

DRURY :

I know of no such examples : the point is that, apart perhaps from sampling experiments, there have been no cross-checks between real tasks and simple laboratory tasks.

OUTLINES OF A HYBRID MODEL OF THE PROCESS PLANT OPERATOR

Jens Rasmussen

Danish Atomic Energy Commission, Research Establishment

Risø, DK-4ooo Roskilde, Denmark

INTRODUCTION

Modelling the performance of human operators as an integral
part of a system is becoming a vital problem to process plant designers. Reviews of major system failures and accidents repeatedly
find that the human element plays a major role in 50-70% of the cases
(Cornell, 1968. Rasmussen, 1969. Scott, 1971). The increasing reliability and safety requirements caused by the rapid growth in production unit size force the designer to include consideration of abnormal plant conditions due to failures of extremely low probability.
For such tasks the operator will not be able to compensate design
deficiencies by his great adaptability, and the interface design cannot evolve through trial and error. This situation is further accen-
tuated by the rapid development of data processing and display equipment with potential for very complex man-machine interaction.

THE PROBLEM

In system analysis and design of modern process plants, the operator is generally considered a vital part of the control system.
He is a flexible - and inventive - data processor transforming information displayed by the plant into appropriate actions according
to his current goal. His data processes must be controlled by a representation of some kind of the functional properties of the plant.
This representation obviously can be derived from different sources;
e.g. from prior experience with plant behaviour; from knowledge of
internal anatomy and functioning of the plant; or from prescribed
rules and instructions. Furthermore, he may use different mechanisms
for the processing; e.g. he may respond "automatically" to a situation or he may identify a problem and "think".

Such features of his data processing must change, when tasks related to infrequent, abnormal plant conditions replace familiar tasks. Reviews of incidents and accidents often reveal difficulties in the operator's proper identification of system state and appropriate goal in unfamiliar situations. The cause can be the complexity and dynamic properties of the plant leading to tasks exceeding the ultimate data handling capacity of the operator. However, for process plants the problem typically is not whether he is <u>able</u> to perform the task, but rather whether he <u>will</u> do it under the actual work conditions; i.e. whether the appropriate mode of dataprocessing is activated.

STUDY OF HUMAN PERFORMANCE IN REAL-LIFE TASKS

Fixation of mental procedures which have proved efficient in frequent applications is a well known human trait. The difficulty of proper identification of serious abnormal plant conditions and the use of improper procedures often indicate such adherence to mental procedures which have proved to be efficient during normal task condition or during more frequent fault conditions - e.g. instrument failures. Therefore, a model of operator behaviour related to plant reliability and safety can not be obtained by adding together results from isolated psychological experiments. It must be based upon study of the performance during the actual, real-life work condition.

The need to identify the internal mental processes of the operator without experimental perturbations of his task raises difficult methodological problems. In spite of the well known difficulties of the method, we have chosen verbal protocols as the source of information for the modelling effort. We have found it possible to get important information in this way, but the appropriate method of analysis and the difficulties met depend upon the type of task considered. Protocols obtained from trained process operators are difficult to analyze and the model we are seeking is needed to structure the analysis. An iterative method must be used for protocol analysis as well as verification by other experimental methods.

VERBAL PROTOCOLS

A significant part of the problem thus is to develop experimental techniques and a work rationale, so that meaningful results can be obtained from protocols. A number of protocols collected during start up of thermal power stations have been analyzed tentatively and some general observations will illustrate the problems:

-The process operator has several different tasks going on simultaneously, and each task has several steps or subtasks implying basically different data processes at different abstraction levels.

-The protocols generally give very little information on the underlying data processes. They are rather a sequence of statements indicating the operator's "state of knowledge" regarding the operational state of the plant, operator tasks and actions, etc. Only when unfamiliar subtasks turn up are more detailed processing of data and observations mentioned.

-Very few observations are formulated as quantitative reading of instruments, and then, typically, only if observations should be related to some prescribed reference value. Observations are generally expressed at a higher level of abstraction related to normal plant state, expected state, next task etc. Rather than reading instruments, the operator seems to ask higher level questions to the system, and individual instrument readings are used as symbols for system states.

-Very little planning is mentioned regarding the tasks to be performed, the instruments to be read etc. The operator seems spontaneously to "know" what is going on and where to focus his attention.

These features of course could be due to difficulties in having operators verbalizing for longer periods, but it seems more reasonable to assume the use of data processes which can not be verbalized. During a long period of interaction with a system a trained operator has developed a large repertoire of complex and partly subconscious routines, which are controlled by a conscious and "verbalizeable" sequence at a high level of abstraction.

This process appears not to be controlled by decisions considering alternatives, but by general conditioning by his "process feel", i.e. a subconscious dynamic plant model.

Processes at the level of observed information are only expressed in unfamiliar tasks, e.g. during plant malfunctions. It is difficult to obtain a reasonable quantity of such sequences from plant operation, and as an example of this type of task we have used electronic maintenance technician's diagnostic task.

The protocols obtained from this task contain detailed information on the data processes used and 4o protocols have been analyzed in detail (Rasmussen and Jensen, 1974). The processes can be described by a sequence of standard subroutines linked by heuristic rules. A few general features are relevant in the present context:

-The basic nature of the processes depends upon the work situation. If information is constrained e.g. by unpleasant or risky observational conditions, the process is characterized by a careful, rational consideration of available information in relation to the anatomy and functioning of the system. In the normal work shop con-

ditions, however, the processes are typically based upon general
search routines which enable the technicians to map the performance
of the system by a rapid stream of judgements of the observations
individually. This search is controlled by a representation - mental model - of the system in the general form of a topographic map
of typical signal flow routes in electronic circuitry supplying convenient measuring points and references values.

In this case it has been possible from the verbal protocols to
identify basically different processes for the same external task.
It illustrates how the process can be controlled by inference rules
and models related to the anatomy and function of the specific system as well as by algorithms specifying the process itself using
only rudimentary models of the system.

The replacement of complex reasoning by general algorithms relieve the cognitive strain, and a pronounced fixation of the familiar
routines was found. Although the mental processes were consciously
monitored and verbalized, they appear not to be controlled by conscious decisions, but rather by subconscious conditioning, chaining
familiar routines according to the law of least resistance. Familiar
search routines were used also in cases for which careful consideration of the information available could lead to efficient short-
cuts.

Comparing the results of analysis of protocols from control
rooms and from maintenance shops, the conclusion is that the behaviour of skilled personel only in special task conditions can be
modelled by a sequential algorithmic process description derived
directly from verbal protocols, as it has been done for subjects
in games and problem solving tasks (Newell and Simon, 1972). In most
circumstances the analysis of verbal protocols collected from process operators can only serve as a guide or intermittent indication
of his activity at several levels.

MAPPING MENTAL ACTIVITY

The efficiency of skilled performance is due to the ability to
compose the process needed for a specific task as a sequence of familiar subroutines which are useful in different contexts. This implies the existence of links in the sequence at standard key nodes
or "states of knowledge" which are characteristic of the specific
skill. The data process stops at such links, the mode of processing
and frequently the level of abstraction changes, and to study and
identify the processes, the activity must be structured according to
such key nodes.

First of all, the activity should be broken down to "subtasks".
Subtasks can be defined at many levels due to the hierarchical struc-

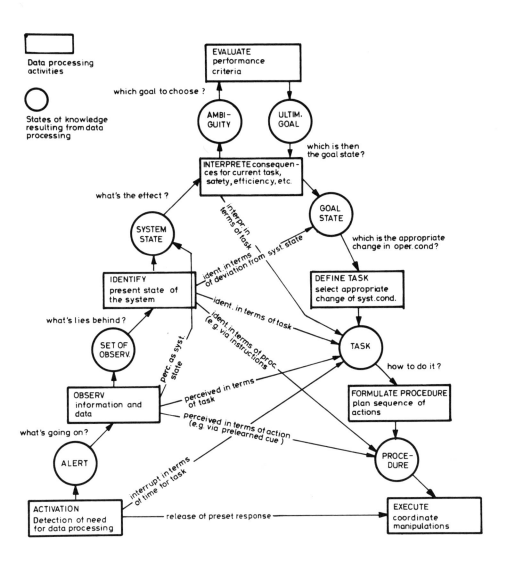

Figure 1. Schematic map of the sequence of mental activities between initiation of the response and the manual actions. The diagram illustrates typical shunting routines in skilled performance. Associative leaps directly between states of knowledge are not shown.

ture of the operator's total task. As a preliminary description for
the present purpose we have defined a subtask as the sequence of data
processing steps and related states of knowledge which connect the
initiation of operator response with the resulting manual action,
e.g. the response following a warning signal. The number of steps in
this sequence depends strongly upon the skill of the operator in the
specific task. Therefore, as a general description typically used
"states of knowledge" from the protocols are arranged in the sequence
which a novice would have to follow. Study of actual, skilled performance may then result in a description in terms of shunting leaps
within this basic sequence, as illustrated by figure 1. The diagram
resembles a "ladder of abstraction". One leg upwards for analysis of
a situation, another downwards for planning of the proper actions.
Short cuts from habits and rules connect the two legs of the ladder.

Frequently, a skilled operator does not enter the sequence at
its entry; his process feel can initiate consideration first of a
step later in the sequence, he may change the order of the steps,
and he only occasionally has to move through all the steps in the
basic sequence. Two types of shunting effects appear to be active.
One is mental activity at a symbolic level leading directly to state
of knowledge later in the sequence, e.g. holistic perception leads to
observation directly in terms of system state or task to perform
rather than observation of separate items of information. Another
shunting mechanism appears to be associations based upon experience
leading to leaps directly from one state of knowledge to another.

Detailed expression of sequential, conscious data processing
is only found if uncertainty or ambiguity is recognized by the operator. If not, either a leap in the sequence takes place or a state
is accepted and the sequence stopped.

The leaps are equivalent to a shunting-out of activities at
higher levels of abstraction which call for complex conscious reasoning; as a result they give rise to a considerable increase of data
handling capacity.

MAPPING HUMAN DATA PROCESSING MECHANISMS

From the preceeding discussion it follows that a variety of
human data processing mechanisms is used for the mental subtask to
transform one state of knowledge to the next. A model of these mechanisms and their mutual interaction is needed to support the analysis
and description of operator behaviour. The model must take into account a wide range of mechanisms including rational problem solving
as well as intuitive and associative reasoning and sensory-motor
skills. A tentative map to serve this purpose is shown in figure 2.
The diagram outlines a hybrid model comprising two basically different data processing systems to represent the low data capacity found

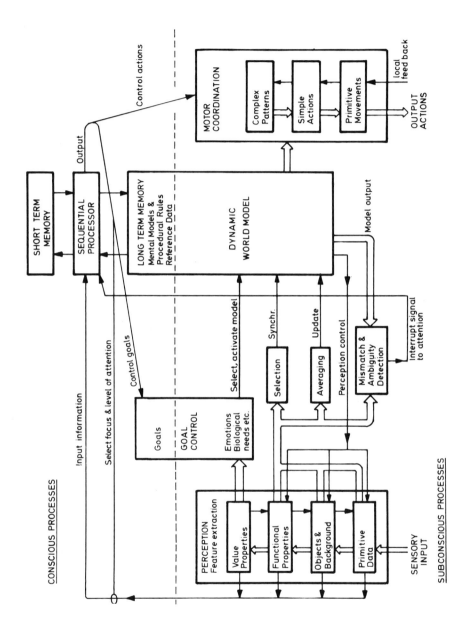

Figure 2. Schematic map of the human data processing mechanisms.

in consciously controlled operations, as well as the ability to respond successfully to situations demanding rapid, high-capacity information processing (Miller, 1956).

A high-capacity, parallel processing system serves the subconscious processes related to perception, sensory-motor responses etc.
It resembles in its performance a goal oriented, selforganizing associative network operating by dynamic matching of input information
patterns to stored patterns. Value properties of the input patterns
- or their verbal representations - controls the process through a
global conditioning, which activates generic stored patterns. These
patterns constitute an analog representation of the behaviour of the
environment, structured in a time-space domain. This internal world
model representing the behaviour of the environment and the body accounts for the ability of efficient feed-forward control of the body
in sequences too rapid to allow for sensory feedback - "the serial
order in behaviour" (Lashley, 1951), for the "process-feel" of the
operator, and it directs and controls his attention. If a mis-match
occurs, i.e. if the behaviour of the environment deviates from the
predictions of the model or a relevant model is not available, this
is detected and the conscious processor is alerted.

The conscious processor is an extremely versatile sequential
processor of limited speed and capacity. It acts as a high-level
coordinator of the subconscious processes and functions in unfamiliar situations demanding unique responses. The variables treated
by the conscious processes can be fetched from the perceptive system at different levels of abstraction, or be purely symbolic variables. The processes can be based upon different types of representations - mental models - of the physical system considered depending
upon the task, e.g. representation of system anatomy and function as
causal models used for rational deductions; representation of typical
system behaviour as used in "visual thinking"; or processes controlled by prescribed algorithms - cook book recipes - rather than
a structured model.

The two processing systems cooperate, and the subconscious processor by its large repertoire of automated subroutines relieves the
limited conscious capacity. The conscious data process controls a
sequence of such subroutines by an executive programme in which the
level of abstraction rises as training increases the complexity and
efficiency of the subroutines. This control, however, is significantly influenced by the subconscious processes directing the attention, supplying intuitive hypotheses etc. The system engineering implications of the model suggested and its psychological references
are discussed in more detail elsewhere (Rasmussen, 1974).

In common life tasks evolution has fitted man to an efficient
interaction with a time-space environment, for which high capacity
parallel processes take care of the lower functions of the ladder

of abstraction. Abundance of redundant information supports feature
extraction and the formation and synchronization of the internal
world model.

In process control, however, an operator controls a physical
process from which only preselected information is presented to him
and typically as symbolic representation of variables individually.
Designers often suppose that he uses rational, conscious processes
also at the lower level tasks, which would lead to complex time
sharing between tasks at different process levels. An important task
when studying process operator performance is to identify the repertoire of ingenious tricks which evolve in operators to avoid this:
he adopts focussing strategies (Bruner et.al. 1956) based upon a
model of normal state, leading to judgements of individual observations separately; he synchronizes his world model by convenient
information which may be secondary, as relay clicks etc; he relies
on intuitive judgements which, due to the nature of the subconscious
world model may be based upon representativeness rather than being
rationally founded (Tversky and Kahneman, 1974); etc.

Fixation to such normally very efficient routines when the task
condition changes during abnormal plant operation is bound to lead
to difficulties, and operator's response to plant malfunction can
only be studied in the light of their normal skilled performance.
We have to consider processes and mechanisms of basically different
nature which are normally studied separately, whereas the problem in
our context is largely related to their interaction.

DATA, MODELS, AND PROCEDURES

A study of this interaction must be based upon a description
of the different types of processes according to a common set of
concepts related to the processes, rather than to psychological or
neurological descriptions. For this purpose the data processes used
to control human interaction with a physical system can be characterized within the following aspects: Data, representing the state
of variables in the systems; a model, representing the structure of
the system constraining the interrelationship of data; and procedures
or rules to control the data process.

So far, we have identified the following types of models to be
considered in our analysis:

-"Physical Models", representations identifying potential data
sources and mapping their spatial relations, e.g., scale models,
topographic maps, anatomical diagrams. Frequently used sets of
sources can be aggregated into objects at several levels, e.g. components, units, subsystems. Such models are typically used when the
process is controlled by a specific, detailed process algorithm.

(Such models are used by Luria's mnemonist to structure the memory (Luria, 1969)).

-"Functional models" identify potential sources of information together with rules or laws specifying the relationship between information from the sources. Such a model can be structured according to the system by aggregating sources into objects such as boilers, pumps, etc. or it can be structured by aggregating sources into functions according to general relations such as mass-balance, feed-back loop etc. The relational rules can be related to the system, being general causal laws, or to the data process used, being e.g. calculating algorithms or heuristic rules. This type of model is found in sequences related to prediction of system behaviour or testing of hypotheses.

-"State models" identify sources of information together with consistent sets - snap-shots - of variables representing typical system states, e.g. "normal operation", "power failure". State models are used when preparing a system for a planned operation, during fault location, etc.

-"Behavioural models" are like dynamic, animate state models and are formed by storing system behaviour from typical response situations, structured in familiar objects and their generic behaviour. The subconscious world model controlling e.g. sensory--motoric responses and animate imagery is placed in this category.

The variables describing the state of a physical system can be represented by data in the mental processes in various ways and at several levels of aggregation or abstraction.

Continuous, quantitative - analog - representation of individual variables in the subconscious modelling system seems to be necessary to account for the precision of sensory-motoric responses and furthermore seems to be used in "visual thinking". Discrete, quantitative - digitized - representation of individual variables can be used in symbol manipulating algorithms. Typically, however, qualitative representations are used in verbal sequences relating variables to a reference state model, e.g. "high", "abnormal", "hot", "rising".

In higher level verbal sequences collective representation of sets of variables are normally used. They are expressed as verbal labels representing system states or functions in relation to reference state models, such as "air system normal", "boiler ready for start up". Verbal statements at this level very likely are also used to initialize and activate process models, e.g. for visual thinking (Bugelsky, 197o) or for judgement of observations.

The need for procedural rules to control a specific data process depends upon the nature of the model available. If the process

is based upon a complex active model performing parallel processing
no algorithm is needed to control a specific process; the process
is completely specified by the elements and the structure of the
model - the problem is transferred to an analogue, physical system
and the process control left to nature. The subconscious data processes have these features. The neural network is capable of the
active modelling needed, considered as a distributed, active network operating by exitation interference pattern (Lashley, 1942)
and some kind of "holographic" memory (Pribram, 1966). The models
can be initiated by a gobal conditioning of the network through
exitation by a reference system which is activated by sensory information patterns or by "verbal labels".

The sequential conscious data processes must be based upon
stationary models and procedural rules are therefore necessary to
specify and control the individual processes. If the model is a
detailed functional model the procedures can be very general. If,
however, the model is more rudimentary, such as state models or
physical models, the procedures will be more specific and implicitly
represent system properties. The low data capacity of sequential
processes is compensated by the extreme flexibility which includes
also the ability of operations on models, e.g. transformation to
other models for which procedures or solutions are known.

CONCLUSION

Analysis of data processes performed by trained process operators must be based upon identification of the structure of the
underlying memory for system properties which includes dynamic patterns of behaviour, structured sets of data and causal relations, as
well as rules for actions and operations; categories which are compatible with memory structures identified by psychological experiments (Piaget and Inhelder, 1973). From this and the "real-life"
conditions of the study it follows that the appropriate method of
analysis depend strongly upon features of the operator's specific
task conditions. Methods developed within different professions have
to be considered, ranging from linguistics and cognitive psychology
to information and computer science and control theory.

When entering a study of human performance in real-life tasks
one rapidly finds oneself "rushing in where angels fear to tread".
It turns out to be a truly interdisciplinary study for which an
accepted frame of reference has not yet been established, and iteration between rather general hypotheses, test of methods, and detailed analysis is necessary. The work presented here illustrates
our approach to the first steps in this process. From analysis of
a number of protocols the outlines of a frame of reference compatible with our systems engineering concepts is suggested. Currently
we are planning the next phase which involves collection and de-

tailed analysis of protocols and interviews from selected task sequences and simulator experiments to verify models of more specific aspects of operator behaviour.

REFERENCES

Bruner, J.S. Goodnow, J.J. and Austin, G.A. (1956), A Study of Thinking. Wiley, New York.

Bugelsky, B.R. (1970), Words and Things and Images. Am. Psychol., 25, 1002-1012.

Cornell, C.E. (1968), Minimizing Human Errors. Space Aeronautics, 49, March, 72-81.

Lashley, K.S. (1942), The Problem of Cerebral Organisation in Vision. In: Visual Mechanisms, H. Klüver (ed.), Cattell, Lancaster.

Lashley, K.S. (1951), The Problem of Serial Order in Behaviour. In: Cerebral Mechanisms in Behaviour, L.A. Jeffress (ed.). Wiley, New York.

Luria, A.R. (1969), The Mind of a Mnemonist. Jonathan Cape, London.

Miller, G.A. (1956), The Magical Number Seven Plus or Minus Two. Psychol. Rev. 63, 81-97.

Newell, A. and Simon, H.A. (1972), Human Problem Solving. Prentice Hall, New Jersey.

Piaget, J. and Inhelder, B. (1973), Memory and Intelligence. Routledge and Kegan Paul, London.

Pribram, K.H. (1966), Some Dimensions of Remembering. In: Macromolecules and Behaviour, J. Gaito (ed.). Appleton, New York.

Rasmussen, J. (1969), Man-Machine Communication in the Light of Accident Records. Int. Symp. on M-M Systems, Cambridge. IEE Conf. Records No. 69 (58-MMS. Vol 3).

Rasmussen, J. and Jensen, A. (1974), Mental Procedures in Real Life Tasks: A Case Study of Electronic Trouble Shooting. Ergonomics, 17, No. 3, 293-307.

Rasmussen, J. (1974), The Human Data Processor as a System Component. Bits and Pieces of a Model, Risø-M-1722.

Scott, R.L. (1971), A Review of Safety Related Occurrences in Nuclear Reactors From 1967-1970. ORNL-TM-3435.

Tversky, A. and Kahneman, D. (1974), Judgement under Uncertainty: Heuristics and Biases. Science, 185, 1124-1131.

DISCUSSION

MORAY :

What part of the information processing mechanism is accessible by protocol analysis ?

RASMUSSEN :

So far I don't know. A simple analysis of the verbal sequence in protocols from skilled operators will only give the structure of a higher level strategy controlling a sequence of - possibly subconscious - subroutines. But a more detailed analysis of the intuitive guesses used by the operators and a linguistic analysis of their statements can possibly give information on the structure and elements of the "world model" behind their sub-conscious subroutines.

DRURY :

Do you know of any studies showing that verbal protocols do not interfere with the process control task ?

RASMUSSEN :

No - and this interference was one of the problems we expected to meet. However, in a study of the mental procedures used by electronic trouble-shooters we discussed the procedures and possible improvements with the technicians after the analysis of some 30 protocols without finding any significant change of the procedures used in the following protocols.

My conclusion is, that it is rather difficult to interfere with the procedures of a skilled person in his normal task - if the verbalization interferes, he rather stops talking, which is also a problem.

THE MAN-ROBOT INTERFACE IN AUTOMATED ASSEMBLY

David A. Thompson

Stanford University

Stanford, California 94305

In recent years there has been increasing pressure for enhanced productivity in the manufacture of capital and consumer goods in order to maintain and expand per capita standards of living throughout the industrialized world. One response to this pressure has been increased attempts at automaticity in the assembly of manufactured parts. More than 3000 industrial ("blue collar") robots are now installed throughout the world, and this number is expected to increase by a factor of 10 in the coming decade. (Johnson, 1975).

Industrial robotics is best exemplified by the parts production of numerically-controlled (NC) machine tools, and more recently by programmable transfer manipulators like UNIMATE and VERSATRAN. Because of the central role that industrial robots play in implementing the production planning of intelligent but "quadraplegic" computers, they will permit substantial improvement in industrial productivity. Not only do they free workers from dull, routine, mechanistic work, but they are now effectively required by the United States Occupational Safety and Health Act to be used in certain hazardous jobs (e.g., punch press part insertion and removal).

However, the future of most manufacturing systems, particularly batch production facilities, is not one of complete automaticity, but rather movement in that direction. At one extreme, a manufacturing system may be mostly manual, and at the other extreme it may be predominantly automatic. But the vast number of systems will contain both human and machine inputs, and although the relative balance may change from time to time, man-machine cooperation will remain a common condition for the forseeable future.

But a man-robot system is sufficiently different from a typical man-machine system and from most man-computer systems that
existing design techniques and approaches provide little guidance
to the production system designer in his selecting that optimal
balance of tasks to be performed by the man and by the robot. Deciding on such a balance of tasks would define the man-robot interface and the associated interface behavior important to the production supervisors, hardware designers, and production system
analysts.

The continuing basis of the man-robot system interaction is
expected to be primarily in the following areas:

    a)   Cooperative man-robot assembly
    b)   Robot programming/teaching
    c)   Robot toolmaking and set-up
    d)   Robot maintenance and repair
    e)   Robot-machine system supervision

The balance of this paper discusses the man-robot interface (MRI)
problems in each of these areas, and suggests some conceptual design approaches that will play an important role in the performance, acceptance, and operational safety of man-robot systems.

COOPERATIVE MAN-ROBOT ASSEMBLY

The production of machined parts, the handling of parts and
materials, and to a limited extent parts fabrication, have been increasingly taken over by NC machine tools. The assembly of parts,
however, has been the elusive but vital link in the fully automatic manufacturing chain. But, although an analysis of the individual task requirements involved in the assembly of mating parts
indicates that some simple assembly can be done by existing "Generation 1" (Driscoll, 1974) robots, this is not true of the majority
of production assembly tasks. The manipulation and insertion of
complex combinations of closely fitting (e.g., $\leq 0.001"$ clearance),
odd-shaped (e.g., large diameter, fine threaded bolts or screws),
non-rigid (e.g., hoses, springs, gaskets) parts defies assembly by
any but a skilled human.

Various improvements in the state of the art of robotics technology are continually being made to expand the scope of programmable assembly, including touch sensors and television feedback
(cf. Brock and Thornton, 1975; IIT Research Institute, 1975; and
Young, 1973). Automatically reprogrammable "Generation 2" robots
with hand-eye coordination and "choreographic programming" are not
expected to become fully commercially available for another decade.
"Generation 2.5-3" robots with context-dependent machine intelligence and adaptive hand-eye coordination are not anticipated for

another five years after that, and would require a "major break-through in artificial intelligence" (Driscoll, 1974).

In the interim, various cooperative man-robot assembly pro-cedures are being discussed which should be very carefully evalu-ated before being put into practice. Because robots are competent at fetching parts from pre-positioning parts feeders and moving them to the assembly area, but have difficulty inserting them, suggestions have been made to the effect that the robot deliver the parts to an assembly worker who then completes the task. The worker would accept the parts from the robot and perform the neces-sary insertion, fitting, alignment, etc. This assigns to each member of the assembly team that function they best perform. Un-less the fetch and the insert/fit/align tasks were time balanced, however, either the worker would be waiting for the robot or vice versa. Moreover, the worker would be very closely paced in work tempo by the robot's cycle, and may find this too restrictive (e.g., too slow in the mid-morning, too fast after lunch) and too rigid (e.g., no allowance for human variability). The resulting job would be worse than that classic example of bad job design, the automotive assembly line.

A possible solution would be to have the robot fetch cycle under the control of the worker and actuated by a foot switch or by completion of the previous assembly. Another solution would involve decoupling the robot and the worker by having the robot lay out a small work-in-process inventory of parts in the immediate vicinity of the assembly area in a manner that would allow easy grasping by the worker for assembly at a pace he found comfortable.

In any event, careful consideration must be given to both the physical and psychological aspects of the man-robot interaction to avoid repetition of the bad job designs robots were intended to eliminate.

ROBOT PROGRAMMING/TEACHING

In both a cooperative man-robot assembly task and in a com-pletely automated assembly task, an important role for the man is that of programmer or "teacher" of the robot system. Because the production system is "down" during programming, it needs to be very fast and efficient. In a batch production environment with much product variety, it needs also to be very flexible in its performance. In addition, it needs to be very accurate, since correcting errors is difficult and time consuming and since errors not detected get replicated in each subsequent piece produced.

One approach to programming that holds promise is that of re-motely moving the robot through its motions in a "teach-by-doing"

mode, rather than the NC-tool software approach to programming.
However, the remote controls developed for this purpose so far
typically do not have satisfactory stimulus-response compatibility---
that is, the worker has to do a complex spatial transformation in
his head in translating the geometric motions needed in the work
area to a sequence of buttons or toggle switches (e.g., "red-lever-
up to extend arm", "blue-lever-up to raise arm"). An ideal programmer would be a master-slave manipulator control, simular to
that used in teleoperator systems, which the teacher would use each
time a new job set-up was required. This would permit the most
natural method for the worker to "teach" the robot the new tasks
required of it.

     One of the more clever approximations of this approach (France,
1974) is a control shaped like a miniature robot, and as the control
is manipulated, the robot moves correspondingly. But even with this
control, the worker cannot just tell the robot what to do spatially
(e.g., reach to this point and grasp this bar), but rather has to
tell the robot how to do it as well (e.g., rotate to the left this
far, tilt upward this far, extend arm this far, open both jaws this
far, close jaws by this amount). This is comparable to the worker
having to tell his own shoulder how much to rotate, his elbow how
much to bend, etc., everytime he wanted to pick up something.

     In a cooperative man-robot assembly environment, the worker
could more naturally define, using the master-slave control, those
tasks the robot was to do and those he wished to reserve for him-
self---giving him more flexibility in locating the man-robot interface during assembly.

     It should be possible eventually to incorporate supervisory
control in the teaching programming, so that the basic motion elements and sensory responses are under computer control (comparable
to spinal reflex) and the worker supervises these being carried
out (Sheridan & Ferrell, 1974). The computer could then substitute
for the worker's relatively "noisy" movements the most efficient
velocity and acceleration patterns appropriate to the robot motions involved.

ROBOT TOOLMAKING AND SET-UP

     A robot's tools are its hands, and extensions of the hands.
To gain control of the objects it moves, positions, and possibly
inserts/fits/aligns, the tooling (typically some version of clamps
or jaws) must grasp the object with sufficient force to grip it
without slippage but without scratching or otherwise damaging it.
The toolmaker who prepares and installs the robot's tooling will
not only have to know the work requirements but also be intimately
familiar with the robot's performance intricacies. He should also

participate in the robot's training in using the tooling to complete its task, and in doing so, enrich his own knowledge about
robot behavior. In a sense, the toolmaker's role is analogous to
that of a surgical nurse feeding tools to a surgeon, except that he
provides the tools much less often and builds or modifies them himself. But he needs a comparable knowledge of the job and of his
robotic colleague.

In cooperative man-robot assembly, the toolmaker must consider
the interaction between the worker and the robot and provide tooling that is compatible with the physical needs of both and which
permits efficient system behavior.

The toolmaker's abilities will become increasingly sophisticated as Generation 1.5 to 2 robots require sensitive, discriminating sensory feedback from their actions. A variety of direct and
remote transducers of location and force will be available for the
toolmaker to choose from in his tooling design, and his "care and
feeding" of the robot will have to increase proportionally. Generation 2.5 to 3 robots will require TV system and control system
knowledge of the toolmaker, and greater involvement in his role of
assisting in the robot's evolutionary progress.

ROBOT MAINTENANCE AND REPAIR

The reliability of the automated system will be a function of
the preventive maintenance and traumatic repair fidelity by the
appropriate personnel. But the maintenance and repair will have
to be characterized by man-robot cooperation in fault identification, location, and display of relatively complex problems, and
automatic fault diagnosis and repair for more common, simple problems. Robots will have to be designed increasingly with built-in
fault diagnostics and self-correcting abilities using redundant
modular hydraulics, wiring, and mechanisms for backup until the next
convenient time to replace or repair the faulty components. Should
a breakdown occur, a robot should say, in effect, "this is why I
stopped working and this is what needs to be done" to the repair-
man, rather than just sitting there defiantly forcing him to figure
out the puzzle on his own. The economics of highly automated production systems are such that the increased cost of robot automatic
fault detection and display (and, perhaps, repair) would be most
probably cost effective.

ROBOT-MACHINE SYSTEM SUPERVISION

As the state of the art evolves from man's direct, active
cooperative interfacing with Generation 1 robots in assembly tasks
to a supervisory and support interaction with Generation 2-3 robots,

new problems will arise. Upgrading a production worker to, or
replacing him with, a supervisor for a group of bank of robot-
machine systems would put him or his replacement in the position of
functioning primarily as a monitor of information flow and physical
activity. But the role of monitor is not one that man typically
plays very well.

The variety of supervisory roles that men eventually play in
automated systems may very well be as varied as the types of systems
themselves. A technique for identifying appropriate tasks for the
man is the Information-Decision-Action (IDA) Chart (Kinkade and
Van Cott, 1972). Once one identifies for all system tasks, the
information needed to make an appropriate decision as to which action
to take, the responsibility for each of these tasks or for parts of
them can be assigned to the man or the machine depending on their
difficulty, duration, and appropriateness for the machines or the
man. IDA charts have been successfully used in other man-machine
system analyses, and should be helpful here.

A poorly designed supervisory role would be one in which the
man has nothing to do but system monitoring most of the time (assuming high system reliability) and then has tasks to perform only
by default.* He needs to be more actively involved in the ongoing
production process, with significant events and data "brought to
his attention" in a timely manner on a master display, and updated
status displays available to him on all of the important system
parameters for planning or problem solving purposes. He may very
well wind up as some combination of programmer/teacher, toolmaker,
maintenance man, and system manager.

CONCLUSION

As automated parts machining, transfer, and assembly progressively permeate batch production systems, the evolving system's
performance, acceptance, and operational safety will depend more
and more on the design of the MRI. This paper suggested several
fundamental concepts of MRI design, from the standpoint of the
production personnel who will interface with the robot, which are
expected to have an impact on the overall production system
efficiency.

---

*This principle holds true for jobs in general, including those of
oil refinery operator, police watch captain, airline pilot, etc.

REFERENCES

1. Brock, T.E., and W. Thornton, 3rd Conference on Industrial
    Robot Technology Proceedings, Birmingham, England, March, 1975.

2. Driscoll, L.C., "Projecting Blue Collar Robot Markets and
    Applications", 2nd Conference on Industrial Robot Technology
    Proceedings, Birmingham, England, March, 1974, pp. F3-21.

3. France, D.W., "USM Robot--Unique Features Include Quick,
    Simplified Teaching", 2nd Conference on Industrial Robot
    Technology Proceedings, Birmingham, England, March, 1974,
    pp. E4-47 to E4-56.

4. IIT Research Institute, 5th International Symposium on Indus-
    trial Robots, Chicago, Illinois, September 22-24, 1975.

5. Johnson, K.G., "Foreward", 5th International Symposium on
    Industrial Robots, Chicago, Illinois, September 22-24, 1975,
    pp. iii-v.

6. Kinkade, R.G., and H.P. Van Cott, eds., Human Engineering
    Guide to Equipment Design, rev., U.S. Government Printing
    Office, Washington, D.C., 1972, Ch. 1.

7. Sheridan, T.B., and W.R. Ferrell, Man-Machine Systems, MIT
    Press, 1974.

8. Young, J.F., Robotics, J. Wiley & Sons, 1973.

THE EFFECT OF COST ON THE SAMPLING BEHAVIOR OF HUMAN INSTRUMENT
MONITORS

Tarald O. Kvålseth

The Norwegian Institute of Technology

N-7034 Trondheim-NTH, NORWAY

Edward R.F.W. Crossman

University of California

Berkeley, California, U.S.A.

Kenneth Y. Kum

Data Measurement Corporation

Santa Clara, California, U.S.A.

INTRODUCTION

Since the first definitive research studies of human visual
sampling behavior by Milton, Jones and Fitts in the late 1940's and
early 1950's (cf. Milton et al., 1949; Jones et al., 1949; Milton
et al., 1950) involving specifically the natural scanning patterns
of pilots during actual flight maneuvers, a number of studies have
been made of the ways in which human operators distribute their
attention between various information sources. The first attempt
to formulate a theoretical model of such behavior was made by
Senders (1955) and based on the simple proposition that the mean
sampling frequency for a displayed signal is proportional to its
bandwidth with a sampling duration that is proportional to the rate
at which the display or instrument generates information. Experimental results by Senders (1964) and Senders et al. (1966) lent

some support to this proposition. Subsequent model formulations
have approached the human sampling-control process from the point
of view of (i) a queueing model in which the server is the human
monitor and the queue members are the monitored instruments (Carbonell, 1966; Carbonell et al., 1968), (ii) an 'internal sampling model' that views the sampling process as one whereby the human operator tries to maintain and update some internal image or model of the
system being controlled and its environment (Smallwood, 1967), (iii)
optimal control theory (cf. Baron & Kleinman, 1969) and (iv) the
'traditional' quasi-linear describing function theory (cf. McRuer
et al., 1967; Allen et al., 1970). Most recently, some reported
studies have analyzed the feedback sampling behavior in manual process control of slow-response systems (Crossman et al., 1974) and
the uncertainty and information processing underlying human sampling (Kvålseth, 1975).

None of these studies, however, has looked specifically into
the possible effects on human sampling behavior of the cost or penalty structure associated with the feedback sampling process and
with control performance in terms of the extent to which real system
response deviates from ideal or prescribed response. It was the
objective of the present study to analyze such possible effects of
sampling and error cost on the frequency of sampling and on the
characteristics of the sampling pattern. The results of such an
analysis would provide some indication of whether sampling decisions
are really determined by an evaluation of probable payoff.

EXPERIMENTAL METHOD

The basic task performed by the subjects was a closed-loop
control task of the regulator type with a constant reference signal
(forcing function) equal to zero. A random disturbance or noise
entered the plant (controlled system), and it was the task of the
subjects to try to compensate for this additive noise through their
control actions. The basic control loop is illustrated in Fig. 1.
It was a four-variate or four-axis control situation in which the
plant consisted of four uncoupled first-order elements each of
which had an impulse response sequence consisting of a train of
points of unit amplitude and was thus slightly unstable. A PDP-8
digital computer was used to model the dynamics of the plants and
to generate the noise, which, when considered to enter the system
at the output ends of the plants, was a general random walk type of
stochastic process. Each component process of this four-dimensional
noise, which was independent of the others, involved a set of independent and identically distributed random variables with a uniform
probability density function over the interval [-0.5, 0.5]. The
noise signals and the input and output signals of the plants were
all time parameter discrete with successive signal values occurring

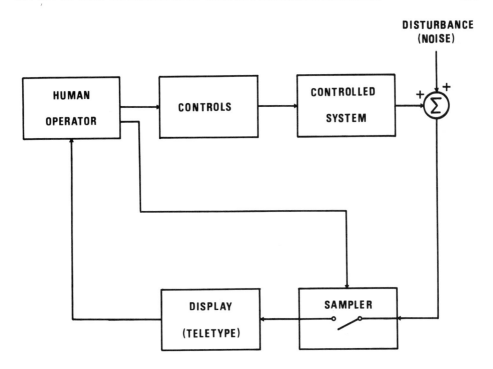

Fig. 1. Basic Control Loop for the Experiment.

at equidistant time intervals of about 1 sec.

The man-machine interface consisted of (i) a teletype on which
the four system output variables were displayed, (ii) a control
panel with four control knobs and (iii) a panel of four sampling
switches or buttons. These three pieces of peripheral equipment
were connected to the PDP-8 computer. The rotary control knobs
(with constant gain) permitted continuous control actions to be made
so that analog-to-digital conversion was required.

Each subject was seated in front of the teletype and a table on
which the control panel and sampling panel were mounted. Whenever
the subject wanted to sample one of the signals, he would depress
the appropriate sampling button and the signal value was then
printed on the teletype. The sampled values of the individual signals were printed in separate columns. Each time the subject sampled a signal he had to pay a prespecified sampling cost. There
was also a given cost per unit value of the amplitude of each control system output signal, i.e., a cost per error unit since the
four reference signals were zero for all time points. The subjects
were instructed to try to minimize the average cost, i.e., combined

Table 1. Alternative Experimental Conditions Involving Different
          Costs (in cents) for Signals 1, 2, 3, 4

Experimental conditions	Cost of sampling				Cost of error			
	1	2	3	4	1	2	3	4
1	0.5	0.5	0.5	0.5	1	1	1	1
2	0.5	0.5	0.5	0.5	2	4	6	8
3	0.5	0.5	0.5	0.5	0	10	20	30
4	2	4	6	8	1	1	1	1
5	2	4	6	8	2	4	6	8
6	2	4	6	8	0	10	20	30

mean sampling and absolute error cost, during each experimental run.
The actual average cost was computed by the PDP-8 and printed on
the teletype once every 30 sec.

Five unpaid subjects were used in this experiment, all of whom
were male university students. None of these had had any previous
experience with similar laboratory tracking tasks.

The six different experimental conditions used are presented in
Table 1 and involve different sets of sampling and error costs for
the four signals being controlled and monitored. The experiment
lasted 5 min for each experimental condition. Each subject was given
a short practice run prior to the experiment and a short rest period
before each new condition. A randomized complete block design was
used that blocked on the subjects.

RESULTS

Sampling Frequencies

The numbers of samples taken by each subject for the four signals during the various experimental runs of 300 sec duration were
obtained from the printout on the teletype and are given in Table 2.
These data seem to indicate clearly that the average sampling frequencies during the 300 sec intervals varied substantially with
variations in sampling cost and/or error cost. While the specific
nature of these variations in sampling behavior is seen to have been
considerably different for the different subjects, the general tendency that the sampling frequency increased with increasing error cos
and decreasing sampling cost was characteristic for all five subjects

Table 2. Number of Samples Taken During 300 Sec* Experimental Runs

Signals	Subjects	Experimental conditions					
		1	2	3	4	5	6
1	1	21	10	1	36	17	4
	2	18	13	8	20	12	8
	3	24	10	3	15	14	0
	4	22	13	0	23	6	0
	5	23	10	9	34	16	4
2	1	20	11	5	19	14	10
	2	12	16	13	16	14	18
	3	22	10	16	15	19	10
	4	14	14	10	14	16	14
	5	24	9	22	14	21	19
3	1	20	38	31	10	16	23
	2	15	23	25	17	9	15
	3	19	18	24	13	18	14
	4	15	21	17	1	8	12
	5	23	29	22	13	22	24
4	1	15	29	41	12	32	44
	2	11	17	22	13	16	21
	3	10	19	28	10	18	18
	4	19	13	19	4	15	16
	5	22	31	21	8	24	26

*A 275 sec experimental run was used for Subject 1 and Condition 3.

When the error and sampling costs were constant for the four signals as for Experimental Condition 1, the data in Table 2 indicate that the rate of sampling varied relatively little between the signals. This was especially the case for Subject 5 for whom the sampling frequency ranged from 4.4 to 4.8 samples per min. For Condition 6, which had the largest variations of both sampling and error costs between the signals, the sampling frequency varied between 0 and 8.8 samples per min. It is also interesting to observe that, for the two conditions involving no error cost but a non-zero sampling cost for one of the signals, i.e., Conditions 3 and 6 (see Table 1), some of the subjects did in fact sample this signal although at a relatively low rate.

Some relationships between mean sampling frequency across the five subjects based on the data in Table 2 and the cost of error and of sampling are illustrated in Fig. 2. Graph 3 in this diagram,

which corresponds to Experimental Condition 3 in Table 1, shows
clearly that the sampling frequency increased with increasing error
cost when the sampling cost was kept constant. For the same constant sampling cost for the four signals but with a smaller differential error cost between the signals than that for Graph 3, a
similar tendency for the sampling frequency to increase with increasing error cost is observed from Graph 2 (corresponding to Condition
2), although a drop occurred between the two highest cost points.
When the error cost was kept constant but the sampling cost varied
between the signals as for Condition 4, the sampling frequency is
clearly seen from Graph 4 to have decreased as the cost of sampling
increased.

An analysis of variance of the sampling frequency data derived
from Table 2 revealed that both the error cost and the sampling cost
had a statistically significant effect on the sampling frequency
with ($F(2,8) = 24.41$, $p<0.001$) and ($F(1,8) = 9.09$, $p<0.025$), respectively. The only significant interaction was that between subjects
and error cost ($F(8,8) = 3.74$, $p<0.05$). The variation in sampling
frequency among the subjects was clearly significant ($F(4,8) = 14.33$,
$p<0.005$).

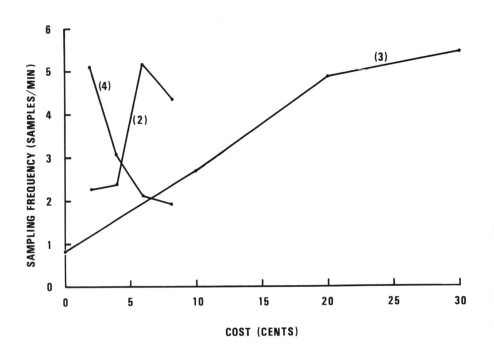

Fig. 2. Mean Sampling Frequency as Functions of Error Cost and Sam-
         pling Cost (the numbers identifying the individual graphs
         correspond to experimental conditions in Table 1).

Transition Frequencies

For the analysis of the sensory load of operators and for the design of instrument panels, another important consideration, in addition to the sampling activities for individual signals, is the sampling pattern formed by various transitions between the signals or the instruments. From a design point of view, the relative placement of instruments ought to have some relationship to their sampling pattern so that any two instruments with a relatively high probability of transition between them should be located relatively closely together. As mentioned in the Introduction, such sampling patterns have been studied by a number of investigators on the basis of both laboratory experiments and real situations involving especially aircraft pilots. However, no reported study has tried to investigate the possible effects of cost of sampling and of error on the structure of the sampling pattern evolved from a closed-loop control task. This was one particular problem that the present study was designed to analyze.

From the printout of the teletype, which gave the sampled values of each of the four signals separately, the relative frequency estimate $\hat{P}_{ij}$ of the probability of transition (P_{ij}) between the i-th and the j-th signal was obtained as the ratio of the number of such transitions to the total number of samples made during each 5 min experimental run. These transition frequencies were obtained for all $i,j = 1,\ldots, 4$ and included consecutive samples on one signal, i.e., transition frequencies $\hat{P}_{ii}$ ($i = 1,\ldots, 4$). Table 3 gives the mean transition frequences across the five subjects for the six experimental conditions defined in Table 1.

The data for the individual subjects indicated that the $\hat{P}_{ij}$ ranged from 0 to 0.38 and tended to be especially high for pairs of signals with relatively high error costs. For Conditions 3 and 6, for example, which corresponded to the highest error cost used for Signals 3 and 4, it is seen from Table 3 that the mean transition frequencies between the two signals were the highest among the 16 different types of sampling transitions. The mean transition frequencies $\hat{P}_{33}$ and $\hat{P}_{44}$ were also relatively high for Conditions 3 and 6. For the various experimental conditions and subjects in general, a substantial number of transitions occurred from one signal and back again to the same signal.

As a single measure of the degree of structure in a sampling pattern that incorporates the entire set $\{\hat{P}_{ij}; i,j = 1,\ldots, 4\}$, the following "sampling entropy index" (SEI) is proposed

$$SEI = \hat{H}/H_{max} \; ; \; \hat{H} = - \sum_{j=1}^{4} \sum_{i=1}^{4} \hat{P}_{ij} \log_2 \hat{P}_{ij}$$

Table 3. Mean Transition Frequencies

Transitions	Experimental conditions					
	1	2	3	4	5	6
1 ↔ 1	0.06	0.04	0.00	0.20	0.04	0.01
1 → 2	0.15	0.02	0.01	0.15	0.07	0.02
1 → 3	0.05	0.02	0.02	0.03	0.02	0.00
1 → 4	0.02	0.08	0.03	0.03	0.06	0.02
2 → 1	0.08	0.07	0.04	0.09	0.09	0.02
2 ↔ 2	0.02	0.04	0.03	0.05	0.06	0.03
2 → 3	0.12	0.03	0.04	0.10	0.08	0.08
2 → 4	0.02	0.04	0.09	0.02	0.04	0.11
3 → 1	0.06	0.04	0.01	0.04	0.02	0.01
3 → 2	0.06	0.10	0.11	0.03	0.09	0.11
3 ↔ 3	0.02	0.12	0.09	0.01	0.01	0.03
3 → 4	0.11	0.08	0.14	0.08	0.10	0.13
4 → 1	0.09	0.01	0.01	0.07	0.05	0.01
4 → 2	0.01	0.02	0.05	0.03	0.05	0.08
4 → 3	0.06	0.19	0.20	0.03	0.10	0.18
4 ↔ 4	0.05	0.09	0.12	0.02	0.12	0.13

where $\hat{H}$ is the (estimated) entropy of the sampling transition structure, which reaches a maximum when all transitions are equiprobable so that

$$H_{max} = \log_2 16 .$$

Clearly, SEI lies between 0 and 1 with increasing values being indicative of decreasing degree of structuring for the sampling pattern.

The values of SEI for each individual subject and for the average performance of the five subjects (based on their mean transition frequencies in Table 3) are given in Table 4 for each experimental condition. An analysis of variance of these data indicated that the error cost was a highly significant factor ($F(2,8) = 4.93$, $p<0.05$), while the variation between subjects was only slightly significant ($F(4,8) = 3.36$, $p<0.10$). Neither the sampling cost nor any of the interaction terms were found to have any significant ($p \gg 0.10$) effect on the degree of sampling structure as measured by the SEI.

Table 4. Values of the Sampling Entropy Index

Subjects	Experimental conditions					
	1	2	3	4	5	6
1	0.80	0.75	0.65	0.81	0.83	0.71
2	0.85	0.91	0.83	0.82	0.91	0.85
3	0.83	0.66	0.71	0.83	0.80	0.56
4	0.86	0.85	0.66	0.66	0.84	0.76
5	0.88	0.81	0.84	0.78	0.92	0.76
Average	0.91	0.91	0.86	0.88	0.95	0.83

SUMMARY AND CONCLUSION

This experimental study has analyzed the effect of sampling cost and error cost on human sampling behavior. The basic task performed by the five subjects was a four-variate (four-axis) closed-loop control task of the regulator type. A general random walk disturbance entered the output end of each of the four uncoupled first-order controlled systems. Continuous rotary control actions were used while the sampled numerical signal values were printed on a teletype. The major conclusion derived from this study was that both the sampling cost and the error cost had significant effects on the subjects' sampling behavior. An increase in the error cost with the sampling cost kept constant tended to cause an increase in the sampling rate. Similarly, the sampling rate tended to increase for a constant error rate when the sampling cost decreased. A 'sampling entropy index' was introduced as a measure of the degree of structure in a sampling pattern. On the basis of the values obtained for this index, which incorporated all transition frequencies between the various monitored signals, it appeared that, of the two types of cost, only the error cost had a significant ($p < 0.05$) effect on the degree of sampling structure.

ACKNOWLEDGMENTS

This work was supported, in part, by Grant GK-37419 from the National Science Foundation.

REFERENCES

Allen, R. W., W. F. Clement, and H. R. Jex. Research on Display

Scanning, Sampling, and Reconstruction Using Separate Main and Secondary Tracking Tasks. NASA CR-1569, July 1970.

Baron, S., and D. L. Kleinman. The human operator as an optimal controller and information processor. IEEE Trans. on MMS, Vol. MSS-10, No. 1, 1969, 9-17.

Carbonell, J. R. A queueing model of many-instrument visual sampling. IEEE Trans. on HFE, Vol. HFE-7, No. 4, Dec. 1966, 157-164.

Carbonell, J. R., J. L. Ward and J. W. Senders. A queueing model of visual sampling: Experimental validation. IEEE Trans. on MMS, Vol. MMS-9, No. 3, Sept. 1968, 82-87.

Crossman, E. R. F. W., J. E. Cooke, and R. J. Beishon. Visual attention and the sampling of displayed information in process control. In Edwards, E., and F. P. Lees, (ed.). The Human Operator in Process Control. London: Taylor & Francis, Inc., 1974.

Jones, R. E., J. L. Milton, and P. M. Fitts. Eye Fixations of Aircraft Pilots; Frequency, Duration, and Sequence of Fixations during Routine Instrument Flight. Air Materiel Command AF TR-5975, Dec. 1949.

Kvålseth, T. O. Quantitative Modelling of the Time-Multiplexing Characteristics of Human Controllers. NSF Rept. GK-37419, Aug. 1975.

McRuer, Duane, Henry R. Jex, Warren F. Clement, and Dunstan Graham. Development of a Systems Analysis Theory of Manual Control Displays. Systems Technology, Inc., Tech. Rept. 163-1, Oct. 1967.

Milton, J. L., R. E. Jones, and P. M. Fitts. Eye Fixations of Aircraft Pilots; Frequency, Duration, and Sequence of Fixations when Flying the USAF Instrument Low Approach System (ILAS). Air Materiel Command AF TR-5839, Oct. 1949.

Milton, J. L., R. E. Jones, and P. M. Fitts. Eye Fixations of Aircraft Pilots: Frequency, Duration, and Sequence of Fixations when Flying Selected Maneuvers During Instrument and Visual Flight Conditions. Air Materiel Command AF TR-6018 (ATI 84010), Aug. 1950.

Senders, J. W. Man's capacity to use information from complex displays. In Quastler, H., (ed.), Information Theory in Psychology. Glencoe, Ill.: The Free Press, 1955.

Senders, J. W. The human operator as a monitor and controller of multidegree of freedom systems. IEEE Trans. on HFE, Vol. HFE-5, No. 1, Sept. 1964, 2-5.

Senders, J. W., J. I. Elkind, M. C. Grignetti, and R. D. Smallwood. An Investigation of the Visual Sampling Behavior of Human Observers, NASA CR-434, Apr. 1966.

Smallwood, R. D. Internal models of the human instrument monitor. IEEE Trans. on HFE, Vol. HFE-8, No. 3, Sept. 1967, 181-187.

DISCUSSION

RIJNSDORP :

Did the subjects experience any difficulties in the lay-out of the display ? Did you apply some kind of randomization to the display sequence ?

KVÅLSETH :

We did not register any lay-out difficulties since the sampled values of each of the four signals were printed in four separate and clearly identifiable columns on the teletype. Throughout the experiment, the display sequence remained fixed in the sense that the sampled values of the i-th signal were always displayed in the i-th column from the left for $i = 1, .., 4.$

SHERIDAN :

Would you say more about any comparisons you made of experimental results with normative or "optimal" sampling rates you may have calculated ?

KVÅLSETH :

In a separate study by Kvålseth (1975), actual sampling rates were compared with normative ones generated by a utility maximization model. The results indicated that the subjects tended to sample a signal at rates that were lower than those prescribed by the model. Furthermore, in another study (Kvålseth, 1975), comparisons were made between the subjective and objective uncertainty based on entropy measurements. The results revealed that the subjects were consistently less uncertain about the state of the monitored process than the normative behavior indicated.

PARALLEL VS. SERIAL INSTRUMENTATION FOR MULTIVARIABLE MANUAL CONTROL IN CONTROL ROOMS

G. Geiser and W. Schumacher

Fraunhofer-Gesellschaft, Institut für Informations-

verarbeitung in Technik und Biologie,

Karlsruhe, F.R. of Germany

SUMMARY

The display of information and the mode of control in multi-variable manual control systems may be designed in a parallel or serial manner. Starting from an experimental comparison of these two design principles, which shows a strong increase of the control error in the serial case, a display and control unit is proposed with parallel, integrated display of information and with serial, compatible mode of control. By means of an experiment it is shown that the control quality with this unit is comparable with that of the parallel instrumentation. Furthermore it is suggested that the operator be enabled to vary the stick signal of the display and control unit continuously by his force of manipulation. The effect of this modification was studied by a further experiment.

INTRODUCTION

Multivariable manual control is often to be carried out by the human operator, e. g. in aircraft guidance or in process control. The operator's objective is to compensate disturbances in each loop or to track the variable setpoints. The performance in this task depends essentially on the design of the displays and controls, which give information about the state of the controlled elements to the human operator and by which he applies input signals respectively. Whereas the pilot of an aircraft is highly

trained in performing this task, the operator in the control room
of a technical plant seldom carries out multivariable manual control tasks, e. g. if the automatic control system (process computer)
has failed. The lack of training is made more difficult by the fact
that there are often control rooms in which several hundred control
loops are to be supervised. In emergency cases the operator has to
control a subset of these simultaneously.

In conventional control rooms the information about the measured variables and the control loops is displayed together in a
parallel manner, and similarly, each input variable which can be
influenced by the operator has its own control device. The displays
and controls of each controlled element are combined in a separate,
panel-mounted display and control unit (DCU) /1/. This parallel instrumentation leads to extremely large control rooms, which are difficult to survey. Furthermore the expenses for instrumentation are
considerable. Therefore it is desirable to reduce the dimensions of
the control room by decreasing the number of panel-mounted DCUs.
This can be reached by representing a subset of controlled elements
by only one DCU, which is to be connected with the actually disturbed
controlled element by the human operator. In the critical case of
several systems being disturbed at the same time the operator has
to connect the DCU with the disturbed systems sequentially. In this
way a serial instrumentation for each subset of controlled elements
is obtained. Fig. 1 shows the parallel and serial instrumentation
principles.

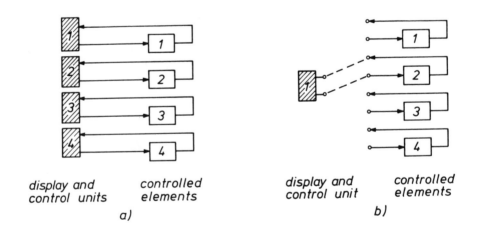

display and   controlled   display and   controlled
control units   elements   control unit   elements
            a)   b)

Fig. 1 : Parallel (a) and serial (b) instrumentation for manual
          control.

In this paper the two instrumentation principles are compared
by means of an experiment. The conclusions drawn from this comparison led to design proposals for an improved DCU which were also
tested by further experimental investigations.

COMPARISON OF PARALLEL AND SERIAL INSTRUMENTATION

In order to compare the human performance with parallel and
serial instrumentation an experimental set-up with four controlled
elements and four DCUs was developed. This development and the experimental procedure are described in detail in /2/. Fig. 2 shows
the block diagram of one controlled element with one DCU and with
the circuit for performance evaluation. The controlled elements have
integral behaviour. A DCU consists of the displays for the control
signal and the output variable (control error) of the controlled
element and of the control for the input variable, which is a three-
position-toggle-switch for the application of positive and negative
control pulses with constant amplitude U_R. The length of these pulses is stored by a hold amplifier of which the output is connected
with the input of the controlled element. Together with the hold amplifier the controlled element has double integral behaviour for the
human controller. As a performance measure the time integral of the
absolute value of the control error beyond the threshold value s is
evaluated. If the control error surmounts the threshold value s a
binary alarm lamp lights up at the corresponding controlled element.
The numerical values of the most important experimental parameters
are listed in Fig. 2.

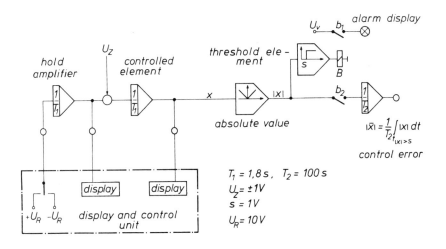

$$|\bar{x}| = \frac{1}{T_2}\int_{|x|>s}|x|\,dt$$

control error

$T_1 = 1,8\,s, \quad T_2 = 100\,s$
$U_z = \pm 1V$
$s = 1V$
$U_R = 10\,V$

Fig. 2 : Block diagram of one controlled element with display and
control unit (DCU) and evaluation circuit.

The disturbance signals which are to be compensated by the human operator are step signals with amplitude U_Z and mean time interval of 50 s; they are added to the input of the controlled elements. In order to disturb several systems at the same time, the disturbance signals are registered on different channels of magnetic tape.

The parallel instrumentation was realized in the experiments by a fixed relation between the DCUs and the controlled elements (Fig. 1a). In the serial case there are less DCUs than controlled elements available; in the limiting case there is only one DCU which is connected sequentially with the disturbed systems (Fig. 1b). In the experiments the variable connections between the DCU and the controlled elements were set up by cables with plugs and sockets.

Independent variables of the experiments were the number of controlled elements and the number of DCUs available. From the 10 combinations, which result from four controlled elements and four DCUs, nine were investigated. The case of one system with one DCU was omitted because there is no difference between parallel and serial instrumentation. Eight subjects performed 10 trials with each combination of the independent variables after an adequate learning phase. The trial length was 200 s, of which only the last 100 s were evaluated. Fig. 3 shows the medians and quartiles of the mean control error beyond the treshold value s as a function of the number of controlled elements and the number of DCUs. The mean values are calculated here and in the following from the sums of the errors of the systems which had to be controlled simultaneously. There is a strong increase of the control error at the transition from parallel to serial instrumentation, i. e. if for a fixed number of controlled elements the number of DCUs is decreased.

MONITORING AND CONTROL ACTIVITIES WITH PARALLEL AND SERIAL INSTRUMENTATION

In order to analyse the reasons for the decrease of control performance in the case of serial instrumentation eye movements and motor activities such as control actions and transfers of the connections between the DCUs and the controlled elements were filmed and analysed. By the films the local and temporal fixation points of the eyes at the DCUs and at the controlled elements were obtained. Furthermore the number and duration of connections between the DCUs and the controlled elements, the sign and the length of input signals and the alarm periods could be determined. These data show that the reduction of the parallel instrumentation to the serial one leads to an information presentation which is not sufficient for the human controller. This is shown by the fact that in the serial case DCUs are also connected with undisturbed systems in

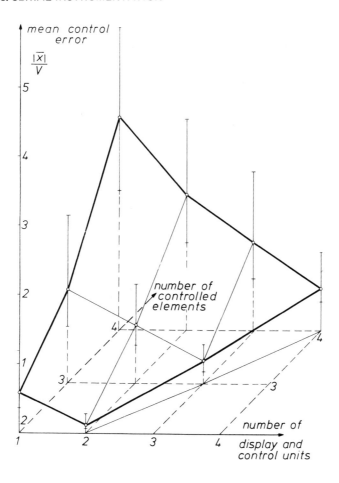

Fig. 3 :   Mean control error (medians and quartiles) versus number of controlled elements and number of display and control units (DCUs).

order to recognise disturbances just in the beginning. With serial instrumentation there is no possibility to attend to priorities for the order in which simultaneously disturbed systems are to be controlled. Because there were only binary alarms with no information about the magnitude of the control error, the order cannot be chosen optimally by beginning with that system which shows the highest control error. Finally it turned out that also with parallel instrumentation control of several systems is performed mostly in a serial manner, i. e. the different control errors are compensated one after another.

DESIGN PROPOSAL FOR A DCU

Display of control errors

The investigation of the monitoring and control activities
shows that the serial instrumentation involves an undue reduction
of the amount of control information. In this method the detection
of disturbances just beginning is made more difficult and the consideration of priorities is prevented during the selection of the
element which is actually to be controlled. Therefore it is concluded that the display of control errors should be maintained in a parallel manner. However in order to reach the aim of better supervision of the control room it is proposed to combine the separate displays of control errors in an integrated display. Integrated displays of different kinds are well-known in the field of aircraft instrumentation, e. g. /3/. In this case a space saving integrated
display with easy interpretation is reached by presenting the control
errors in polar coordinates (Fig. 4a). With restriction to a subset
of at most four controlled elements the angles $\varphi_p = k \cdot 45°$ and φ_n
$= 180° + \varphi_p$ (k = 0,1,2,3) characterize the different controlled elements and the sign of the control error. The length of the radius
vectors indicate the amount of the control errors. The realization
of such an integrated display can be achieved by means of a cathode-
ray-tube or by rows of light emitting diodes, which are arranged in
a radial manner with 45° angular distance.

Control Device

Even with parallel instrumentation, i . e. with equal numbers of
controls and controlled elements, several   simultaneously disturbed
systems are controlled in a serial manner by selecting them one after another. Therefore the application of input signals can be
performed by a single control device which can be switched over to
the different controlled elements. Important design criteria for such
a control device are the compatibility with the corresponding display and the ease of transferring the connections between the control and the controlled elements. In /4/ a high similarity between
the display and the control is recommended. A joystick with eight
movement directions corresponding to the integrated display in polar
coordinates satisfies these conditions. Its functional diagram is
shown in Fig. 4b. The control has eight switching devices with angular distance of 45° and allows the application of positive and negative control pulses for four controlled elements.

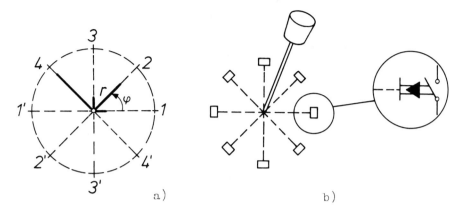

Fig. 4 : Integrated display (a) and compatible control (b) of the
proposed display and control unit (DCU).

    The combination of the proposed display and control devices
represents a DCU which is a compromise between parallel and serial
instrumentation. It consists of a parallel integrated display and
a serial compatible control.

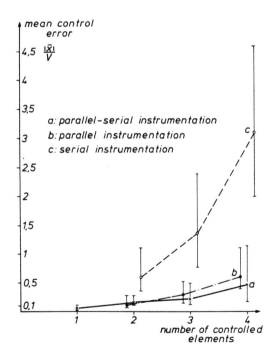

Fig. 5 : Mean control error versus number of controlled elements.

For this parallel/serial DCU a laboratory set-up was established
and an experimental investigation was performed. In order to be able
to relate the results of this experiment with the previous comparison of parallel and serial instrumentation the experimental procedure chosen before was retained. Fig. 5 shows the measured results,
where the mean control error beyond the threshold value s is plotted as a function of the number of systems which were simultaneously
to be controlled. For comparison of the results as obtained with
the former experiment, the results with parallel instrumentation
(n systems, n DCUs; n = 2,3,4) and with serial instrumentation
(n systems, 1 DCU; n =2,3,4) are also shown (curves b and c). It appears that the control performance with the proposed parallel/serial
DCU is comparable with that obtained with the conventional parallel
instrumentation.

LINEAR VS THREE-MODE CONTROL

The analysis of the behaviour of the subjects shows that it is
often not possible to compensate the disturbances without overshoot.
One of the possible reasons is, that the manipulation intervals of
the three-mode switches with constant control signal amplitude must
decrease with the control error. Because the human choice of short
time intervals is inaccurate and limited to a minimum value of 0.1s
approximately fine minor control is difficult. Therefore as modification of the parallel/serial DCU a linear controller for variation of the amplitude of the control signal is to be taken into consideration.

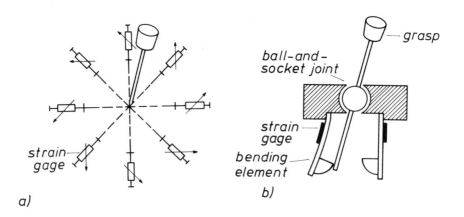

Fig. 6 :   Control with force transducers
           (a) principle (b) realization for one axis

In /5/ the binary choice of the gain of the control signal is recommended as an aid for coarse and fine control respectively in a two-dimensional positon control task. But there the choice of the control gain represents an additional task for the human operator. Furthermore there was no proprioceptive feedback of the control gain. But the performance with this kind of binary selectable control gain was improved without markedly affecting the self estimated workload. On the other hand it is shown in /6/, that a three-mode switch permits better performance than a linear control stick if a one-dimensional system with more lag than double integration is to be controlled. Even with a linear controller the human operator tends to control difficult controlled elements in a bang-bang manner.

To investigate the influence of linear controllers in the multivariable control task a control device was developed for serial application of continuous control signals for four controlled elements. The desire for a simple equipment configuration led to the

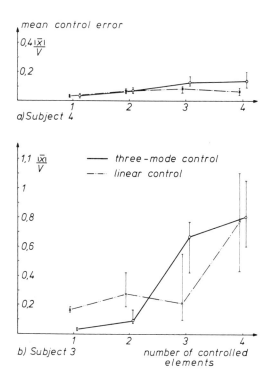

Fig. 7 :   Mean control error versus number of controlled
           elements for two subjects (a,b).

utilization of strain gages as force transducers for the manipulation force of the human operator. Fig. 6 shows the principle of
the controller (a) and the realization for one dimension (b). By
this controller the range of the control signal was $0 \leq U_R/U_{Rmax} \leq 1$.
A further experiment was performed to compare the DCUs with linear
and three-mode controller. In Fig. 7 the results of this comparison are shown for two subjects which turned out to be characteristic for two kinds of behaviour. One group of the subjects
(Fig. 7 a) performed the control task with low control error, nearly independent of the number of controlled elements. A second group
showed an increase of the control error with the number of controlled elements. By analysing the stick signal it can be seen that
only the first group makes use of the continous control signal of
the linear controller, whereas the second group operates with both
kinds of controllers in a bang-bang manner. Finally there is a
slightly lower control error with the linear controller in the first
group. Closer analysis of the former experiment with the three-mode
control (Fig. 5, curve a) also led to the discrimination of these
two kinds of performance, namely increasing and nearly constant
control error as a function of the number of controlled elements.

REFERENCES

/1/ Geiser, G., Kollmann, E., Nürnberger, W., Schulz, H., Towae,
     K.: Anthropotechnische Gesichtspunkte bei der Gestaltung von
     Kompaktregler-Leitgeräten. Regelungstechnische Praxis 17 (1975),
     82 - 86, 120 - 124.
/2/ Schumacher, W.,: Experimenteller Vergleich paralleler und se-
     rieller Stelleingriffe in einen gestörten Prozeß. Fachtagung
     Prozeßrechner 1974, Lecture Notes in Computer Science, Vol. 12,
     Springer-Verlag, Berlin, Heidelberg, New York (1974), S. 246 -
     256.
/3/ McCormick, E.J.: Human Factors Engineering. McGraw-Hill, New
     York, 3. ed., 1970.
/4/ Poulton, E.C.: Tracking Skill and Manual Control. Academic
     Press, New York, 1974, S. 299-302.
/5/ Rothbauer, G., Krüger, W., Kruse, W.: Untersuchung der binär
     wählbaren Bediensignalverstärkung bei einer Positionierungsauf-
     gabe. Forschungsinstitut für Anthropotechnik, Bericht Nr. 8,
     Meckenheim, 1972.
/6/ Young, L.R., Meiry, J.L.: Bang-Bang Aspects of Manual Control
     in High-Order Systems. IEEE Trans. on Automatic Control, vol.
     AC-10 (1965), 336-341.

ACKNOWLEDGEMENT

This research was supported by the project "Prozeßlenkung mit DV-
Anlagen (PDV)" of the F.R. of Germany.

DISCUSSION

SOEDE :

In practical situations very many control units are involved to control a plant. Your experiment considered up to four units. What do you expect about your results and conclusions (mean error and parallel vs serial instrumentation) if you have to deal with the more usual numbers of control units ?

GEISER :

The experiments showed a more or less strong increase of the control error with increasing number of controlled elements with serial and parallel instrumentation as well as with the proposed parallel/serial DCU. This increase will continue for more than four controlled elements.

The maximum number of controlled elements which can be controlled with the parallel/serial DCU is mainly determind by the human ability to discriminate angular directions of the control device. This limit has to be found ; however much more than eight directions (corresponding to four controlled elements) cannot be used.

If there are more than four controlled elements there are two possibilities for the equipment of the plant with the parallel/serial DCU. Firstly, one DCU can be serially switched over to several subsets of, e.g., four controlled elements. Secondly, the plant can be equipped with several DCUs in a parallel manner, each being related to a subset of, e.g., four controlled elements.

PERCEPTUAL ORGANISATION AND THE DESIGN OF THE MAN-COMPUTER INTERFACE IN PROCESS CONTROL

H.T. Smith

Psychology Department

Bradford University

The advent of the second generation of process control computers has brought about a considerable change in the role and importance of the human operator. In place of several individual, semi-independent control units there is a trend towards more complex hierarchical systems. The operator increasingly occupies a supervisory function in co-ordinating and regulating information supplied by, and to, automatic sub-systems. Lower level machines implement the actual continuous control; the operator is principally concerned with making short to intermediate term plans in the face of anticipated or unexpected events. Such systems place great emphasis on the development of the operator's supervisory technique; which is dependent on the design of the man-computer interface. This paper is concerned with interface design, particularly the use of computer generated displays to present information in perceptually 'assimilable' forms. An experiment is described which demonstrates how the representation of a control problem may inflence the interactive program user's performance.

There has been considerable interest in the role of the human operator in computer based control systems (eg Rasmussen 1974, Edwards and Lees 1973 and 1974), particularly with respect to the design of displays and controls. Although considerable evidence is available to demonstrate the importance of suitable coding schemes in the design of conventional displays (eg McCormick 1964), there has been only a relatively small number of studies involving computer generated displays. Recent work has for example focussed on such topics as state diagnosis (Rasmussen & Goodstein 1972), manual versus computer display panels (West & Clark 1974) and predictive displays (Ketteringham & O'Brien 1974). However there

is as yet little prescriptive information available to help the
designer of hierarchical control systems. These differ most notably
from their more traditional counterparts in that the operator is
placed in parallel with a semi-automatic control system. By utilising 'local' control the process may continue to run (within prescribed limits) without direct operator intervention, thus freeing
the operator to devise plans for the short term future of the
system. For this purpose, access is often provided not only to
the lower control levels but to a simulation model of the controlled
environment. The underlying rationale is that interactions between
complex processes may prove to be too difficult for the operator to
resolve without some form of decision aiding. The simulation provides information about the outcomes of alternative actions without
disturbing the ongoing control of the process. The success, or
otherwise, of this approach depends upon the operator's ability to
use the 'online' model to identify a member of the class of acceptable solutions. However very little attention has been directed
towards establishing the difficulty of this task. Memory limitations
for example may lead to acceptance of superficial solutions when a
large number of actions are possible. Moreover deciding which
system states constitute acceptable solutions, given restricted time,
is a problem in its own right.

In this context Smith and Crabtree (1975) investigated the
ability of subjects, in an experimental control situation, to utilise
a simple simulation facility. They concluded that those memory
limitations which prevented direct prediction of action outcomes
also affected the ability to successfully use the simulation model
to reduce the solution space to be searched. One approach to this
problem is to incorporate a model of the operator's strategy in the
system model; the most promising developments in this area utilise
Artificial Intelligence techniques. For example Sheridan (1972) and
Freedy et al (1971) describe supervisory schemes for teleoperator
control that involve the machine learning parts of the operator's
strategy. Sime et al (1975) adopted a similar approach based on an
AI production system - the simulation model incorporated a dynamic
rule stack which was automatically invoked by system conditions.

Another possible approach to the problem of extending the
solution search lies with changing the task representation to one
in which human working memory limitations are not so apparent.
This may be done either by allowing system states to be more easily
evaluated in terms of goals, or by reducing the memory load associated with storing search patterns. Krolak and Felts (1971)
exemplified this approach in a travelling salesman problem. A
computer was used to group, into clusters, places within a criterion
distance of each other. The user was then able to quickly connect
the clusters into a minimum tour by eye. The experiment to be
described in this paper is similarly concerned with how the apparent

structure of a problem may be altered to help the user. Although
centred around a form of resource allocation problem that frequently
occurs in discrete industrial process situations (eg routing and
scheduling) the approach may be generalised.

An Experiment to Investigate Solution Search
as a Fuction of Problem Representation

Two groups of subjects were each given a set of problems to
solve with the aid of an interactive computer program and visual
display. The problem sets were identical but differed in the form
in which they were represented to the two groups. The first representation was that of a resource allocation task in the context of
a PERT type process network. The second was an apparently unrelated
reasoning task involving pattern substitution and matching. In both
cases the subjects were given a simulation facility which enabled
them to investigate various alternative actions in their search for
an optimal solution. No answers were supplied to the subjects –
they were instructed to terminate their search when they had discovered the 'best possible solution'.

A typical network problem is shown in figure 1. Activities
(processes) are indicated by the dashed lines with an alphameric
character name. By convention the network graph starts on the left
hand side at day zero and, via a simulation program whose progress
is controlled by the subject, proceeds to the right hand side. As
each process completes the dashed line is replaced with a solid
counterpart so that at the network completion time all lines will
be solid. The subjects had to find an activity sequence/resource
allocation that completed the network in a minimum number of days.
The activity sequence could be altered subject to the usual network
constraints (eg an activity cannot start until its predecessor(s)
have completed, parallel branches may be worked simultaneously or
one given precedence over another). An activity could only be
started if there were enough resources available to satisfy its
requirements. In these problems, resources were of just one type
(men) and the time that each activity took depended upon the number
of resources employed. Only limited resources were available for
each network problem which effectively restricted the number of
options open to the subject. The simulation facility allowed the
subject to inspect the state of the network at any projected time
from the initial to the completion point. (Figures 1a and 1b show
the network states at days 12 and 15). In the absence of subject
decisions a simple heuristic dispatcher allowed the program to run
forward in (simulation) time. When changes were made to the sequence,
or resource utilisation, of an activity this default mechanism was
not invoked. All subject actions were selected via a display 'menu'
and associated screen cursor.

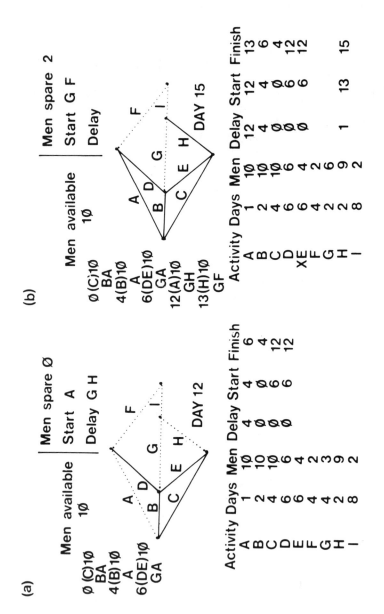

Figure 1. The Network Representation

The second representation of the resource allocation problem
was adopted from a suggestion by Battersby (1968). The problem is
presented as the packing together of a set of rectangular boxes into
an enclosure in such a way as to minimise the empty space (see
figure 2 for the pattern form of the problem shown in figure 1).
In these problems the height of the enclosure is fixed and the left
hand wall is placed on the extreme left hand side of the display
screen. The right hand wall is free to move and always assumes a
position immediately to the side of the rightmost box. If this
box can be moved to the left (eg by stacking it upon another) then
the wall will move to the left and, most probably, the amount of
wasted space inside the enclosure will decrease. There are two
restrictions to this strategy however, (i) the fixed enclosure
height and (ii) certain constraints on where the boxes may be placed
with respect to each other. In the first case the boxes may not fit
neatly between the floor and the ceiling without gaps. It is possible to overcome this constraint by allowing the shape of the boxes
to alter to some extent. For example a tall thin box may be trans-
formed into a squat long one provided that its area remains constant.
In practice the subject is allowed to choose from a restricted set
of shape combinations for each box. Limitations on the relative
placement of boxes are indicated by letters in the top right or
bottom left corners of a box. The former indicate those boxes that
must lie to the right and the latter those that must lie to the left.
The pattern position restrictions are the logical activity sequences
that are so clearly depicted in the network representation of these
problems. Similarly the shape (height/length) of a box is an equivalent form of an activity's resource/time usage in the network representation. However there is one additional problem to be accommodated
in this representation that relates to the identification of each
resource element as a unit rectangle on the wall of the envelope.
Sometimes certain spaces inside the enclosure will become isolated
from their neighbours and apparently not be usable. This problem is
overcome by allowing boxes to be split into two or more vertical
sections when this situation arises (see box I in figure 3). Alterations to the position of a box (or its size) were made via a menu
technique utilizing a screen cursor driven by a 2D joystick.

Method. Fourteen postgraduate students were randomly assigned
to one of the two groups. Neither group knew about the other condition and specifically the pattern group did not realise that there
was a direct analogy between their reasoning task and one involving
activities and resources. The subjects were given six problems to
solve and allowed to spend as much time as they wished on each problem (although this was taken into account by a bonus scheme). They
were asked to rate the quality of each solution (ie the likelihood
of it being an optimum selection). In order to investigate the
memory load associated with state recall the problem was then reset
to its initial position and the subjects required to re-create their

(a)

COST 250 SPACE LOST 26%

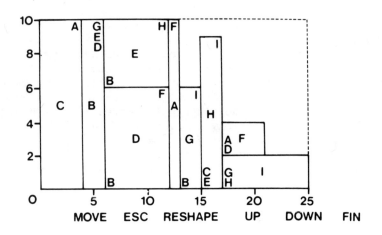

MOVE ESC RESHAPE UP DOWN FIN

(b)

COST 250 SPACE LOST 26%

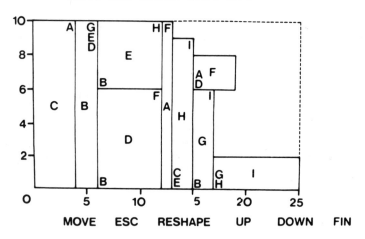

MOVE ESC RESHAPE UP DOWN FIN

Figure 2. The Pattern Representation

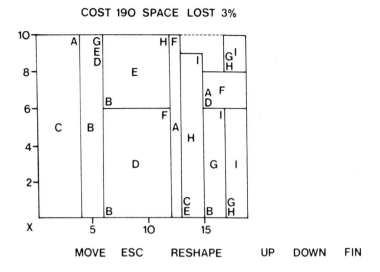

Figure 3. An optimal solution of the problem shown in figure 2

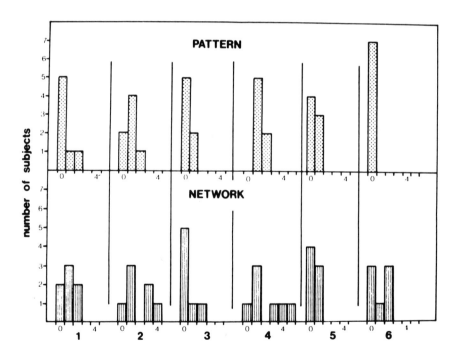

Figure 4. Solution quality for both groups and six problems

solution. Only ten minutes were allowed for the completion of this
recall phase. The subjects took between four to five hours to perform all six problems and this time was split between three sessions.

Results. The solutions that the subjects attained for each
problem were scored in terms of their distance from the optimal
solution. This is not a measure of the number of transformations
that are required to turn a solution into the optimal but simply the
category of solution ie optimal, second best, third best ... and so
on. These scores are plotted in histogram form in figure 4 for the
six problems and two conditions. (0 means optimal, 1 means second
best, 2 is third, etc.) It can be seen that in terms of the number
of subjects in the different solution categories the Pattern condition is clearly superior in four of the six problems. Statistical
analysis (one tailed Mann-Whitney U test) indicated a significant
difference (p $<$.003) between the two groups.

Subjects from both groups found it difficult to recall and
hence re-create their solutions. The analysis of group differences
is complicated by the fact that the number of transformations required to get back to the solution obviously differs for each type
of solution. However is a simple count is made of the number of
successful recreations the Pattern group is slightly better than
the Network group by the ratio of 22:18. Nevertheless this shows
how difficult the re-creation phase was since the total number
possible was 42.

Discussion. The solution category results appear to be
explained by differences in the search strategies adopted by the
two groups. These differences may be characterised as 'wide' versus
'deep' search. The Pattern group for example investigated approximately 50% more actions than the Network group. Whereas the latter
tended to explore changes to action sequences in an incremental
manner (corresponding to the position of branches in the network
graph), the Pattern group concentrated on trying to make fairly
gross alterations to the 'shape' of the total pattern picture. The
re-creation results suggest that the Network group's behaviour was
a function of their relatively difficult memory load associated with
returning to previously visited states. The types of search strategies observed tend to support this hypothesis. However further
experiments are required to establish whether the pattern representation is clearly superior for other problem types.

The problems given to the subjects in this experiment involve
only two dimensions of constraint - sequence and resource usage.
In multi-dimensional problems it will not be possible to use this
form of pattern representation (although pairs of constraints could
be displayed separately). Accordingly some work has recently begun
on the use of computer generated polar plot displays (Wolff 1970)

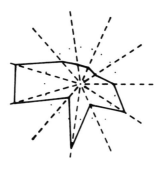

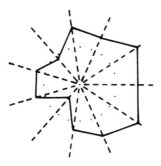

Figure 5. Examples of polar plots for the 11 variable case

in multivariable control systems (figure 5). In order to study the applicability of such displays experiments on operator recall and diagnostic capability are currently being performed. Initial results . promise considerable advantages over more conventional displays.

Acknowledgements

The greater part of the research described in this paper was performed at the MRC Social and Applied Psychology Unit, Sheffield, England.

References

BATTERSBY A and BERNERS-LEE M, 1968, Communication through interactive diagrams. In Computer Graphics in Management (Edited by E Green and R Parslow) (London: Gower Press)

EDWARDS E and LEES F, 1973, Man and Computer in Process Control (London: Instn. Chem. Engrs.)

EDWARDS E and LEES F, 1974, The Human Operator in Process Control (London: Taylor and Francis)

FREEDY J, HULL F, LUCACCINI L and LYMAN J, 1971, A computer based learning system for remote manipulator control. IEEE Trans. on SMC, SMC-1, 356-363

KETTERINGHAM P J and O'BRIEN D D, 1974, A simulation study of computer-aided soaking pit scheduling. In Edwards E and Lees F op cit

KROLAK P and FELTS W, 1971, A man-machine approach toward the travelling salesman problem. Comm. ACM. 15,4, 327-334

McCORMICK E J, 1964, Human Factors Engineering (New York: McGraw-Hill).

RASMUSSEN J and GOODSTEIN L P, 1972, Experiments on data presentation to process operators in diagnostic tasks. Danish Atomic Energy Commission. Riso Report 256

RASMUSSEN J, 1974, The Human Data Processor as a Systems Component. Danish Atomic Energy Commission. Riso Report M-1722

SHERIDAN T B, 1972, Supervisory Control of Teleoperators. In Displays and Controls (Edited by R Bernotat and K Gartner) (Amsterdam: Swets and Zeitlinger).

SIME M, FITTER M and GREEN T, 1975, The Congenial Computer? MRC (Sheffield) Social and Applied Psychology Unit Memo 67

SMITH H T and CRABTREE R, 1975, Interactive Planning. Int. Jnl. Man-Machine Studies, 7, 213-231

WEST B and CLARK J A, 1974, Operator interaction with a computer controlled distillation column. In E Edwards and F Lees op cit

WOLFF H T, 1970, The hospital ward - a technological desert. In Instruments in Working Environments (London: Adam Hilger) p 90.

DISCUSSION

THOMPSON :

 With respect to the polar representation of 11 variables, we have developed at Stanford University an interactive computer graphics display program which permits not only polar plots but also a "stack" of such plots representing several states or points in time. The "stack" can be tilted, if desired, and modified by the user to group the variables differently (by importance, relevance, interrelationships, etc.).

SMITH :

 Please ship directly !

MORAY :

 In the box displays such as fig. 3, what is the significance for action in the real world of a box being split, (such as Box I) ?

SMITH :

 This situation is caused by the identification of each resource element as a unit length on the Y axis of the envelope. No problem is caused by the splitting up of a box into two or more points unless a particular resource is required at a given time.

ELLIS :

 If one of the rules of the pattern representation task is that "if X men can do a job in Y days then Y men can do it in X days", then does it not follow that shapes need not be rectangular and that even more space might be saved.

SMITH :

 It does indeed. In the experiments reported in this paper the subjects were constrained to work with only rectangular shapes. Further work is required to determine the useful limits on pattern partitioning.

PROCESS CONTROL - SIMPLE AND SOPHISTICATED

DISPLAY DEVICES AS DECISION AIDS

B. Shackel

Department of Human Sciences

University of Technology, Loughborough, U.K.

INTRODUCTION

Following the aims of the symposium, this paper will describe
and relate together one type of current practice and one new
research result, and will suggest some areas for research.   The
process control tasks are of the type which involve the human
operator in minute-to-minute control of relatively complex systems.
The decision-making is sequential, ie. requires successive separate,
though often inter-related, decisions.   The systems involve expensive resources, and even the possibility of risk to human life if
an error occurs.   Therefore, improvements in speed and especially
in accuracy and reliability of decision-making are important, as is
improvement in job satisfaction and reduction of strain for the
controllers.

Two display devices which appear to be useful decision aids
for such tasks are described. The first has been in regular and
unchanged use for 7 years;   the second is a new invention with
good laboratory results soon to be tried in the field.   These
contrasting solutions are then discussed and finally some research
needs are suggested.

THE STATEBOARD AS A PLANNING AND MEMORY AID

An ergonomic re-design of the control function and the
control offices in the ESSO Refuelling Control Centre at London
Airport was carried out in 1967-68 (for a full description see
Shackel and Klein, 1976).   From the ESSO control office and truck
depot men and trucks are allocated and sent out to aircraft by a

429

Controller.   After landing, aircraft are parked at one of the 165
stands on the long-haul or short-haul aprons.   In the turn round
time of about 30 to 75 minutes, not only are fuel and passengers
loaded but also cleaners, caterers, maintenance engineers, baggage
handlers, etc., need to park near and work on the plane.   When
speed is essential, refuelling trucks go to the apron before the
plane arrives.

The Tasks of the Controller

For information about aircraft movements the Controller had
the arrival and departure schedules from the airlines each day,
which thus gave the expected load.   Changes and the specific
fuel needs were supplied by telephone or other links from the
various airlines.   Minute-to-minute information about the approach
and arrival of aircraft was received by two ticker-tape machines
from the air traffic control centre.   For information about the
men and trucks he had a list of men from the duty roster, and in
racks at each side of the desk the truck logs of each available
truck.

When the Controller knew the needs of an aircraft he would
check how many vehicles were in the truck depot, which ones were
filled, and which operatives were available.   He assigned men to
a truck and gave them the truck log sheet.   The operatives did the
job, returned to the control centre and completed the log sheet.
This was then returned to the Controller, who checked and passed it
to the plant office and recorded the operatives on his list of men
as available again.   In due course the truck would be re-loaded
under the direction of the Depot Fuelling Chief, who was in the
plant office next to the Controller and had to attempt to meet his
needs for loaded trucks.

On the surface, the Controller's job appeared simple.   However, with only a limited number of men and trucks he had a
managerial problem to match the available resources with the demands
for service.   This problem was increased by the difficulty of
predicting how long before men and trucks would become available
again, because of the variability in aircraft refuelling time.
He also had a supervisory problem in that he had to organise a
shift of men who were doing a job which could at times be fairly
unpleasant.   Other difficulties were the demands made on short
term memory, the relentless flow of complex information, the noise
associated with it, and the constant worry of the ultimate 'crime'
of causing a delay to an aircraft departure.

Fig. 1   The control room and desk before design.

The basic information sources are the four air schedule boards at
the back, the ticker-tape of aircraft movement running across the
desk top, the electrowriter link at the left, and four telephones.
The clutter is obvious.

Fig. 2   The control room and desk after redesign.

The Controller's right hand is near the telephone key unit which
selects up to ten lines; his radio microphone is mounted on the
wall.   The basic information sources are more visible, with the
aircraft schedules and ticker-tape directly facing him.   His left
hand points to the stateboard.   The Shift Supervisor looking over
his shoulder can easily review the current situation.

The Control Room before the redesign (Fig. 1) shows the working conditions for the Controllers and the complexity of their inform- ation sources. It was also difficult to reach the schedules at the back and to read the ticker-tapes, so that the Controllers almost always stood up, especially during peak hours. Several telephones could ring at once, and the Controller could only stop one of them at a time.

The Redesign

The redesign is shown in Fig. 2. The desk is now L shaped, and lowered to a more comfortable height. The separate telephones have been amalgamated into one lamp and key unit which enables the Controller to 'hold' calls. The ticker-tape has been raised to eye level, and the schedules have been placed within easy reach above the ticker-tape. The truck logs are now in a sliding store above the desk top to the Controller's left, which is more readily accessible and also backs directly onto the Depot Fuelling Chief's office. Thus, both Depot Chief and Controller can handle the logs easily, in step with their work, and above all the log of a reloaded truck, when available again, is put in its right place directly by the Depot Chief.

The Stateboard

A magnetic stateboard was designed to give the Controller an exact representation of the state of his resources (see Fig. 3). It has tags representing men, trucks and aircraft, to be placed as appropriate in the various marked columns. The handwritten list of men, in the old system, is replaced by a column space for men tags – a separate tag for each man with his name on it. These men tags are colour coded by the working shifts, and can be written on, which helps the Controller easily to take account of the various end-of-shift and meal-break times (which are of great importance for the job satisfaction of the operatives). The old meal-break board on the wall is replaced by a separate column on the right side of the stateboard. The truck tags are also coloured to show truck type and numbered, while the aircraft tags are larger white ones upon which flight numbers are written; all stick magnetically.

The Controller operates the stateboard by placing men and truck tags onto an aircraft tag which, when the men are actually sent out, is placed in the central part of the board. Thus he has readily visible the current location and duties of all the men and trucks available on that shift, and he is also able to use the tags to plan his decisions step-by-step in advance, by building up modules ready for allocation.

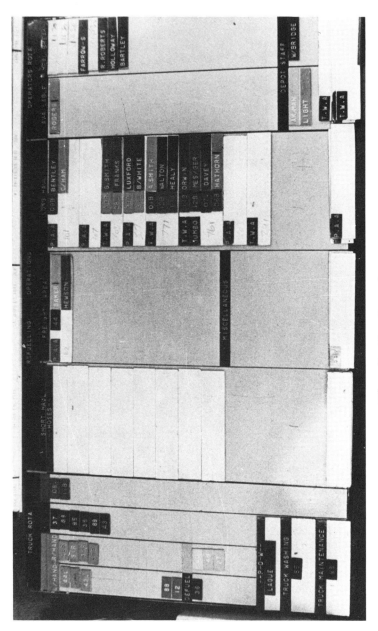

Fig. 3 The Stateboard

The tags representing men and trucks available are on the right and left.
After allocation to refuel an aircraft they are mounted on aircraft tags
and placed in the central part. Thus an overview of the current location
and work of all resources is always available.

A full laboratory simulation experiment in 1968 tested this display system (Hatfield et al. 1969), after which it was installed in 1968, evaluated on site in 1969, and remains unchanged in full use (latest visit September 1975).

Comments

Although the use of such stateboards is still not very common, their design is a simple procedure, requiring only a thorough implementation of ergonomics design principles which start with a full decision analysis of the controller's job (the exact sequence of decisions, all information needs for each decision, etc.). Excerpts from this analysis are shown in Table 1.

The reasons for the success of this type of stateboard solution are considered to be: economy and compatibility of information presentation; gathering all the needed information within a limited area and organised format; enabling the user to record and update relevant information simply and quickly; and relieving the memory load by enabling a record of every decision step towards the full allocation, so that the telephone and other frequent interruptions do not reset the decision series back to the start.

Other aspects of this and related decision aids are discussed more fully by Brigham (1976).

PROBABILISTIC PREDICTIVE COMPUTER DISPLAYS FOR DISCRETE DECISION TASKS

The results and text in this section are principally the work of my colleague Dr. L. Laios.

Many decisions in industrial and other control situations are subject to information uncertainty. In many systems, decisions already made determine the context for subsequent decisions. Often decisions need to be made quickly and on the basis of incomplete or uncertain information. This uncertainty makes predictions and decisions difficult; nevertheless it is imperative to extract as much as possible from the uncertain information. Further, existing computer aids fail to assist the essential part of the control process, which should concentrate on future events.

Table 1: Excerpts from full decision analysis of Controller's job.

Decision	Information Needed	Information Sources	Consequential Action/Record Old Method	New Method
1. Next aircraft to be handled	ETA of the several relevant aircraft	Flight schedules Ticker tape from ATC	Remember; later write on job ticket	Write Flight No. on aircraft tag
3. Which truck(s) to be sent	Which trucks of various types (capacities) are available, loaded and accessible	Truck logs Visual inspection of depot yard	Remember or pull out truck logs and pile on desk	Pick relevant tags (can be presented to show info. needed) and put on A/C tag
4. Which men to be sent	Who is available and has had longest rest pause	Record of men updated as they arrive on shift or back from jobs	Write names onto job ticket and cross off from 'men list'	Pick relevant men tags from top of column and put on A/C tag
10. When should man X go to meal break	Time range relevant Has he had break already	His duty shift Record	Find name on meal break board – ticked with time due back?	Colour of man tag Time written on it?
11. Where is man X	Job he is on, or his work duties for the day, or meal break data	Day's shift rota Meal break record Job allocation record	Look at shift rota, meal break board, men list or past job ticket carbons (in desk drawer)	Find his tag on stateboard
12. Is A/C Y being handled and with what resources	What trucks and men allocated, have they gone and where are they	Job allocation record	Find job ticket carbons (under pile on desk or in desk drawer)	Find A/C tag on stateboard

From research (Laios, 1975) into such decision tasks, Laios and Shackel (1975) have devised various forms of Predictive Computer Display (PCD) to provide a dynamic analogue representation of the situation, allowing the operator to see the changes in the states of the controlled system and to manipulate alternative configurations so that the system objectives are best satisfied.   There is already extensive work going on in the area of predictive control, mostly in the United States (Kelley, 1968; Poulton, 1974).   However, this work is mainly concerned with the control of continuous processes, especially in the field of slow response systems and vehicles (Bernotat, 1972; Crawley, 1974; Edwards and Lees, 1974).

The Problem

The type of Predictive Computer Display (PCD) discussed here has been designed for industrial applications in stochastic discrete control systems.   In contrast to traditional predictive displays it is not necessarily based on a detailed fast time simulation.   It is recognised that a large majority of control situations are ill-defined as far as the operator is concerned, and in such situations complete automation may not be possible, or may be too expensive or undesirable for some other reasons.   At present, unaided operators control these ill-defined problems without very great success.   It is envisaged that the PCD in one or other of its possible forms may improve such control.

Consider the simplified scheduling problem of Fig. 4.   A number of items I_1, I_2, ..., I_n arrive at random times t_1, t_2, ..., t_n and they are allocated to different operation lines L_1, L_2, ..., L_n of varying efficiencies.   The controller has to make allocations according to a number of criteria.   Let us assume that the main criterion is a constant output flow of finished products.   Now there is a wide range of O.R. techniques (eg. linear programming, dynamic programming, queuing theory, etc.) which can be applied to deal with such problems, but they fail when the problem involves many criteria with changing priorities, stochastic elements, etc., in the input arrivals and system operations.   Under these ill-defined conditions it is necessary to use a man with his inherent flexibility and adaptability.

However, the man can be a weak element in the system in other ways.   He is particularly bad in making arithmetic calculations, although he is a good pattern recogniser.   Therefore the first step towards aiding him is to provide the system parameters in an analogue form or in other forms compatible with his abilities. The second step is to introduce the time element onto the display. Since the past is uncontrollable, the present is presented and at

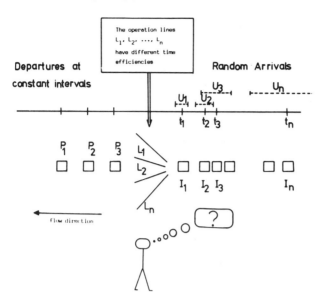

Fig. 4 An example of a discrete stochastic control problem.
The product items I_1 etc. arrive randomly at different times t_1 etc.
with associated uncertainties U_1 etc. The controller should
allocate I's to L's to achieve a constant flow of completed products
P_1 etc.

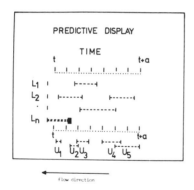

Fig. 5 A predictive display for the problem of Figure 4. U_1, U_2
etc. are predicted intervals within which the items will arrive for
allocation.

$\vdash--\dashv$ are trial allocations set in by the controller which are
implemented automatically when the items arrive. $\models===\blacksquare$ shows
that an item has arrived, been allocated to this line, and is being
processed with end time at $\blacksquare$.

All these blocks $\vdash--\dashv$ step one unit space to the left after each
time unit.

each time unit the future is moved toward the present on the
display.   The prediction span should be adequate to allow for
long-term satisfaction of objectives.   The third step is to
introduce an interactive mode.   The controller should be able to
manipulate system configurations and find out which is the best.
The fourth step is to introduce information about uncertainty.
Clearly the controller will work better when he knows that
arrivals will occur each within a given time range, instead of
having only estimates of arrival times and their uncertainties.

The Display

     The result of all these considerations is a probabilistic
predictive display which may typically be like the one in Fig. 5.
This display has most of the facilities needed by the controller.
One of the many advantages is that it is very simple to generate.
In essence it is a type of computerised dynamic planning board
particularly suited for on-line minute-to-minute control, because
it represents the fluid aspects of the situation and enables an
adequate number of different trial allocations to be explored.
A similar display has already been tested in the laboratory and
has achieved considerable success in improving control performance,
reducing errors by an average of 77%.

     The complexity of the computer model needed to generate this
display depends mainly on the system requirements.   It is,
however, the authors' opinion that predictive aids of this type
should be simple to operate and easy to interpret.   This will
also make them cheap and easy to generate in small portable
computer equipment.   In theory a computer is not essential for
the PCD but in practice it is likely to be for the most useful
versions.

     Additional facilities may be added to make the controllers'
task easier.   For example, under certain conditions it may be
possible to incorporate automated Bayesian processing to cut down
the uncertainty size.   A second possible facility is to use some
algorithmic rules or heuristics to cut down the number of
alternatives which the controller has to consider.   In each case
the potential advantages should be examined before making the
predictive facility more complex.

     It is clear that there are basic differences between the
traditional fast-time simulation predictive displays, which have
been described in a variety of texts and scientific reports, and
this PCD facility.   Some of the differences are summarised in
Table 2.

Table 2:   Main differences between the present Predictive
            Computer Display facility and the traditional
            predictive displays.

Traditional fast-time predictive displays	PCD
Control of continuous slow response systems	Control of discrete on-line multi-stage decision systems
Based on an accurate fast-time simulation model of the system	Based on a computer model of varying complexity according to system requirements and operator considerations
Research made mostly on military and space applications	Research made with industrial applications in mind
No provision for input uncertainties. Deterministic Predictions	Designed particularly for systems with uncertainties in the input or within the system
Inflexible on internal variations of the controlled elements. Wrong predictions may occur.	Flexible on internal variations. Possible to include variations due to failures of human or mechanical elements.

DISCUSSION

These two different decision situations have led to solutions which contrast in several ways; but they also suggest several similar conclusions about the characteristics needed for a useful decision aid for these types of process control task. Both solutions provide for considerable pre-processing of information but are essentially displays (rather than eg. decision units); both provide economical and compatible displays which match the tasks and the human user's needs; both display all the needed information in a closely integrated group; both display the results of past decisions for as long as they are relevant; both are interactive and flexible (but the PCD much more so); and both especially reduce the memory load.

The contrasts are equally obvious. The stateboard provides for integrating the relevant information from a large assemblage by a simple and ordered presentation of all the wanted information; although time is an element in the task, spatial organisation of resources is the main feature. Because there is no inherent limit on physical size, the stateboard can show at a glance the status of the whole system, thus allowing the controller to adjust his schedule and develop heuristic strategies otherwise difficult to envisage. However, it is essentially a static decision aid, and cannot enable the exploration of many alternative courses of action.

The PCD, on the other hand, computes the time domain consequences of possible solution patterns and displays them in the form of an analogue spatial pattern. At the same time, the display is dynamic in real time and thus particularly solves a difficult combinatorial problem for the human with his limited calculating capacity. Moreover, the PCD presents both current status and future input information on the same display, with uncertainty data added, all in a compatible form. The research results (Laios, 1975) show significant increases in exploration of alternatives with the PCD. Thus, as has already been emphasized (eg. Edwards and Lees, 1972), the valuable skills of the human operator are complemented with the advantages offered by the computer.

However, comparison between these two solutions may also remind us that computers should never be used for their own sake, but only because there is no cheaper way that is equally efficient. Applying the stateboard manipulation concept to the PCD decision task, one could envisage some form of mechanically driven belt moving at the appropriate speed, with the user manipulating different, colour coded, lengths of plastic block at appropriate places on the belt to explore different patterns. We are in fact applying this type of simplistic approach to several similar but simpler process control situations, with some success.

RESEARCH NEEDS

From the above studies and related work on process control,
I would propose five subjects for discussion as potential research
needs.

1. The essence of process control, as with vehicle control, is
    prediction from past and present to future states of the system.
    More research is needed into methods and displays (of which the
    PCD is but one small example) to aid this basic part of the
    controller's decision task.

2. However, even more important perhaps, we need more experience
    of the implementation and working life of ergonomics designs.
    We need to develop a 'case-law', such as engineers have, of
    process control ergonomics.

3. The compatibility between the computer interface and man is
    still minimal. Imagine a computer-supported display and
    control system for the ESSO stateboard situation; at present,
    ignoring the cost difference, it could not possibly be
    accepted because the controllers would be seriously impeded
    by the limitations of the hardware. Major research and
    development is needed to realise compatible computer equipment
    for process control tasks.

4. Equally, on the human side of the question (of how far computers
    can aid the controller), much basic research is needed to
    clarify and define the characteristics of those decision tasks
    which could be aided by computers and those which could not,
    say for the next 10 years, given the amount and expected growth
    in computer compatibility with man.

5. Perhaps the most interesting subject will be a specific aspect
    of man-computer allocation of function. These two display
    devices offer information, in an ordered or pre-processed
    form, but do not offer decision patterns for acceptance or
    rejection. However, given appropriate algorithms the computer
    could do so. The question is when precisely is this useful
    and when is it counter-productive?

REFERENCES

Bernotat, R.K.   1972   Prediction display based on extra-
                              polation method.   In 'Displays and
                              Controls' edit. Bernotat, R.K. and
                              Gartner, K.P. Amsterdam, Swets and
                              Zeitlinger.

Brigham, F.R.   1976   Decision-making problems in industrial
                              control tasks.   Applied Ergonomics,
                              7.1, in press.

Crawley, J.E.   1974   The present and future contribution of
                              the human operator to the control of LD
                              Steel-making.   In Edwards and Lees, 1974,
                              pp. 249-259.

Edwards, E. and   1972   Man and Computer in Process Control.
Lees, F.P.   London, Institution of Chemical Engineers.

Edwards, E. and   1974   The Human Operator in Process Control.
Lees, F.P.   London, Taylor and Francis.

Hatfield, M.,   1969   Some control room methods evaluated by
Harrison, R.G. &   simulation.
Pritchard, Wendy   Ergonomics, 12, 768.

Kelley, C.R.   1968   Manual and Automatic Control.
                              New York, Wiley.

Laios, L.   1975   Decision-Making and Predictive Aids in
                              Discrete Multi-Stage Decision Tasks.
                              Unpublished Ph.D. thesis, Loughborough
                              University of Technology.

Laios, L. and   1975   Improvements in or relating to Predictive
Shackel, B.   Display Apparatus.
                              British Patent Application 37904/75.

Poulton, E.C.   1974   Tracking Skill and Manual Control.
                              New York, Academic Press.

Shackel, B. and   1976   ESSO London Airport Refuelling Control
Klein, L.K.   Centre Redesign - an ergonomics case
                              study.
                              Applied Ergonomics, 7.1, in press.

DISCUSSION

SOEDE :

Can you tell something about the attitude of the operators during the transition from the old system to the new one ?

SHACKEL :

Because many of the ESSO operators had been involved with the laboratory simulation, most were already in favour of the new design. This was installed in May 1968, but the stateboard system was not implemented then because the summer heavy load started one month earlier that year. We planned the final implementation in October 1968 ; however, before the date planned the Supervisors and Controllers themselves implemented the stateboard entirely on their own. The evaluation study in 1969 revealed very favourable attitudes to the new system (see Shackel and Klein, 1975, for further details and some direct quotations).

AUTONOMOUS I/O-COLOUR-SCREEN-SYSTEM FOR PROCESS CONTROL WITH VIRTUAL

KEYBOARDS ADAPTED TO THE ACTUAL TASK

R.Grimm

Fraunhofer-Gesellschaft, Institut für Informations-

verarbeitung in Technik und Biologie,

Karlsruhe, F.R. of Germany

SUMMARY

An autonomous input-output-system for process-control with virtual keyboards adapted to the actual task is obtained by combining a
colour television monitor with a highly integrated microcomputer and
working memory, a floppy disk memory and a light pen. The system
allows an optimal man machine communication with regards to human engineering as well as an economical design and manufacture of control
rooms.

INTRODUCTION

Control rooms for automated technical processes set high physiological and psychological demands to the operators since these demands mainly spring up unexpectedly during complex start-up and breakdown situations. These problems become more difficult with the increasing size of plants and the growing of economical as well as environmental problems.

In 1950 the number of displays and controls in typical control
rooms of power stations for example, with a controllable generator or
network power of some 100 MW, was about 400. By 1970 the power had been
increased to 1000 MW with about 1300 displays and controls in the
control rooms (Fig. 1). Considering power stations with nuclear fuel
the number of displays and controls is now about 3000 (Fig.2)/1,2/.

Fig. 1: Control room of a power station in 1970

PROBLEMS OF MAN MACHINE COMMUNICATION

        The increasing size of plants makes it necessary to display
the state of the process in a way best suited to man and task. The
flow of information at the man machine interface must be in accordance with man's capacity for processing information during the operation of technical processes. Low error rates of recognition as
well as of operation must be the aim. Within the near future it
will not be possible to develop a true mathematical model of the
complex and highly adaptive way of acting of the operator. This is
even true for the simplified example of human optical information
perception shown in Fig. 3. But some rules of thumb can be given /3/:

(1) Account for parameters of human sensory organs (e.g. range of
    vision, angular decomposition of the eye).
(2) Select the design of instruments according to the task (e.g.
    the importance of reliability, accuracy or speed when reading
    the instruments).

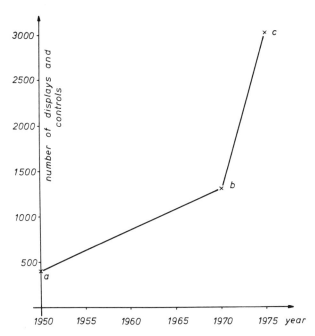

Fig. 2: Number of displays and controls in typical control rooms of
power stations
a) power station with fossil fuel and controllable power of
some 100 MW
b) power station with fossil fuel and controllable power of
1000 MW
c) power station with nuclear fuel

(3) Select a solution directly matching with the task (e.g. high accuracy can be given better by digits than by a scale).
(4) Avoid the display of information irrelevant to the task (e.g. automatic change of displays depending on the actual situation).
(5) Respect the habitual codings (e.g. potentiometer turned right
gives a higher value).
(6) Use a homogenous design of a display element and the corresponding control element (e.g. red needle, red control knob).
(7) Instruments belonging to the same process units should have
common characteristics (e.g. special colour, nearby arrangement).
Because of the increasing number of displays and controls (Fig. 2)
it becomes more and more difficult to take these rules into account
in conventional control rooms. Also, the costs for control panels increase. On the other hand the prices decrease for computer components
allowing a larger information processing power. Prices in 1980 may
be as low as

        1/8 for central processing units (CPU)
        1/10 for mass storages
        1/2 for electromechanical devices

based on the price of 1973 /4/.

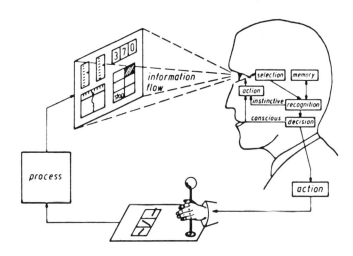

Fig. 3: Problem solving with human factors partial models /3/.

A SOLUTION

New control panels have to be developed which allow optimal man machine communication as well as economical design and manufacture of control rooms: Instead of specially manufactured equipments and arrangements for each individual process standardized devices should be installed in the control rooms. These devices must then be composed for the individual process in an efficient way.

One solution is the input-output-colour-screen-system (shortly named: IOC-system) described in this paper. (Fig. 4 shows its operating console) This device combines a colour display screen device with a highly integrated microcomputer and working memory, a small disk memory and a light pen. The display screen device is a colour television monitor because in the present state of the art an economical multi-colour display cannot be otherwise obtained. The construction of an IOC-system for an individual process is performed by composing standardized hardware devices and software packages, described later, and by 'interactive programming' on the screen via light pen whereby no special knowledge of the software of the system is necessary.

Two requirements have to be met for establishing such a system:

(1) The disadvantage of the small screen size has to be compensated. To achieve this the screen refreshing memory has been integrated into the working memory. Now the process charts can have the size of up to nine times the size of the screen, and in conjunction with a joy stick these process charts can be 'rolled' over the screen. Thus the instinctive movement of the head is replaced by an instinctive movement of the hand.

(2) The keyboards have to be adapted. Real keyboards are expensive and different keys have to be manufactured for different processes and control panels. By using virtual keyboards - i.e. keys are symbols on the screen - all necessary keys can be generated and their functions easily adapted to the individual process. Furthermore the keyboards can be adapted to the actual task (e.g. keys not used for the actual task are not displayed on the screen).

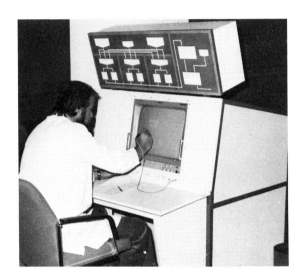

Fig. 4: Operating console of the IOC-system

THE HARDWARE OF THE SYSTEM

The IOC-system (Fig. 5 shows its block diagram) is realized by integration of a colour TV monitor with a low cost microcomputer. The working memory of the computer is simultaneously used as a screen refreshing memory and enlarged by a floppy disk memory where momentarily unused process charts and process data are stored and documentation is performed.

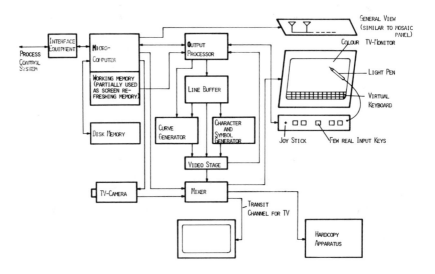

Fig. 5: Block diagram of the IOC-system

An interface equipment connects the IOC-system to the bus of the
process control system whose process computer is now completely re-
lieved of the process display and documentation functions. The data
flow thus merely contains comprised data, reports and instructions
(including reference values and thresholds).

An output processor controls the cyclic line-by-line transfer
of the displays from the screen refreshing memory to a line buffer,
initiates the necessary recomputation of addresses (particularly for
rolling), and determines the screen coordinates from the light pen
signal. The displays are prepared for colour reproduction by a character and symbol generator, a curve generator and by a video stage.
Process states that are difficult to codify can be superimposed on
the graphic process display in the form of real scenes obtained by a
TV-camera and a computer-controlled image mixer. Instrument recorders are the most expensive display elements in conventional control
rooms and have to be maintained very often which makes them responsible for high costs during process control. To avoid these high
costs the IOC-system allows curve representation to be inserted into
the process charts. Without any extra devices outside the IOC-system
up to seven curves can be displayed at the same time, each having a
resolution of 126 points in the y-direction and 126 or 252 points in
the x-direction depending on the selected time scale /5/. In the IOC-
system virtual keyboards with keys selectable by a light pen are used.
These keys can be automatically adapted, with respect to size, number of keys, image, place and shape, to the momentary state of the
process. Thus the operator's eyes remain accomodated to the display
screen.

The use of standard instrumentation and standard programs is accomplished for the IOC-system by the autonomous writing of lists during the generation of process charts with the aid of the light pen, whereby a symbol, relative place of the symbol, its name and data array is coordinated to each process element, and by the simultaneous use of the name as a telegram address via the bus. Further descriptions of the characteristics of the IOC-system are given in /6,7/.

THE SOFTWARE OF THE SYSTEM

The IOC-system is programmed for three different running modes which communicate via common datas in a list structure and basic programs (Fig. 6). The data lists are subdivided into symbol and keyboard lists, one configuration list, linkage lists and lists for the measured values. The common basic programs are the executive system of the microcomputer, start and restart, screen refreshing and rolling, light pen acknowledgement, selection of process charts, and system messages.

The chart generation is done in five steps:

.Defining symbols and keyboards
.Drawing of process charts
.Drawing of curve fields
.General labeling and colour coding of process charts
.Defining linkage lists and process elements

All these steps are done on the screen with the aid of a light pen and allow the operator- and process-oriented 'programming'; that means the adaptation of the standardized IOC-system to the individual process. Different keyboards exist for chart generation:
. keyboards containing the symbols for process graphic, a few digits and instruction keys.
. keyboards with alphanumerical symbols, keys for colour coding and instruction keys.
An example with one symbol and two alphanumerical keyboards is given in Fig. 7.

If the IOC-system is installed in a process control system, the process control computer provides the IOC-system with telegrams which transmit analogue and digital values together with the name of the signals. The values are in a redundancy reduced form /8/. In a stand-alone implementation the programs for data transmission control as well as for data processing are installed in the IOC-system depending on the demands of the implemented process. Other programs dealing with process control update the process charts as well as curve fields, transfer the process data to the documentation disk, allow the modification of reference values and thresholds, the input of binary commands (such for switches) as well as the input of continuous

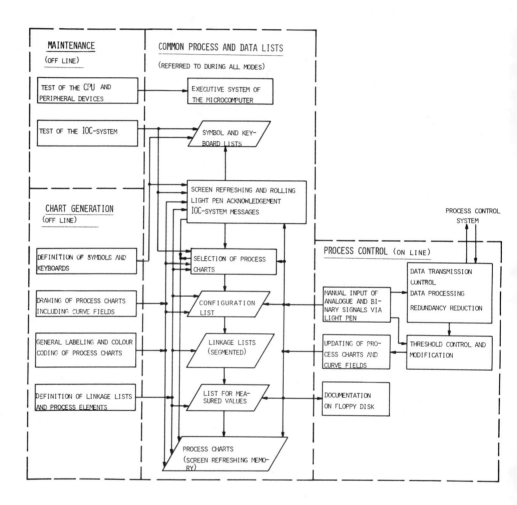

Fig. 6: Program and data structure

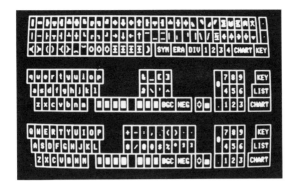

Fig. 7: Keyboards for chart generation

control signals. The latter is done with the aid of a joy stick and with parallel integrated displaying of some process signals codified as vectors under different angles and with serial control of these signals /9, 1o/.
Programs for system maintenance include tests for the CPU of the microcomputer, its peripheral device, a test for the whole IOC-system including its software.

AN EXAMPLE

Fig. 8 shows a process chart of a chemical reactor and its corresponding curve field with a resolution of 126 x 126 points. The actual time (hours and minutes) is written below the origin, the numbers at the time axis give the hours back from the actual time. Different time scales and resolutions are possible. In this example the labeling field contains values for six measuring points.

The lower part of the graphic contains an example of a virtual keyboard with instruction keys for the process on the left side (underneath the process chart). The selection of an instruction key can be plausibility-controlled by the system: a valve can be opened or closed, an engine or an electric break can be switched on or off. Reference values or thresholds can be modified by selecting 'COR' and then the desired digits. A new process chart can be selected either by rolling or by selecting 'CHART' and then the corresponding number.

SUGGESTIONS FOR INCREASING THE RELIABILITY OF THE SYSTEM

The operating reliability of the system can be increased in the following way:

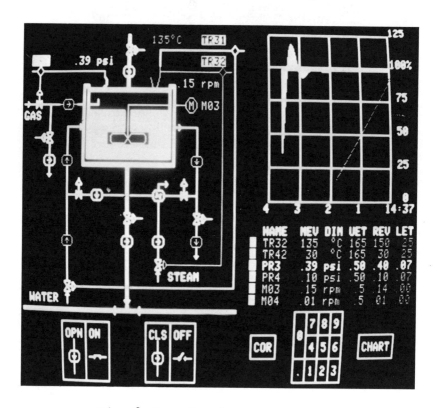

Fig. 8: Example of a process chart

(1) IOC-systems oriented: Two floppy disk drives are provided thus
    allowing one to fail. The increase of reliability can then be
    reached by other redundant equipment like a second light pen, a
    second light pen control, a second monitor attached in parallel.
    This goes as far as to duplicate the IOC-system where the two
    systems normally perform two different operational tasks but in
    case of failure the undisturbed system performs all operational
    tasks.
(2) Process control system oriented: In the IOC-system an emergency-
    break-switch is provided for the process; the transition to decen-
    tralized manual control is possible. Besides these, equipment
    for the parallel central manual control of a few important con-
    trol elements (binary and analogue) may be installed.

CONCLUSION

The described autonomous input-output-system for process control
with virtual keyboards adapted to the actual task is obtained by combining a colour television monitor with a highly integrated microcomputer and working memory, a floppy disk memory, and a light pen.
The system allows
- an economical design and manufacture of control rooms:
  . The construction of the system is done for an individual process
    by composing standardized hardware devices and software packages
    and by 'interactive programming' on the screen via light pen.
  . Substantially all functions of process control panels including
    recording and documentation are performed completely and auto-
    nomously by the system.
- a better man machine communication:
  . Various forms of information coding are possible, e.g. colour,
    time, blinking, size of symbols.
  . The same display screen is used for monitoring and intervening,
    the instruction and command keys are on the same screen as the
    process charts, thus guaranteeing the same accomodation of the
    operator's eyes.
  . The disadvantage of the small screen is highly compensated by
    the roll-function.
  . The system can be adapted to an actual task especially during
    process disturbances; for example by displaying automatically
    the process chart with the disturbed process element and/or by
    displaying automatically the necessary virtual keys for this ac-
    tual task.
A pilot implementation of the described system will be tested in a
chemical process.

REFERENCES

/1/ Syrbe, M., Bacher, F.: The Role of the Human Operator in System
    Control. Real-time Control of Electric Power Systems, Elsevier
    Publishing Company, Amsterdam/New York, 1972, page 279-291.
/2/ Geiser, G., Syrbe, M.: Problems and Prospects in Large Control
    Rooms. Proceedings of the 13th International Automation and In-
    strumentation Conference 'Human Engineering', Nov. 1974,
    Milano, page b1-b19.
/3/ Syrbe, M.: Anthropotechnik, eine Disziplin der Anlagenplanung.
    ETZ-A, 91 (1970) Heft 12, S. 692-697.
/4/ Paul, M., Schuler, H.: Marktübersicht: Prozeßrechner 1975. Re-
    gelungstechnische Praxis rtp, 1975, Heft 10, S. 297-305.
/5/ Heger, D., Trück, H., Rauth, A.: Verfahren und Anordnung zur
    Darstellung mehrerer Kurven auf einem Farbsichtgerät. Patent-
    anmeldung P 25 44 489.7 vom 4. Okt. 1975.

/6/ Grimm, R., Syrbe, M., Trück, H.: Ein-/Ausgabe-Farbbildschirm-
    system. Patentanmeldung P 25 10 632.5 vom 11. März 1975.
/7/ Grimm, R., Syrbe, M., Trück, H.: Input-/Output-Colour-Screen-
    System. Application for Patent in the USA on Oct.10, 1975.
/8/ Steusloff, H., Grimm, R.: Verfahren zur Nachrichtenreduktion
    bei der Systemsicherung mit Prozessrechnern. Lecture Notes in
    Computer Science. 3. Jahrestagung der Ges.für Informatik. Springer
    Verlag, 1973, S. 394-404.
/9/ Geiser, G., Schumacher, W.: Verfahren zur parallelen integrier-
    ten Darstellung der Regelabweichungen und zur seriellen, kompa-
    tiblen Stellimpulseingabe bei der Regelung mehrerer Regelstrecken
    durch den Menschen. Patentanmeldung P 24 60 605.1 vom 2o. Dez.
    1974.
/10/Geiser, G., Schumacher, W.: Parallel vs Serial Instrumentation
    for Multivariable Manual Control in Control Rooms. Proceedings
    of the NATO Symposium on Monitoring Behavior and Supervisory
    Control, March 1976, Berchtesgaden.

ACKNOWLEDGEMENT

    This research was supported by the project 'Prozesslenkung mit
DV-Anlagen (PDV)' granted by the Ministry of Research and Technology
of the F.R. of Germany.

DISCUSSION

MORAY :

    What safeguards are used with the virtual keyboard to make sure
the light pen accesses the correct key ? How long does it take to point
to a virtual key compared with hitting a real electromechanical keyboard ?

GRIMM :

    To make sure the light pen accesses the correct key the following
aids are given :

- the light pen emits a light circle onto the screen surrounding the
  area which the photodiode can detect,

- during process control the selected key is blinking until the
  instruction is executed,

- instruction keys are plausibility-controlled.

To point to a virtual key, it takes about the same or less time compared with hitting a real electromechanical key. The system recognition time is 20 ms at the most.

HAMMOND :

What type of microprocessor is used ? What is the capacity of ROM and RAM storage used ?

GRIMM :

A mini process control computer (Siemens 310 S) is used at present with 32 k words (16 bits) RAM storage and 256 words (16 bits) ROM storage.

SOEDE :

I read in the list of references that you applied for a patent. What are the specific elements of your system that you mentioned in your request for the patent ?

GRIMM :

Some of the specific elements of the system are :

- input of commands without real keyboards,

- adaptation of the virtual keyboards to the actual task and situation,

- hierarchical information structure,

- pointwise curve generation on the same screen (superimposition of process graphics and curves),

- two-dimensional rolling of the image by means of a joy-stick with selectable speeds,

- computer-controlled image mixer for real scenes of process information that would be difficult to code.

GRAPHIC VIDEO DISPLAYS FOR PROCESS AND MAN-VEHICLE

CONTROL

Dr.-Ing. Rolf Zimmermann

DORNIER SYSTEM GmbH

799 Friedrichshafen, F.R. Germany

1.   INTRODUCTION

Over the last few years great progress has been
made in the field of visual displays. Today such displays are not only passive devices like typewriters or
plotters but more active devices for an interactive
dialogue between men and computers. With the cathode
ray tube (CRT) as the most common output device for
todays visual displays we can generally find two kinds
of displays. There are the so called vector-displays
(or X-Y-displays) with a mostly analogue random deflection of the electron beam and with stroke writing
generators; there are the so called raster-scan-displays
with a deflection usually in a standard television
raster, with point raster generators and using normal
television monitors for the image output.

The progress made with devices of the first kind
has culminated in displays with very high resolution and
special multiphosphor penetration tubes which are able
to show pictures in e.g. four colours. Such systems are
excellent for line drawings like in computer aided
design and construction.

The refresh rate of about 50 Hz wich is necessary
for a flicker-free picture, as well as the bandwidth
of deflection devices and thereby the writing time for
a line, nevertheless limit the number of lines which can
be shown. Normal maximum-quantities are generally
sufficient for line drawings, but they are not however

for extensive bar graphs and other kinds of shaded areas.

By far the most commonly found, are the other type of
device, the raster scan displays or so-called television
displays. These devices are predominately employed for
the representation of texts, tables and other alphanumeric
information. Complex systems are moreover able to repro-
duce block diagrams and similar simple graphic displays
as well. When these devices produce standardized video
signals, then they can be used for the reproduction of
pictures of commercial size television monitors. In this
way the costs are low, maintenance is easy, and almost
limitless screens of any size, as well as projection systems can be connected directly or at a removed distance.
The display potential includes almost any colours, brightness and blinker frequencies. The mixing with television
pictures of other sources (e.g. from cameras) is also
possible, and shaded areas can also be produced.

A disadvantage with the television raster scan displays is the relatively small resolution of pictures, the
visible dot structure especially with sloping lines, and
the very high cost of hard- and software for the production of graphic displays.

2.   DEMANDS FOR DISPLAY SYSTEMS FOR PROCESS AND MAN-
      VEHICLE CONTROL

Contrary to the tasks of computer aided design, the
high resolution is not necessary for numerous applications
in control and monitoring systems. Especially in those
cases where the digitally produced picture is to be mixed
with the picture from a TV camera, it would be hardly
logical to display the digitally produced picture with
better resolution than the camera picture.

Such applications are e.g.:
-    Control monitors for remote piloted vehicles (RPV's),
     with which e.g. in the camera picture transmitted
     from the aeroplane, piloting symbols of all sorts
     (Horizon flight height, route angle, speed etc.)
     should be superimposed.
-    On board systems with similar characteristics to the
     afore mentioned RPV systems.
-    Military situation displays with tactical symbols
     over a map in which the symbols show by their posi-
     tion, movement, form, blinker situation etc., the
     position, movement, status and operation of the
     military systems with which they are associated.

Traffic control and vehicle dispatching systems, in which buses, taxis, police cars and fire-engines as symbols   are shown on a faded-in city map.
- Large area observation systems e.g. for air-pollution monitoring, with graphic displays of test data on a faded-in map of the area being observed.
- Dispatching systems for trains and underground, in which the present location of trains, the position of signals and points, and the security of block sections are graphically shown.
- Special systems for controlling experiments and simulations, which due to increasing complexity, require new-style forms of data test representations.

The list of examples goes on and on. The displays which are used, must however posess the following characteristics:
- Representation of texts, individual signs and additional symbols at any place in the picture.
- Representation of simple block pictures, diagrams and tables.
- Representation of shaded bar and column diagrams.
- Representation of curves.
- Representation of simple line drawings.
- Rapid assembly of whole pictures.
- Rapid change of any single parts of the picture (transferring, erasing, shifting, colour changes).
- Sufficient resolution of the picture.
- Fading-in of already existing pictures of other forms (Photos, radar pictures, TV cameras).
- Representation in different colours, brightness, blinker frequencies.
- Adaption of the brightness and contrast of the picture to the brightness of the room.
- Use of screens of appropriate sizes.
- Connection of parallel screens, eventual possibility of projection.
- Connection of devices for picture recording, transfer and copying.

3. PROBLEMS OF MIXING TV PICTURES AND DIGITALLY PRODUCED SYMBOLS

With most of the examples of application mentioned in the previous passage the mixing of digitally produced symbols with normal TV pictures is necessary. For this various solutions are possible, with different advantages and disadvantages.

The most simple solution is to show the required
symbols on a display device of any sort (e.g. a vector
display), to scan this picture with a TV camera and to
mix the video signal thus poduced with the video signal
which is to be faded-in. As both the video signals which
are to be mixed are simultaneously present, the TV picture can simply be suppressed at the points where the
symbols are to be faded-in. However a very large amount
is spent on devices, since an additional monitor and a
camera are needed for the mixing. Further disadvantages
are the loss of sharpness in the camera picture, eventual
problems with synchronisation and with "running" black
bars which that causes, and an especially important disadvantage, being the fact that symbol representations
in several colours are practically impossible.

Roughly the same disadvantages as described above
are also found in a more sophisticated technique in which
the symbols are written in a scan convertor. In synchro-
nism with the television signal the content of the scan
converter is read and the signals can be mixed.

The fading-in of symbols into TV pictures can occur
not only by mixing 2 simultaneously present video signals
but also by the consecutive reproduction of the TV picture
and symbols. For this the TV picture can normally be re-
played on the CRT and the symbols are written during the
image fly-back period (about 2ms). Due to the brief
amount of time available for this, the electron beam must
be deflected in a random scan.

For the deflection two different control methods
are therefore required and the number and the distribution of symbols which can be displayed, is very limited,
being dependent on the deflection speed of the electron
beam; shaded symbols are almost impossible to achieve.
Due to the various methods of deflection no mormal TV
monitors can be used for replays. Only penetration displays are perhaps suitable for colour replays.

As the symbols and the TV picture are independently
produced it is not possible to supress the TV picture at
the points held by the symbols. In this way the colour
and the brightness of symbols is greatly distorted. E.g.
according to the brightness of a green background picture
a red symbol appears in colours varying between yellowish
green, yellow orange and red.

All the disadvantages mentioned in the process, which

have so far been described can be avoided if the symbols
which are faded-in are directly produced in the TV raster
and mixed synchronously with the other TV picture. In
this way the legibility and correct colouring of symbols
is guaranteed, owing to the fact that the TV picture is
suppressed everywhere,where symbol points are faded-in.
If the suppressed part is slightly enlarged, then the
symbols become even clearer with thin black borders at
the sides.

This last solution however, permits the fading-in of
digitally produced coloured symbols and graphics in TV
pictures which is required for many applications. The
problem with this technique is however, that until now
there were almost no TV raster displays with low hardware and software costs permitting the production of
coloured graphic representations which can be finely
placed in position and rapidly changed.

4.   NORMAL TV RASTER SCAN DISPLAYS

Normal TV raster scan displays employ the usual European TV norm with 625 lines. In order to achieve a flicker-
free picture, the inter-lace process is however abandoned
and 2 identical frames of 312 lines are produced.

The total number of lines and line time are however
not available for a rectangular bordered field on the
screen. Because of the electron beam fly-back times and
the border areas which cannot be used, only about 270
lines and about 45 µs per line are available. A flicker-
free, digital image for representation on TVs of normal
band width and number of lines, therefore usually has a
raster of e.g. 256 lines each with 384 raster points.

Signs, vectors and other picture elements are constructed from dots of this raster. Alphanumerical signs
usually fill up a field of 5 x 7 points, vectors consist
of a lining-up of raster points and therefore, according
to banking, have a more or less graduated effect. 32 text
lines, each with 64 character places, that is up to 2048
characters can be displayed with a raster of 256 x 384
points, a character size of 5 x 7 points and each with
one point space between.

4.1   Alphanumeric and Semi-Graphic Displays

Normal TV raster displays are used for storing and
displaying of alphanumerics. The principle construction
of such a device is shown in Fig. 1. Fig. 2 again gives
an example for the display potential. Characteristic for
devices of this sort is the fixed correlation between
character place and the address in the picture refresh
memory. At each character place exactly one symbol can be
displayed, its code being recorded under the corresponding
address of the picture refresh memory. If only the 64 characters of the SCII codes are used, 6 bits are sufficient
for the code. If additional lower case letters circuit
symbols, parts of bars etc. are used and besides, several
colours and blinker states, then correspondingly more bits
are needed e.g. 12.

Devices of this type are well suited for block diagrams, tables, bar graphs and other simple graphics. Random curves and drawings are however not possible by this
process; especially not when lines intersect. But even
slight changes of position of individual characters (e.g.
for high numbers and indices) are just as impossible to
produce as slight dynamic shifts, lengthening or turnings
of lines and characters.

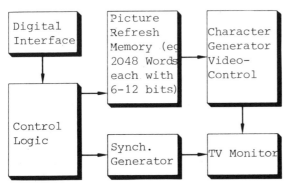

Fig. 1

Block diagram of a
TV raster display
with fixed correla-
tion between charac-
ter place and memory
address

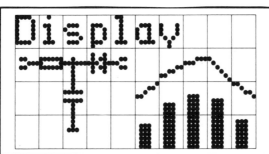

Fig. 2

Semi-graphic repre-
sentations on a
character orientated
display

4.2 Point Raster Video-Graphic Displays

With these devices the picture refresh memory contains the information already separated for each point of the picture raster. In the case of a raster of e.g. 256 lines and 384 columns, it consists of almost a hundred thousand words. With one bit per word, monochromatic displays are possible, with 3 bits per word e.g. 7 colours or 7 shades of grey. Additional bits are necessary for information about blinker frequencies.

The construction of a picture occurs point-wise as in a storage-tube display; on the other hand however, a point-wise clearing is possible. With many devices the displayed picture must be calculated point for point and transmitted by the computer. Most devices do however have their own character and vector generators, so that the data transfer is limited to initial addresses and character codes or terminal addresses. Due to the large number of words to be stored, digital discs are also frequently used as well as shifting registers for picture refresh memories.

Devices of this sort permit the displaying of line drawings and shaded pictures with the given point raster. Due to the usual cyclic memory (shifting register or disc)a cycle of the whole memory is needed with most devices for writing all points of a vector. The writing rate is then with 50 vectors or 50 characters per second, so low that dynamic representations are hardly, or not at all possible. A further disadvantage of this device is that e.g. in clearing a line which cuts another line or symbol, all the intersecting points are also erased, Fig.3 right above, right below.

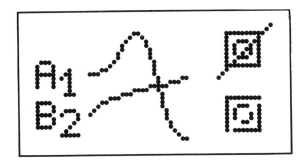

Fig. 3

Graphics on a point orientated display. Difficulty right hand side, when one of two intersecting symbols is erased.

A point raster video-graphic display is therefore
suitable for any graphics which are only limited to TV
rasters. A very high storage cost is however required
especially for coloured displays and this kind of device
normally does not permit any very dynamic representations
as the writing and clearing times are relatively long.
Also, due to the above-mentioned clearing of intersection
points, a lot of software-management is necessary.

5.   A NEW VIDEO-GRAPHIC DISPLAY WITH POSITION-INDEPEN-
DENT CODED STORING

With the video displays which have so far been described, it is common for the structure of the picture
refresh memory to be screen-orientated. Each place in the
picture refresh memory corresponds to a character place
or a raster point on the screen. In the case of the
applications of displays only a part of the character
places or only a very small fraction of the controllable
raster points are necessary for the representation. Therefore it would be more favorable to store in a coded form
only the relevant information for the picture which is to
be displayed, and in such a way that the size of the picture refresh memory corresponds to the number of picture
elements actually to be displayed. When for all that,
the degree of freedom of a video-graphic display (passage
4.2) is achieved and its disadvantages are to be avoided,
then each picture element (character, symbol, complete
bars, vectors, vector segments etc.) independent of its
position on the screen, must be stored in one word. This
word, besides the character code, the bar length etc.
also contains the exact initial coordinates and further
details about the colour and manner of display of the
picture element and is hence relatively long.

This optimal manner of coding and position-independent storing is normal with X-Y displays and causes no
difficulties there, as the individual picture elements
can also be written in any order, due to the random controlled deflection of the electron beam. With TV displays
the electron beam movement is however given. If temporary
storage was abandoned, then during the display time of a
picture point (about 100ns) the whole picture refresh memory would have to be read to see whether and how (e.g.
in which colour) these picture point can be displayed.
Such a solution cannot be realized at the present moment.
A TV raster display with position-independent storing of
picture information therefore needs a sufficiently large

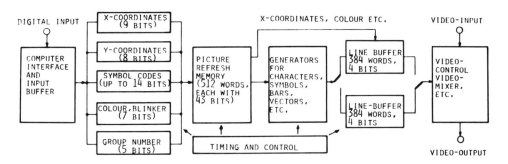

Fig. 4: Block diagram of the new video-graphic-display

temporary memory. In this temporary memory the relevant information for a certain part of the screen (e.g. a line) is written while the picture refresh memory is being run through and the relevant information is being calculated.

In the system which has been realized (Fig. 4) the picture refresh memory has a size of 512 words and can therefore store up to 512 picture elements. The contents of this memory is completely processed during a TV line (64μs) and the picture point information which is thus gained about the next TV line, is at the same time temporarily stored. The temporary storage consists, with 384 picture points per line, of 384 words, with every 4 bits being able to display up to 15 colours. Of these memories two are necessary to act as change buffers, which are alternately filled and read out.

For the processing of each word of the picture refresh memory, there are with 512 words and 64 μs total time, only 100 ns available. The processing can however also be done in several time steps lasting roughly 100 ns. At a low cost, only simple operations are possible in such a short time, like for example:
- Testing to see whether parts of the picture elements came in the next line.
- Addressing of temporary storage on the basis of stored x-coordinates.
- Line - addressing of character generators on the basis of stored Y-coordinates and the Y-coordinates of the lines to be temporarily stored.
- Reading the character generators and picture point transfer in the temporary storage.
These operations can be carried out in the given time.

Therefore long lines are put together from short
segments, whose form is derived from a special symbol
generator from a field of 8 x 8 points. Such a line segment consists of up to 8 points and is described by its
initial and relative terminal point (-7 to +7 points in
the X-Y direction).

The horizontal and vertical lines or bars can on the
other hand have any length, their production follows
according to another principle.

A data display device with this technique requires
very high internal data processing speeds. On the other
hand however, it does permit any coloured graphics at a
low amount.

The block diagram (Fig. 4) shows the computer
connection (16 bits parallel with FIFO Buffer), the input register, in which the words to be stored are put
together from various information, and the picture refresh
memory.

In the various symbol generators the points for the
next TV line to be displayed are determined and these are
deposited in temporary line storage.

Before the input into the picture refresh memory, the
picture elements can be provided with some coefficients
(group number, 5 bits). It is then possible to change
simultaneously all picture elements in the same group with
a single order e.g. to change their colours, to shift
these elements, to completely erase or temporarily not to
display.

For the repetition on colour monitors, the signals
R, G + B (red, green and blue) and the synchronizing
signal S are separately given out. In this way it is also
possible, e.g. to provide 3 monochromatic screens with
different pictures from the same display controller or
to connect another source (e.g. with S remote-synchronized
TV camera) instead of one colour out-put of the display-
controller and in so doing, achieve a simple type of
picture mixing.

An additional circuit permits the real mixing of a
digitally produced picture of any colour, with an equally
random picture from another source. The legibility of
characters, symbols and lines is guaranteed by displaying
them independently from the background in the right colour
and optionally with thin black side borders.

The realized device thus fulfills all requirements for displays for monitoring and control. Its special characteristics are:

- Colour graphic representations at low storage cost with absolutely free positioning of all picture elements within the screen raster.

- Expansion in as many colours and gradations of grey as are needed, with at the same time only a small amount of storage expansion.

- Easy picture manipulations (e.g. erasing, shifting, colour change) by means of only one instruction for all picture elements of one "group number" (fig. 4).

- Rapid data transfer, a free place in the picture refresh memory is available in 0.1 to 64 µs.

- Programmable shades of colour with 15 bits for each colour code.

- Colour correct mixing with camera pictures, symbols optionally with black side borders.

- Expansion to shaded areas similar to cartoon film representations. Shaded areas are defined by their left and right-hand edges.

The limits of the display unit are given by the limited resolution of the picture and by the maximum number of 512 picture elements, which suffice for almost all the applications which have so far been planned.

6. REFERENCES

Kreitzer, N.H. and Fitzgerald, W.H.: A video display for image processing by computer. IEEE Transact. on Comp. C-22 (1973), 128-134.

Sherr, S.: Technology and equipment. SID-Symposium New York 1973, Symp. Digest, 172-173

Thornhill, D.E. and Cheek, T.B.: Raster scan tube adds to flexibility and lower cost of graphic terminal. Electronics (Feb. 7, 1974) 95-101

Zimmermann, R.: Grafische Darstellungen bei Datensichtgeräten mit Anzeige nach dem Fernsehprinzip. Regelungstechnische Praxis 17 (1975) 167-176.

DISCUSSION

RIJNSDORP :

In your video-graphic-display, a long vector has to be built up from short segments. Did you also consider the possibility of coding vectors by initial and final coordinates ?

ZIMMERMANN :

The command structure of the display controller already includes a write instruction for long vectors. In this command the final point of a vector can be given by absolute co-ordinates or relative distance to the initial point.

At the present moment, the conversion of this command into the codes of start segments occurs not by the display controller but by a computer software routine ; a conversion by a microprocessor is planned.

It will be possible with another planned extension of the display controller to store also the codes of long vectors in the picture refresh memory. Owing to the longer processing time these codes cannot be stored consecutively and therefore the number of long vectors which can be stored will be limited, e.g., to 32 or 64.

Workshop Reports

INTRODUCTION AND SUMMARY

T.B. Sheridan[*] and G. Johannsen[**]

* MIT (Mechanical Engineering)
  Cambridge, Mass.

**Forschungsinstitut für Anthropotechnik (FAT)
  5309 Meckenheim, F.R. Germany

1. ORGANIZATIONAL BACKGROUND

Four parallel workshops were held in conjunction with the Symposium on the second and fourth days, two hours each afternoon. The purpose of these four workshops was to provide opportunity for all participants to talk informally in small groups and to answer the same general questions : Computers and new display technology are changing the human operator's role toward that of a monitor or supervisor. What is, or what should be, the nature of this new role ? In view of this new role, what should be the priorities for research ? What implementation problems are foreseen ? What new institutional or interdisciplinary arrangements are advisable ? On the fifth and final afternoon the chairmen of the four workshop groups gave reports of their groups' deliberations and recommendations, and a plenary discussion was held.

The four workshop reports follow this introduction and summary. They show consensus in technical and scientific respects, but reveal differing viewpoints on the value of various problem approaches and the social relevance of applications of this technology. The main ideas are paraphrased in the following summary.

2. NEW ROLE OF HUMAN OPERATOR

Computers and new display technology are changing the human operator's role in man-vehicle and process control systems from that of a controller toward that of a monitor or supervisor. It is felt that the human operator should remain in future systems in order to cope with unpredictable events, and also for predictable tasks when economic considerations preclude complete automation. Of course there are also compelling psychological and social reasons for retaining the human operator.

However, the human operator usually lacks operational experience for very low probability events, and human reliability may therefore be low. These factors affect training and selection, as well as the development and evaluation of skill. Therefore, the use of simulators is highly recommended for training and evaluating, since by this means low probability events can be experienced.

A proper and well-defined function allocation between computer and human operator is required. Various criteria must be considered. Not only system effectiveness and reliability, but also workload and job satisfaction are of great importance for systems design and operation. Opportunity and challenge exist for generating more coherence and meaningfulness in human jobs.

3. RESEARCH PRIORITIES

In view of the new roles of the human operator, the corresponding human capabilities and limitations in performing these new tasks should be determined. Modeling is generally considered to be a useful tool. Models of human monitoring and supervisory control behavior, human information processing and decision-making exist, but are often primitive or not well matched to applications. A demand for normative models as performance base-lines has been expressed.

It is felt that the internal model concept is very useful. However, more information is needed on what features of the world are internally represented in the human and what utility functions he internalizes in various real tasks.

For the near future, it may well be that more results can be expected from models pertaining to specific tasks. The interaction between general and application-oriented models has to be clarified. Modeling of complex tasks and tasks under stress is a continuing need. Finally, the ever-present problem of validating models needs attention.

The man-computer interaction in automated systems is a focal point. The allocation of functions between human and computer has to be clarified. Better design rules are needed, and the appropriate hierarchical level at which the human operator should interact should be easier to determine in a given application. Allocation conflicts may exist between system performance and job satisfaction. It is therefore necessary to find the correct degree of responsibility for the human operator in view of all of the criteria cited above. The methods found for allocation of functions should be extended to allocation of duties in multi-man groups working with complex automated systems. On the other hand, micro-miniaturization, especially of electronics, may allow individualized design of processing and control equipment for operators and supervisory.

The interaction between human and computer may be improved if the computer has as a reference its own internal model of how the human operator normally behaves. On the other hand, the actions of the computer must be transparent to the human. Displays should be designed to monitor the performance of the increasingly complex "slaves". In short, the computer should assist man by active monitoring of his performance, and the computer functions should be adapted to monitoring by man. Thus, computer and man may check each other, thereby improving overall system reliability and performance.

Techniques for measuring (and thereby operationally defining) work-load, job satisfaction, human reliability, and design criteria are needed. Workload measures should be relatable to task meaningfulness. Integration of data concerning human performance degradation under combinations of stressors is recommended. Physiological criteria, in addition to system performance, should be used more. It is desirable to work toward a theory which interrelates performance, reliability, workload, measurement techniques, and design criteria (e.g., goals, utilities, job satisfaction). Since many human problems of judgment exist in ill-defined situations, some means are needed to provide a more measurable set of goals or utilities in real decision-making tasks.

4. IMPLEMENTATION PROBLEMS

Existing human factors methodology is not as widely applied as we would like. Not enough professionals are trained in human factors, especially managers. Better links between industry and universities are needed for this purpose. However, more and more educational institutions are now engaged in training competent human factors experts ; when these people go into industry, implementation of human factors may become more commonplace. While human factors experts should continue to try to influence modes of thinking in industry, there is no guarantee of immediate implementation, and patience is called for.

Experimental results should be put into a form usable by persons of other disciplines, e.g., design engineers. However, the designer must decide whether to try to apply published human factors information directly, or to call in a human factors expert. Small companies may be better off to seek advice from an external human factors institution. Thus, profit-motivated human factors consulting firms should remain viable in addition to publication-motivated human factors research teams.

Implementation could be facilitated by human factors and safety standards. However, these standards should not be couched in terms of physical configuration but rather in terms of system performance. Job satisfaction should also be considered in standards for systems design.

Models must be applicable to industry, not only to laboratory situations. As computers are becoming more used for data collection and reduction, there is the danger of overloading of displays and providing incomplete information. Experimental work should be done at various points on the continuum between abstract laboratory situations and field applications. The use of simulators is recommended all across this con-tinuum for the education and training of human operators, for the study and test of alternative designs, and for basic research.

5. INTERDISCIPLINARY AND INSTITUTIONAL ARRANGEMENTS

The interaction between disciplines should be encouraged (an example is the interaction between human factors and neurophysiology in workload research). While basic scientific research is more mono-disciplinary, application oriented research is multi-disciplinary. Both should occur, be parallel, and they should interact with each other. Cooperation be-tween the disciplines is necessary in order to solve practical problems. A common language for all disciplines may be found in system theory.

Governments should actively stimulate interdisciplinary research. Human factors experts should recommend institutional means, including legislation, etc. to improve links between industry and human factors groups. That may be part of the increasing government effort of humaniz-ing industry. A directory of people from different human factors subdis-ciplines could be organized to help them share their knowledge with each other and with the wider community.

The organization of short courses in human factors for engineers, designers, etc. is regarded as an important activity to continue. These courses should now focus on the new roles of the human monitor and supervisor.

WORKSHOP DISCUSSION REPORT

GROUP I

Chairman : Dr. A. Rault

Secretary : Prof. J.E. Rijnsdorp

Participants : Verhaegen – Rasmussen – Bauer – Burdorf – Dilling – Hansen – Lemke – Liebl – Pitrella – Peroyannakis – Kalsbeek – Hammond – Moray – Bauerschmidt – Curry – Malecki – Baatvik – van Lunteren – Moraal – Schmidt – Parks – Willumeit

Workshop theme : Computers and new display technology are changing the human operator's role toward that of a monitor or supervisor. What is, or what should be, the nature of this new role ?

From the various discussions the following points emerged :

- The definitions of supervision and monitoring were considered and formulated as follows : Monitoring is essentially the answer to the three following questions : What is the present state of the system ? What will it be in the near future according to the internal model I have of the system ? Are there any hardware failures ? Supervision encompasses monitoring, action and/or control and includes the capability of dealing with new situations.

- In allocating functions between man and machine the job satisfaction of the human operator should be considered. Further, it is difficult to apply existing lists of recommended function allocations between man and machine especially when the specific problem is not clearly specified.

479

- It was agreed that the notion of the internal model refers to an internal representation the human operator has of selected aspects of the external world, and is, as such, a set of hypotheses operating under certain conditions.

Research priorities are :

- Research should be done towards answering the question : How should we resolve man-machine allocation conflicts which sometimes occur between job satisfaction and system performance or productivity goals ?

- There are a variety of performance measurements and design criteria which may be applied to man-machine systems. A comprehensive theory which interrelates human performance, workload, measurement techniques and various design criteria (e.g. goals, utilities, job satisfaction, etc.) is highly desired.

- Model making is well acknowleged by everyone and even though the control engineer has some tools in his bag, still a strong effort should be made to improve them. The representation of the human operator's internal model is one of the most important problems of man-machine systems and the goal pursued should be to understand what features of the world are embodied in such representations within human beings.

- In the comprehension of human behaviour one of the most critical steps is information processing. There is a need for a comprehensive model of information processing useful for various kinds of complex tasks. Present classical information theory tools are insufficient.

With regard to implementing knowledge of man-machine systems a certain number of recommendations can be given :

- Actions of the computer should be "transparent" to man in a way that permits him to coordinate his actions with those of the computer.

- Computers can assist man in many ways, thereby permitting him to handle higher level tasks. More sophisticated man/computer interactions can be expected in the future (e.g., man instructing the robot's computer for various situations as described in Thompson's paper).

- Computers perform very well in data collection and reduction tasks and can therefore replace or unburden man. This may be true for other tasks as well. It is astonishing that computer-driven devices such as predictive and integrated displays are rarely implemented. However, improper function allocations or use of computers can lead to overloading of displays or the presentation of incomplete information and must be avoided.

- In as much as it is possible, computer functions should be adapted to man's abilities. The computer should be used to check the operator and vice versa.

Analysis and design of man-machine systems requires the application of knowledge and expertise from several disciplines. Interactions between these disciplines should be strongly encouraged. An attractive idea is to set up a directory organized according to problem area interests of people prepared to share their knowledge with colleagues of other disciplines (psychologists, control engineers, physiologists etc.). Interdisciplinary interests should also be encouraged at the university level. Some research grants and special training sessions should be organized to help solve interdisciplinary problems.

WORKSHOP DISCUSSION REPORT

GROUP II

Chairman : Prof. H.G. Stassen

Secretaries : R.W. Allen ; J.J. Kok

Participants : Merhav – Pfendler – Stein – Strasser – Kvålseth – Hosman – Chenchanna – Lemaire – Kaiser – Geiser – Ellis – Bossi – Stockbridge – Kirchhoff – Ahlin

A breakdown of the background and/or interests of the audience was :

- Control- and system engineering, modelling and simulation	11
- Workload measurement and secondary tasks	3
- Performance criteria and tests	2
- Education and psycho-social problems	2
Total	18

MANDATE

The general mandate was : What do we want to tell our governments and colleagues about :

- Research project priorities

- Implementation problems

- Integration of disciplines

- Institutional arrangements.

SESSION 1

From the suggested topics to be discussed the audience felt that the priorities of research projects and the integration of the different disciplines were the most important items. Due to the fact that the majority of people had a background in modelling, identification and system theory, the discussion centered around the theme "Modelling the human operator". From the discussion the following questions or comments were derived :

1. Should we start with conceptual (verbal) models, or can we learn enough from models based on quantitative analytical techniques ?

2. Models should be developed in relation to the application, or to real world problems.

3. What do we need in addition to models ?

4. Is there a need for general models or for specific application-oriented models ; what is the relation between these to modelling philosophies and how do they interact with each other ?

5. What is the relationship between system complexity and model complexity ? Do we need hierarchical models ?

6. There is a need for a better understanding of human capabilities and limitations.

7. What is the significance of internal models ; what are the human's capabilities for developing internal models ?

8. Are we using and/or can we use the available knowledge of human behavior and models ?

9. How do we keep operators attentive and involved in tasks ?

10. What is the optimal level of automation for individuals and for the society ?

11. What about the psychosocial implications ?

From these questions we felt that 5 additional important main questions could be derived. Therefore, the secretaries and the chairman formulated these main questions so that they could be discussed in more detail during the second session. The questions were :

1. What is the utility of modelling, and how can models be applied ?

2. Given any complex system, what considerations or factors dictate the degree of automation ?

3. What is the definition of an internal model, and what is the utility of the internal model concept ?

4. Relevant scientific research is mostly a mono-disciplinary activity; relevant problems of interest to society are multi-disciplinary in nature and thus their solution requires a multi-disciplinary approach. How can we encourage this view; what does it mean for education, team effort, and so on ?

5. How should workload be conceptualized ? What is the relationship between workload and performance ? How should we include workload in modelling ?

SESSION 2

With reference to those five questions the following comments and questions were made during the second session.

Modelling utility

The goal of modelling activities is to obtain basic laws such as in physics. Here it should be noted that the more general models become, the simpler they probably become (e.g., cross-over model). There is a strong need for basic laws rather than detailed models; i.e., after long research we can then accumulate more basic laws. It was felt that some framework is necessary; therefore conceptional models are very important. Models like the Bolt, Beranek, and Newman-optimal control model probably can lead to such a general concept; also the internal model concept promises a better understanding. Furthermore, it was mentioned that one should derive a general theory of models to compliment practical research just to make both theoretical and practical work easier in the future. Finally it was mentioned again how important it is to know human capabilities and limitations.

Factors dictating the degree of automation

Presently the "second generation" of man-machine problems can be recognized. The first generation was more or less involved with problems in adapting the physical environment to human beings and pure data processing capabilities. Nowadays we are able to automate processes to such an extent that factors like job satisfaction and the nature of human tasks and functioning are becoming important. Problems such as determining the appropriate hierarchical level at which the human supervisor should interact with the machine, are extremely important. Perhaps, automation should be set to a level that leaves some degree of meaningful responsibility to the human operator. The question is, can this statement provide the basis for optimal automation in the future ? Some consideration should be given to inter-human relations.

Scientific versus application-oriented problems

It was felt that only if cooperation between the different disciplines becomes more and more common, can sufficient scientific knowledge be built up in order to solve certain practical problems. The various disciplines may specialize, but an integrated presentation should be made at an early stage in the educational process. If required system theory will probably provide a language common to the various disciplines. Governments should stimulate interdisciplinary research. This should be a matter of national policy.

Workload

The problem is that we cannot define workload and/or mental load strictly. We have only indirect measurements of workload. We felt the best definition of workload for certain conscious tasks could be based on rate of conscious "moments of decision". It may be that an integration of human engineering with neurophysiology may lead to a better understanding of the concept of mental load.

RECOMMENDATIONS

1. More research is needed on the utility of human operator models, with a strong demand for conceptual models ; the main question is to find out human capabilities and limitations.

2. Scientific and application-oriented research should be parallel and interact.

3. To solve the second generation of man-machine problems one may start with the definition : An optimal degree of automation must lead to a correct degree of meaningful responsibility of the human supervisor.

4. Multi-disciplinary activities should be stimulated by governments.

5. Workload and performance problems and criteria would be an excellent topic for the next NATO-conference.

SUMMARY

Main questions

- Utility of models

- Internal model concept

- Optimal degree of automation

- Scientific versus application research

- Concept of workload

Utility of human models

- Demand for general models (laws)

- Interaction between general models and application oriented models

- Human capabilities and limitations

Degree of automation

- Second generation of man-machine problems

- "Correct" degree of meaningful responsibility

- Human relations

Scientific vs. application-oriented problems

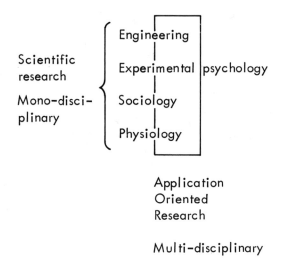

Scientific
research

Mono-disci-
plinary

{ Engineering

Experimental psychology

Sociology

Physiology

Application
Oriented
Research

Multi-disciplinary

⟶ Need for integration of disciplines

Workload ; Performance

- Need for applicable definitions

- Measurement

- Integration of disciplines

- Next NATO-conference

WORKSHOP DISCUSSION REPORT

GROUP III (first session)

<u>Chairman</u> : Prof. B. Shackel

<u>Secretary</u> : Dr. L. Laios

<u>Participants</u> : Wahlström – Brémond – Aschenbrenner – Bernotat – Ficht-
bauer – Henning – Kokoschka – Meyer-Delius – Schumacher –
van Heusden – Mulder – Wewerinke – Singleton – Drury –
Hebenstreit – Pack – Roscoe – Weltman – Smith – Richter –
Schubert

On the first afternoon it was decided to discuss the general issues
proposed, namely research priorities, implementation, communication among
disciplines and institutional arrangements. On the second afternoon topics
such as monitoring of low probability events, methodology in process
control etc. were examined in more depth.

The questions dealt in the first session were :

<u>Q1.</u>   Why do we fail to implement human factors knowledge ?

<u>A.</u>   Human factors methodology is not made to be widely applicable.
It can be expensive and often there is not time to carry out designs
according to human factors criteria. The design objectives are often
irrelevant to human factors objectives. Also, human factors training
does not necessarily produce people confident to use their own data.
It may be that many people cannot use the textbooks etc. Another
factor may be that managers come mainly from a non human factors
background and thus do not appreciate the contribution of human
factors specialists. It appears nevertheless that the situation is slowly
changing.

Q2.   We speak a lot about control or system performance ; why are physiological criteria not used more extensively ?

A.   It appears that in most work situations physiological measures are considered to be within normal limits. Consequently, these measures tend to be used more in extreme environmental conditions. However it has been found that in some cases minor changes in environmental conditions have detrimental effects on decision performance, but these phenomena have not received adequate attention by physiologists.

Q3.   How do we get more implementation of human factors findings ?

A.   It may be that human factors experts need to know more engineering in order to become good system designers. However care should be taken so that human factors people are not converted to be engineers. It is true however that in the U.S. some of the best human factors experts have engineering background. Nowadays a lot of institutions train competent human factors experts. When these people come to industry, implementation of human factors findings may become easier. In industry it is also essential to promote those human factors facets which are most likely to produce economical benefits. If a company is small it may be better to get human factors advice from an external human factors institution than to employ fulltime human factors staff.

Q4.   How can we get more implementation of human factors research findings, particularly in process control, monitoring, etc. ?

A.(1) Attempts should be made to publicize this symposium to other professional institutions, stressing the relevance to their own field of work (i.e. process control etc.).

  (2) Models from the laboratory may not be applicable in industry. Therefore more general models applicable to both industry and laboratory may be needed before implementation can be successful. Care, however, should be taken not to create a total climate of applications research as it would then be difficult to get money for basic research.

(3) Implementation could also be promoted by setting up human factors companies with profit motivated human factors staff. The objectives of these staffs would be different from those human factors experts who carry out research for publications, etc.

(4) There is a need for better links between industry and universities. One method to help this is for postgraduate students to carry out part of their research in industry, which could lead to better appreciation of human factors research.

(5) There are today increasing government efforts to humanise industry. As part of this process, human factors experts should recommend institutional ways, legislation etc. to improve links between industry and human factors groups.

(6) Organisation of short courses for engineers, designers etc. should also be promoted. There is a need to gather teaching materials for some of these courses (e.g. in quality control, process control, etc.).

(7) There is no guarantee of immediate implementation of human factors knowledge. There may be some influence but its effect may not be felt for some time to come (e.g. only now there is clear evidence of the influence of ergonomics in the design of motor cars). But the human factors people should always try to change the ways of thinking in industry.

(8) Finally, implementation could be facilitated by convincing governments to introduce human factors and safety standards. However, some problems may arise. Human factors standards may not be standards for dangerous conditions and therefore implementation may be difficult. Also, premature application of human factors may produce suboptimal standards. To prevent this the aim must be to go away from the usual dimensional basis for standards and instead to develop performance standards ; in these the requirement is for the equipment not to be of a particular size but to reach a required performance, within certain accuracies and within certain time limits, in a controlled test experiment with defined samples of human subjects.

WORKSHOP DISCUSSION REPORT

GROUP III (second session)

Chairman : Prof. C. Drury

    The main direction of the discussion was on research needs. It was not felt appropriate to prioritize needs as this should be a responsibility of individuals and separate governments.

    Our main question was whether we are behind application needs with respect to computer control. While realizing that many "mopping-up" jobs exist in industry which only require existing expertise, it is felt that the next generation of problems still requires modelling.

    For example we can now model well (but never as well as we would like) simple situations, such as monitoring of multiple discrete channels (Senders) or simple sequential tasks (HOS, Siegel & Wolf) or reliability of simple system events (SHERB, etc.) or continuous tracking tasks (Baron ; McRuer + Jex, etc.). But we cannot model these same tasks well under stress nor can we model the complex tasks best suited to the human operator's complexity.

    To take the first problem a literature search and (quantitative) data integration (c.f. Teichner) needs to be done on human performance degradation under combinations of stressors.

    For the second problem we must realize that computer enhancement of input information has taken us away from the "threshold" situation. Instead we are into the uniquely human problems of judgement in ill defined situations. We may not have an easily-measurable set of goals or utilities in these decision-making tasks.

Three particular research questions were asked :

1) How far can normative models take us in such tasks ?

2) Can we formulate better rules for function allocation (and even function expansion) in such tasks ?

3) How can displays be designed to monitor the performance of increasingly complex "slaves", with respect to what they are doing, why they are doing it and what will they do next ? Do we need an active monitor who interrogates the "slave" via Wiener wiggles ?

WORKSHOP DISCUSSION REPORT

GROUP IV

Chairman : Dr. J. Miller

Secretary : Prof. J. Senders

Participants : Pasmooij – Soede – Kimmel – Witt – Dey – Ninz – Trück – Grimm – McLeod – Smit – Linn – Skans – Rouse – Andow – Edwards – Niemann – Thompson – Bargl – Chatelier

The following points, listed in the order of their importance, are those on which there is substantial agreement within the working group :

1. The role of the human being appears to be shifting from a predominantly controlling to a predominantly monitoring function. Is this appropriate ?

   What are the effects on training, the generation of skill ?
   on the selection for talent ?
   on the maintenance of skill ?
   on the evaluation of skill ?

   These latter questions arise particularly because of the fact that many of the tasks of the human operator are concerned with low probability events for which no operational experience can exist. These then generate questions about human reliability.

2. A major problem is that of defining work content as well as optimum workload such that system effectiveness, reliability, and job satisfaction are properly considered. Proper workload estimation a priori has effects on design, on manning requirements, on training system specification and on reliability of systems.

3. Micro-miniaturization of processing and control equipment could completely change the concept of human engineering by allowing for

individualized design for operators and supervisors. The question is :
how do we begin to explore this possibility ?

4. There are serious problems which arise from the allocation of duties.
   Should each man in a multi-man group have a specific task component,
   should all men participate in all task components, or should there be
   some optimum mix of the two concepts ?

5. How does one measure (and achieve) validity ?

6. Is human reliability meaningfully looked at in the same way as the
   reliability of physical system components ? How can it be measured
   and estimated ?

7. Job satisfaction must be considered as an element in system design.

8. There are serious questions which arose and were not completely
   resolved relating to the problem of putting experimental results into a
   form such that they can be used by persons in other disciplines, such
   as design engineers. One approach appears to be that of tabulating
   prescriptions, proscriptions, and exhortations. There appear to be some
   vague boundary conditions which the user of human factors information
   should use to decide whether to apply information or to call in an
   expert in human factors.

9. Are there possibilities for tutorial interaction between automatic
   computer-based system controllers and the human monitors ?

10. The human being apparently should remain in future systems to cope
    with specific predictable or with unpredictable events. There are also
    social, psychological, economic, and technological reasons which
    apply here.

Additional comments by Prof. W.B. Rouse

I don't think we should ask whether or not automation should occur – it is inevitable. Instead, we should be concerned with how humans should interact with automated systems. This should include consideration of overall human-computer system performance <u>and</u> the human's role in such systems in terms of the coherency and meaningfulness of the human's role.

Currently, there are many non-automated jobs where humans act in rather incoherent and meaningless roles (e.g., automobile assembly lines). Automation offers the opportunity to change this <u>if</u> we can determine what roles are appropriate and meaningful for the <u>human</u>. I think this should be the first research priority. Further, I do not think that current workload measures relate at all to task meaningfulness. A new approach is needed.

With increasing efforts in automation, computers will at least appear to be more and more intelligent (especially to the non-sophisticated user). If such intelligent systems are to react appropriately with humans, we must give the computer models of how humans behave. If the computer can only react to the human's current state, interaction between human and computer may be poor in much the same way that a human is a poor controller when he has an inadequate model of his environment. Thus, I think the second research priority should be development of models that can be used by the computer to understand the human.

Appendices

Appendix A

GLOSSARY OF SPECIAL TERMS

allocation of functions

Assigned division of required functions to one or more human, machine, and/or computer elements. Also that part of the design process for accomplishing such assignments. Allocation of functions affects, e.g., the attention and effort required of the human operator.

control theory

Mathematical theory dealing with the means by which some variables in a system are forced to remain constant or are driven to match changing input or reference variables in spite of disturbances.

crossover model

A mathematical differential equation describing the open-loop behavior of the human operator and the controlled process in series, and accurate near the frequency of crossover (at which loop gain is unity). The model implies that the human operator adjusts his response so that the open-loop response of man-plus-machine equals that of an integrator plus a time delay.

descriptive model

A model based on what actually does happen.

display

Format or mechanism for presentation of information. Examples of visual displays are: cathode-ray tube vector and TV displays; dials; arrays of lights; signs; photographs; windows through which to see actual events. There are also: auditory displays of voice segments or sound patterns; tactile displays such as knob shapes; tactile maps for the blind; olfactory displays of leaking gas, etc.

expected utility (EU)

Linear sum of utilities of all possible mutually exclusive outcomes weighted by their true probabilities.

expected value (EV)

Linear sum of objective values of all possible mutually exclusive outcomes weighted by their true probabilities.

subjectively expected utility (SEU)

Linear sum of utilities of all possible mutually exclusive outcomes weighted by their subjective probabilities.

subjectively expected value (SEV)

Linear sum of objective values of all possible mutually exclusive outcomes weighted by their subjective probabilities.

false alarm

Decision that a given event occurred when in truth it did not.

hierarchical control

Where the highest level control loop determines the goals or parameters of a lower level control loop (and, if there are more than two levels, the latter in turn determines parameters of a still lower level control loop, and so on).

ideal observer

     One who operates as signal detection theory says he should (maximizes expected value).

information theory (or communication theory)

     Mathematical theory dealing with the contingent probabilities of alternative events at either terminal of a communication channel, and yielding ensemble measures of "input information", "output information", "noise", "equivocation", and "transinformation".

integrated display

     Many signals presented in pictorial or interrelated fashion in a small area (usually one CRT).

internal model

     A representation (usually internal to a person) of his comprehension of the external (real world) system or environment. If the internal model is valid, test signals which characterize the input to the external system can be input to the internal model and it should yield output signals which approximate the output variables of the external system.

Kalman filter

     A recursive optimal estimator of system state variables (least squares estimation) for dynamic systems.

man-machine system

     A functionally interrelated set of elements arranged so that the interaction of one or more persons with one or more devices can occur with the intent of accomplishing a definite objective. Examples are : car and driver ; many cars and drivers and pedestrians and traffic police-men ; pilot and aircraft ; many pilots and aircraft and ground controllers and ground-based instruments ; nuclear reactor and operators ; secretary and typewriter.

missed signal

Decision that a given event did not occur when in truth it did.

monitoring

Observing displays or an information field in a purposive fashion to insure that system operation is normal or as desired. If available information suggests abnormality, additional information is sought and a diagnosis of the difficulty is attempted.

noise

(first meaning) Signal energy which is unwanted, spurious or unaccounted for.

(second meaning) Signal energy which is (or appears) random and has a broad range of frequency components.

normative model

A model based on some theory about what should happen.

objective function

A scalar function of all relevant variables which defines the worth of system performance. It is usually defined in such a way that best performance is achieved by minimizing the objective function.

optimal control model

The prediction and characterization of human dynamic performance as optimizing an objective functional within certain psychophysiological constraints such as time delay and perceptual noise.

predictor display

An instrument which calculates an estimate (most probable) of the future states of a usually slowly-varying process or vehicle shown to the human controller to aid in control.

process control

Control of large scale complex processes where men or machines continuously process some commodity. Examples are : chemical plants ; discrete parts production ; mail sorting (as contrasted, for example, with control of vehicles).

queueing theory

Probabilistic theory dealing with the formation and reduction of queues (waiting lines) of objects or events to be serviced, e.g. aircraft waiting to land or information waiting to be processed.

remnant

Measured signal remaining after a certain fraction has been accounted for by a deterministic (usually linear) model.

sampling strategy

Procedure by which to select what information to observe and with what frequency or under what contingency.

secondary task

A task which the operator is asked to do in addition to his primary task. Two types are : "non-loading" (the operator attends to the secondary task when he has time) to measure "spare capacity" ; and "loading" (the operator must always attend to the secondary task) so as to cause performance degradation on the primary task.

shadow controller

Human operator which observes the same display and activates the same type of hand control as the active (real) controller, but the shadow controller's hand control is not connected to the controlled element.

signal detection theory

A theory of detection performance based on both the detectability of the signal (which includes the sensitivity of the observer) and the observer's tendency to favor reporting one signal over another. Symbols d' and β are used for detectability and tendency to favor one signal over another.

supervisory control

Controlling a semi-autonomous system through the intermediary of a computer. The computer receives information from sensing devices, makes decisions according to its stored programs, and issues commands to effector mechanisms. The human supervisor performs upper level goal-oriented functions such as planning system activity, programming the computer, monitoring system behavior when computer-controlled, adjusting parameters on-line when appropriate, and intervening to take over control in emergency or for normal reprogramming or repair.

task hierarchy

Classification of tasks where tasks at lower levels combine to form tasks at higher levels.

transinformation (or transmitted information)

An average measure of the degree to which occurrence of particular symbols from an "input message" set determines occurrence of particular symbols from an "output message" set. Transinformation gets larger as the message set becomes larger and its symbols occur with more equal probability.

utility function

The magnitude of worth of a thing or event as a function of one or a set of attributes (dollar cost, number of accidents, amount of time).

verbal protocol

Description of activity rendered in natural language by a person doing that activity or by an observer. Also a procedure for systematically obtaining and organizing such verbal descriptions.

vigilance

A state of readiness to detect and respond to certain specified small changes occurring at random time intervals in the environment.

white noise

Noise signal whose power density (power per radian per second) is the same at all frequencies.

workload

The level of activity or effort required of a human operator to meet performance requirements or criteria. There are various and conflicting ideas as to how to best measure (and thereby operationally define) workload because several factors can affect the required level of activity including operator skill, task difficulty, amount of work to be performed, etc. Examples of workload measures are : scores in a secondary task ; physiological measures ; subjective ratings of activity level or task difficulty ; the number of units to be processed ; the highest difficulty value of a task (e.g., greatest turbulence) which the operator can perform while still satisfying some performance or error criteria.

Appendix B

PARTICIPANTS

Belgium

  1 P.K. Verhaegen   Katholieke Universiteit te Leuven
                             Winksele

Canada

  2 N. Johnston   Brock University (Psychology)
                           St. Catharines

  3 R. Johnston   Brock University (Psychology)
                           St. Catharines

  4 J.W. Senders   University of Toronto (Industrial Engineering)

Denmark

  5 J. Rasmussen   Danish Atomic Energy Commission
                           Roskilde

Finland

  6 B.G. Wahlström   Technical Research Centre of Finland (VTT/SÄH)
                           Helsinki

---

* Session Chairmen

France

7   J.E. Brémond   CERPAIR
                            Saint-Cyr-L'École

8   D.G. Cavalli   ONERA
                            Châtillon

9   A. Rault   ADERSA (GERBIOS)
                            Vélizy-Villacoublay

Germany

10   H. Aschenbrenner   Bundesministerium der Verteidigung
                            Bonn

11   R. Bargl   Deutsche Lufthansa AG (Flightengineer's Office)
                            Frankfurt

12   W.P. Bauer   Technische Hochschule Darmstadt (Regelungstechnik)

13   R.K. Bernotat[*]   Forschungsinstitut für Anthropotechnik (FAT)
                            Meckenheim

14   S. Bossi   Standard Elektrik Lorenz AG (Bahn-Steuerungstechn
                            Stuttgart

15   R. Burdorf   Vereinigte Flugtechnische Werke - Fokker GmbH
                            Bremen

16   F. Burkardt[*]   J.W. Goethe-Universität (Psychologie)
                            Frankfurt

17   P. Chenchanna   Technische Universität Berlin (Landverkehrsmittel)

18   D. Dey   Vereinigte Flugtechnische Werke - Fokker GmbH
                            Bremen

19   J. Dilling   Bundesanstalt für Straßenwesen
                            Köln

20   S. Fichtbauer   DFVLR (Luftfahrtpsychologie)
                            Hamburg

21	G. Geiser	Inst. Informationsverarbeitung Technik Biologie Karlsruhe
22	R. Grimm	Inst. Informationsverarbeitung Technik Biologie Karlsruhe
23	N.P. Hammer	Bundesministerium der Verteidigung Bonn
24	D.-P. Hansen	Bundesamt für Wehrtechnik und Beschaffung (BWB) Eckernförde
25	P. Haubner	Siemens AG Karlsruhe
26	K. Henning	Technische Hochschule Aachen (Regelungstechnik)
27	G. Johannsen	Forschungsinstitut für Anthropotechnik (FAT) Meckenheim
28	F. Kaiser	Technische Universität München (Psychologie)
29	K.R. Kimmel	Forschungsinstitut für Anthropotechnik (FAT) Meckenheim
30	U. Kirchhoff	Technische Universität Berlin (Luft- und Raumfahrt)
31	S. Kokoschka	Universität Karlsruhe (Lichttechnik)
32	Lemke	Technische Universität Berlin (Landverkehrsmittel)
33	L. Liebl	Flugmedizinisches Institut der Luftwaffe Fürstenfeldbruck
34	K.-O. Linn	Universität Karlsruhe (Biokybernetik)
35	J. Meyer-Delius	Flugmedizinisches Institut der Luftwaffe Fürstenfeldbruck
36	K. Niemann	Daimler-Benz AG Stuttgart
37	N.R. Ninz	Technische Universität Berlin (Luft- und Raumfahrt)

38   C. Pfendler   Forschungsinstitut für Anthropotechnik (FAT)
                           Meckenheim

39   F.D. Pitrella   Forschungsinstitut für Anthropotechnik (FAT)
                           Meckenheim

40   B. Richter   Volkswagenwerk AG (VW)
                           Wolfsburg

41   G. Schmidt   Techn. Univ. München (Meß- und Regelungstechnik)

42   E. Schubert   Forschungsinstitut für Anthropotechnik (FAT)
                           Meckenheim

43   W. Schumacher   Inst. Informationsverarbeitung Technik Biologie
                           Karlsruhe

44   W. Stein   Forschungsinstitut für Anthropotechnik (FAT)
                           Meckenheim

45   H. Strasser   Technische Universität München (Arbeitsphysiologie)

46   B. Tilemann   Technische Hochschule Aachen (Regelungstechnik)

47   H. Trück   Inst. Informationsverarbeitung Technik Biologie
                           Karlsruhe

48   H.-P. Willumeit   Technische Universität Berlin (Landverkehrsmittel)

49   H. Witt   Technische Universität München (Psychologie)

50   R. Zimmermann   Dornier-System GmbH
                           Friedrichshafen

Greece

51   C.G. Peroyannakis   Scientific Group for Space Research
                           Athens

Israel

52   S.J. Merhav[*]   Technion (Aeronautical Engineering)
                           Haifa

Netherlands

53	A.R. van Heusden	Twente University of Technology (Chem. Engng.) Enschede
54	R.J.A.W. Hosman	Delft University of Technology (Aerospace Engng.)
55	J.W.H. Kalsbeek[*]	Institute for Preventive Medicine TNO Leiden
56	J.J. Kok	Delft University of Technology (Mech. Engng.)
57	P. Lemaire	Institute for Road Vehicles TNO Delft
58	A. van Lunteren	Delft University of Technology (Mech. Engng.)
59	J. Moraal	Institute for Perception TNO Soesterberg
60	G. Mulder	University of Groningen (Experimental Psychology) Haren
61	C.K. Pasmooij	Institute for Preventive Medicine TNO Leiden
62	J.E. Rijnsdorp[*]	Twente University of Technology (Chem. Engng.) Enschede
63	J. Smit	National Aerospace Laboratory (NLR) Amsterdam
64	M. Soede	Institute for Preventive Medicine TNO Leiden
65	H.G. Stassen	Delft University of Technology (Mech. Engng.)
66	P.H. Wewerinke	National Aerospace Laboratory (NLR) Amsterdam

Norway

67	E. Baatvik	University of Trondheim (SINTEF)

68   T.O. Kvålseth   University of Trondheim (Industr. Economy Organ.)

Sweden

69   J.E. Ahlin   Royal Institute of Technology (Design Methodology)
                           Stockholm

70   S. Skans   LUTAB
                           Bromma

United Kingdom

71   P.K. Andow   University of Technology (Chem. Engng.)
                           Loughborough

72   E. Edwards   University of Technology (Human Sciences)
                           Loughborough

73   K. Ellis   Admiralty Research Laboratory (Applied Psychology)
                           Teddington

74   P.H. Hammond   Warren Spring Laboratory (Control Engineering)
                           Stevenage

75   L. Laios   University of Technology (Human Sciences)
                           Loughborough

76   P.D. McLeod   Medical Research Council (Applied Psychology)
                           Cambridge

77   J.W. Miller   USA Office of Naval Research
                           London

78   N. Moray   University of Stirling (Psychology)

79   B. Sayers   UK Atomic Energy Authority (Systems Reliability)
                           Warrington

80   B. Shackel   University of Technology (Human Sciences)
                           Loughborough

81   W.T. Singleton   University of Aston in Birmingham (Applied Psychol.

82 H.T. Smith   University of Bradford (Psychology)

83 H.C.W. Stockbridge   Quest Research
                              Tilford, Farnham

84 T.R. Warren   Applied Ergonomics (Editor)
                              Haslemere

USA

85 R.W. Allen   Systems Technology, Inc.
                              Hawthorne, Calif.

86 D.K. Bauerschmidt   Rockwell International (Marine Systems)
                              Anaheim, Calif.

87 P.R. Chatelier   Naval Air Systems Command (Human Factors)
                              Washington, D.C.

88 R.E. Curry   MIT (Aeronautics and Astronautics)
                              Cambridge, Mass.

89 C.G. Drury   State Univ. NY, Buffalo (Industrial Engng.)
                              Amherst, New York

90 W.J. Hebenstreit   Boeing Aerospace Co. (Crew Systems)
                              Seattle, Wash.

91 G.S. Malecki[*]   Office of Naval Research
                              Arlington, Virginia

92 R.W. Pack   Electric Power Research Institute
                              Palo Alto, Calif.

93 D.L. Parks   Boeing Aerospace Co.
                              Seattle, Wash.

94 S.N. Roscoe   University of Illinois (Aviation Research)
                              Savoy, Illinois

95 W.B. Rouse   University of Illinois (Coordinated Science Lab.)
                              Urbana, Illinois

96   T.B. Sheridan   MIT (Mechanical Engineering)
                             Cambridge, Mass.

97   D.A. Thompson   Stanford University (Industrial Engineering)
                             Stanford, Calif.

98   G. Weltman   Perceptronics, Inc.
                             Woodland Hills, Calif.

99   R.J. Wherry Jr.   Naval Air Development Center (Human Engng.)
                             Warminster, Pa.

100 R.C. Williges   University of Illinois (Aviation Research)
                             Savoy, Illinois

INDEX